Voyaging On A Small Income

By Annie Hill

Illustrated by John Blackburn

Badger, Greenland, 1991. Disko Island is in the background. It is hard to give an impression of the size of a berg, but Badger is sufficiently far off to be out of its wind shadow. Note patches on sails.

P. O. Box 447
St. Michaels, MD 21663
410-745-3750

Layout and design by Tiller Publishing.
Published in the UK by Waterline Books
an imprint of Airlife Publishing Ltd
101 Longden Rd, Shrewsbury, England

Photos supplied by the author, except as noted.

Tiller Publishing
P. O. Box 447
St. Michaels, MD 21663
Voice: 410-745-3750
Fax: 410-745-9743

Acknowledgments

Most of the information in this book has been passed on to me over many years, by cruising people we have met and talked to along the way, who were always ready to lend a helping hand or make suggestions. Thanks to all of them. Thanks, too, to David Cox, Cornwall's premier marine surveyor and naval architect; to Spring Electric Company of Canton, Ohio; to Lesley and Chris Rowntree for encouraging me to continue; to Tom Cunliffe for all his support and ideas; to Tom Fake of the Benford Design Group for his sketches and to John Blackburn for his wonderful illustrations.

Dedication

To Pete, without whom it never would have happened.

*Annie and Pete Hill enjoy a 'memorable picnic' in
Mallorca, February, 1991.*

Table Of Contents

Badger *in St. Michaels, Maryland, December, 1991, while*
visiting her designers, Benford Design Group.
Jay R. Benford photo.

Foreword
by
Tom Cunliffe

Unless you are already living creatively on the uttermost boundaries of the monetary system of Western civilization, you should read Annie Hill's book with the greatest caution.

The work you have in your hands purports to offer a series of hints concerning the art of **Voyaging on a Small Income**. So it does, but if you think that is all you are getting, you have been misled by a remarkably innocuous title. What you are about to read is a volume dealing with the business of sailing in its broadest context, but which also poses a number of serious questions about the true priorities of life for the long-distance mariner. In case this makes you want to dump the thing like a hot ballast pig, don't panic. Annie Hill and her skipper, Pete, are emphatically not "drop-outs", pushing half-baked philosophies to the disenchanted.

They are members of the Royal Cruising Club and are the most successful capitalists I have ever met. The fascination of the following chapters is that for many of us, they may serve to redefine the meaning of "success".

I first crossed tacks with Pete and Annie in 1975 in the Canary Islands. My wife and I were bound out for Brazil in a 32-foot gaff cutter. I cannot remember whether or not we had proper lifejackets, but we certainly had no liferaft. A radio set, even a VHF, was consigned to the realms of fantasy. We had a fine boat, however. Our rig was strong and efficient, our garboards were well caulked, and we shipped a fine array of ground tackle which represented our only insurance policy. The Hills, aboard their tiny catamaran *Stormalong*, were similarly equipped, as were most of our fellow-rovers. Few of us came to serious harm, and those that did went to their Maker in the way most of us would one day choose to go.

Times have changed. I recently attended a seminar on ocean cruising in which a large part of the weekend was taken up, not with urgent questions about self-help, how to make do with imperfect charts, and how strong and reliable the Trade Winds blow in real life, but on such matters as juggling your tax problem, insuring your production yacht and the offsetting of her capital depreciation.

My own little talk was swiftly re-written on the back of a programme and ended up with a quote: "Where your treasure is, there will your heart be also".

Annie Hill takes us gently, but firmly by the scruff of our consumer necks and leads us back to the all-but-forgotten green pastures of simplicity. She never patronises us for missing the point, she merely offers us rest from our labours and our stress. Even as we squirm and wriggle to find the flaw in her logic, the truth begins to dawn that there isn't one. To those with the courage to re-examine their lives and their needs, this book presents the possibility of genuine freedom experienced by only a few, even amongst people who are now sailing the great oceans.

So take thought before you dive into these pages. They might change your life, as my own was changed by a foreword from Weston Martyr, whose work also occupies the first paragraphs of Chapter One. Martyr caught my imagination as a thirteen-year-old in the middle of England by referring the reader to his probable irritation with the troubles and boredoms of everyday life. He compared these with the achievements of W. A. Robinson who sailed the small, uncomplicated *Svaap* successfully around the world on a diminutive budget. He finished up with seven words which scorched themselves into my whole future.

To anyone who read and enjoyed Robinson's book and was moved by its message, Weston Martyr offered only one course of action:

"By Gum, go and do thou likewise."

Now read on. Annie's message shines through the muddled thinking of our time like Venus breaking through a pre-dawn overcast.

Tom Cunliffe
Pilot Cutter *Hirta*
Falmouth UK

Chapter 1

The £200 Millionaire

In 1934, Weston Martyr wrote a book of short stories. The first story and the one that gave its name to the book was **The £200 Millionaire**. This wonderful little story, only 24 pages long, was about a meeting between a couple on a sailing holiday in Holland, and an elderly gentleman. The old chap was sailing his little sloop around the length and breadth of Europe on £200 a year, and even in those far-off times, that was not a princely sum. He told the couple of his experiences and adventures, and of the pleasure he derived from his simple way of life; his conversation was an inspiration to them. The story itself, subsequently inspired many other people, not the least of whom were Peter and Anne Pye. In just 24 pages, Weston Martyr managed to conjure up a man's personality and his whole way of life. Times change, however, and reading the story today, people may well believe that it is the sort of life that could have been led 50 years ago, but is no longer possible. (*See Appendix VIII for this story.*)

In writing this book, I am hoping to be able to show that the £200 Millionaire's way of life is still possible. Admittedly, the figure of £200 has increased, but the main point of the story, the fact that it is quite simple to live a civilized and pleasurable life on a very small income, is as valid now as it was then. In this book, I am hoping to help sailing people who, inspired by such an idea, find that they too want to undertake extended cruises on a limited budget. In it, I have attempted to compile all the information that I wished I had when I first started voyaging in 1975, green as grass and as ignorant of both life and sailing as it was possible to be.

Anyone reading this book will, I trust, come across ideas that they haven't thought of before and find ways of doing things more cheaply than has previously been the case. However, the book as a whole represents a philosophy of life, developed by Pete and myself during the years that we have lived and sailed together. Many of the ideas are interdependent because they are part of a whole, but most can be adopted by themselves to suit the needs and desires of the individual. I don't pretend that they will

work for everyone or that everybody could live as happily as we do by this philosophy. What I can say is that the whole book is written from hard won experience and that the ideas work.

The title of this book was chosen with a great deal of care, because I wanted to put over, in the minimum of words, what it is that I am trying to write about.

According to Alan Villiers, a voyage is a "setting-out from a home port and an eventual return, with all lesser goings and comings in between reckoned as passages, each part of the whole". I feel that this is an excellent definition, and even if you don't really have a home port, there is usually a place from which the voyage started and to which one will eventually return, or a place where the planning took place and the shape of the voyage grew up. Voyaging therefore, is about sailing as a continuing way of life, not something done between long periods at anchor doing other things. Circumstances force the most determined of us to stay somewhere for weeks, months or even years, but to voyagers this is an unfortunate event preventing us from enjoying our true vocation — that of travelling over the world's seas.

The Oxford dictionary defines income as "periodical (usually total annual) receipts from one's business, lands, work, investments, etc.". This book is about voyaging on an income rather than on capital simply because the need to replenish capital interferes with voyaging, unless that is, you can do something to earn money whilst you are actually underway. As well, a large part of our philosophy is that one's energies should be devoted to the way in which one is voyaging rather than the means whereby one goes voyaging.

As for "Small"——well, each person has a different definition of what constitutes a "small income". For the sake of the record, our fixed income, on which we live, is £1,300 per annum. In fact, we have about £300 per annum extra, but this is reinvested against inflation and doesn't really count.

The whole of the title was inspired by Maurice Griffiths who wrote **Yachting on a Small Income** just before the Second World War, because I hope to encourage people to appreciate the more simple and wholesome type of boats and cruising such as Maurice Griffiths designed and about which he has written so wonderfully.

Perhaps the most important part of our philosophy is that we *choose* to voyage on a small income rather than doing it out of necessity. We actually enjoy living on a small amount of money and have no real desire to have any more. Quite often, we talk to people about going off cruising and they will say, "If I couldn't go out for meals or have a drink in a bar, I'd rather not bother, thank you very much". Your first reaction might be to agree with them, but when you analyze the statement it is quite ludicrous. Are you seriously saying that you would rather carry on working than sacrifice the odd meal out and visits to bars? Are these things so important that you would trade them for the pleasure of living your own life on your own yacht, travelling to different places, doing things in your own time and having the time to appreciate the beauty of the world? If you feel that you can't do without any of your 'comforts', perhaps indeed you prefer the dream to the reality. So many of the things that people regard as necessities are luxuries unheard of 50 years ago. Many of them are in fact, society's compensations for sending you out to work. When you are in charge of your own life, with the freedom to live as you wish, you don't need these compensations.

It is a worthwhile undertaking to read the classic voyaging books. Harry Pidgeon, Frank Wightman, Edward Allcard, Peter and Anne Pye, Annie van der Wiele, Erling Tambs and many others sailed modest and simple boats on splendid voyages and thoroughly enjoyed themselves. Who, reading Eric Hiscock's books, has not felt that with the advent of the large *Wanderer IV* into their lives, the Hiscocks lost a lot of their pleasure in sailing? We live in a consumer society; in order for it to function correctly, new objects have to be made and a demand has to be created for them. It is an interesting exercise to examine earlier voyages and to try analyzing which of the many gadgets now available, would truly have been of assistance during them and improved the pleasure and satisfaction that they gave.

Economists talk a lot about Cost Benefit Analysis, the system whereby the cost of an item is set against the benefits derived from its possession in order to ascertain its worth. To take an example: a GPS navigation system costs about £1,000 or two-thirds of our yearly income. These systems are supposed to enable us to sail across the oceans of the world with a pinpoint knowledge of where we are. However, in 70,000 miles of voyaging, we have never been in a situation where we have been *seriously* concerned about making a landfall due to lack of a good sight or uncertainty as to our position. As well, a GPS depends on electricity and sophisticated components. With an input of effort and money the former can be more or less sorted out,

but there is no way that the average voyager could dismantle the black box for running repairs, should it go wrong. If it does go wrong, and every prudent sailor must assume that this may well happen, you will need a sextant and the appropriate tables anyway, and as everyone knows, familiarity and practice with a sextant are a large part of getting accurate fixes. Therefore, it is necessary to keep in practice in case the GPS goes wrong. To this, we also have to add the fact that should it go wrong, we then have to instigate a series of complicated manoeuvrers to post it to be repaired, pay for the cost of the repair, have it posted back to us and then try and get it through Customs without having to pay an onerous amount of duty. All this costs money, takes time and trouble and in the meantime, it is sulking in a corner doing nothing while the money invested in it is wasted.

BADGER'S G.P.S.

So, why do we have it on board? If we are concerned about a landfall, can we not heave-to until we can get a sight? In certain places, we may well be very worried about our position, but surely these concerns are part of the challenge of voyaging. As well, we should also take into account the satisfaction of finding our way upon the face of the oceans by our own efforts and this must be weighed against having to rely upon lots of other people having done their jobs correctly.

Having considered all the evidence pro and con, then the decision can be made. Self-steering makes sense — it allows time for so many things and permits a crew of two to get sufficient sleep; man-made fibre rope and sails make sense — they last longer; modern sealants make sense — they keep the boat dry and your possessions and the boat herself are the better for it. We believe in using Cost Benefit Analysis all the time and in all sorts of circumstances from the purchase of a Mars bar to that of an echo-sounder.

I believe that one of the great pleasures that we derive from voyaging is that of independence and we have found that the best guarantee of that independence comes from simplicity. Take the yacht herself. If she is a sophisticated boat, with electronics, generators and high tech equipment, your independence will be reduced in relation to the amount of this equipment you can look after by yourself; if you need specialist help then you have to sail to a place where such help is available, which interferes with your freedom of choice. Indeed, essential maintenance in itself controls your actions. The less the necessary maintenance the freer you are. Financially, you may be a lot better off by playing the money market than by committing yourself to one safe form of investment. However, life will become complicated by the necessity of keeping in touch with what is going on and the need to contact your broker. You'll probably need some sort of communications system and then what has happened to the peace and tranquillity of a long ocean crossing? In short, the fewer things there are to go wrong, the less there is to worry about and the more time you have for sailing. Moreover, if there's nothing to go wrong in the first place, then you won't need to spend anything on putting it right.

PYE'S MOONRAKER

Living on a small income is immensely pleasurable. Because it demands many 'sacrifices', the rewards are consequently greater — when you have worked out just how little is necessary, you then realize that everything else is actually a luxury. Because of cost benefit analysis, you have a high quality vessel on which to sail — by buying the best you can afford you are saving on maintenance or replacement costs in the future. Because your boat is simple you enjoy her. Because you sail as independently as possible, you get increased satisfaction.

With boats, small is beautiful. "The smaller the boat, the greater the fun", runs the old saying, and there is a lot in this. Why have a big boat? In bad weather there are very few boats that could truly be described as comfortable and in the light winds which are prevalent in so many places, a smaller boat will generally sail so much better. A large vessel will cost much more in the first place, and think of all that time spent working to earn this money, when you could have been sailing. A big boat will be more expensive to run and take much more work to keep smart; smaller boats will be off voyaging while you find somewhere to haul out your leviathan and spend a week putting antifouling on its enormous bottom.

If you voyage on a small income, you will rarely feel out of place in the countries you visit-even poor ones. You will not feel a spoilt child of a wealthy nation; you won't be buying gimcrack toys to stave off boredom as you try to spend more money than you will ever need.
Instead, you will also be stretching what you have as far as it will go. You'll enjoy doing it, too. I hope to convince you that voyaging on a small income makes sense: it's easy, satisfying, efficient and above all, it's a joyful way of life.

VAN DE WIELE'S OMOO

ALLCARD'S TEMPTRESS

Chapter 2

It's All Right For You Two, But...

When I met Pete, I was 18 and he was 23. I, straight from school, was working and studying to qualify, in the fullness of time, as a valuation surveyor — the same occupation as my father. My mother was a teacher. Pete was doing temporary work in the same office — he had spent a year at University, been in the Royal Navy as an Officer Cadet for a couple of years and had recently completed an HND in Computer Studies, with the intention of becoming a computer programmer. What he really wanted to do was to go sailing. His father was an Engineer for British Leyland and his mother a Civil Servant. Pete's grandfather and great-grandfather had been seafaring men and only colour-blindness had prevented his father from following the family tradition; so, for what it's worth, you could say that sailing is in his blood.

Even at this stage, Pete's interest lay in *simple* cruising, having been inspired from boyhood by such great writers as Joshua Slocum, Bernard Moitessier, James Wharram, Harry Pidgeon, Peter Pye and, perhaps more than any, by Peter Tangvald, and as such, I suppose his case was pretty hopeless. However, young and innocent in the ways of the world I knew nothing of this. At the time I met Pete, he had nearly completed *Stormalong,* a 28 foot, Wharram catamaran, but had run out of money — hence the temporary work. His plan had been to complete her and sail off to the West Indies — he hadn't planned on meeting me. He persuaded me against my better judgment, that I would enjoy sailing, and inveigled me into painting and varnishing and helping him complete his boat, while I tried to keep my nail varnish intact. Eventually *Stormalong* was launched and we went sailing. Pete, with typical gallantry, lent me some cast-off oilskins, with a distinct lack of buttons, and snuggled down in his new Henri-Lloyds, no doubt thinking they wouldn't fit me any better than the others — even if they did fasten up. Such is the strength of teenage infatuation that I went back for more.

Pete had done a fair bit of dinghy sailing at school and had experience in larger yachts in the Royal Navy,

including being 'lost' during one race (as usual, the crew were the last to realize that they were meant to be lost). His most important experience, however, had been in 1972 when he helped another chap, David Gaffyne, deliver *Aloha VII* from Newport, RI to Alicante, after that year's Singlehanded Transatlantic Race. At Alicante, David had to return home and Pete took the boat back to France by himself. His enjoyment of this passage was such that he came back to *Stormalong* with renewed enthusiasm.

The summer *Stormalong* was launched, Pete and I went on our 3 week's summer holiday sailing from Morecambe Bay to the Isle of Man, down to the Scilly Isles and back again. *Stormalong* had no engine and no log and it never occurred to me that this was anything out of the ordinary — where 'ignorance is bliss'.... We had a successful holiday, in spite of the usual English summer weather. The following spring, we were debating what to do. We had realized somewhere along the line, that we were going to stay together, and we were discussing in a desultory way where to live. One evening we were sitting in a pub and, with a distinct lack of enthusiasm, Pete was talking about buying a house in Fleetwood and doing it up so that we would have somewhere to build a bigger boat — *Stormalong* being too small for two people to live on. He seemed pretty depressed about the whole thing.

"Well, what do you *want* to do?" I asked.

"Quite honestly, Annie, I'd like to get into *Stormalong* now and sail off to the West Indies", he replied.

"Yes, but that's silly, she's too small for both of us."

"I know," he said glumly. He went to the bar for another two pints of mild beer (Pete had long since weaned me off gin and tonic — it cost too much) and when he came back I said:

"If we were to go in *Stormie,* when would we have to leave?"

"About early August."

"Well, we've got three months to sort it out — and by the way, Mum and Dad will do their nut if we go off 'in sin' — we'd better get married first! How long does it take to organize a wedding?"

"I've no idea."

Between us I doubt if we had £1,000. Pete's parents, still labouring under the illusion that I'd be a 'good thing for him and make him settle down' were all for us getting married and I think, hoped the *Stormalong* trip would be his final fling. My father took it on the chin, liking Pete and wanting me to be happy above all, but worried sick about the thoughts of me sailing off into the wide blue yonder. Having waited nearly 20 years to say it, he asked Pete if he would keep me "in the manner to which she would like to be accustomed". Without batting an eyelid, Pete said he hoped so. Little did I realize the brainwashing that would be necessary before I enjoyed the manner that Pete had in mind. My poor mother at first didn't want to know — her daughter had been intended for much better things than marrying a long-haired, bearded chap who didn't seem over fond of work and had no money. All in all, it was rather traumatic all round.

I'm bound to confess that the wedding was regarded by both of us as a rather expensive necessity — we couldn't believe the number of ridiculous things that were apparently essential and kept looking at our dwindling resources. We had to stock up *Stormalong* for a year and buy charts, etc. for the voyage. I hadn't a clue about any of these things — to be quite honest, I didn't even know how to cook, in spite of my mother's best endeavours to "domesticate" me, as she termed it. Pete reckoned that baked beans and soya mince should be a good basis for provisioning and somehow we got stuff together and, even more surprisingly, did a fairly good job of it, for a first effort, although we had nowhere near a year's supply of food. We bought charts with great profligacy and for the first and last time, had all that we were likely to need. By the time we left, we had about £400 in the kitty and no prospects. Pete's parents gave us a Walker log as a wedding present — most of the other presents were put away for our return, with the exception of a kettle, a pan and some cutlery, which I decided we'd take with us.

The prospect of the voyage should have scared me to death — in fact it hardly worried me — I'd no idea at all what I was letting myself in for and as I couldn't imagine what might happen, I couldn't worry about it. In fact I will now come clean and admit that, having announced to everyone that we were going to sail to the West Indies, I had to sneak a look in Daddy's atlas to see where they were — it still didn't mean much.

We set off in the middle of August, 1975 and did the classic 'milk-run' — Northern Spain, Madeira, the Canaries, Barbados and up the islands to the British Virgin Islands, Azores and UK. We skipped Bermuda because, by then we only had £15 left and wanted to have £5 for when we got back. We always seemed to be chronically short of money, which shows what hopeless managers we were. In today's terms, I reckon that £400 must have been worth at least £1,000 and we could easily manage to live on that these days, especially with a fair amount of provisions on board. I distinctly remember going into a shop in St John's, Antigua to stock up. I forget how many dollars we had, but there wasn't much selection and all we could afford were sardines. We bought 59 tins — I still recall the figure; I suppose we didn't have enough for the 60th. If only we had known about eating pulses then, how much easier it all would have been.

After all these years, I can't really remember how I felt at the time. I know that quite often, I was frightened and miserable. We had our fair share of adventures; we were dismasted twice, fortunately each time coastal sailing and weathered a couple of gales — a lot of wind for 'a weekend cruiser/racer', which is how Jim described his *Tane* design. Much of the time we were very wet — a large wave swept over the bow the second day out of the Canaries, flooding the dorade box and soaking the only bunk we could sleep on (the other being full of gear) and our sleeping bag. Later on, one of the bulwarks got broken — by another large wave — and needless to say it was on the same hull, so that the dorade box kept filling up and, as it was some weeks before we could carry out repairs, many of our stores were spoilt by water. The hatches used to leak too, whenever it was rough. We couldn't sleep on deck in the West Indies because it rained a lot and, after a while the awning started to leak; we didn't enjoy sleeping down below, because our 'double bunk' was a bit warm being 20 inches at the wide end and a foot at the bottom. There was nowhere for us both to sit down below in any sort of comfort, and, when cooking with the hatch shut, there wasn't enough air for the single-burner Primus, Pete (sitting behind me) and me, so that I periodically fainted — coming round almost immediately due to there being more air available low down.

On the other hand, I came to discover that one of the best things about voyaging is the people you meet — we still keep in touch with people we met that year. I gained in self-respect from overcoming fear and learning new skills such as navigating. I learned how to cope with apparent disasters and discovered that they were usually merely incidents. We had a lot of fun, soaked up the sunshine and visited many fascinating and beautiful places. We decided to go back and build another boat so that we could do it again, but this time in some comfort. Norway in 1980, for the summer and then south for the winter was what we planned.

Returning to an England of high unemployment and high inflation, we realized that the first thing that we had to do was save as much as we could. I'm afraid that I must have been a pretty hopeless housewife in those days — I seem to remember that we had £25 a week to live on and I could only just manage — these days we live in comparative luxury on the same amount. We moved into a flat at the end of a country house and Pete got a job as a computer programmer. It was some distance away, so we reckoned that we needed to run a car. (These days, of course, we'd live where the work is or get another sort of job. Running a car costs an awful lot of money because there are all sorts of hidden costs that aren't readily apparent). In order to pay for this flat, I acted as charwoman and Pete did some gardening. In its favour was the fact that there was somewhere for us to build The Next Boat. We sold *Stormalong* and so had some capital with which to start off.

I should like to draw a veil over this attempt on The Next Boat, but honesty says I can't. Because at this time epoxy was not available in the UK, we decided against plywood due to maintenance considerations and decided to go for GRP, which seemed cheapest. I now think that we overestimated the amount of work that plywood needed in the way of maintenance, even without being treated with epoxy. We constructed a female mould, which was a mistake to begin with, and then started laying up in June, under a plastic cover. It was a disaster. When the sun came out, the temperature soared and when it went in, the temperature plummeted. Going to work on the hull on the morning of the third day, we were horrified to see that the moulding had started to collapse inwards. All we could do was to scrap everything and cut our losses. Back to the drawing board.

A couple of days later, Pete still being on holiday, we decided to drive up to Glasson Dock to "look at the boats" — probably to reassure ourselves that such things still existed. We wandered around and saw an old yacht for sale; she had been a beautiful boat in her prime, but was now very run down. As much out of curiosity as anything else, we asked for the keys and had a look over her. One of the first things we noticed was that she was built by the Herreshoff Mfg. Co. "A real classic", we said, "what a shame to let her go like this". She was very small down below; although 27 ft. overall, I doubt that she had as much room as a Folkboat. Still, she intrigued us and we wondered whether in fact it would be a good investment to buy her and do her up, thus getting more money for The Next Boat. We had her surveyed, made an offer and bought her and so *Sheila* came into our lives.

I don't suppose it could have been more than a month later that we came to the conclusion that we couldn't tolerate living in a house any more and decided to move aboard — once we'd rebuilt the accommodation. By the middle of February, the double bunk under the foredeck was finished and, although the rest of the hull was completely stripped out, we moved on board. How else would we get her finished? In the winter, half of the weekend was taken up by Pete's gardening chores and it was impossible to get the work done on *Sheila* and so we decided that by living aboard we should make better progress. There was a kitchen and a day room at the marina and we could use those until *Sheila* was a little more sorted out. The owner of the place nearly had kittens when he realized that we had moved on board and were living in his shed, but didn't really have the heart to throw us out on the street. Indeed, he even let us move onto a boat he was selling, which had central heating on board — "to keep it aired", he said, which was rather decent of him.

Having a boat again, we started to make plans. *Sheila* wasn't at all the ideal, but we felt that it would be possible to go places in her. We took a summer cruise down to the south coast that year, 1978, planning to base ourselves at Southampton where I would go on a secretarial course, in order to have some marketable skills, and Pete should be able to get a job as a programmer. All that went according to plan. However, living aboard and sailing *Sheila*, we came to realize that she would only be a temporary solution as she wasn't suitable for what we ultimately wanted to do. We hoped perhaps to go to Brazil in her and then come back and build The Next Boat. Pete had now persuaded me that The Next Boat should be junk rigged. We'd been to the Southampton Boat Show, and he had taken me to see Sunbird Yacht's working model of a junk sail. Having seen how it worked, I was an instant convert — at last a rig that an undersized coward like me could work singlehanded — and, like all converts, I am now rabid in my beliefs.

Unable to find anywhere we could live on the Hamble, we lived in East Cowes Marina on the Isle of Wight. It was the coldest winter for about 30 years and we discovered that our charcoal heater was not a good idea, because no one sells barbecue charcoal in the winter. Instead, we ordered one of Taylor's paraffin heaters — which arrived in April. I don't think I've ever really forgiven them for that; we nearly had a divorce because I can't tolerate being cold and Pete refused to buy an electric heater because the Taylor one would arrive any day. In the end we did buy a fan heater, which was just as well, but found that it only seemed to heat the air so that the boat was never really warm, especially as we were both out all day. It was a pretty grim winter, actually, but I remember it with pleasure for one particular thing — that was the time we decided to try eating beans.

This may not seem a particularly spectacular event, but in fact it was probably the first positive step we took towards living on a small income, as opposed to struggling on one. Pete was on good wages, for once, and I had a grant, but our commuting expenses were very high and we were trying to save for our trip in *Sheila*. As far as possible, we tried to live on my grant and I found that the cost of food seemed outrageous. Being brought up in an exceedingly meat oriented household, and with both of us having good appetites, I was used to buying a pound of meat for a meal. Neither of us are fond of offal and I didn't really know what to do with all these much vaunted "cheap cuts". I suppose most people would have gone out and bought Good Housekeeping's cookery book, but having been talking to several people about beans, I decided to try to learn to cook in a way that would also make economic sense. The first book I bought was an American one, and although the food was not bad, it didn't do a lot for us, and we would cast longing looks at pork chops and buy chicken for a 'treat'. Then I discovered **The Bean Book** by Rose Elliot — who should be nominated for an Order of the British Empire, I reckon. Suddenly I was producing delicious meals that came from an incredibly cheap basic product. In those halcyon days, I was paying about 7p for the meat substitute of our meal — saving approximately 93p per meal. What's more, these wonderful beans were *designed* for storing on a boat, they took up hardly any room and needed no special treatment. We had taken our first major step forward and realized it when we no longer regarded buying a lump of dead animal as a treat.

On completing my course we set off in the hope of circumnavigating Ireland. We beat all the way to Cork and then proceeded to beat all the way long the South coast, at which point I mutinied.

We sat down and discussed things. *Sheila* was not the sort of boat in which we, or at any rate I, wanted to go cruising: she was too wet when sailing and too damp in harbour; there was no proper place to keep many of the things we needed; she had no permanent double berth (we had early abandoned the bunk under foredeck — the condensation was beyond a joke) and it was no fun making up a bed every night; she couldn't carry sufficient gear to be independent; reefing or changing sail was a nightmare for me; the hatch leaked. Poor boat, we tore her to shreds and decided that if we wanted to go voyaging we should stop fooling around and sort ourselves out, otherwise 10 years hence, we would be sitting down in another boat making the same sort of comments and really be no better off. The only thing to do, we said, was build The Next Boat now. We couldn't afford to buy one that would satisfy our requirements, we had a chance of earning reasonable money now, which would be reduced if we went off cruising (computer programmers soon get out of touch) and we had somewhere to live while we were building, a bit of money saved up, and the prospect of selling *Sheila* at

the end of the building process, which should give us some money on which we could cruise.

We sailed back along the South coast of Ireland and up to Glasson Dock where we set about building The Next Boat, *Badger*.

We chose Glasson Dock because we had contacts there and were also quite near to our parents. Jobs were in short supply of course, in 1979. However, I found one in the village after a lot of false starts — a temporary job for 2 1/2 days, but once I had my foot in the door, they were scuppered. It didn't pay too badly and was handy. Pete, in the end, didn't get a job as a programmer, because he would have needed to travel and we didn't want to buy a car — we were learning — but he managed to find a rather less well paid post at a local teachers' training college, as a technician in the mathematics department, which had computers. The nice thing was that he was only employed during the term time, so had long holidays for boatbuilding.

Having had our setbacks, we were now even more determined to get away. Our original goal of 1980 was the following year and that continued needling us and kept up our resolve. Once we had paid for a year in the marina, we had very little behind us and on working out how much we'd earned over the past couple of years, we were staggered at how little we had to show for it. From now on, we decided, we'd make sure we saw some tangible return for all those hours spent at a desk. In future, we would try to avoid living on capital, ending up back where we started when a cruise was ended. In the meantime, all Pete's money would go on The Boat and we would live on mine and save what we could out of it.

When we started building, we had the choice of buying good quality power tools and looking at them or buying some wood and using it as best we could. We decided to use second-hand pitch pine, readily available in that part of the world, for all the solid timber and so had to buy a decent saw and plane to rip it up — a lot of it came in 12 inch square, 12 foot lengths. For the rest we used do-it-yourself tools and they cost us a lot more in the long run. Our saw and plane we sold easily when we finished *Badger,* but we totally wore out 3 drills, 2 jigsaws and an orbital sander. How the latter kept on as long as it did is beyond me. This experience reinforced our opinion that it makes sense to spend money up front on good equipment that will last and not go for false economy. However, if we were in the same situation again, I suppose we'd still buy the wood and get started.

Glasson Dock is a place of dreamers. I'd hate to think how many people have built, completed or bought boats there with the idea of 'going off', but have never made it. Quite a few projects have never been finished. Several of us have succeeded, but there were plenty of reminders there of how easily it could all go sour. I suppose this helped us in many ways, and whenever we felt like taking time off, we had only to look about us to change our minds. We worked full time earning money, of course, but then we came home and worked full time on *Badger.* I believe it was the only way to do it, if we wanted to get sailing in a reasonable amount of time. The years we put into building and working were years we could never get back. By this time, we had become quite paranoid about

going out to work, regarding it as a complete waste of time that could be much better spent, and have never got over that feeling. Our subsequent freedom has merely emphasized how much better one's time can be used. I was made redundant after 2 1/2 years (without, alas, a British Steel type payout) and concentrated on *Badger.* Pete also quit work to finish her off and this was when we really learnt how to pull in our belts. The point was that she took longer to build than we had anticipated (well, they always do) and once we had stopped earning money, we were living on savings. We had paid the marina fee, I had saved £3,500 when I was working and we'd got £4,000 for *Sheila.* Invested, this gave us £15 per week and on this we managed to live. There was still money in the boatbuilding kitty, but that was about finished when *Badger* was complete. It was good training and we also realized how much satisfaction we got from our independence. Both of us could have found more work, but we took the decision to be poor and free rather than wage slaves, which sounds trite, but is true.

When we set off in *Badger,* we were cruising for the first time on income, rather than on capital and the sense of freedom and security that this gave was something quite wonderful. We effectively had money behind us for emergencies and could sail for as long as we wanted with no need to look for work unless we wished to. We made up our minds to accept work if offered, so long as it was fairly agreeable and didn't prevent us from carrying out a particular plan upon which we'd decided. The reason for this was, I suppose, almost superstitious as we felt that we shouldn't look a gift horse in the mouth. In fact, this has served us very well.

In the Virgin Islands, we couldn't afford the prices and wanted to stay longer. Pete was offered work, and then I got work and we managed to save a lot of money. Then a friend in America offered us work on a boat he was fitting out, so that we not only earned some money, but experienced living in a Mid-West town for several months, something we'd never have done otherwise. We've both worked since then, but have kept our weekly allowance the same since 1985, content with living on that amount and allowing the surplus to accumulate so that we can reinvest for a larger income in the future, if and when that becomes necessary. We have spent a fair bit on improving *Badger* — fitting an engine, buying expensive material to build a new suit of sails, fitting a new keel, buying better blocks and winches and generally upgrading her equipment. The longest stint we have spent working was during a two year stay in Falmouth, when we both put in 12 months full-time work and some part time. However, this came about because we had returned to England due to family illness and decided, amongst other things, to change our existing ferro-cement keel for a cast-iron, wing keel. As well, we didn't want to make an issue of the illness and everyone is always ready to believe that we *need* to earn money.

While we were in Falmouth, we bought ourselves a little 20 foot Westcoaster to play with, and had a lot of fun with her, doing her up and re-rigging her as a junk. In the Summer of 1989, we spent three months exploring the Brittany coastline and canals in *Missee Lee*, something we couldn't have done in *Badger*. Then we sold her to a good home and made a profit, which money was also invested in a separate account, to provide capital for a large project such as replacing the engine. And so things work out; we don't feel that we've done much work, but in fact have increased our wealth substantially without losing our feeling of freedom.

Missie Lee — '*The smaller the boat the greater the fun.*
Neil Trevithick photo courtesy of Annie Hill.

I realize that only a part of our philosophy has come out in the above, but I hope that the background will help when reading what follows, and that other parts will become apparent, so that the whole ties together. If you want to go voyaging on a small income, it is my hope that you will find ideas in the book, that will help you to do so successfully and above all, enjoyably.

In an attempt to disarm criticism, I shall state here and now that this book is about *ideas* and not about *facts*. To learn about voyaging as such, I would recommend that you read such books as Eric Hiscock's **Voyaging Under Sail**, Bob Griffith's **Blue Water Sailor** and Hal Roth's **After 50,000 Miles**. Pete and I have done the major part of our voyaging in just two boats — a 28 foot Wharram catamaran, *Stormalong* and a 34 foot Junk rigged, Jay Benford designed monohull, *Badger*. Therefore, I write from my experience from these boats and the two other boats we have owned and in which we made mainly coastal cruises, with only one or two offshore passages.

Many of my comments are controversial — possibly even radical. The reasons for this are really quite obvious — we voyage in a way that is radically different from what many people consider to be the norm. I would add, however, that a great many people who voyage *as a way of life,* have more similarities than differences with us. You may well disagree with a lot of what I say: that's fine — at least I've given you an alternative point of view and made you consider the issue. Sooner or later, I know you're going to say, "Oh, it's all right for you two, but it's different for me!" So when you do, please try and remember that:

1) This book is meant to be about voyaging on a small income.

2) Pete and I have spent more than 15 years thrashing out our way of life — you're probably trying to take it all in at one reading.

3) Our way of life works successfully for us and our ideas have all been tested out by experience — they are not half-baked theories conjured up from armchair sailing.

4) What works for us may not work for anyone else — but I really don't believe that we are so eccentric!

Having got all that straightened out, I hope you will bear with me when you find what I say clashes with your opinions. It may be easier for you to do this if I relate how it was that we came to develop our philosophy in the first place.

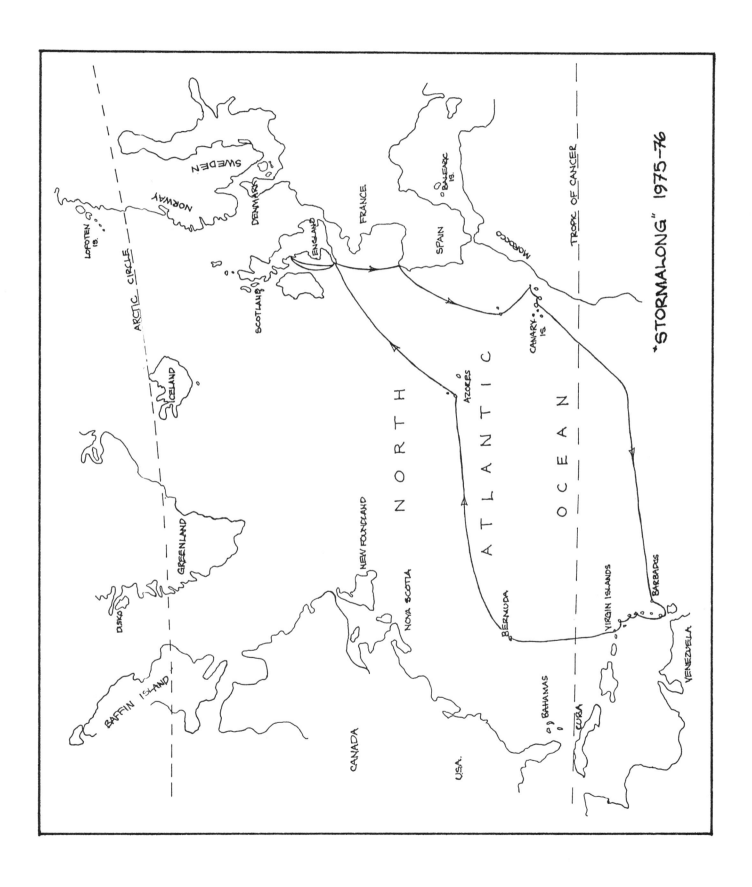

MODERATION IN ALL THINGS

Chapter 3

Moderation In All Things

Choosing the right size yacht in which to go voyaging, is as much of a compromise as anything you can think of. Ideally, they should be telescopic: big and fast at sea and tiny in harbour, with enormous accommodation and infinite load carrying capacity. However, in reality things are rather different, but bearing in mind that they all cost money both to buy and to run, there's a lot to be said for making a virtue out of necessity and thinking small rather than big.

The boat in which you voyage on a small income, should not be too small however, because a very small boat will stop you from being independent. This independence is not only psychologically satisfying, but perhaps even more importantly it is financially sensible. If your little ship is large enough for you to carry plenty of stores, spares, tools and miscellaneous bits and pieces, this means that you will be able to take care of your boat or any problems that crop up, with what you have on board. The capacity for carrying a reasonable amount of cargo will allow you to take advantage of bargains, such as cheap food or cut-price varnish and means that, with the exception of fresh food, you should rarely need to buy anything in an expensive place. Indeed, when we sailed up to Greenland, we did not even need to buy fresh food, as I stocked up with onions, potatoes, carrots, cabbage and garlic in Madeira and the Azores, and these stocks lasted from early May until mid September when we could again buy affordable food, in Nova Scotia.

A very small boat, although initially cheaper, may end up making for a more expensive lifestyle, particularly as it is less likely to be a comfortable home in which you will be happy to live in harbour, thus subjecting you to the temptation of going out at nights and spending money.

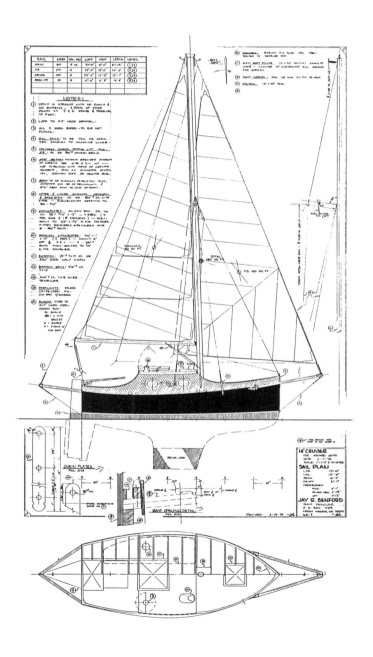

This size of boat is definitely capable of cruising most places, but her low initial cost is the only saving you'll make. She's too small to carry a cargo so you'll have to buy most things you need at whatever price is being asked.

On the other hand, we don't want to get carried away and end up sailing around in a huge boat, laden down with everything we might conceivably need. A yacht should be small enough that she is still fun to sail, easy to handle and capable of fitting into any anchorage that takes your fancy. You don't want a very light boat that will be uncomfortable as soon as the seas get up, but on the other hand, do you want a very heavy boat that will be a dog in light winds? Your ship will be a large part of your investment and insuring her would take too much of your income, so that you have to accept the fact that one day you might lose her and that if this happens, you need to be able to afford to lose the amount of money that she represents. Therefore, if you have a large and valuable boat, you have to be pretty wealthy or take the risk of losing her and being left on the beach, which is a worry that would certainly spoil my pleasure in voyaging. As well as being cheaper to buy (build), a smaller boat is cheaper to run and it's also a lot less work to keep smart.

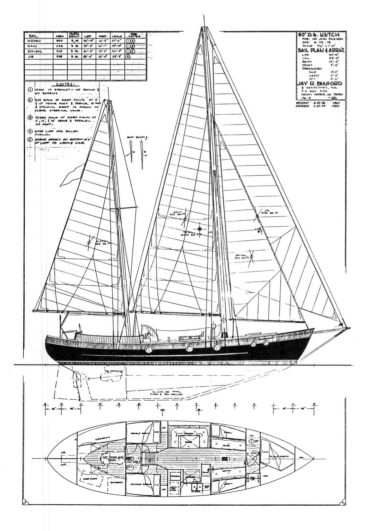

This boat will also take you anywhere you want to go, but take all of your small income to run — even if you could afford to build her.

I think satisfaction is a forgotten factor in this discussion. One of the reasons that we go voyaging on a small income, is that we find the whole way of life extremely satisfying. Part of this is undoubtedly due to the fact, that by sailing a fairly modest boat, with just two people, we get a greater sense of achievement at the end of a voyage. Let's face it, it's an awful lot easier to sail around the world in a 70 footer, with all the electronic aids at your disposal and a crew of half a dozen, then it is for two people to do the same thing in a simple 30 footer. However, I doubt that the people on the 70 footer have a quarter of the fun that the couple have on the smaller boat. Just think of all the hassle in harbour, finding a space in which to put her; they probably worry about being robbed, too, and wherever they go there will be a certain element trying to divert some of that wealth.

In fact, one of the drawbacks of having a large yacht is that other yachties think that you're rich. I remember when we were in northern Spain on *Stormalong* and were sailing in company with our friend, Steve on *Rolling Stone*, who had built the boat himself and was not over endowed with wealth. We came up to anchor one afternoon and Steve rowed over. "We're all right tonight!", he said.

"Whatever do you mean?", we asked him.

"I've just been talking to the people on that big schooner," he replied, "and they've invited us round for about 6 o'clock this evening. I'm sure we'll be able to wangle dinner from them."

Well, we went round and had a drink and a yarn and the time passed. Before too long we realized that there was no chance of a free feed on this particular yacht: Ted and Irene had built 54 foot *Pen-Y-Ddraig* themselves and they didn't have two pennies to rub together either. They were amused by our mistake, when we finally admitted it, but I'm bound to say that nobody has ever made the same one about us.

When you come to think about it, what is the point in having anything bigger than you need, anyway? People like to talk about the virtues of big boats, for example pointing out that big boats are faster, but who's in a hurry? If you want to get somewhere quickly you'd be better going by 'plane. Again, people say that fast passages are safe passages, because you're not spending as much time at sea, but against that is the argument that most boats are lost near the shore, not at sea, and a well found boat should be able to take any weather that you are likely to encounter, in the normal course of events. Anyway, while you're on passage you can't spend any money, which is one of the best ways I know of saving it. Although a lot of people would disagree with me here, Pete and I actually enjoy making long passages, it's one of the reasons we go voyaging. I wouldn't want to blast across the Atlantic in 13 days. There is also a lot of talk about the increased comfort of a large yacht, but on the other hand, a small boat is much more compact, so that if you do get thrown about, you haven't as far to go and are less likely to get hurt. In really heavy weather all boats are pretty uncomfortable — it's the way they are sorted out that makes the difference. No doubt I'm prejudiced, but I've found *Badger* much more comfortable than several larger yachts on which I've sailed.

However, I think that for small income voyagers, the final thing to keep in mind is something that Dick Newick said: "I can design you a boat that has any two of the following three attributes — Speed, Comfort and Economy". I don't know about you, but I'll go for the last two.

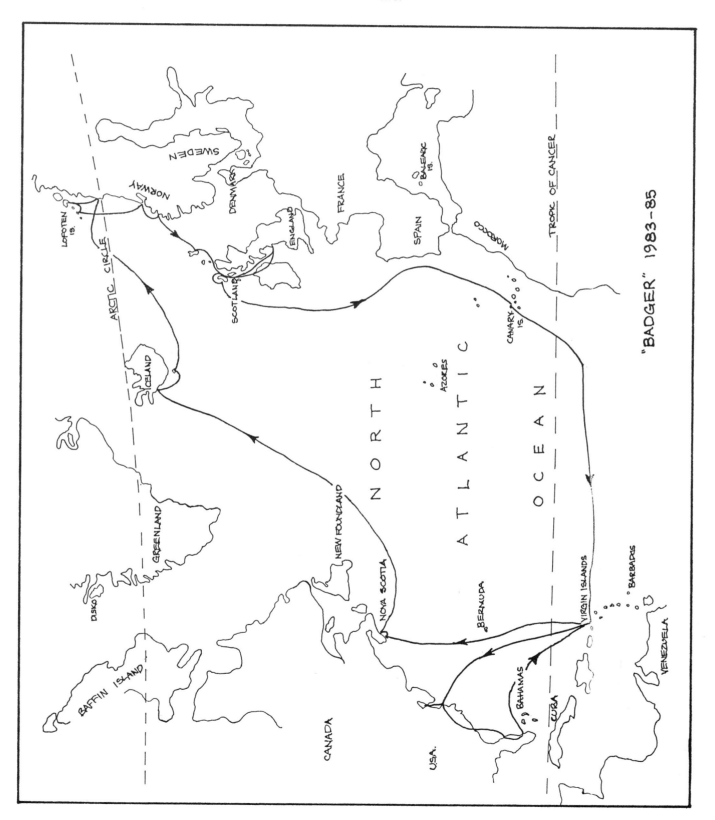

CUTAWAY DRAWING OF
BADGER PARTING WITH HER CONCRETE KEEL

Badger changed keels, from a conventional fin to a winged Collins Keel, decreasing her draft by about six inches in the operation. The hard work required to remove the original keel was a testament to the solidity of her design and construction.

Chapter 4

One Pauper's Luxury Yacht

After innumerable discussions, covering the topics in the preceding chapters and many more besides, Pete and I eventually drew up a list of requirements for our ideal boat. Obviously, even with the ideal, there have to be some compromises, but it was amazing how difficult it was to find a design that fitted our ideas. Everything we looked at would have some major defect as far as we were concerned, with which we would be unable to live. Eventually, we were in the position of having the site on which to build, the money to start and no design. We had started to get desperate when Pete remembered seeing a design on *Rolling Stone*, which he had traced and put in *Stormalong's* log book back in 1976. "It was a dory," he said, "designed by Jay R Benford. Let's write to him for study plans and see if it's anywhere near what we want". Meanwhile, we continued to search through books and magazines looking for our boat. One day a package came from America and in it were the study plans for a variety of dories. Looking at the design for the 34 foot version, we immediately realized that here was the boat for which we had been looking for so long.

Badger suits us perfectly, but I wouldn't pretend for a moment that she is everybody's ideal yacht. Details of the design are given in Appendix IV, but I have listed below the reasons we chose her, believing that it may be of interest to see how our way of life influenced the design of *our* 'Dream Ship'.

(1) We wanted a plywood boat because it would be easy to build and we thought the WEST System® sounded ideal for us. We chose plywood because we like wood as a material and because it is an economical material for building. Although we couldn't afford to buy top quality marine ply such as Bruynzeel™, we bought the best external that we could. The glue is the same and they choose the hardwood veneers with care. In all the pieces we used, we didn't come across a single void. From what we have seen, cheap marine ply seems very inferior and often has voids. Plywood is also easy to repair and easy to alter. We liked the idea of the WEST System as it eliminates the main worry of plywood — that of water getting into the end grain — and so should produce a long-lived vessel. Although the cost of epoxy seems high, you don't need to buy expensive bronze or stainless steel fastenings as you can use ordinary steel ones to hold the boat together until the glue has set and then take them out. We also liked the idea of monocoque construction for its strength and for the fact that *it doesn't leak*. Our original idea was to build a cheap and simple boat (budget £8,000) but we got a trifle carried away and ended up with a *yacht* (total cost £11,000) complete with teak decks; we've never regretted it.

(2) We wanted a boat of about five tons displacement, which was all we could afford to build. The cost of a boat varies with its displacement. To a large extent a 26 foot boat displacing five tons will cost as much as a 34 footer displacing the same. Our homework had helped us in the costings. We could have built something smaller and therefore cheaper, but that brings me on to the next point.

(3) We wanted a boat of about 30 feet. Actually, we still say that *Badger's* length is one of her few drawbacks — thirty-four feet is really rather longer than we wanted. We needed a boat that would be big enough to carry a year's supply of food — well, beans, pasta and rice anyway and that would carry all the gear that we need, but she should not be so heavy that she would encourage us to overload her. She had to be big enough to be able to take advantage of cheap supplies so that we could stock up with local bargains. She had to be big enough to carry all our charts and pilots so that we could return to places we'd enjoyed, without needing to buy them all again. She had to be big enough to be our home and hold all our books and clothes for all climates. She had to be big enough that she wouldn't frighten me to death in heavy weather. On the other hand, she had to be small enough that we could sail in and out of anchorages and enjoy the fun of handling a

boat in close quarters, without worrying unduly about hitting anything. She had to be small enough to enter tiny harbours. She had to be small enough that she would be accepted by locals in poorer places, who wouldn't immediately assume we were wealthy and to be fleeced. She had to be light enough to ghost in light airs and not need an engine. She had to be light enough to float like a cork and give to the seas rather than fight against them and hurt herself. She had to be small enough for either of us to sail single-handed in case of necessity or the desire so to do.

(4) We wanted junk rig, so that I could do all the sail handling by myself and wouldn't need to wake up Pete to reef or make sail. This would add both to the comfort and safety of our sailing. We liked the idea of not having to go on deck, being lazy sailors and of not having wet sails down below. We also liked the low-tech rig — cheap to build and easy to repair and we loved the idea of eliminating rigging — the expense, worry, strains on the hull, windage and noise. Until you've sailed on a boat with free standing masts, you've no idea how much disquiet is induced by the shriek of the wind in the rigging. It's nice too, to realize that unless you are actually sailing, the masts put no strain on the hull — and even then the loads seem fairly light — unlike the massive tensions set up by Bermudian rig. Best of all, for a small income sailor, the rig is incredibly cheap to run — the sails last for ages, you only need small, inexpensive rope and you can do everything yourself.

(5) We wanted a built-up cabin for strength and added room. Coachroofs are notoriously weak structures and we also like the appearance of a full width cabin. There is an enormous sense of space created by this type of cabin and the boat seems huge inside.

(6) We wanted a double-ended design because we like them. We feel that outboard rudders are the only logical way to go on a heavily used boat — easily attended to— and we like the pointed stern. Another advantage of a pointed stern is that if you overload the boat, you still leave a clean wake and do not end up dragging the transom through the water. If we were to build again, we would probably put on a tombstone stern — like many dories have. This would make it easier to mount the self-steering gear and also we would have the option to fit an outboard engine. I'm less fond of a transom stern; I used to find the noise of the waves slapping against *Sheila*'s vertical counter, when we were alongside, very irritating. However, as we hardly ever go alongside, maybe it's not something I really need to think about.

(7) We wanted moderate draught for more flexibility. An astonishing number of places have thin water. Even deep water areas such as Scotland often offer the best anchorages in a shallow spot. With anchorages getting more and more crowded you can often wriggle to the back of the fleet and drop your hook in water too shallow for them. *Badger* was designed for four feet, six inches, draught, but either Mr. Benford was a trifle

optimistic, or he didn't count on her being a home, because we ended up with about five feet. However, the wing keel that we fitted has brought the draught back down to four feet, six inches. It would be nice to have less, but we need to make too many compromises to achieve that.

(8) We like hard chine boats. After having lived on *Sheila,* I had become somewhat disenchanted with boats that looked absolutely gorgeous out of the water and sailed like a witch to windward. No-one could deny that *Sheila* was a beautiful boat both in and out of the water —however, you paid dearly for that exquisite wine glass hull at anchor. She could roll — God, how she could roll! I remember one anchorage where she rolled so badly as to fling cups off the table. In the end we rowed ashore, unable to tolerate the motion and, watching her, we wondered that the mast could stay in. Downwind too, she could pick up an appalling motion. Reading Eric Hiscock's description of *Wanderer III* rolling down the Trades had done nothing to reassure me that this fault was purely *Sheila*'s and I didn't want a boat that rolled. Hard chine boats have flat sections which damp out rolling — *Badger*'s dory hull looked an even better bet. Building in plywood, a chine boat is a logical way to go, but we actually both like the clean lines of hard chine. We were right too, *Badger* doesn't roll and, contrary to popular prejudice, she doesn't pound going to windward because she heels to present a "V" shape to the waves. She may not look a delight to the eye out of the water, but she looks lovely afloat and is comfortable to live in, both sailing and in harbour.

(9) We wanted a boat with room for a separate double cabin, full size chart table and decent galley. Neither of our boats had any of these and we decided that we needed them. We disliked having to make up a bed every night — it's uncivilized and means that you always have to go to bed at the same time. 99% of the time we do so anyway, but sometimes one or other of us will want to sit up and finish a book while the other one wants to go to bed. Equally, it's awkward for the one who gets up first to have a cabin full of bed. We wanted a full size chart table because we were tired of 'navigating on the crease'. It is truly amazing how often the bit of chart you need is right on the middle and you ruin them if you start folding them a different way. We also wanted a chart table divorced from the galley, on which a chart could lie in safety, available for perusal as required. A big galley is, in my opinion, a necessity on a boat and we were impressed with the fact that Mr. Benford's design was one of the first we'd seen with a proper galley. In order to prepare food, serve it out, etc., you need a large work surface. I now enjoy cooking and like having enough room to put things down and to have what I need to hand.

(10) We wanted a monohull. We still have a soft spot for catamarans, but both agree that the only decent looking ones are designed by Jim Wharram, without much in the way of bridge deck accommodation. Unfortunately, you need a fairly big one in order to get a reasonable

amount of space and cargo carrying ability and we don't find that the split accommodation works so well in a cool climate. You always need to go from one hull to the other which, if it's raining, means togging-up first. Either that, or you end up living in one hull and carrying the other round as a sort of spare — and you still have a thundering big boat in harbours and a small one for a party down below.

(11) We wanted a good looking boat. As far as we're concerned, if a boat doesn't look attractive, or at least have a certain *je ne sais quoi*, we're not interested. We like to row away and enjoy the sight of our little ship sitting quietly at anchor and we delight in looking for her when we're ashore and admiring her. True, "beauty is in the eye of the beholder," but she had to look beautiful to us.

Many of our ideas had come from *Stormalong*, the rest had come about with living on *Sheila*, from speaking to other cruising people and from our reading. We wanted a lot of different things in one design, but we were determined to have each one, feeling that for us and for what we wanted to do, they were essential requirements. I'm happy to say that even after sailing *Badger* over 50,000 miles, we've not changed our minds on any of them and we have yet to see the boat we prefer.

(For more about *Badger*, see Appendix IV.)

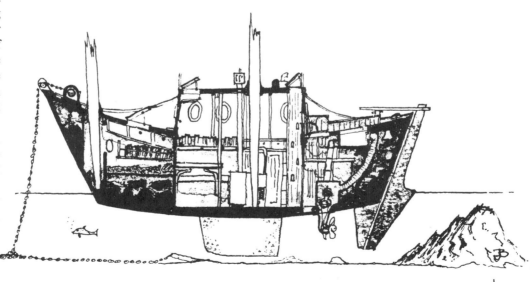

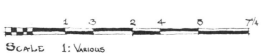

SCALE 1: Various

'BADGER'

~ ACME ILLUSTRATIONS ~
~ HUDDERSFIELD ~

Chapter 5

The Wind Isn't Always Free

Generally speaking, the average cruising boat is rigged as a Bermudian sloop, ketch or cutter. Any other rig is an exception. One might be forgiven for assuming that this is because these are the three best rigs for cruising; in fact the reason that most boats are rigged in this way is because that is how they were designed and the owner bought the boat with the rig that was in it and never gave it a second thought.

The main advantage of the Bermudian sloop is that it is very efficient to windward — indeed, some might say that this is its only advantage. Because of this, it is popular with racing yachts, where the windward leg can be the make or break point of a race and, as usual, cruising boats follow behind. However, for an out and out cruising boat, the modern Bermudian rig has a lot against it and cruising people should not be brainwashed into having such a rig, simply because 'that's what everybody else has'.

Just for the sake of interest, it's worth mentioning some of the disadvantages of this rig, several of which we discovered ourselves, when sailing with it. For a start, windward performance depends to a large extent on the cut of the sails, and after two or three years of hard use, Bermudian sails will be far less efficient than they were when new. It is also necessary to maintain a bar taut forestay to achieve this efficiency, which means that the boat is under constant heavy loads. Whilst on the subject of loads, it is also worth bearing in mind that the loadings from sheets and halliards are also a lot higher than on other cruising rigs.

Bermudian rigs rely on having a large variety of sails for varying wind conditions. In fluky winds, these involve a lot of sail handling and with a small crew, can cause tiredness on an otherwise uncomplicated passage, which will at best spoil their pleasure and in the worst case, lead to poor decisions being made. Sails are expensive to buy and bulky to store and changing them entails going on deck in bad conditions. Should you decide to avoid deck work by having roller furling equipment, you will have high-tech, expensive pieces of equipment to buy,

which if fitted to an existing boat, will tend to mean that you are undercanvassed in light airs and have inadequate and ineffective storm sails in heavy winds. A more modern Bermudian rig may well have a fractional rig, which in many cases, means more complicated rigging.

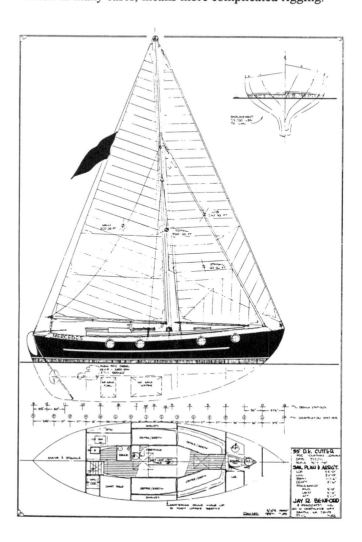

Voyaging people tend to choose downwind passages, and for sailing down wind, the Bermudian rig is hopeless. Indeed once the wind is much abaft the beam, the sails lose a lot of efficiency and with a small mainsail rig, many people drop the main altogether, as the only way to keep the headsail full. Once the wind is on the quarter, you then have to fool around with booming out poles and boom vangs to keep everything out to the side, and then you're really up a gum tree should you want to alter course in a hurry. Even then, your mainsail will be doing a lousy job, as it will be nowhere near squared off, in order to avoid chafe on the spreaders (which may well be swept far back, so as to avoid even more complicated rigging). Then of course, you can consider a spinnaker, but in spite of all its fans, in spite of spinnaker socks and other taming devices, I know of very few sailors who regularly fly a spinnaker on a lightly crewed cruising yacht. And again, in fluky wind conditions, they involve a lot of sail handling. Finally, I don't like the looks of those white triangles. It is an interesting and little known fact that the average non-sailor, whose sense of aesthetics is unsullied by any prejudices or knowledge of the subject, prefers the looks of gaff, lug, dhow or junk rig to Bermudian rig, which must say something. Artists, too, seem to prefer quadrilateral sails to triangular ones.

Instead of accepting the popular wisdom that Bermudian is best, it seems to me to make more sense to look at what is required of a rig that is going to be fitted to a voyaging yacht, whose owners are on a small income. I think that the ideal could be best described as being cheap, simple, efficient and pleasing, and these objects should be kept in mind while deciding on what type of rig would suit your requirements.

If you still like the idea of a Bermudian rig, it can be made a lot more acceptable by treating it rather radically. For example, a large mainsail with plenty of reef points and a small self-tacking jib will result in a boat that is much easier to handle. The large mainsail would give more drive down wind; the small jib, especially if fitted with reef points, would save a lot of foredeck work and by being self-tacking would make short handed sailing in close quarters more fun and less tiring. Because you wouldn't need a large number of jibs, you would get more room below. Admittedly, such a rig wouldn't win you any races, but it would make your passages easier and therefore more pleasant. On the other hand, you would still need storm sails and probably a light weather ghoster, all of which need to be stored somewhere and you would also have to go forward in heavy weather to change down the jib.

One of the rigs that deserves a lot more attention from cruising people is gaff rig. One of its greatest advantages is that it is a low tech rig, which means that it is cheap to set up and cheap to run. Nick Skeates put a gaff rig on *Wylo II* and thinks very highly of it (See Appendix V). However, he gave the matter of weight aloft, an oft cited drawback of the rig, some consideration and

went for a high-peaked sail with a short gaff. Instead of fitting *Wylo II* with massive gear, in the way of so many older boats, he made the gear as strong as was necessary for the type of hard use it would get, without going overboard. In this way, he overcame the disadvantage of having a rig that is too unwieldy to handle easily. *Wylo II* has a large mainsail, which gives the boat a lot of drive off the wind. The gaff sail has this advantage over the Bermudian, an advantage that is increased by the fact that the sail is a quadrilateral so that there is a lot of the sail high up, where the stronger wind is blowing. Because gaff rig often does not have spreaders that chafe the sail, it can be squared out a lot further than a Bermudian sail. With a cutter rig, it is divided into smaller sails, easier for a crew of one or two to handle, and the topsail is an extremely simple and efficient first reef. The rigging is not set up bar taut and so the boat is not under great loads (although with *Wylo II* being built out of steel, no doubt she could easily tolerate such loads) and can be set up on lanyards, which are cheaper than rigging screws. Having sailed in company with *Wylo*, I can say that she goes to windward extremely well — the short light gaff does not sag off anywhere near as much as a longer, heavier one. Nick sails the boat singlehanded much of the time and drives her to make fast passages — faster, I would say, than the majority of yachts. With gaff rig having lots of sails spread out over the boat, it is easy to set enough canvas for gentle breezes, without having to resort to special, large, light-weather sails. When the breeze gets up you simply take sails down, rather than having to replace them with smaller ones.

*Wylo II in the BVI, Spring 1985. The gaff rig is fast downwind. Sailing in company with **Badger**, who has the same waterline length, we found **Wylo** faster to windward, the two boats exactly the same speed from close reach to broad reach and **Badger** faster downwind.*

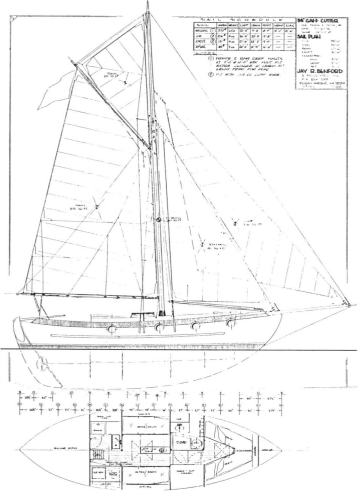

To shake out the reefs, you simply slack off the sheet, the yard hauling parrel and downhaul and heave on the halliard.

However, there are a considerable number of other advantages to junk rig, rarely mentioned. Gybing is quite painless with this rig — you simply bear further and further away until the sail swings over. This is because you can sail by the lee quite happily, due to the fact that the sail is squared right off, and thus it will not gybe until the wind is almost on the beam. This means that at the end of its gybe, the sail is virtually feathered, and all the force has been spent.

The rig is extremely low-tech and can be built on the proverbial shoestring — Donald Ridler used it on *Erik The Red.* It is quite unconcerned as to what you use for sail material and actually works perfectly well with great holes in the sail. *Badger's* original sails were built out of canvas — it cost us £18 — and eventually the sun and rain rotted them. It got to the stage that we would tear the canvas each time we put the sails into their crutches and one panel had a great hole in it, which I reckon you could have climbed through. When we came to make our new sails, we took off the old ones and folded them up. On trying to lift them up, the corners tore away — they couldn't take their own weight, and yet these sails had taken us from the Virgin Islands to the US and back, already pretty rotten. Because they are sewn in vertical panels and have battens running horizontally, a hole or split seam will not go any further.

The junk rig makes for a highly manoeuvrable boat, not in the least because you can actually see where you are going under sail — no deck sweeping genoa on this rig. If the head seems disinclined to pay off, the sail is easily backed to swing her round. *Badger* has two sails and we can tack up the narrowest of channels by putting someone on the foredeck to back the foresail, thus guaranteeing her tacking even if she has hardly any way on. She can be made to turn in just about her own length by gybing her with the foresail sheeted in hard — she will simply spin round when you put the helm down. As well, the ease of reefing means that you can slow the boat down easily, enabling you to sail in close quarters in full control of the situation. Junk rig is superb downwind. The mast should be raked slightly forward as gravity will then hold the sail out even in light airs and a slop. Because there is no rigging, the sails can be squared right off and we sail *Badger* wing-and-wing (or wing-and-wong as we junkies say) as soon as the wind comes noticeably abaft the beam. We actually derive a great deal of innocent amusement from watching sailors with other rigs attempting to do the same, not realizing that the wind is actually on the quarter.

One of the things that everybody asks is, "How well does she go to windward?" Unfortunately, those with junk rigs are constantly dwelling on the fact that Bermudian rigged boats go better to windward, instead of looking at all the other advantages of the rig — in just the same way as multihull magazines are obsessed with

Badger (see Appendix IV) is fitted with junk rig, another much maligned rig. There are two ways of going with junk rig. You can either follow the Chinese ideas in their entirety or you can go for the simplified version, specifically modified for short-handed sailing as developed by 'Blondie' Hasler and Jock McLeod. On *Badger* we went for the latter. Sailing the boat is simplicity itself with only four running lines to each sail and no need to touch anything when tacking. The most obvious advantage of junk rig is the ease of reefing and making sail — it is possible to reef both sails on *Badger* in under a minute. To reef, one simply eases off the halliard until the first batten sits on the boom — while this is happening, the sheet automatically slackens off, thus taking the pressure off the sail. You then top-up the yard, take the slack out of the downhaul (used in heavy weather when gravity alone is no longer sufficient to get the last panel or two down) and haul in the sheet until it is adjusted correctly. There is no need to tie in any reef points — the pull on the sheet keeps the battens together. As many reefs as you want can be put in at one time, stacking the battens one on top of the other.

capsizing. Undoubtedly, a Bermudian rigged boat is faster and more powerful to windward. However, if it came to tacking up a narrow channel, the junk might well win, because we simply put the helm down and round she goes — no cranking of jib sheets. We'd certainly do it with a lot less effort. In truth, we find it difficult to compare *Badger* with Bermudian rigged boats, because we so rarely see one beating to windward — they generally seem to motor sail. When we do make comparisons with other cruising boats, they rarely outpoint us, but generally sail faster. However, one of the prices many of them pay for this is sailing on their ear — junk rigged boats do not heel as much, because the rig induces much less heeling moment.

Badger *sailing off Man O'War Cay in the Bahamas, Spring 1990.*

Badger is slower to windward than she would be with Bermudian rig, but for cruising this is arguably an advantage, as it means that we can sail to windward day after day and be perfectly comfortable and content, which is just as well, as we seem to 'enjoy' more than our fair share of headwinds! With *Sheila*, (our ex 6-metre), we could never slow her down to comfortable speed, she would either do five-plus knots, regardless of how small her jib was, or you could take off the jib and go at two knots. We could never get her to sail at a comfortable four knots. And in the meantime the spray was flying. Other sailors, with boats that go superbly to windward, have told us the same and live to curse their weatherly ship, with its noise, spray and vile motion. *Badger* will sail contentedly at four knots and we're all happy — until a light, cruiser-racer comes on the scene!

Junk rigged boats don't point quite as high as Bermudian rigged boats in flat seas, but on the high seas, there doesn't seem to be a lot in it and we've found that Bermudian rigged boats, with older sails, rarely outpoint us. Although in light airs, one might wish for the sail to be a better shape and give more drive, in strong winds, the junk sail comes into its own. We have driven *Badger* to windward in a Force 9 (in sheltered water) and were astonished how well she went — far better than we had anticipated. It must be because the sails are so flat. If you care to motorsail to windward, you will find the junk ideal: because you heel less, your engine will be able to keep itself lubricated and the fully battened sail can be sheeted in hard and won't flutter, however close you point.

The sail battens themselves, are not without their uses. When hoisting sail, there is no flogging canvas and no thrashing blocks, because the battens tame the sails. A spin-off from this is that you can stop the boat by simply letting go the sheets and sit quite quietly while you think what to do next. The boat can also be hove to by sheeting in the sails hard and putting the helm down a little. She will then jog along happily, forereaching slowly and be very comfortable. The battens are also useful when conning your way through rocks, coral or ice, as they are fairly easy to climb and you get a good view from aloft.

The masts are unstayed, a great advantage, and with wooden masts, there is sufficient weight to give the boat an easy motion without having rigging to make a lot of windage — very lightweight rigs can make for an unpleasantly 'corky' motion. Finally, the sails, like great butterfly wings, look beautiful— especially spread out on either side, powerfully shoving *Badger* through the water at seven knots.

It's fun to cruise in company for a few days, with friends, to compare boats and meet each evening to talk over the day's sail. It's also a good opportunity to take photos of one another's boat. Lesley Rowntree took this one while sailing around Mallorca. I am on the centredeck photographing **Cameleon**.

In my opinion, regardless of what type of rig you have on a voyaging yacht, there is a lot to be said for being able to do all the sail handling from the cockpit or better still, the companionway. One of the reasons that I like this idea is that I have a rotten sense of balance and am not at all happy moving about on deck in any sort of weather. However, you do not want the cockpit to end up with a mass of spaghetti in it, and I think that half a dozen longish lines are more than enough to keep in order. The odd short control line should be a little more easy to find a home for. I would not like to have the cockpit or coachroof cluttered up with (expensive) jammers, and any line of much over 20 feet will need a box or bag for it, rather than just a cleat, which must be easy to use at sea. Well sorted out, such a system is a boon for the more fainthearted of us. On *Badger*, we have four running lines to each sail — the halliard, the sheet, the downhaul and the yard-hauling parrel, which tops the yard into the mast. The halliards are on four-to-one purchases and the foresail and mainsail sheets are on five-and-six-part purchases, respectively, due to the number of battens on the sails. However, the light loads mean that we only need 10mm polypropylene (hemp lookalike) rope for the sheets and halliards, so the rope doesn't take up too much room. The yard-hauling parrels and downhaul, of 8mm line, only have short tails — usually about a couple of feet and only about 25 feet when fully reefed, and so don't really need a home. All the sail handling can be done from our little deck hatch, in which we can be braced securely. We only need oilskins when it's raining, in which case we generally just slip on a jacket.

On a yacht sailed by only two people, one person should be able to do any sail changes that are necessary, without too much effort. While this is obviously important in case one person is incapacitated, it also means that when the person going off watch goes down below, they can turn in knowing that their time off is guaranteed. My own view is that there are few things more squalid than turning in 'all-standing' and few things are more unpleasant than having to go on deck from a warm bunk on a filthy night, with no time to get dressed. In order to avoid both, we went for a rig which would require neither.

Ideally one should try to avoid the expense of winches on a boat. If you need one, it is an idea to mount it centrally, so that it can be used by several lines. However, if you are doing sail handling from the companionway, you will be losing out a lot on your body's leverage, so one or two winches may prove necessary. The use of blocks and tackles should reduce both the quantity and size required. For example, a sliding gooseneck and a block and tackle downhaul may mean that a halliard winch is unnecessary; a purchase on the jib sheets may be possible so that a smaller winch can be used. As with most things, if you do need winches, it's worth buying the best you can afford in order that they will be reliable and last for many years. However, it is not particularly difficult to get hold of second-hand winches in good condition — a lot of people find that production boatbuilders, in order to cut

costs, have fitted winches that are really too small and so need to replace them with larger ones. On a boat with only a couple of crew, self-tailing winches have a lot going for them and we have fitted them on *Badger* to use with the halliards. They are really for my use so that I can get the last panel of sail up when I'm working in the hatchway and have no leverage; we also have a smaller snubbing winch (not self-tailing) for each sheet, which I use when we're reefed down and going to windward. None of them is really necessary when I'm handling the sails from the cockpit, although I would sometimes have a struggle without them. Pete doesn't use them at all.

The cost of sails can be considerable and it is worth having a rig that does not need an extensive wardrobe of sails, taking up space that could be better occupied by strings of onions or bottles of wine. Certainly, it's worth avoiding having to change sails, and having sails that can be reefed should be considered. With a cutter rig particularly, the staysail can have a row of reef points, which will be a lot cheaper than a new storm jib. If the sail is on a boom, the fact that it will need to be of heavier material will not matter as much, as a boomed staysail will not set quite so well anyway. On a gaff rigged boat, the rig will be even more flexible, as there are usually two jibs to come in before the staysail needs reefing. They will, of course, take up room down below, but they tend to be relatively small sails. The Wykeham-Martin roller furling gear is of use here; this piece of kit simply furls the sail around itself, it is not a reefing device, but it leaves a sausage to stow, which strikes me as being simpler than dragging down a recalcitrant sail and stuffing it into a bag. Admittedly, as the sail is set flying, it will not have a bar taut luff, but one can't have everything.

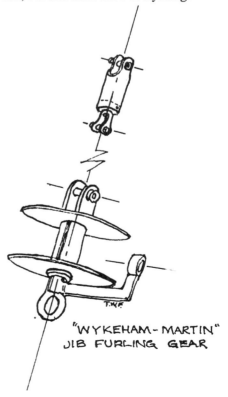

"WYKEHAM-MARTIN"
JIB FURLING GEAR

Unfortunately, most rigs still require you to have a storm trysail and jib. One of the advantages of the junk rig is that with such light loads on the rig, storm sails are not necessary. We've never felt the need for them and I don't think that we've been particularly fortunate with our winds nor have we sailed only in gentle climates.

Another advantage of a low-tech rig is that you only need low-tech sails, which means that you can build them yourself. With junk rig, the sails haven't got any shape to begin with and as most sailmakers will never have made one, they've no more experience than you. With a gaff mainsail, you set the shape yourself, to a large extent, when hoisting it. There are a number of books to help you with building all different types of sails; it's a continuing source of amazement to me that many people will happily loft out and build a boat, but are scared of tackling the sails. As Tom Colvin says, "How bad must a suit of sails be not to work at all? I have never seen such a suit, and I have seen sails on all types of vessels all over the world. Indeed I cannot conceive of a sail so poorly made that it will not function. I don't mean to win races, but just propel the boat — and this is the function of sails." However, once again, small is beautiful: handling big sails and heavy material needs a lot of room and a powerful sewing machine.

The cost of a high-tech rig is much higher than many people seem to appreciate. A good example of this is illustrated by the story of *Badger*'s 36-foot sister, *Donna*.. She was built in Alberta, Canada by a home builder in 1976 for about $25,000.00 (Canadian). Her owner and builder, Fred Schreiner, then sailed her from Vancouver to Mexico, Hawaii and back to British Columbia. The boat had performed well and he was very pleased with her, but felt that with the low gaff ketch rig, she tended to get becalmed in the bottom of the Pacific swells and also lacked light-air performance. I think that if I had owned the boat, I should have been tempted either to completely re-rig her as a gaff cutter, with a topsail or to add topmasts to the existing masts in order to be able to set topsails. However, Mr. Schreiner decided to go for a modern Bermudian rig.

In conjunction with Mr. Benford, he completely re-designed the rig, adding height and increasing the sail area. He then bought the mast and rigging and had the new sails made for the boat. The final cost of the new rig was more than the boat had cost in its entirety, when launched.

When we built *Badger*, the masts, sails, blocks and running rigging came to less than £300. After about 8,000 miles, we made new sails and another 30,000 miles later, we replaced the running rigging and replaced the blocks with larger ones of better quality, although most of the original ones were still in sufficiently good shape that we could sell them. We don't expect to spend any more money on the rig for the next five years, although the sails will probably need the odd repair, which we will do ourselves. We may not sail quite as fast as other yachts, we

may not point quite as high, but if you make comparisons on a cost per mile basis, I think that you will begin to realise that that last 5% of efficiency comes very expensive.

Until recently, it was most extraordinary to see a boat without any standing rigging, but largely due to Gary Hoyt's hard-sell techniques, it has become more acceptable to have free standing masts. There is a lot to be said for this idea. Quite apart from the fact that rigging is expensive, it also makes a lot of drag in high winds. Bearing in mind that wind 30 feet above the water is blowing a third faster than it is at water level, the windage on a tall, rigged mast is quite considerable and something to consider when choosing your ground tackle. Phil Bolger talks about this matter of windage in **Different Boats**, where he points out that in a blow, motor boats with tuna towers will sit more quietly than low hulled sailing boats with tall masts and rigging. As well, the noise of the wind in the rigging is frequently unpleasant and occasionally downright worrying — we have often been visiting other people and started to become concerned about the wind getting up, only to find that it's the noise of the wind in their rigging. How on earth do they put up with it, we ask ourselves. Rigging is also a weak point in a vessel. Being dismasted twice in *Stormalong* has made us rather aware of such things. In our case, to be fair, it was the rope lashing that let us down in the first instance (ultraviolet deterioration — people weren't so aware of it then) and the second time was possibly as a result of having come down once before — the mast just fell down. However, when we think of the stories some of our friends have told us about cracked tangs and corroded fittings, we feel that we'd rather be without the worry. If you have a rig that requires standing rigging, I would think that it is worth designing it for the very minimum number of shrouds and stays and making those well oversize. A final point — rigging is a surprisingly large task when building the boat and needs a lot of checking and maintenance afterwards.

I should very much like to have my masts in tabernacles. Chinese junks used to have their unstayed masts set in tabernacles and the mast was counter balanced with a heavy weight — just like a Broads cruiser. In a Tai-phun (typhoon) they would lower their masts and lie ahull until the blow was over. I can't imagine how they got them up again, but facts is facts and Weston Martyr mentions seeing it done in **The Southseaman**. I must say, I think it would be nice to be able to do it on one's own boat. However, tabernacles have a further advantage in that they are also easier for maintaining the mast (and rigging) because the whole lot can be brought down to your level. Having a mast in a tabernacle can open new cruising grounds where you need to be able to get under bridges, such as the European waterways, and can also save you money when you wish to stay somewhere for a while, as you can sneak up to the top end of the creek, under the bridge, where no-one will charge you. We used to think they were incompatible with unstayed masts — in spite of the Chinese - but Phil Bolger has designed several. We fitted **Missee Lee's** mast in a tabernacle and were delighted with the results. However, she is only a little boat (20-feet and about one ton displacement) and what works on her may not work on a larger vessel, although if we were to build another boat, I think we'd try it out. I love the idea of the counter-balanced mast, but unfortunately they need to go through the deck (in order to have the pivot point high enough upon the mast and low enough down to work the sails), which weakens the boat's structure and somewhat interferes with the accommodation. But it would be great to 'shoot' the bridges on the Intracoastal Waterway, while everybody else was waiting for them to open!

As far as I'm concerned, I can see no argument in favour of aluminium masts. They are unattractive and cold down below, they are noisy — particularly if they have internal halliards, not that easy to repair and rather more vulnerable in the case of rigging failure. On the other hand, wooden masts are quiet, beautiful, easy to alter or repair and strong in and out of compression. As for the maintenance, this can be dramatically reduced with modern techniques. **Badger's** masts are made of laminated douglas fir, sheathed in epoxy/glass fibre and polyurethane painted. They were put in the boat in January 1983 and we have done nothing to them since, apart from repainting them after 6 years because they had chalked rather badly (we finished them with clear polyurethane over the top to stop that from happening again), but that was for cosmetic purposes — the paint was still protecting them. They have done '50,000' miles and, although the sails are held to the mast with parrels of 8mm rope, which have been sawing backwards and forwards for all those miles, there are no signs of chafe.

A lot of people seem to be frightened at the thought of building a wooden mast — although I don't believe that there is anything particularly difficult about the job — and therefore want an aluminium mast. Others believe that they will withstand the compression loads better and prefer aluminium for that reason. They can be obtained fairly cheaply by buying a mast kit, and assembling it yourself. Another idea is to go to a manufacturer and see if he has any that have damaged anodising. They will often sell these off at a substantial discount and the problem is easily cured by painting the mast with a light shade of two-part polyurethane, which make the mast look more attractive anyway. In fact, most American yachts have painted masts and they look much more handsome than silver, gold or worst of all, black anodising. A second-hand mast can be smartened up with similar treatment. Broken racing spars are often a good source for a second-hand mast, especially with a smaller boat, which doesn't need a particularly tall mast.

When Bermudian rigs first began to appear on yachts, they were often know as Marconi rigs, because people thought that they looked like one of Mr. Marconi's radio aerials, so tall and thin and with all that rigging. They seem to be going back that way again. The drawbacks of a tall mast lie not only in its increased windage and heeling moment when it's up, but also in the problems it creates when it's down. A mast that is a lot longer than your boat cannot be safely stored aboard when she's hauled out. It also makes it difficult for you to take the mast out and cruise down a river or canal system where bridges prevent you having it up, because it will overhang either end of the boat by an alarming amount. With the increasingly tall masts on high freeboard yachts, more and more boats will be finding that even the Intra Coastal Waterway (maximum height from truck to waterline 65-feet.) will be closed to them, if they keep their masts in, but few owners would care to motor down it with the mast sticking out 10-feet at either end. There's a lot to be said for a low rig; however, it's not always easy to have low masts and spread enough canvas for light airs. Once again, the smaller, lighter boat is going to prove easier to sort out than the bigger, heavier one.

At the end of the day, a low-tech rig is cheap to set up, cheap to run and easy to maintain. As far as I can see, this makes it extremely efficient and means that you can sail more miles for less money and with fewer worries. It seems to make sense.

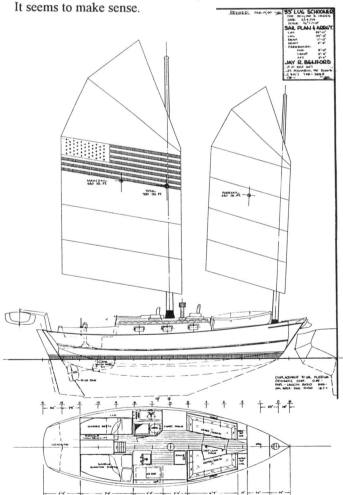

The designer of this steel schooner, Jay Benford, suggests that she could have the same sort of interior layout as **Badger**, *which would make her an excellent voyager.*

AND DON'T APPLY FINISHES IN
TEMPERATURES MUCH OVER 70° F

Chapter 6

Shipshape

When it comes to maintenance, there is no such thing as the perfect material and when you come to select your boat for voyaging, you will, in fact, find yourself considering the Osmosis 32, the Dry Rot 30, the Anode 35 or the Rust Bucket 31. Whatever the advertising blurb says, none of them will be 'maintenance free' and all of them will have both virtues and drawbacks. For voyagers on a small income, the most important thing is that they should be able to maintain the boat themselves, so it makes sense to buy a boat that is built of a material that you understand. On the other hand, we met a chap called Michel in Guadeloupe who was building a steel boat. He explained his choice — 'I'm a carpenter and I know too much about wood, but nothing about steel', which I suppose has a certain logic to it.

It is worth remembering, too, that although steel, for example, is easy to repair and there are welders all over the place, by Sod's law, you will end up on a piece of rock shaped exactly like a can-opener and find out that you're on a desert island. Therefore, unless you have a welding set and generator on board, you can't guarantee being able to carry out cheap repairs. Similarly, with a wooden boat you need spare wood and fastenings, plywood and epoxy; on a ferro boat you should have mesh and cement and so on. Because on a small income, you can't necessarily afford to have professional repairs done, it's worth having both the materials and the skills with which to do your own. As well, being ripped off by an unscrupulous yard after an accident can turn an incident into a disaster. If you *know* that you can do your own work, then at least you have a choice, even if you prefer to have it 'professionally' done.

Take a long-term view, when choosing your boat for voyaging on a small income. The bargain of today may become expensive in the long run, if she needs a lot of money spending on her in order to maintain her to the standard you require. As well, a boat that needs an inordinate amount of time spending on her to keep her smart, will limit the amount of cruising you can do.

Maintenance as such, should not be considered as work. Work is what you get paid for — everything else you do by choice! Even when doing a job like putting on antifouling, I keep reminding myself that I could be toiling in an office instead — and for somebody else, too. I believe that if you love your boat, then the maintenance becomes enjoyable and no longer a chore. To have a boat which is both handsome and of smart appearance is a continuing source of satisfaction, giving renewed pleasure each time you see her. For myself, I thoroughly enjoy doing a spot of varnishing and we both like *Badger* to look like a yacht. The so-called 'work boat' finish that some yachties adopt would not be accepted by a lot of working seamen, whose boats are usually kept very smart, and I don't think that it really takes a lot of effort to keep a boat presentable.

Quite apart from the considerations of pride or aesthetics, there is a lot of common sense in keeping your little ship in good order. Such things as rigging failure, engine failure and sails blowing out could often have been prevented by routine maintenance. A boat that is in fine shape is easy to keep that way, but when you let her go, you'll find yourself running to stand still. All that paint and varnish is not only to make the boat look tiddly, it is there to protect her as well. Yes, I know that teak will put up with a vast amount of abuse and can survive when bare, but if you compare the condition of a varnished covering board with its neighbouring deck plank, you will see how much even teak suffers from weathering. On the other hand, if you detest maintenance, it is much better to paint the whole lot than to kid yourself that you'll do the varnish some day. It is also worth bearing in mind that if you should want to sell your boat in a hurry — dire financial straits or the boat of your dreams at rock-bottom price — it'll be a lot easier getting someone interested in her if she looks in good condition.

As with so many things, when maintaining your boat it is worth investing in good quality products. In the **£200 Millionaire,** the old gentleman tells his visitors how it happened that each time he'd saved a bit of money: "I tried to get rid of some of it by buying extra fine gear for the boat, but I found that scheme merely saved me more money in the long-run. For instance, I scrapped my Manila running rigging and replaced it with best hemp at twice the cost, but I'll be bothered if the hemp hasn't lasted four times as long as the Manila already!" I am sure that the same still holds true.

When we built *Badger*, we used teak above decks wherever there was going to be varnish because, particularly in the Tropics, trying to keep any other type of wood looking up to scratch ends up breaking your heart. Having tried several types of finish, I have found that the type that suits our situation best is two-part, polyurethane (with an ultra-violet filter) such as is sold by Structural Polymers of Cowes, WEST System products or International Paints. The only drawback of some of these is that the hardener will go solid if exposed to air, so that you have to keep decanting it into smaller and smaller pots. Although not cheap, the varnish lasts incredibly well and looks superb. It is possible to apply more than one coat in a day and it goes on beautifully. If damaged, it doesn't seem to lift and the moisture doesn't get under it. When you want to freshen it up, you sand it down one day and touch up the damaged areas. The next day you sand down those spots again and then put two coats on and that's it for another year. From time to time we have left *Badger*'s brightwork for longer than that and it has still looked better than that on most other boats. We know of people who have used a similar finish on a conventionally built wooden boat and they have also been perfectly happy with it. Incidentally, I have never had any problems in getting varnish to stick to teak, and nor has anyone else that I've spoken to, who is interested in the job. The secret, if there is one, is proper preparation and enough coats.

We have also used two-part polyurethane on *Badger*'s topsides in the past and this too, looked very well. However, on the negative side are the facts that in warm places, the salt dries on it and makes a white film that is difficult to remove and unsightly on black topsides. However, a month or so in temperate latitudes is enough to remove this — the rain seems to dissolve it after a while. The other problem is that damage from such things as unfendered dinghies doesn't get touched up straight away, because we tend to be lazy and too mean to mix up such a small batch. In the end, we decided to use polyurethane on the cabin sides, which are painted cream and use ordinary gloss paint on the black topsides.

Incidentally, when using two-pack polyurethane paints, it is not that difficult to get a good finish if you are careful and don't apply the finishes in temperatures much over 70 °F. However, a truly excellent finish can be obtained by overcoating with clear polyurethane, which brushes better. It is also easier to repair than the coloured finish, because there is no problem with fading and subsequent colour matching.

When using oil-based paints, we have generally used good quality house paints and found them as good as those 'formulated for yachtsmen' and a lot cheaper. The gloss often seems better, too, which helps its longevity — an instance where the more expensive is not necessarily the best.

Traditional wooden boats are supposed to take the most maintenance, but if they are in good order, I don't think that is the case. It is a damn' sight easier to put on a coat of paint than it is to polish the topsides of a fibreglass boat — let alone repairing scratches and gouges and especially if you are doing it afloat, from a dinghy. Eric Hiscock reckoned that maintaining *Wanderer IV*, built of steel, involved considerably more work than caring for her predecessor and that she never looked as smart. Certainly, the thought of grit blasting a steel boat every 10 years or so, is not a happy one for the sailor whose boat is also his home. Ferro-cement is very easy to care for — once you've got the paint to stick, but like steel, it is sensible to paint the hull in a dark colour as a little rust goes a very long way on white topsides. The sort of paint that is used on rendered houses makes excellent deck paint, incidentally and must be ideal for a ferro boat. It comes in tasteful, pastel shades, which are restful to the eyes and has a good non slip finish. The fans of aluminium point out that it does not need painting. While this is beyond dispute, I'm sure that most people do not find the appearance of unpainted aluminium attractive and I certainly wouldn't want to live with it.

The most important maintenance for an unsheathed wooden boat, is in keeping a good coating of antifouling on the bottom. Marine borers are a worry and no joke. It is, however, possible to get a paint-on latex from Davey & Co. (who else?), which will give the little beasts acute toothache if they try to get through it. A cold-moulded or plywood boat should be sheathed with epoxy and cloth to keep out borers. All voyaging boats, however, need antifouling and good quality antifouling paint is horribly expensive. When we originally built *Badger*, we mixed cuprous oxide with epoxy and coated her bottom with that. It worked quite well, with periodic scrubbing, (to expose fresh copper), but had to be abandoned when we fitted the engine with an aluminium saildrive. We've since heard that one should use pure copper powder, rather than cuprous oxide, but do not know what the correct proportions are — as much as you can add so that it can still be readily applied, I'd guess. If you get a good deal on antifouling paint, it's worth stocking up and, although the shelf life is supposed to be limited, we've never found old stuff to be any less effective than new. However, good deals are not always as good as they seem — we bought a famous brand of antifouling in Venezuela at £15 per gallon, but found it was quite useless after only a few weeks! Hauling out in order to slap the stuff on can also be expensive and it is worth having a boat which will dry out happily.

This has been brought home to us because *Badger* was always difficult to dry out. The flared topsides and angled-in cabin sides made it tricky to ensure that she stayed upright. No doubt we were a trifle neurotic, but we felt it better to be safe than sorry. However, in 1989, we fitted one of Mr. Warwick Collins' Tandem keels, which has a great delta wing at the bottom, that makes her a lot more stable when dried out.

To assist in this, we decided that *Badger* should have legs. However, we didn't really fancy the idea of lugging round thundering, great hardwood legs for the foreseeable future and so invested in some of Mr. John Franklin's Yachtlegs™. These are manufactured of marine grade aluminium and being telescopic, take up far less room than conventional legs — in fact we can store them down below. Because of *Badger*'s great flare, Mr. Franklin had to do slight alterations to the basic kit; they are all effectively made-to-measure and it was nice to deal with somebody who obviously cared about his clients. Once again, we had to put down quite a lot of money for good quality equipment. However, gains are made from the fact that, since we bought them, we have not needed to pay for a haulout for antifouling. As long as we keep visiting tidal areas, we should be able to avoid this and if we do need to be hauled out, we can be firmly secured on our legs. Also in tidal areas, we can explore much more thoroughly knowing that we can dry out if necessary. Had we had legs for *Badger* when we went back to the UK for 2 years, we could have found ourselves a snug berth for the winter up a creek somewhere, and saved a lot of storage bills.

When building *Badger*, we decided to put on teak decks, overlaid onto the plywood. Following the Gougeon Brothers' advice, we only used 3/16" teak — which kept both the cost and the weight down — and have found it very satisfactory and showing no real signs of wear, in spite of the fact that the after deck has been down about 10 years and continually walked over. We chose teak not only because it looks so nice and is a good non-slip surface, but also to keep down the cost of maintenance. We actually varnish the king plank and covering board, for the appearance, but they don't really cost anything to maintain. The experts say that scrubbing teak decks is bad for them, so we don't need to do that, either. In fact, as long as we avoid going alongside and cities, which we try to avoid anyway, the decks don't get dirty. On *Sheila* we had painted, canvas covered decks which were very attractive.

However, the paint stained easily and we were always repainting them to keep her smart, which on a boat the size of *Badger* would cost a fair bit of money. It seems to be the oddest of things that make a hole in your budget.

Down below, we have tried to avoid paintwork, because of the problems of repainting a boat on which you are living. *Badger* is fitted out in pitch pine, because it is a fairly light colour, attractive to look at and was cheap (second-hand stuff, which we ripped up ourselves). From the beam shelf down, everything is varnished, as are all the bulkheads; the varnish can be kept like new by washing down with warm, soapy water and then drying and polishing with a chamois leather — often just a wipe over with a damp chamois will suffice. However, we decided that with everything varnished, it would be too dark and that the deckhead and the cabin sides, front and back should be white. For this we used white melamine. Although it does tend to attract the dirt, particularly when we had a solid fuel fire, it washes down easily with a bit of Jif and doesn't yellow in the way that paint does. We also used varnish in the lazarette and inside the lockers — varnish doesn't show the dirt like paint — on the other hand it doesn't reflect the light either! If we'd had more money we'd have used melamine there, too.

All the time we were building *Badger,* we tried to make things easy to maintain, while at the same time keeping to a yacht finish. Although, as I said, we don't really regard maintaining our boat as a chore, it is good to know that we can spend a lot of time sailing and stay in harbour out of choice rather than out of necessity.

Postscript: **WoodenBoat** magazine (Number 100, May/June 1991) did a survey of boat yards specializing in yacht maintenance and asked them, in their opinion, what was the boat that needed least maintenance. The result? A cold moulded wood/epoxy hull with a Dynel-over-marine-plywood decks and cabins, all surfaced with modern urethane paint, equipped with anodized aluminium spars and the most rugged and straightforward gear available.

YOU ARE IN AN AREA WHERE SECOND-
HAND BOATS ARE FEW AND FAR BETWEEN

Chapter 7

Fools Rush In

A lot of small income voyagers sail boats that they built themselves, but this possibly reflects their individualism rather than suggesting that this is always the most logical way to go. The decision to build your own boat is not one that should be taken lightly, and it is well worth while sitting down and working out the pros and cons before taking on such a project.

Although we have friends who have built their boat on the proverbial shoestring — Nick Skeates built his 32 foot *Wylo II* for $4,000 (New Zealand), generally speaking, you don't necessarily obtain the cheapest boat by building your own. In order to do it on the cheap, you have to invest a vast amount of time begging, scrounging and hunting out bargains. You also have to build the boat totally, not simply fit out a hull and buy in items like the rig and sails. If you are in a good job, it may be worth putting a price on your time to see if it is actually cost effective to build. However, having said that, it is quite possible to build for a reasonable outlay and end up with a good, high quality vessel. We built *Badger* between May 1980 and May 1983. When we set off from Glasson Dock, she had cost us a total of £11,000. That figure includes all the materials in the boat; the equipment for building her, such as electric drills (three!), circular saw, etc.; rental of the area in which we built her (including the cost of transport from one site to the other when we were evicted from our first site); consumables such as sandpaper and paintbrushes and everything else associated with her — even two new sets of oilskins! We believe that we have a much more suitable boat than we could have bought off the shelf, better built than a production boat and she probably cost less than a third of the price. We did get some fantastic bargains, but then so do most people who build their own.

There are a lot of good buys on the second hand market, particularly among the smaller boats and especially with plywood and ferro cement, neither of which materials is generally popular. If you can find out who built the ferro boat and exactly how it was done, it could

prove a good buy. However, without damaging the boat, it's impossible to check the construction after she's been built and there are a lot of very poor examples about. If you can't be certain that she was well built, it would be too risky to choose such a boat for *voyaging*. With plywood, a point to consider is that it is actually fairly cheap and easy to replace a whole side, so that one that is quite seriously damaged may be worth taking on, if the underlying structure is sound. If you find one in good condition, you could burn her off and dry the hull out, before covering it with cloth and epoxy, in order to keep out rot and worms. If you do this job carefully, you will end up with a boat that will last for many years with little maintenance, and for a reasonable initial outlay. If you feel that you could manage major work on a traditional wooden boat, these are also worthy of consideration, as labour costs frequently mean that no-one is willing to take on a wooden boat that is in poor condition. The same applies to a fibreglass boat with osmosis — again professional repairs are expensive, but a lot of the cost is in labour. A boat that needs five hundred hours work on it could well be written off by the insurers, and yet the material costs to put her back into good order may only be a couple of hundred pounds or so. Thus it's well worth looking at second hand boats before committing yourself too far.

Basically, the reasons to build your own can be summarized as:

● You are very broke, but are just able to get together what you need to build the most basic boat, which will get you off sailing.

● You are in an area where second-hand boats are few and far between.

● You are unable to find what you want on the second-hand market and adapting what is available is not really feasible.

● You want to build a boat.

The first and the last reasons will probably ensure that you are pretty successful about the whole deal. When there is less incentive to build your own, starting from scratch may end up as too great an undertaking — investigate bare hulls and unfinished projects, but remember that they may end up more expensive.

If you are building due to near bankruptcy, I would strongly advise reading **Erik the Red** by Donald Ridler. In fact, I'd recommend it anyway, because it's such a good book. He chose a design called a *Mouette*, which can still be obtained from the Eventide Owners Association, who advertise in **Practical Boat Owner** and **Yachting Monthly**. He built his boat from largely second-hand wood, rigged her as a junk (good man!) and then sailed across the Atlantic and back. Some years later he set off round the world and had almost completed the journey, when he was wrecked, I think in the Cape Verde Islands. As value for money, there have been few better boats and no-one reading his book could deny that he had a lot of fun, too.

ERIC THE RED

If you want to build a boat, nothing is going to stop you, so you might as well go ahead. However, it is worth considering whether she is going to suit you at the end of the day. If you have never lived aboard or done extensive cruising, it is very likely that the first boat that you build will turn out to be quite different from what you really want. Therefore either build something that will be easy to sell, or prepare yourself for having to make fairly major changes. Of course, best of all, convince yourself that she's perfect, even if she isn't. Whatever else you do, don't build too big — she will end up breaking your bank balance as well as your heart; and don't take too long about it. Remember that you will probably not be insured and should you be unlucky enough to lose the boat, you would be throwing all those years of your life away. We spent three years building *Badger* and I felt that we needed to get at least three years sailing out of her. After that, we started winning and whilst I would have difficulty in coping with losing her now, at least I'd feel that we'd had a good return

for our investment of time in her, to say nothing of the money.

We both went out to work while we built *Badger*. The one thing that this has to recommend it is that when you go over budget, and 90% of people do, you will still be getting money in to pay for what you need. You will also be working so incredibly hard that you will have no time for any social life, so that you will be saving money on entertainment too, which, if looked at the right way, can also be considered an advantage. I'm not exaggerating either; if you're out at full time work and are building everything yourself to a halfway decent standard *and* you want to get away in the foreseeable future, you will have to spend every spare minute on the boat. When we were building *Badger*, we reckoned that we each put in a 40-hour week on her, as well as doing our "day jobs". (It must not be forgotten either, that someone has to do the cooking, laundry, housekeeping, etc. to keep you going in your present home). I suppose that what I'm trying to say is that it's not much fun, and if you move on board before you've finished, it will be even less fun — I know, we did it. Someone wanted to buy *Sheila* and so we hadn't much choice, really, but it was hard on our sense of humour at times — everything ended up with WEST epoxy on it somewhere. The other difficulty with living onboard as you're building, is that there is even more temptation to go off before the boat's finished. Mind you, to be realistic, no boat is ever completely finished and if you waited until she was perfect, you'd never get away.

We came across an example of this where we were building *Badger*. A man there had bought a catamaran. In fact he had bought this boat about the time we went off in *Stormalong*, five years before we started *Badger* and at that time he was intending to alter her interior to suit himself and his family. Over the years, the galley was rebuilt three times and the rest of the interior at least twice, while he got the boat perfect. As far as I know, he is still there, planning to go away "next year". I suppose that he didn't really want to escape because if you want to get away enough, you will.

At the end of the day, we are happy that we built *Badger* and we'd do it again. Ideally, we would build full time and if we ever need to replace *Badger*, due to losing her or to having somebody come up to us and offer us an outrageous amount of money for her (well, everyone's allowed to dream, aren't they?), we'd happily build another boat. However, we both enjoy boatbuilding and would like to build more boats anyway.

Of course, the great thing about a boat that you've built yourself is that you have done the best job that you can and I'm not sure that there are many boats built these days, about which the same comment could be made. I think that it's fair to say that once you've built your own boat from scratch, you'd find it very difficult to trust anybody else's — so make sure it's the right one. Remember the old saying: 'Rich men build boats for poor men to buy from them'— and you're not even rich!

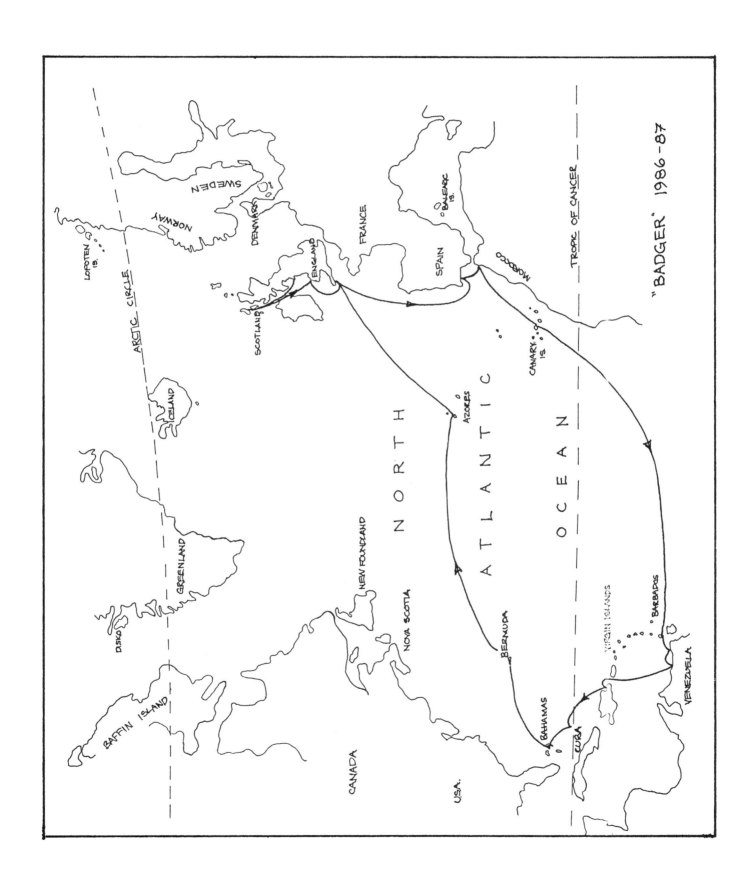

Chapter 8

The Heart Of The Boat

Never mind the chart table or the saloon, the real centre of a voyaging yacht is its galley. On passage, it is actively used more than any other part of the vessel and in too many cases, it has had the least attention paid to it.

In the average production boat the galley is at best barely adequate and at worst a joke. This is hardly surprising, as these boats are made for people who rarely use the galley except to brew up, heat up the occasional tin or make breakfast in the marina. As well, building in drawers and lockers takes time and skill, whereas building bunks costs very little. This was brought home to me at a recent boat show, when I was looking over a French built 34-footer, comparing her with *Badger*.

"Where's the cutlery drawer on this boat?" I asked the salesman.

"Oh, we don't fit drawers on this boat", he replied, "people put the cutlery on that narrow shelf behind the settee, normally. The 40-footer has two drawers on it,'" he added helpfully, "but that's the smallest boat we fit drawers to".

One of the aspects of voyaging on a small income is that you tend to do quite a lot of cooking and the galley should enable you to do this job with the minimum of problems and the maximum of pleasure. Above all, this should be the case at sea when good food is so important, particularly in bad weather when morale can be low.

The first thing about a galley is that it should be as big as possible. The average, weekend, macho skipper likes to go on a boat and pour scorn on the galleys "built for the ladies". This is because he thinks that sailing should be uncomfortable and squalid and undoubtedly goes in for such senseless practices as turning in 'all-standing' in a damp sleeping bag and then wonders why he feels cold all through his watch on deck. But I digress. The galley, I say, should be big. The reasons for this are manifold, but a long work surface is the primary one. A long counter enables you to dish up more than one serving at a time, it allows you to put plates down, to get out what you need to make a meal, to prepare vegetables, to roll out pastry and to make bread. It gives room for crockery and pans and allows you to spread yourself out when you want to cook

something a bit special. It also means that there is plenty of locker space underneath. Locker space is useful at the best of times, but essential for the pauper cook. You will use plenty of herbs and spices to enhance the flavour of cheap food, particularly as curry will probably be on the menu a fair bit. (Curry powder does not keep its flavour very well and is not always easy to obtain. It makes a lot more sense to buy fairly large quantities of the individual, whole spices, when they are available and use them for your curries, which incidentally end up tasting more interesting.) If you are going to eat beans — and what small income voyager won't be — you will need room to put all your most often used pots in the galley. There are few things more annoying for either the cook or the crew than having to rummage under the settee, each time you want to make a meal. You will also want lockers for tea, coffee, lemon juice, dried milk, tomato purée, soya sauce, baking powder, jam, yeast, etc.

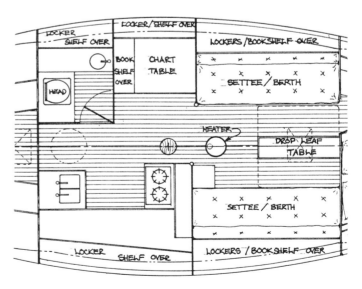

On *Badger*, my galley is essentially U shaped, but it is a U with a long base and short arms. The first thing that strikes a lot of visitors is that the cooker is athwartships. Originally, we had a diesel range that could not be gimballed anyway (because of the chimney), but I had already decided to have the cooker athwartships for several reasons. For a start, if you are going to have a gimballed cooker, you are going to waste a lot of space to allow it to swing. Not only that, but the only realistic place to put it is in the middle of the counter, thus breaking the work surface into smaller units. While it is possible to use the athwartships area that would otherwise be filled by cooker, this is far less satisfactory, as everything will always slide down to leeward and placing fiddles across will take you back to square one. Another disadvantage of a gimballed cooker, for those who enjoy cooking, is that it is difficult to see what's going on in the pan when it is leaning away from you. Maybe I find this a particular problem due to my lack of height, but I'm not the only hobbit in the world. The final reason that I like an athwartships cooker is because in heavy weather, when even the best of gimballs can be put out of action, I am not standing downhill of any hot pans or boiling liquids that may decide to come away from their proper place — they will end up all over the cabin sole and not all over me. If you have a gimballed cooker, it is essential to fit a crash bar so that if the boat lurches and the cook falls towards the cooker, she will not hit it and knock it off balance, spilling boiling food about.

Badger's cooker is at the forward end of the galley and, since we changed back to paraffin, has one of Davey & Company's nifty bronze mushroom ventilators over the top, where the chimney used to be. This lovely bit of kit has two glass lights let into it, thus providing a little more illumination, as well as ventilation. The screw holes exactly fitted those of the chimney surround, so it was obviously Meant. Forward of the cooker, stretching across most of the counter is a tiled area for hot pans. There is a removable fiddle that fits there at sea, to stop the pans sliding downhill. At the outboard end is space for the kettle to sit. Underneath the cooker is a pan locker which holds three saucepans, a frying pan, wok and the pressure cooker. The wok sits upside down over the frying pan, otherwise none of them is stacked. Under the pan locker is stored water and detergent and there is room for bottles of olive oil, vinegar, etc. Between the cooker and the counter is a rack which holds the sharp knives and the steel. Incorporated in this is a place in which the pressure cooker lid can fit, so that there is a safe place to put it when it is very hot. There is also a hook for the galley lighter. Inboard of the cooker is a laminated rail, which usually has the tea-towel hung on it.

As *Badger* has a full width/raised-deck cabin, there seems to be lots of room in the galley. On the deckhead at the after end we have a rack for wineglasses, like they have in pubs. Along the sheer clamp is a long shelf on which I have about a score of little plastic tubs which hold herbs and spices. Under this shelf is locker space, with four doors. The first two hold ready-use beans, coffee, dried milk, and such things as the pepper mill and tomato purée. The third one has a divided box which holds

dessert bowls, breakfast bowls, saucers and tea plates and the fourth one has more ready-use tubs. The counter itself is 6 feet long, made of teak-faced plywood and varnished with two-part polyurethane varnish. Under the counter in the base of the 'U', are five drawers and a full height locker door. The drawers contain: (1) cutlery and cooking tools, (2) dinner plates, dessert plates, mugs and cups, (3) tea-towels and tea cosy, (4) glasses and bits and pieces, (5) glasses. The door gives access to a large locker, with three shelves, the upper two of which are each divided into six sections. At the forward and more inaccessible end are stored items for long-term use. The after two sections contain such things as ready-use pots of nuts, dried fruit, etc., jars of jam, mayonnaise, peanut butter and so on. The bottom shelf holds the bread bin, a couple of flasks and water containers.

At the after end of the galley is a double sink. The two basins are very small, but deep, to save water and there are two hand pumps. The sinks are also made of teak-faced ply and varnished and have been very successful. Against the companionway bulkhead is a rack for washing-up liquid, etc., and a paper towel holder. Under the sink, outboard, is a shelf for the cake tin, containers for oats and pasta, measuring jugs, etc.; directly under the sink is another shelf and in the space below are stored the muesli tub, the flour tub, fresh vegetables and the two containers for water — a five-gallon one for fresh and a two-gallon one for either fresh or salt water, depending on the availability of the former and cleanliness of the latter. (See Chapter 10, **Waterworks**)

I hope that all the above isn't too tedious, but I think it shows how a very efficient galley can be built just by paying some attention to the details. I'm not saying that *Badger's* galley would be everybody's ideal or that there is no better way of doing it, but the ideas we've used come from hard won experience and they all work. For example, the pan stowage works very well; a lot of people buy stacking pans to try and save space, but somehow you always seem to want the one in the middle and then there is nowhere to put all the lids, while you get it out. A good home for condiments is essential and they need to be able to stay dry. Ideally, you don't want them behind the cooker because it would be dangerous to reach over for them and you certainly don't want them under a lifting hatch in the counter, because there will always be something on it when you need to get under. In fact, lifting hatches of any sort in a galley counter are an abomination.

At times, I will be the first to admit that our sinks are inconveniently small, but for the number of occasions that you need a large sink, it is better to stow a large plastic bowl away and not waste water the rest of the time. Also, because the sinks need so little water, we can use fresh water in which to wash up, which means that everything is more pleasant to use.

The fact that the galley is U shaped makes it easy to work in. I have a galley strap which runs across the base of the U and lean against that when on the starboard tack. It is made of 2-inch Terylene™ webbing and has a sail hank at one end and a snap hook at the other. At sea, it is left in place until we change tack and use it at the chart table. Because everything is to hand, I don't need to be constantly re-fastening it and I find it very comfortable to use and am able to reach counter, cooker and sinks.

Being largely of varnished wood, *Badger*'s galley is a pleasant place in which to work; I think that lots of plastic and stainless steel make a galley feel like an operating theatre. Tiled counters are noisy and encourage broken glasses, as well as being unsatisfactory for bread making; they are also difficult to keep clean enough for food preparation. On the other hand, the small tiled area which I have for pans does work well — it has room for four pans side by side and I don't need to worry about how hot the pan is. A useful tip, if you are having a tiled area, is to use darker coloured ones with which you can use a dark coloured grout. White grout is constantly getting stained and it is very difficult to clean — bleach will eventually destroy the grouting. Melamine counters are very popular, but do eventually get scratched and stained and look, in my opinion, less attractive than varnished wood. I found out the hard way that the two-part polyurethane varnish is heat proof; I put down a very hot plate and scorched the wood underneath without affecting the varnish at all! When it eventually gets scratched, it is no big deal to revarnish.

With good stowage for crockery and glassware, we have very few breakages — no more than we would in a house. Cheap pottery costs very little money and is much nicer to eat from than plastic. We have a couple of wooden platters we use at sea. Actually, this is more to stop the food sliding off the plate, than because we are worried about breakages. Plastic glasses are horrid to drink from and, as you can buy glass ones for virtually nothing, I cannot understand why people use them. Whenever we have broken a glass, it has generally been while washing it up; I can't remember one ever being thrown across the cabin by a wave. On the other hand, we do put them down carefully, so that they are very unlikely to get thrown about — we can't afford to spill the contents.

It's difficult to decide just what is essential in the way of cooking utensils. The best method I have found is not to buy something until its lack becomes so irritating that I know I really need it. I try not to let the galley get cluttered, because it will then become inefficient and less of a pleasure to work in.

Badger's galley is to one side of the passage fore and aft and this is a happy situation. The poor cook will be sorely tried if constantly interrupted by people pushing past. Believe me, one smallish man can become a 'constant interruption by people pushing past', if he is jumping from chart table to companionway for a bit of tricky pilotage. This is perhaps a good place to mention that wherever possible, the chart table and galley should be separate. Fierce and bitter become the arguments between cook and navigator when a work surface is meant to be shared.

One of the nice things on *Badger* is the two opening scuttles in the galley. They help enormously in ventilation and are useful for disposing of bio-degradable items such as vegetable tops and tea leaves, as well as allowing the cook to watch the world go by. If you have side decks, long arms are useful — on *Sheila*, we always seemed to have bits of garlic peel scattered about.

When I had the diesel range, I had a free oven all the time and very nice it was, too. On returning to paraffin, we debated whether to get a cooker with oven or not, and decided against one as the cooker becomes rather tall and we felt it might be expensive to run an extra burner. Although I sometimes miss the oven, I don't regret the decision and rather enjoy seeing what I can produce with the pressure cooker and frying pan. I certainly would not sacrifice space for an oven and would put one into the luxury category.

If we were to build *Badger* again, I would keep the galley just as it is and I would hate to move on to a boat with a small or badly designed galley. We are both convinced that at the end of the day, the time and effort spent in creating a good galley are well spent. A decent place to work will encourage the cook and result in savings in food costs as well as an improved quality of life for all concerned.

A LITTLE LOVED ITEM ON ANY SHIP

Chapter 9

They Bored A Hole
Within The Hull ...

I'm never very happy about putting holes through any part of a boat, but particularly underwater. That little ditty has a lot of truth in it:

> They bored a hole within the hull
> To let the water out
> But more and more with awful roar
> The water in did spout!

Amusing as the verse is, it is also true that boats have been lost through failure of a skin fitting. Not very long ago, a famous American sailor took delivery of a brand new yacht. A short while after, he was sailing along and noticed water over the floor boards; however, there were so many seacocks and the water was coming in so rapidly that he could not examine each one and the yacht had to be abandoned — sinking soon after. If my memory serves, there were 14 seacocks altogether and one would have been enough to sink the boat.

Seacocks are expensive items, need maintaining and are a weak point in the boat. Personally, I believe that there's a lot to be said for doing without them altogether, if possible. One less hole in the hull is one less worry. In fact it's rather ironic that, after years of trying to make boats watertight and having finally achieved this desirable state of affairs due to modern materials and technology, today's yacht builders seem to go out of their way to make the bottom of a boat look more like a colander than anything else. Having said this, it is obvious that some of the items for which these holes exist are essential, the question is, are the holes themselves essential?

I think that the least justifiable hole below the waterline is one made for a wash basin in the heads. As the wash basin itself is certainly a luxury (there's always the galley sink), to put in a skin fitting below the water line, for the sole purpose of draining it without any expenditure of effort, is more than a little decadent. There are two other ways in which a basin could be emptied: the simplest is to have a removable bowl and pour the contents down the heads (which would certainly not be harmed by some soapy water) or into the galley sink, and the alternative method is to install a small pump which enables the water to be pumped out over the side, through a fitting *above* the waterline.

The galley sink itself, can be most irritating when fitted with seacocks to let it drain. On a lot of boats it is not uncommon for the water to surge up the plug holes when the sink is to leeward and apart from the fact that it gurgles infuriatingly, anything in the sink floats about in a most annoying manner. I remember sailing on a friend's boat where the sink had been put in so poorly, that not only would the water come up the plug hole, but it would then overflow onto the counter and ultimately into the bilge. As this particular sink was not even fitted with a seacock, the set-up was potentially lethal. Of course, you can turn the seacock off each time you use the sink, but it's a real bother and even so, the sink may well not drain properly when it's to leeward. Another nuisance is that the pressure on the plug may well be sufficient to push it out and then all your hot water becomes rapidly diluted with cold seawater. On *Badger*, we have a pump for our galley sinks and are perfectly happy with the arrangement. Mr. Hiscock says that the pumps can get blocked with food bits, etc. and although I hesitate to disagree with The Master, I have to say that after four years of living on *Sheila*, where we had the same arrangement and ten years on *Badger*, we have never had a blocked pump. Of course, being poor is an asset here — our plates are always scraped clean. On smaller boats, a bowl makes a perfectly satisfactory sink, as long as the washer-up remembers to check for cutlery before he empties the bowl.

The sea toilet is a little-loved item on board any ship. I think that everyone has their favourite story about them and most skippers can tell gruesome tales of having to disembowel the beast as sea, after it went wrong. A lot of them are less than pleasant to use when the boat is under way: if the seat isn't actually wet before you sit down, the bowl is so shallow as to give you very unpleasant sensations of insecurity. Visiting landlubbers need a course before they can use them and are then terrified that they will turn the wrong knob and sink the boat. Add to this the fact that fear of blocking the damn' things up, is enough to induce constipation in anyone and one begins to wonder why we bother with them at all.

When we lived on both *Stormalong* and *Sheila*, we had what yachting writers used to refer to as a "sanitary bucket". It had a lot in its favour — it never got blocked, was easily overhauled and serviced and was very cheap. Against it was the fact that the rim was wet, it slid about in a seaway, (but then it didn't have its own locker) it was not very discreet to empty in the daytime and, in winter because it lived outside, it was very cold to sit on. However, on odds I was happier using our bucket than our friends' sea toilets, so that when we came to build *Badger*, we discussed the matter at some length, particularly as we didn't want holes in the hull. On the other hand, I felt that it would be nice to be a little more civilized. After looking around, we came across what we consider to be the ideal compromise — the Khemi Kaze. Before you reel away in horror with memories of Girl Guides' camps, I would point out that chemical toilets have come a long way in the past few years, largely due to the increased popularity of caravanning. They consist of a holding tank and a fresh water tank for flushing. The modern ones are in two pieces and to empty them, you separate the flushing unit and bowl from the holding tank, which can then be taken to a toilet ashore or emptied over the side. The chemical liquid is put straight into the holding tank and prevents any smell while starting to break down the contents, making it more ecologically responsible to use.

We fitted one of these to *Badger* and I am bound to say that we are very pleased with it. It is a fairly small unit and with two of us on board, it is quite happy being emptied once a day. One of the nice things about this is that the contents can be dumped at night, which is rather more discreet than a bucket and better than a conventional sea toilet too, where solid matter is often pumped into the surrounding water during daylight hours and when people are swimming. As well, the toilet never gets blocked so that one doesn't need to terrify visitors with a list of things they must not do. For that matter, being so simple to use, it is far less embarrassing for landlubbers, who are unlikely to have to come back into the cabin apologizing that they have forgotten which knob to turn next.

Even in this Eden there is, however, the odd serpent. One must remember that the holding tank can get full and empty it in time — and discourage one's more hygienic visitors from using it as a bidet. The chemical is not particularly cheap and the unit has to be emptied regardless of the weather. Admittedly, it has the advantage over a bucket that it only has to be emptied once a day, but on *Badger*, it does strike us as rather ludicrous that the only time anyone has to leave the shelter of the cabin, is to go out and empty the heads! However, it is pleasant to use at sea, because the bowl is never full of water. It can be lifted out in its entirety, which makes it very easy to clean around and being a plastic moulding, the unit itself is no effort to keep clean. And, of course, it doesn't need any plumbing with the added bonus that it is quite legal in areas that demand that marine heads are fitted with holding tanks. Another less obvious advantage, is that if you are hauled out or dried out, you can still use the boat's heads. In fact, Pete and I both regard our little Porta-Potti™ as more civilized than a conventional sea toilet, on the principle that civilization equals simplicity and contentment, not complication and worry.

The most difficult of all through-hull fittings to avoid are those caused by the engine. The average engine as well as having a water intake, also has a stern shaft which goes through the hull and whose bearing, in many cases, is actually designed to leak at a controlled rate. There is not really a lot you can do about these on an existing arrangement and not even I would suggest chucking out a perfectly good engine for the sake of eliminating an underwater skin fitting. However, if you're are about to consider changing your present engine or if you are building from scratch, unnecessary holes below the waterline can be avoided.

The simplest solution is to fit an outboard engine. Unfortunately, aesthetics apart, this is not always feasible for a number of reasons. However, an outboard engine can be used as an inboard/outboard fairly simply, on quite a number of boats. In this case, the engine itself will be either in a watertight locker or surrounded by a coffer-dam, so that the hole that is made in the hull for it will, to all intents and purposes, be above the waterline. Phil Bolger actually designs the odd boat with a false stern, that has a structural transom in front of it, on which is mounted the engine and also incidentally, the rudder. This means that you have the simplicity of an outboard, with the appearance of an uncluttered stern; the engine will function better further away from the end of the boat and will also be protected from the elements. With the advent of diesel outboard engines, this becomes an even more attractive concept.

A more sophisticated inboard/outboard arrangement is provided by a saildrive unit, and many people would prefer one of these as they are often fitted with a diesel engine. Again these can sometimes be installed with a coffer-dam for absolute security, although I have never heard of any of the rubber gaskets around the drive leg ever failing. It is also possible to get units in which the drive leg is bolted to the underside of the boat and the engine attached to the inside, so that there is no great hole through the hull. With some saildrives, you only have one hole below the waterline, as the cooling water is drawn up through the leg.

Another way to reduce the number of underwater holes required, is by installing an air-cooled engine, which also has the advantage of discouraging you from using it, due to its being a very noisy form of propulsion.

People also drill a hole through the bottom of their boat in order to install an electric log and speedometer. Once again, there are other ways of achieving the same end and as well as the traditional towing log such as is made by Thos Walker, there are also electric logs available whose rotator is towed at the end of a short line. I believe that another advantage of either of these types, over and above that of eliminating a through hull fitting, is that, should the rotator become fouled by weed, it is a lot easier to clear and it is also easier to repair if damaged.

Underwater skin fittings are sometimes necessary in order to drain the cockpit of a boat when she is heeling. Drains are very useful things to have in a cockpit, if only to prevent it from filling up with rainwater. Indeed, the paltry little drains whose diameter is reduced still further by crossed pieces of metal, which are fitted to a large number of production boats, are only up to the task of draining out rainwater. On **Badger**, our cockpit is two feet square and a foot deep. We have two, one-inch unobstructed drain holes and as an experiment we filled the cockpit to the brim and timed it emptying — it took the best part of two minutes. I hate to think how long it would

take some of the cockpits I've seen on 'blue-water cruisers' to empty. And, yes, we have had it flooded. If the boat that you have is fitted with seacocks for the cockpit drains, it may be possible to raise the cockpit sole further, in order that the skin fittings can be placed above the waterline. A shallower cockpit is not necessarily a disadvantage either, as you may find that with what is effectively a lower seat, it is more comfortable to sit in and that it is easier to brace yourself. Anyway, it could be worth a try. If you can have pipes that have a fairly straight run to the side or stern of the boat and don't need to cross one another, it will mean less congestion under the cockpit. You will also be able to do away with the cross-wires in the plug hole because it will be possible to clear the pipe out should it get blocked, something that is difficult to do when there is a seacock at the end of the pipe.

If you would prefer to keep the self-draining conveniences that are fitted to the yacht, another idea is to have a number of pipes draining into a small, isolated sump which has but one seacock. Although this will not add to the simplicity of your vessel, it would have the virtue of reducing the number of seacocks required. All in all, I think that a good look at the underwater through hull fittings that there are on your boat, could give you the opportunity to simplify the vessel and also to reduce the possible chances of becoming like the unhappy boat in the little bit of doggerel quoted earlier.

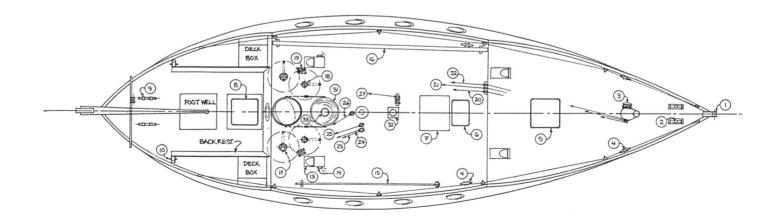

AN ADEQUATE SUPPLY OF WATER IS NECESSARY

Chapter 10

Waterworks

One of the essential requirements for successful and happy voyages is that there should be sufficient water. To have to count every drop consumed or to be forced to eat equal quantities of salt with your rice and potatoes, is not something likely to add to your pleasure or quality of life. People seem to use vastly differing amounts of water, some struggling on a gallon per day and others thriving on two pints. Pete and I manage quite successfully on between five and seven gallons per week between us, which amounts to a maximum of four pints per person per day. To achieve this, we don't seem to try very hard, but we do have water-saving methods, which make it easy and painless to be economical with our water use.

Generally speaking, most yachts carry their fresh water supply in one or more fitted tanks. For voyaging purposes, it is essential to ensure that you have more than one tank, in case you should be unfortunate enough to pick up contaminated water or to develop a leak in a tank. However, on *Badger*, we have gone to the logical extreme of this concept by effectively carrying our water in about three dozen separate tanks — in short, we have no built in tanks but carry the water in 1 gallon polythene containers. This somewhat radical solution came about for a number of reasons.

Firstly, with having a flat-bottomed boat, we have no bilge in which to install a water tank and were not keen on fitting tanks under the settees, the most logical space, because we would then lose stowage in one of the more accessible parts of the boat. Secondly, because we dislike going alongside and avoid it where possible, we needed a large supply of jerricans in order to be able to replenish our water, without having to make an inordinate number of trips ashore; these jerricans needed to be fairly small because of the difficulties that I encounter when trying to heft five gallon containers about. Thirdly, we had lived happily without proper water tanks on both *Stormalong* and *Sheila* using jerricans in both cases and finally, the jerrican solution was infinitely cheaper and simpler than installing tanks.

The system has other advantages, too. By using these small containers, we can stow them away in lockers that are less accessible and therefore less useful and can also spread the load evenly around the boat. By keeping all our water in separate containers we have minimized the problems of cross-contamination and leakage and although we have never taken on board water which would have made us ill, we have frequently suffered water that tasted pretty awful and would have spoilt the taste of the rest in a large tank. Our day to day supply is kept in a five gallon container under the galley sink and a pipe leads into it from a pump. To top it up we use either a funnel or a siphon if it's rough, and can keep a very accurate track of our water consumption, knowing to the nearest gallon what we've used. The containers are easy to obtain either very cheaply or gratis and therefore no problem to replace. Should we be planning a particularly long passage, we can also supplement our stocks with more of these containers which are small enough to find a home for down below, thus meaning that we can avoid a lubberly and unsightly deck cargo of plastic containers. These small containers are much easier to keep clean than a large tank, too, not in the least because they are completely emptied each time they are used and can be thoroughly rinsed out. Watering the boat is, of course, a very straightforward operation as one simply rows the jerricans ashore in one or two trips and fills them at the nearest tap. Being on a small income, we have found this particularly useful in places that generally charge for water. No-one begrudges you getting the odd couple of gallons, but they will make you pay up if you bring your yacht alongside. By using a little tact and patience, you can replenish supplies for free without upsetting anybody. There are two slightly more *outré'* advantages to this method of storing water. If you are unfortunate enough to run aground and need to lighten the boat, you can easily take off the water and either pour it away or put it in the dinghy, if you fear you can't replenish it. The other point is that should you be forced to abandon ship, you will have a plentiful supply of emergency water containers.

With self-sufficiency the name of the game, there is a lot to be said for being able to collect your own water when it rains, rather than having to rely on shore supplies. When we were in the Virgin Islands, we had some friends who collected rainwater as it ran off the cabin roof and they had better water than the locals without ever having to pay for it. Their method, which we have installed on *Badger*, was to fit a little 'toerail', without scuppers, either side of the cabin roof and put pipes at the after end. After allowing the rain to wash off any accumulation of dirt and salt, they usually found that the one gallon containers at the end of the pipes would fill up as fast as they could empty them, in a typical tropical shower. On *Badger*, as we are not solely tropic birds, we have fitted copper piping inside the boat, one in the galley and one in the heads (where spilt water doesn't matter) and have put a tap on the end so that we can fill our containers without standing in the pouring rain. How soft can you get? It is of course, important to make sure that the deck is thoroughly clean, but the first few gallons of water can always be put to one side for washing clothes or oneself. Although we have heard of people who have not needed to go ashore for water for years, I don't think a voyager can rely on this. We have been some places where it hasn't rained for weeks at a time and on other occasions have stayed places where we would feel unhappy about the cleanliness of the rain. We have also found it very unusual to be able to collect rain while on passage, as it is so often accompanied by wind, so that there is too much spray about. However, it can make you quite independent of shore supplies.

If you are concerned about the purity of the water that you have picked up ashore or from your own collecting system, it can easily be purified. Although a number of people use water purifying tablets, we have found them to be both expensive and unsatisfactory. They don't seem to dissolve very well and give a horrid taste to the Earl Grey. Instead, I use ordinary household bleach or Milton.

Some containers give the percentage of chlorine in the bleach, but if they don't, you can assume that it's in the region of one percent (the minimum usually available). To purify the water, you add 45 drops per gallon using an eyedropper. (If the water is turbid or coloured use double the amount; if your bleach is 10% chlorine, use four to five drops per gallon, etc.) Any flavour is hardly noticeable. However, it is important to ensure that the liquid only contains chlorine, since such bleaches as Domestos often contain other substances, which might be injurious to your health.

Milton and similar sterilizing solutions, are available from either a chemists or a large supermarket. The directions for water purifying are given on the bottle and as they may vary from manufacturer to manufacturer I shall leave it for you to find out. A further use for this product is to sterilize jars for processing food, or containers for salting down, etc. — a lot easier than trying to boil them all.

If you do get water that has an unpleasant flavour or if your water pipes seem to give it an odd taste, it may be worth fitting a water filter. When we use one, we have the charcoal type and our system has a container which holds the filter, a separate item that can be thrown away when no longer functioning correctly. The advantage of this type of system is that if you are in an area of good water you don't need to bother with using a filter, which cuts down on expense. We don't actually drink much water as such, but I can always notice odd tasting water in my tea and I am, therefore, quite fussy about its flavour.

With fresh water being a valuable commodity, it is worth having the sea on tap. If you have an engine with a seacock for cooling water, it is well worth running a line from this seacock into the galley for having salt water on tap. On *Badger*, we have a two gallon water container under the sink that we fill with seawater. This works quite well, as we can fill it with fresh water before we start on a passage, thus having two extra gallons, and we can top it up with seawater before coming into harbour in an area where fresh water is scarce, thus feeling sure that the seawater we're using is fairly unpolluted. A lot of people are great believers in using seawater wherever possible, and originally I was of the same school of thought. However, although I use salt water for washing vegetables and hands, over the years I have come to the conclusion that sea water is generally not much use for other purposes. Cooking in all salt water produces excessively salty food, in my opinion, although I often use one 'squirt' of sea water to four of fresh for rice or pasta, etc. If you are cooking vegetables in a pressure cooker, it is possible then to use all seawater as long as the vegetables are in their separators on the trivet, because the vegetables won't actually be in contact with the water. Indeed, if you want to economize on using water you are far better to cook your vegetables in the pressure cooker anyway, as boiling them in separate pans uses a lot of water. They taste better, too.

We used to wash our dishes in sea water and if you have a large sink that requires a lot of water, I don't suppose that you have much choice. However, the trouble with using salt water is that the dishes and counter top never really dry off properly, particularly in cooler climates and the tea towels are always horrid. Pete, the chief washer-upper, has perfected the art of doing a day's washing in a couple of pints of fresh water in our small sinks. I don't watch, as I hate to think what it looks like, but the pots and pans always seem clean and everything is much nicer to eat from than when it's been washed with salt. We even wash up in fresh water on long passages, but if water is running short it is an obvious and easy economy. Washing up once a day has undoubted appeal to the more lazy of us.

The wash basin in *Badger's* heads is supplied from a one gallon container and it is a real treat to be able to rinse the salt from your face with a flannel soaked in fresh water. With a small, fairly shallow bowl, four 'squirts' or a mug full of water is sufficient and there are about 20 mugs to the gallon so that one gallon goes a long way. As Pete doesn't bother too much about such niceties, one gallon will often last for the whole passage. If you feel like a more thorough wash down, it's often worth heating up lots of salt water and washing down with this before rinsing off finally, with a small amount of fresh. Salt-water soap, by the way, is useless and unpleasant and you'll have much more success using liquid soap, a shower gel or shampoo. Detergent is really too powerful to use on your skin on a regular basis.

Personally, I wouldn't bother with pressurized water on a boat. Using a hand pump is not particularly onerous and it is much more efficient than using electricity to pump water. Indeed, any boat that is stopped for any length of time and whose crew does not wish to irritate either themselves or their neighbours by running an engine or generator may soon find themselves wishing for a hand pumped system. When we wintered in Mallorca, we had several neighbours who relied on engines or generators for charging their electricity (and there would have been insufficient sun or wind for an alternative supply). The wharf to which we were tied had no electricity laid on and diesel was extremely expensive. Some of our neighbours ended up having to pour their water out of jerricans into kettles and pans — usually with a fair amount ending up all over the galley because they had no alternative to pressurized water and did not want to flatten their batteries. The water in Palma was particularly dreadful, so that nobody wanted to use it for drinking. However, we were the only people who could use both drinking and washing water from our galley pumps, because we had our tiny tanks and unpressurised water. We were also the only people there who had a shower when we wanted to and as was normal on our boat. We also had the simplest and supposedly least civilized yacht.

However, I seem to have digressed a little. Quite apart from the initial expense and added complication, a pressurized system undoubtedly encourages wasted water, particularly when there are visitors on board. With hand pumps, each stroke of the pump measures out the same amount per squirt — usually about two fluid ounces. Because of this, when making tea you know that it's four squirts per cup, for rice it's six squirts and so on, so that you measure out exactly the correct amount and avoid waste. With running water, even if you use a measuring cup, you are more likely to get waste by spilling water or turning the tap off too late. Such things as brushing teeth can waste a lot of water if people rinse the brush under a steady flow. Some friends of ours were once tormented by two crew who could not be persuaded to economize with water and used it as though they were in a house. The yacht in question, a 54-footer, had huge tanks, but even

these were eventually exhausted. Ted decided that as the two crew had used most of the water they could fill it up. He gave them each a five gallon jerrican, pointed to the tap 100 yards away by dinghy and told them to fill the tanks. It took them all day and from then on they never wasted a single drop!

Hot water systems are a great temptation, especially if you use your engine fairly often and can fit a calorifier to it. With manual pumps and great self-discipline, you can probably justify fitting one, particularly if you don't envisage doing a lot of passage making. For voyaging yachts, however, I think that they will simply mean that you spend a lot more time fetching water. One drawback with a lot of such systems is that you have to run off cold water before getting to the hot, which seems very wasteful. On the right sort of boat, a Heath Robinson system, consisting of a deck tank, painted black with a pipe leading to a tap down below, might be of use, but on odds, putting the kettle on isn't that much hard work. The main charm of hot water is for a shower and we got round the problem on *Badger* in a highly satisfactory, if unsophisticated manner. We use a Sun Shower™, a heavy duty polythene bag with a black lining and hose leading to a small shower rose. The idea of it is that you put it in the sun and it heats up from solar radiation. In practice, it only works in fairly hot sunshine, so that we generally heat up a kettle to fill ours with hot water. We then hang it on a hook in the heads and find that one gallon gives a very adequate shower and the small shower rose ensures that it lasts for quite a long time. It is rather pleasant to have in hot places too, as you can keep it on deck and use it for rinsing the salt off after a swim — particularly appreciated by those of us with a lot of hair.

You will undoubtedly have read and wondered about water makers. At the moment, the running costs make them too expensive a proposition unless you intend to cruise solely somewhere like the Bahamas, where you have to pay for every gallon of water (but even there, you could probably catch enough rain). The initial cost of the unit is no longer prohibitive, but the filters are very expensive and will not last long at all if you use them in harbours where the water is not as clean as it might be; they are also hard on their pumps because the systems work at such high pressure. Watermakers are actually quite energy efficient, if you keep your water usage moderate, so if the prices of the filters drop substantially, they could well be worth consideration.

It doesn't really matter how much water you carry, but the feeling that you have a plentiful supply of water is essential to your quality of life afloat. Learning to make the best use of what you have seems to me to be the solution to gaining this feeling. With water, as with so many things, we have come to the conclusion that the simple and easy ways not only work, but at the end of the day, seem to be the most efficient and the least hassle.

UNDER THE DOUBLE BUNK

Chapter 11

A Place For Everything

On any boat used for voyaging, I think that it's fair to say that you can't have too many lockers. It is truly amazing the amount of stuff that is stowed away on even the smallest of boats. I remember that when we moved from *Sheila* onto *Badger*, the amount of gear that we had to shift was nothing short of astonishing.

When we first loaded up *Badger*, we had two enormous galley lockers in which everything was carefully stowed. However, never having had large lockers before, we hadn't taken into account the obvious fact that lockers are not always packed full and found that the contents used to slide around making the most appalling racket about six inches away from the ear of the off-duty watch. As you can imagine, we soon got fed-up with that and decided to divide them up. However, these two lockers go under the galley counter and into the corner, so that their furthest recesses are somewhat difficult of access. Pete solved the problem in his usual inimitable style, by making a kit of parts suitably notched so that the longitudinals could be put in first, with the cross pieces going in afterwards and notching over, in order to end up with a fitted dividing unit. Each locker is thus broken up into six smaller sections and they have been perfectly satisfactory. It is a point worth bearing in mind, because quite a lot of boats are built with huge and undivided lockers, which end up like the Midshipman's chest with "everything on top and nothing to hand".

That old adage about a place for everything must have been coined by a sailor. As Arthur Ransome put it in, **Racundra's First Cruise,** "Houses are but badly built boats so firmly aground that you cannot think of moving them". On the other hand, boats are moving all the time and I suppose that living on a boat is not dissimilar to living through a continuing earthquake, although generally somewhat less traumatic and a good boat is built accordingly. Because of this, it is necessary to have a home for everything — anything that doesn't have a home will simply end up on the floor and probably in several pieces. When we were living on *Sheila*, her sheer lack of size prevented us from achieving this happy state of affairs, so that each time we went sailing, everything had to be wedged in or secured against damage. (There was no room for anything on *Stormalong*, either, but at least she didn't heel.) It used to take us ages to get ready for sea and the preparations involved were enough to put you off going out for just an afternoon. We swore to ourselves that we wouldn't allow this to happen on *Badger* and have generally managed to keep to this resolve. Normally, in order to get underway at a moment's notice, all that is necessary is to move any unwashed bits and pieces in to the sink and to check that the scuttles in the galley and heads are secured. Everything else can, and does, stay put. Quite apart from making life more civilized and enabling you to enjoy using the boat as a daysailer, keeping the boat ready to sail means that you can get out of an anchorage in a hurry if needs be, without turning the event into a drama. Our worst temptation is the chart table, because such a large, flat surface seems to be crying out to have things put on it. (Cox's law of horizontal surfaces, which states that all horizontal surfaces will end up covered until no usable area remains.)

A dry boat is a great boon when it comes to stowage. With modern materials and building methods, there is really no reason for there to be any unwanted water down below on most boats and the eradication of any leaks should be a major priority, as most things can easily be spoilt by being damp for any length of time. Putting things in polythene bags will keep them clean, but polythene is by no means waterproof when it comes in thin sheets. If you have anything wrapped in polythene lying in water, the water will manage to get in, even when there are no holes and I can only assume that some process of osmosis is at work. Large polythene containers such as ice cream comes in, seem to be perfectly waterproof, however, although total immersion will usually defeat the lid/container seal. In the form of jerricans, buckets and boxes, one can beg or buy this type of container and maybe even get some Tupperware™ from devoted family for presents, although I don't have any myself (Tupperware, that is, not devoted family). We use these containers for food, but our water, paraffin, meths, diesel and petrol "tankage" are all in the form of polythene containers.

Because *Badger* is a dry boat, everything else we have, just gets put in lockers and doesn't come to any harm. Our clothes are kept in shelves or under the double bunk. A fairly efficient way of keeping clothes for another climate in some sort of order, is to store them in soft grips. These can also be used if you go visiting and can be stowed flat when empty. Spare sail material also lives under the bunk, as does flag-making cloth, a couple of blankets, spare lamp glasses, spare compass, etc., etc. Our tools live in the lazarette and we keep items such as chisels, screwdrivers and spanners in tool rolls. The lazarette also contains such things as paint, ropes and fenders. More rope and fenders live in the forepeak. Pilots have overflowed from the chart table bookshelf to live under the saloon floor and most of our food is stored in the saloon and galley lockers. I hate to think how much stuff we have on board — enough to open a small shop, I should think.

The lazarette is probably the most useful area of storage on board *Badger* and is used mainly for boat gear.

In many ways, it serves the same function as cockpit lockers do in other boats, but has several advantages. Being inside the boat, it is a much drier area than lockers would be, especially as the sides and deckhead are all insulated. As well, with the after hatch dogged shut and the hurricane hatch fitted in way of the pram hood, there is no way that water can penetrate below, except by way of the ventilators — cockpit lockers always strike me as very vulnerable in this respect, particularly should the boat be pooped and the cockpit fill up. Because the lazarette lockers are approached from the side, rather than the top, they are easy to divide up and in fact we have a total of seven lockers either side, with a large locker below containing three five gallon drums of paraffin/diesel. In the stern of the boat there is another area of storage, which is divided into space on the bottom of the boat, a large athwartships shelf above that (containing charts and the legs) and a smaller one above that. Outboard are hooks on which to hang ropes.

Rope storage is something that rarely seems to be well sorted on yachts; coils of rope tend to be simply thrown into a heap at the bottom of a locker. I think one of the reasons for this is that not many people know how to make a coil with an eye incorporated for hanging it up. It is really very easy to do. You coil down the rope in the normal manner until there is about four feet of rope left. Holding the coil in one hand, you double the four foot length with the loop thus formed, at the top. You then pass this loop around and through the coil and half hitch it under itself. You do this a second time ending up with two crossed hitches and a now substantially smaller loop coming out at the top of the coil. This loop can be used for hanging up the rope. Alternatively, the coil can be put in a locker, but is much less likely to come undone and get tangled than is usually the case. Hanging up ropes is the better option, though, because it is easier to select the one you want and they can dry out properly, if they have been put away damp.

All lockers, big or small, benefit from ventilation. However, now and again some things seem actually to generate condensation and the problem of a chronically damp locker can sometimes be cured by moving one or two of its contents to a larger, airier one. The louvered doors that a lot of yachts have fitted are good for ventilation as are caned door fronts. Our locker doors on *Badger* are made up of panels of wood with slots cut in between some of the panels. An idea that has worked well, too, is to drill two finger holes in each door for opening them which also adds to the ventilation and is cheaper than a door knob. When you are voyaging on a small income, storing things in dry conditions is particularly important as you can't really afford to allow things to get spoilt so that they have to be thrown away.

I store a fair number of food items in glass jars, and we also usually have bottles of booze on board. The reason I mention this is that I know a lot of people seem to think that glass on a boat is not permitted. Once again I think it comes down to organizing things properly. There can be few things more unpleasant to have to cope with than a broken jar of jam or honey, but on the other hand, if things are put away properly, they shouldn't get broken in the first place. As well, if you put a ban on glass on the boat, you're doing yourself out of home bottled produce, jam and marmalade as well as many products that you would otherwise buy. If I saw jars of cheap mayonnaise or bottles of cheap olive oil, I'd be after them like a flash and wouldn't think twice about the glass. Obviously, you'd be pretty stupid leaving a bottle on the galley counter while underway, but you wouldn't want to do that with a plastic bottle either. You might not end up with glass everywhere, but the container would probably still split and spill the contents all over the place. In fact, there are occasions when glass bottles are an advantage. When we were living on *Sheila*, I put a plastic bottle of cooking oil in the bilge, and unbeknownst to me, it chafed on something, with the result that it spread itself all over the bilge. It was two or three weeks before I noticed it — we didn't go under the floorboards very often and *Sheila* didn't require much pumping — and I never managed to get the bilge thoroughly clean again afterwards. If the bottle had been glass, this would never have happened.

One of the real problems with living on board is that you start acquiring stuff. You buy a bargain or something is given to you; you replace a halliard and keep the old one and before you know where you are, you can't move for all the dross. When this happens, it's time to have a good sort out. Throwing things away is good for you and actually becomes quite addictive. Alain Gerbault writes in **The Fight of the *Firecrest***, "... I put things shipshape down below, throwing overboard the things I had found useless. This always gives considerable pleasure, for it is one of the joys of the sea that you are not obliged to keep with you things you dislike." You can always tell cousin Maud that her knick-knack got broken when you were knocked down off North Cape — she won't know any better. It is not always easy to assess what you need, however and quite often you will look at something and think "I'm sure that I need that from time to time, I really shouldn't throw it away". If this happens, the best thing to do is to write the date on it. If you don't use it during the next year, I think it's a safe bet that you can chuck it out.

Possessions can tend to become a real tie and I think there's a lot to be said for being ruthless with them. I tend to be very sentimental over my bits and pieces, but Pete is far more pragmatic and says, "For Heaven's sake, it's only an object and if you can't remember an old friend or a place you enjoyed without a tangible souvenir, then the person or event can't really be that important to you." I must confess however that I still keep old birthday cards, but at least I can hide those in books. Boats are really too small to have filled up with miscellaneous rubbish and more pleasant to live aboard when they are not filled with gew-gaws and godwottery from a little island in such and

such a place or a divine harbour somewhere else. Of course, often things are important because the person who gave them to you thought long, hard, carefully and lovingly before choosing or making it. Unfortunately, even these objects can rarely have a home aboard.

Bearing in mind, however, that there is always a certain amount of miscellany in any home, it is worth providing a boat with what we call 'the third drawer down', in order to try and keep it under some sort of control. On *Badger*, the third drawer down is the drawer that contains whatever it is we are looking for and can't find, to say nothing of odd lengths of string, shoe polish, rolls of 35mm film, batteries (often dead), a whistle, flux and soldering wire, an instruction book for my camera, a clothes brush, a refill cylinder for our self-inflating lifebuoy (does it work? I wonder), playing cards, barograph papers, Primus™ spares and Heaven knows what else. All in all it is what is commonly known as the junk drawer — every house has one and I'm sure that every boat needs one, too.

We also use a drawer for storing the sextant. This happened quite fortuitously, when we brought our new sextant onto *Badger*, long before she was finished and were looking for somewhere safe to put it. We discovered that it fit in the drawer, but that we couldn't close it because the box was too high. However, when we removed the lid of the box, it fitted perfectly and we found that we had instant sextant stowage. The drawer is fairly stiff, which has the advantage that it can be left open when the sextant is being used, so that the instrument can simply be passed down and placed in its box where the navigator can read its scale at leisure.

Drawers are an excellent way of storing things and not difficult to make in the form of a plywood box. We have faced ours with pitchpine and glued a wedge underneath so that they lock in place at sea and have to be lifted up to open them. We have five in the galley, which I have mentioned elsewhere and have four by the chart table. The top one is a shallow drawer divided into six sections and is useful for pens, pencils, loose change, etc. The second one contains cassettes for our "lo-fi", the third drawer is the one for odds-and-sods and the fourth contains our Zeiss™ sextant and the back-up Ebbco™. There is also another drawer next to my settee, over a locker full of paperbacks. This little drawer, another shallow one, is divided into sections in which I keep needles, thread, button, pins and so on.

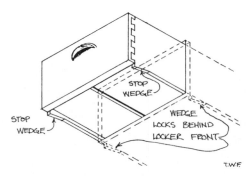

Books can be a problem on a boat, particularly if the crew are avid readers and like to collect books, like what we do. The ideal for bookshelves is athwartships, but this is not always possible. We have three sets of bookshelves: one either side in the sleeping cabin, one either side behind the settee backrest and a pair of athwartships shelves on the bulkhead, abaft the chart table. They are always solid with books. The ones in the sleeping cabin follow the sheer of the boat and are six foot long with a removable fiddle. They were designed for paperbacks, but even the weight of those is sufficient to bend the fiddle so that they end up on the bunk when we are bashing to windward. In the end we solved this in a rather unorthodox, but eminently satisfactory manner, by putting a sliding clamp at the end of the books, with the fiddle between the handle and the bar of the clamp. The clamp is tightened into position onto the shelf and stops the books from sliding forwards. It also stops the fiddle rail from bending and the whole thing is very successful.

The bookshelves behind the settee have about a four inch fiddle at their inboard side. The books are somewhat jammed in fore and aft and the shelves are divided into three. The odd pair of gloves stuffed behind them tends to stop them sliding back and forth. For many years we intended to do something to keep them in place should we be knocked down, but got away with it for so long that we kept procrastinating. The day eventually came and over we went in a North Sea gale — far enough

for all the books to come out and for two or three of them to go through the melamine to the cork insulation underneath on the opposite side of the cabin. Claud Worth did the most damage, followed by Bill Tilman and **The Times Atlas**! Pete was on watch at the time and later said that he was lucky to escape being brained by **Heavy Weather Sailing**. We now have rope going along the top, secured at each end and at the divisions and so far, the books have stayed in place.

Securing stowed gear against heavy weather is something that really comes with trial and error. I think that keeping the lockers small or divided up is a help and once again, if everything has a proper home, it does make life easier. In rough conditions, particularly in the galley, you want to have what you need to hand and in its accustomed place, so that you don't have to go rummaging for it. One of the things that is quite astonishing, is how even the most densely packed of lockers can shake itself down on a long windward leg so as to produce annoying rhythmic rattles, as soon as you start going downwind.

One of the problems at sea can be filling the oil lamps or cooker. We have overcome this to a large extent by having a little pump for the paraffin, the type of pump that is used for changing oil. This is secured to the bulkhead in the lazarette and a pipe from it leads into a five gallon container beneath. The tap is over a little bowl, which catches the drips. The ultimate refinement is to have a funnel under the tap, so that if you overfill the lamps, the spilt paraffin drains back into the container and can also be used for filling up the tank, but I've never been able to persuade Pete to do this; he wants the storage space under the bowl for his pots of fastenings. For filling the cooker, we pump paraffin into a jug and use that to pour through a filter funnel into the cooker's tank. The paraffin line is also fitted with a fuel filter. All our paraffin is stored in five gallon plastic drums. They were much easier to install than putting in proper tanks and can be taken ashore for filling or filled from smaller containers. When we are using the heater, we can fill one or more of these containers with diesel, so that they are in fact, interchangeable; they are also easier to clean out than are fixed tanks. Incidentally, when we had the diesel cooker, we made the header tank out of plywood and epoxy and it proved very successful. It would be a lot cheaper and easier to install tanks into a boat using this method rather than having them made out of stainless steel — they could even be bonded directly to the side of a wood or fibreglass boat.

Weight distribution is, of course, always a problem, but a modicum of common sense when designing the boat, can make life easier here. By ensuring that there is plenty of storage space amidships, you can reduce the temptation of putting too much in the ends of the boat, or perhaps more accurately, you can put more gear in the middle. Although I'm a great believer in carrying plenty of spares and am compulsive about stocking up, we always try to bear in mind the amount of weight in the boat and how it's spread out. We don't want to ruin her performance by overloading her — but it's an uphill struggle.

A lot of people like to have a stowage plan for all their stores and equipment. Whether or not you need one depends on your type of mind. I can remember where I put anything, even several months previously; Pete can't remember where he put something down half an hour ago. However, one thing that I find very useful is my 'Little Brown Book'. This is a note book that I use to mark down all our provisions. Each type of bean, tin and things such as packs of tea or pasta, has a page of its own on which I note the type of containers used, the number of the container, in which locker it's been stored, what date it was started and what date emptied. This allows me to keep a very accurate track of consumption and helps for re-provisioning. I also put down the price paid for each item which helps me compare costs. I mark all the containers with a masking tape label, which sticks very well, but also peels off easily and costs virtually nothing. As the bulk of items in the LBB is kept either under or behind the two saloon settees, there is no reason to make a complicated stowage plan and I tend to keep everything in its own area. For example, the lockers behind the settee backrests are divided into six and top-middle-starboard is for tea, top-middle-port for peanut butter and so on. On a small income, it is obviously essential to keep a close eye on your supplies and such a system does seem to work well.

As far as possible, all the boat's gear should be stowed below. While, of course, such things as a solid dinghy have to be stowed on deck and while it is often useful to have the boathook there and its length may prevent you from keeping it below, the majority of deck cargo with which many a cruising yacht is lumbered, is quite unnecessary. Extra jerricans of fuel are really no more than a nuisance — on a long passage extended motoring is unpleasant and will take away the satisfaction of having made a passage under sail using only the winds and your skills. As well, you are spending money that could probably be better utilized and wasting non-renewable fuel for no real purpose. One of the latest excrescences to ruin the appearance of a yacht is the ubiquitous wind surfer. This is apparently now considered an absolute necessity and yet we hardly ever see people on yachts rigging and using the things. However, they insist on carrying them about, usually lashed to the guardrails, ruining the looks of their yacht and a positive menace in heavy weather when their resistance could easily bend the rails or even rip them out of the deck. Any deck cargo is a hazard in bad conditions, with the worry of it shifting or going overboard and the danger caused by cluttered decks when you most need them to be clear. If you want your boat to look at her best and wish to appear seamanlike, keep everything below and avoid the appalling lubberliness of jerricans and fenders all over the decks.

Sorting out stowage may not seem to have a lot to do with the theme of this book, but in fact good stowage prevents spoilage, breakages and wastage, all of which cost money and add nothing to the pleasure of cruising. It also makes it easier to run the yacht efficiently, which make the whole business of voyaging that much more pleasant and civilized and therefore, more enjoyable.

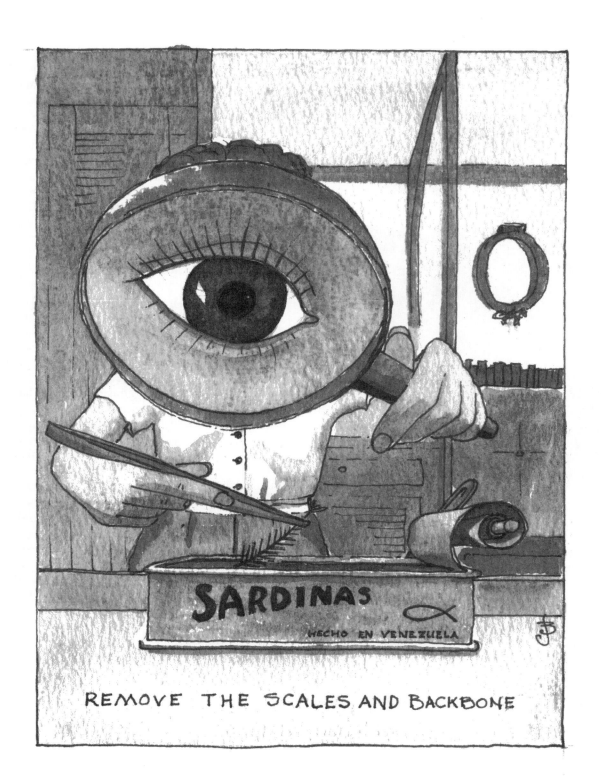

REMOVE THE SCALES AND BACKBONE

Chapter 12

How To Eat Like A King
When You Haven't Got A Bean

The Wind is Free is one of my favourite books and I have read it many times. However, one of the few arguments I would have with Frank Wightman would be about food. Not for a moment do I believe that food is a bore. Indeed, I think that eating is one of Life's great pleasures and, as it is something that we have to do like it or not, it seems to me to be plain stupid to think otherwise.

When we are on passage, the main meal is the highlight of the day. I spend an inordinate amount of time in thinking about it and compared with many other cruising people, an inordinate amount of time in cooking it. Maybe we eat a rather boring and monotonous diet, sometimes I wonder if we do, but we enjoy each meal and look forward to them. It is rewarding at any time, to make cheap ingredients tasty, filling and satisfying, but at sea with a heaving galley, no oven and fresh food according to your own ingenuity in keeping it, the sense of achievement is even greater. I am very proud of the fact that we have never missed having a properly cooked main meal at sea, on *Badger*, apart from those times when I have been seriously incapacitated. Admittedly, in the worst conditions, it has been a one-pot curry or chili, but even then it has been made with at least some fresh vegetables, the beans soaked for the usual time and then pressure cooked in the normal way. To take pleasure in such basic achievements may mark me out as being incredibly simple-minded. I prefer to attribute it to having a low threshold of contentment. They may be one and the same thing.

At anchor, we eat more or less the same meals as we do under way. There are a number of what I believe to be good reasons for this. For a start, it means that the meals that you eat at sea tend to be from tried and trusted recipes. Knowing them they are easier to cook and more likely to turn out well. Also, when I'm feeling a bit queasy and reaching for the old Stugeron™, the fact that I can cook them with one hand tied behind my back, so to speak,

makes it more bearable. The ingredients tend to be on board, as well. Another advantage of this is that sea life and harbour life are less separated. If we decide in the middle of the afternoon that we'll sail now rather than tomorrow, I don't need to start panicking because the meal I planned isn't a sea-going one. Provisioning becomes a lot easier when you don't need to take into account a load of special items — you can concentrate instead on getting the local bargains, to enjoy at the next stop whose specialties are different. That reminds me of one of the rare justices of voyaging. In England, tinned tomatoes are cheap (although, alas, leaping up in price). In other countries they are more costly, *but* fresh tomatoes and better still, fresh plum tomatoes become available, saving your tinned stock for some place like Norway where you can't afford to buy *anything* other than bread and cinnamon buns.

A further advantage of this policy of sea and harbour food being the same is that we don't suffer from the — "Oh, won't it be wonderful when we get to anchor and can eat such and such again!" to the same extent, which means that we find that we enjoy our time at sea that much more.

I think a lot of people have been led to believe that one doesn't really cook at sea. Because when I first went sailing with Pete I was (a) trying to impress him and (b) so ignorant that I didn't know better, I tried to cook proper meals — not that I knew how to cook either, but at least I tried. When I think of *Stormalong*'s galley with our single-burner, Chinese paraffin stove, I realize the true depth of my ignorance. Most crew would have said there and then "No can do" and left it at that. I suppose that I was lucky(?).

Anyway, what I'm getting at is that there is no reason not to cook at sea, given a reasonable galley and sufficient determination. Much as I admire the Hiscocks, I should have hated their diet at sea. The list of stores in the back of **Voyaging Under Sail** sounds like a supermarket salesman's dream. Lots and lots of tins of this and that. (Pete's eyes take on a nostalgic gleam at the thought of Fray Bentos Steak and Kidney Puddings.) Mind you, if hotting up food was good enough for Swallows and Amazons, I suppose it should be good enough for the rest of us. The tins you will find on *Badger* should you be inclined to come aboard for a rummage, when we have just provisioned in the UK would be:

Tomatoes (15ozs)	48
Baked Beans (15ozs)	48
Sardines (4ozs)	24
Pilchards (8ozs)	48
Tuna (8ozs)	24
Pineapple in own juice (8oz)	6
Water chestnuts (8ozs)	6
Bamboo shoots (8ozs)	6
Sharwoods curries (15ozs)	6
Assorted cooked peas and beans	12

Tomatoes and baked beans are essentials and cheaper (and better, in the case of baked beans) than most other places. Sardines make a useful starter, 'treat' (i.e., expensive!) lunch or 'tapa' (hors d'oeuvre), when mashed into a sort of paté, with a little tomato purée, thyme, pepper, a dash of hot sauce and mayonnaise. (I always remove the scales and backbones, which causes a certain amount of ribald laughter from my better half.) Pilchards are gob-smackingly cheap in England — I hate to think what the poor beggars who fill the tins get paid in some God-forsaken sweat shop — and can be made into fish cakes, with the judicious addition of loads of fresh parsley or one-half teaspoon of dried thyme. They can also be spread on toast as a 'treat' lunch or eaten with fried rice and stir-fried vegetables (heated up for a couple of minutes by splitting them down the middle, removing the backbone — chopsticks are excellent for this — breaking them into pieces and putting them on top of the vegetables with the lid on the pan for just a minute or so). The 8-ounce tins aren't always easy to get hold of, so should be grabbed when you get the chance. Those in brine are better for fish cakes, but the tomato sauce is good otherwise.

Pineapple, water chestnuts and bamboo shoots are combined with vegetables (including root ginger, if possible), two tablespoons soya sauce, and one tablespoon vinegar into a glorious sweet and sour sauce, to which the tuna is added towards the end, just to heat it through. Actually, thrift will often raise its ugly head and only one of the tins of Chinese vegetables will be used and chick peas will be substituted (very successfully) for tuna, to get more meals from the tins. Of course, more pineapple will then have to be bought. Good with Chinese noodles, but when they run out, rice will do quite nicely. Prawn crackers are carefully hoarded, too (and I even deep fry *those* at sea, in the sort of calm conditions when we are allowed such an extravaganza. With any luck, half-way

day, birthdays, the third anniversary of the day I bought my bathing suit and similar milestone events will fall on a calm day and allow one to have a real celebration). The best prawn crackers we've ever had were bought in Cuba, imported from Vietnam. When fried they were lovely and thick and beautifully crunchy.

The Sharwood curries are a real extravagance and completely unjustifiable. One tin is not really enough and if you have the odd tin of peas or chick peas in your locker, they combine very well. They are ideal for the times when you've been ashore all day and come back too weary to cook. As well as being instant, they are quite delicious and will be thoroughly heated by the time the brown rice has cooked in the pressure cooker (eight minutes at fifteen pounds pressure). In fact they're so good that the smell of them may revive you enough to crisp up some poppadoms on your toaster, using a low heat.

We also have the occasional tins of ham, corned beef or salmon on board, which have usually been given to us and have enjoyed tinned bacon and tinned sausages (especially the ones from Harrod's, courtesy of *Saecwen*). Generally speaking though, we're not very fond of tinned meat and don't bother with it. It's also very expensive. I don't use tinned or packet soups very much either, finding it as easy to make one with pulses and/or fresh vegetables in the pressure cooker, though it's useful to have the odd one in for a quick lunch. I don't generally care for tinned vegetables apart from butter beans and so forth, so that we don't have any of those either.

If there is one food of which you are particularly fond, it's often worth stocking up with it before you set off. While you may find that is costs less elsewhere, there is every chance that it will cost more or even be unavailable and only experience and picking other voyagers' brains will help you there. For example, you can't buy muesli in the States, or unsweetened peanut butter in Portugal or semolina in Canada. Often things are very cheap simply because a country imports them in vast quantities. For example, tea and instant coffee are quite cheap in England. Ground coffee is also cheaper there than in a lot of countries, Venezuela being one notable exception. But then it always is. We use loose tea, which works out cheaper than teabags, is more compact and more accurate. If we're making two cups of tea, we use one spoonful, if we're making four cups we use two spoonfuls. Just like teabags. But, what happens if you want three cups — do you have three weak cups, three strong cups or waste four squirts of water? You can't really cut a teabag in two, but you can measure out half a spoon of tea, which means that you can make just what you need. It's not just a case of penny pinching, either; saving water makes sense on voyages and having a cup of tea just the way you like it (and made in a pot) is one of the little details that adds quality to life. Most people, quite rightly, object to having tea leaves in the bottom of the cup, but seem also to have forgotten about a nifty little device called a *tea-strainer*. I make coffee in a pot, just like tea, which saves fooling around with filter papers (more expense) and so forth — the tea strainer is used for this, too. It tastes really nice, but with the present craze for filter coffee, it can be difficult to get medium ground coffee. Cafétières are improving this situation. We used to grind our own, but have got too lazy. It doesn't taste *that* much better, to our jaded palates anyway.

If you use tomato purée and who doesn't, the tubes are almost impossible to buy out of England and the tins and jars will work out expensive or grow mold, which amounts to the same thing. Tomato purée grows mold at a quite incredible rate. If all else fails, oil poured over the remaining paste will stop it growing moldy, but open tins of tomato purée are not pleasant things to have about at sea. In a hot climate, the contents can ferment a little once you've opened the tubes and they sometimes swell up quite alarmingly. However, I've always used the tubes up in spite of this and they taste OK and never seem to have done us any harm.

Mayonnaise is something that can be very cheap in some countries, such as the UK and the USA and very expensive in others, such as France. If you find a supply of good, cheap stuff, it's worth stocking up. We've never had any problems with not storing it under refrigeration, although after being opened for several weeks it may start to taste a bit stale. The anti-glass mob point out, quite rightly, that it makes an awful mess if you break a jar, but we've never broken a jar yet, (touch wood) and they make excellent storage jars or paint brush cleaning jars.

Real peanut butter can be a bit tricky to buy, although it is getting easier. That ghastly, smooth stuff that they sweeten with sugar or dextrose is quite easy to buy, which just goes to show. Perhaps you like it? A great British love is Marmite, which is either impossible to buy or outrageously expensive. It makes a good gift to other Brits, but for one's own use, the health food shops sell Barmene, Vegecom and yeast extract, all of which are perfectly acceptable substitutes and a great deal cheaper. Some places sell Barmene in bulk — bring your own jar. Honey can be a bit expensive, try your friendly health food shop for that, too. When you are cast adrift in an open boat, you could take your jars of honey with you — good energy. It keeps forever, virtually; apparently it has been found in Egyptian tombs of the Phaeroes era, quite fit to eat. When people are deprived of a favourite food, it can start to assume a quite disproportionate importance. We have heard of an American couple who decided to give up cruising because they missed their Cheese Whiz™. Only those who have ever sampled this delicacy can realize the true relevance of this story!

For milk we take as much sterilized as we can store and then make do with various dried substitutes. Sterilized full cream milk is not to everyone's taste and that includes me. What we use is the skimmed milk, which we find very palatable. It's also cheaper and incidentally, arguably healthier. We'd carry a lot more because it's not always easy to find, but unfortunately it takes up rather too

much room. In the Canaries we can buy dried, whole milk and prefer Kerrygold. It mixes well with a whisk and tastes very good. It's compact and well packaged and lasts for ages as long as the packets aren't opened. Once opened something happens to it that prevents it from mixing, but this takes several months. We also use skimmed milk granules for tea and coffee or when we can buy no other type, but it is bulky and takes up a lot of room.

When voyaging on a small income, the amount of money spent on meat seems to become rather excessive. We found that the best way to overcome this problem was to abandon buying meat altogether and become largely vegetarian. We started a vegetarian diet in 1978 when we decided that it cost too much to eat meat. Initially, it was quite difficult changing over, but eventually I discovered **The Bean Book** by Rose Elliot, which has become my bible. It's published by Fontana and I can't recommend it too highly; without it we'd still be struggling. In those halcyon days, you could buy dried peas at 15p per pound and even chick peas were only 30p. However, since the Yuppies decided to adopt vegetarianism the prices have gone up — but it's still substantially cheaper than eating meat. Usually, in England, there is a co-operative or wholesaler somewhere around and diligent searching will turn one up. Then, when buying by ten or twenty pounds at a time, you'll find the price tumbling. For our two hearty appetites, I used to buy a pound of meat. Now a pound of dried beans costs 60p at worst, but wait a minute — you only use four ounces so your "meat equivalent" costs 15p. In many ways, I do use pulses as a direct substitute for meat. Whole lentils replace mince in spaghetti bolognaise, we have our chili with extra kidney beans and 'sin carne' and use whole peas, for example, in curry. Admittedly, it does take longer to cook, but I always use a pressure cooker, whereas I might not with meat. It could be argued that you spend more on fuel, but I reckon that there aren't many people who eat as cheaply and *as well* as we do. Cooking pulses in the pressure cooker reduces the cooking time substantially. I don't cook any for more than twenty-five minutes and lentils, black-eyes, split peas and butter beans cook in eight to ten minutes without even being soaked. (At fifteen pounds pressure, that is — if you've got a Continental pressure cooker, it might well be ten pounds).

Another advantage of eating pulses is that they are very compact. The average tin of, say stewing steak, contains fifteen ounces of steak, gravy, etc. However, the tin itself weighs a couple of ounces. On the other hand, you only need four ounces of pulses. If you add to this the fact that you can fit ten pounds of the smaller pulses into a one gallon water container (ex vinegar, tomato ketchup, etc.; easy to obtain free from such places as canteens) and then think how much space forty, fifteen ounce tins would take up, you begin to appreciate that beans and boats go very well together.

People often say, "But what about the water?", which seems to be a valid question. However, I have found that for a half cup of beans — a standard double serving, I can soak them very successfully by pouring over them a cup of boiling water and leaving them for an hour before draining and cooking them in another cup of water. I wouldn't generally recommend cooking them in the water used for soaking as it contains the substance known as the 'fart factor', although once used to a bean diet, the body adapts and I tend to use the soaking water on passage, when I'm watching water consumption extra carefully. On the other hand, the beans that I don't soak: whole and split lentils, split peas, black-eyed peas, mung beans and butter beans, all get cooked in one and a half cups of water to a half cup of beans. They don't seem to induce antisocial tendencies — in us, anyway. The cooking water can then be used in the sauce, if one is to be made. Don't add salt when actually cooking the beans, by the way, or be tempted to use sea water as this makes the skins tough and can prevent older beans from softening at all. I don't think that this shows that beans mean an extravagant use of water and, as I've mentioned elsewhere, a gallon of water a day is plenty for both of us.

While I'm putting across the advantages of beans, I ought to point out that they are high in fibre, which has recently been the subject of much discussion among medical and nutritional experts. For the average yachtsman on long passages, the important thing is that fibre 'keeps you regular' as they used to say, meaning that you won't have to torment your unfortunate body with laxatives, to overcome a common problem of offshore sailors.

Beans keep for a long time, which is another great advantage and robust polythene containers are much less vulnerable to damp than are tins. This means that it is feasible to stock up in countries where the conditions are right for buying beans, to have them on board for other places. By the right conditions, I mean countries that do not sell them infested with weevils, cockroaches and other equally delightful hitchhikers. Should you find some really cheap ones of dubious ancestry, I'd suggest keeping them isolated and eating them first. I'm not being neurotic here. When we were in the Canaries in 1983, we went to the local mill for freshly ground wholemeal flour. The flour came straight from the grinders into our bags, which were brought back to our boats and loaded into sundry containers. All three boats subsequently found the flour to be *heaving* with the larvae of what turned out to be tiny moths. I'm not particularly squeamish, but even I ended up throwing fifteen pounds of the stuff away. The worst thing was that the blasted creatures managed to migrate and enter cellophane bags of muesli and rolled oats. They were, fortunately, only into grains and left the beans alone. In Morocco I stocked up with perfectly good cumin seeds, only to discover about three weeks later that they had doubled in bulk and were moving. Closer examination revealed equal parts of cumin seeds and weevils. They look so similar that sorting them out was impossible and, once again, the whole lot went overboard.

I have since been told that if you put a piece of cotton wool, or tissue, soaked in alcohol into a container, it will kill existing weevils or keep potential interlopers at bay. I have tried this and it does work. It is unnecessary to use pure alcohol, gin or rum will do quite adequately. I've put bay leaves in containers to keep weevils out and while I've never had weevils in any containers treated in this way, we have so rarely had them on board that I couldn't categorically state that they work. They certainly don't keep other insects out and would not kill existing weevils. If you buy whole nuts or spices about which you have doubts, sterilizing by heating in a low oven or a dry pan seems to work well. However, this is not feasible for large quantities.

We eat a lot of popcorn, which is also compact, easy to store, etc. Once again from the halcyon days of 15p per pound it is now 50p, but two ounces will provide an enormous bowlful and make a very cheap pre-prandial snack. To cook it, I cover the base of a large saucepan with cooking oil and then put it over a medium heat. When the oil is hot I put in about three dessertspoons per person. A one pint pan will pop 2 teaspoons of corn, a two pint pan four, and so on. The corn should start popping almost immediately, but don't use too high a heat, or you'll burn it. I always shake seasoned salt all over it as I can't stand sweet popcorn. I discovered this condiment in the States and stocked up with some really cheap stuff in Venezuela (where else?), but I haven't yet seen it for sale in the UK. You can make your own by mixing together celery salt, garlic salt, onion salt, chili seasoning and cumin in whatever proportions take your fancy. Once, when I provisioned *Badger*, I thought that I'd put tons of popcorn on board, knowing that it's not always easy to buy. I stocked up with twenty pounds, but it only just lasted a year. It just shows how many times people come on board for drinks! Nearly everybody seems to love it and it's an awful lot cheaper than crisps and peanuts.

It's well worthwhile taking the provisioning of the boat seriously. With a sound boat and a year's supply of food on board, you are in a very strong situation. When we set off in *Stormalong* (in our pre-bean days), we didn't have much money and we had even less idea of how to live on it. We provisioned the boat quite well, but not knowing how to keep many of the items we had on board made for a fair amount of wastage. As I mentioned earlier, when we were in Antigua, we looked at our small amount of money and the food on the shelves and eventually had to settle for fifty-nine tins of sardines. I must confess that it took several years for me to get interested in sardines again, after that voyage. Although we never actually went hungry on *Stormalong*, it was a near thing at times and from then on, I've always tended to over-provision. However, it does give us great security, because even if we lose our money or have problems getting hold of it for some reason, we will still have enough to eat. Indeed there have been several occasions when we have had to 'live off our fat' and not found it any great inconvenience. If push comes to shove, we can always start sprouting our beans and grains for fresh produce. Another advantage of being over-provisioned is that you are often in a situation to help out other people who maybe underestimated their consumption or overestimated their bank balance, or have had supplies damaged.

When buying in provisions for the boat, it is worth thinking in terms of months, or even years rather than just weeks. A lot of foods have a much longer shelf life than people realize. Tins will last for two or three years quite happily, if they are kept dry and as cool as possible. Dried foodstuffs, including fruits as well as pulses, rice and pasta will also keep several years in good, airtight containers, preferably in a dark place and again, as cool as practicable. There is a certain amount of trial and error in seeing how long things will last and you should always be aware of which foods suffer what nutritional losses with lengthy storage; however by taking a long-term view, you can often make use of buying in quantity for a year or two at a time, saving money both now and later on.

With living on an income and a small one at that, we sometimes have to juggle money to take advantage of bargains or to stock up the boat for any length of time. We have an arbitrary starting date for the year and then work from that, which means that if, for the sake of argument we need £200 at the start of our year, we take that from our total income and divide what's left by fifty-two to work out how much per week to allow ourselves. This may happen several times in a year, so that by the end of the year we are on only £10 per week, but in that case we will have all our staples on board, several luxuries and be well stocked with fuel. Another way in which we adjust our money is by taking the next two weeks' money to spend, just before a passage that we reckon will take about a fortnight. This enables me to buy in fresh food and other things to see us over the next couple of weeks. At times it all seems to take a lot of organizing, but it's good fun and it's also satisfying to see how many years end with us having lived and fed well without having spent all our income.

Because we often have large supplies of food on board, bought at different times, it is very important to make sure that it is rotated carefully, eating the oldest stocks first. For this I make use of my Little Brown Book (c.f. Chapter 11, **A Place for Everything**) which shows me where everything is stowed. I note down the date I bought things and when the containers are labelled, I also number them and write this number in the book. Then, when one container is finished I can look up in the book to see what the next number is and ensure that stocks get used in the correct sequence. I also number the tins and note in the book when these are bought so that I know that a new batch starts, for example, at number 36 and use all the previous numbers up first.

One aspect of provisioning with which you need to be accurate is with fresh produce. Without refrigeration and in hot climates, the keeping of fresh fruit and vegetables can be a headache and there is precious little

accurate information about. However, our forefathers (foremothers?) managed and so should we. The books that do cover fresh food for cruising people, skate over the details and one book that I have read, specifically about feeding sailors and written by a very well-known cruising lady, who should have known better, simply suggests keeping most things in a "cool, dark place". Well, we all know that; what one wants to know is what to do when there aren't any cool, dark places. When stocking up for a passage you need to check out what is available, what you want and how much it costs. Then make your list and check it against the probable shelf life of the different items, crossing off things as they get past that time. For example, even though peaches may be dirt cheap, you can only take as many as you can eat before they go off and so a fortnight's supply is probably the very maximum you would buy.

From long and frequently painful experience, I have gathered together my knowledge on keeping different types of fresh food and assembled it in three appendices at the back of this book. Appendix I is for such things as dairy produce and also covers one or two things such as pasta. Appendix II is for fruit and Appendix III is for vegetables.

When we were in Venezuela, fresh food prices were extremely low and there was a superb variety available. We would load ourselves up with all this lovely grub and then sail off somewhere like Los Roques or Laguna Grande, where we would be unable to buy any more food. We would eat up the fresh stuff — some of it would have to be guzzled before it went off, some would easily last until we could shop again and some would last for several shopping trips and we discussed, interminably, whether we should install refrigeration in *Badger*; a system that would take up no room, no electricity and hold bushels of delicacies such as curly endive and string beans. After we left Venezuela, our interest in the subject waned and we no longer even consider the idea. Indeed, it is only in a very hot climate, where markets are few and far between that we ever feel we could do with some sort of refrigeration on *Badger*. However, refrigeration is becoming increasingly popular aboard cruising yachts and a number of boats even have freezers. For those on a small income, the concept of being able to buy food cheaply and keep it fresh or frozen seems very attractive and possibly worth the initial expense, particularly bearing in mind that most people considering going off voyaging have never lived without refrigeration.

Unfortunately, the facts make refrigeration a luxury and not a truly realistic proposition on the sort of boats we have been discussing. Leaving aside the initial cost of such a system, the space requirements are something worthy of consideration. Because these systems will be of most use in the Tropics, the insulation must be designed for high temperatures, in order to avoid wasting energy and so it will be necessary to use a minimum of four to six inches of insulating material, which will make the external dimensions of even a modest unit quite sizable. Pete and I worked out that a one and a half cubic foot unit, (far too small to be of any use for stocking up with vegetables) with six inches of insulation, would need four and a half cubic feet of space, i.e. two feet by one and a half by one and a half, which is a lot of room on a smallish boat. It is not easy to decide how large the unit should be. On the one hand, it has to be large enough to put in a month's supply of perishable foods for an ocean passage, but what would be a month's supply? Well, for a start, two dozen eggs (two dozen in a locker for the first fortnight), twelve pints of milk, two pounds of butter, ten pounds of meat, three pounds of cheese, three lettuces, four containers of orange juice, four pounds of bacon, one pound various cooked meats, four cucumbers, two pints of yoghurt, a jar of mayonnaise, two pounds of thin carrots, one pound of french beans, one cauliflower and maybe some more salad ingredients. In fact this list would not last two people anywhere near a month, but I've written it to give you some idea of the quantities of food you might be talking about and hope that you might be able to visualize how much room it would take up. As time goes by, this is going to get depleted and it's going to take a lot of energy to keep it cold. Being a cunning soul, you will no doubt get round that problem by filling your fridge with beer, but then you'll start to enjoy ice cold beer and need a larger unit to take a month's supply of fresh food *and* keep your beer cool, etc., etc. Whatever size you decide on, it will mean that a fairly substantial proportion of storage will be given over to the refrigerator and its heat-excluding epidermis, in return for storing a fairly small amount of food, much of which is in the "luxury" category. An astonishing number of these things will keep for a fortnight, without refrigeration. Indeed, the only vegetables that really need refrigeration are those that have already been refrigerated and broccoli, non-hearty lettuce, mange-tout peas and string/french beans. And these will keep more than a couple of days even in the Tropics. The running costs of refrigeration are also very high. A large, well-designed unit can quite easily be run from a compressor from the engine, running for two hours a day — but who wants to run an engine two hours a day? An alternative is to have a mega wind generator such as the unfortunately named Wind Bugger™, but this may well not give sufficient power when running down wind and as you would most certainly want your cold storage on an ocean crossing, you would be best to have a back up in the form of a water generator and prudence would dictate having a large bank of batteries for the times when you are becalmed — all of which are perfectly possible, of course. No doubt you could run your engine in a calm, but this would cost money and as well, the object of the exercise is meant to be to improve your quality of life. Maybe you could get around the above problems by fitting large solar panels which could be adjusted to the sun (although they

could be in the shadow of the sails, for much of the time, when you are heading south). However, apart from being very unattractive, these units, usually perched on a stern rail are both dangerous and vulnerable at sea, as soon as the boat starts moving about.

Having overcome the problems of powering your refrigeration ("I couldn't possibly survive without fresh meat or lettuce") and got it set up and running, I am bound to point out that refrigerators do not seem to be the most reliable of devices on boats and are not particularly easy to repair. However, as it is much more efficient to buy the compressor, etc. and build your own unit (with generous insulation) rather than buying a ready-make job, at least you would have a good idea of how to tackle any work on it. Don't forget the Freon™ bottle!

A lot of boats have ice-boxes. Those fitted into British production boats are usually a bit of a joke, with minimal insulation on the sides and bottom and none at all on the lid (to save space). However, most of the time in the British climate, you don't need refrigeration anyway, which is just as well as it's damn' difficult to buy ice in Britain. Actually, it's not particularly easy to buy ice in a large number of other countries, either. In the USA they understand these things rather better and build superb (and enormous) iceboxes. However, they will cost you an arm and a leg to run in most places (especially as a portion of your small income) with the notable exception of Canada, where the Government wharves have ice for sale for the fishermen and will sell it to yachties for a song, or even give it away. In fact, it's only any good relying on an icebox if you intend to go coastal cruising in a limited number of areas. On the size of boat with which we are concerned, I very much doubt that you could carry enough ice (and food, don't forget!) for a month's passage. Incidentally, an icebox needs to be properly designed so that water can be drained away without all the cold air going with it. If the water can't be drained, the ice melts more quickly and your food ends up floating in water, which doesn't do it any good at all. I have lived with an, admittedly very basic, ice-box on occasion and quite honestly find them more trouble than they are worth. By the way, an ice-box without ice is probably one of the worst places you could possibly store fresh food: warm, humid and unventilated.

Once again, it is necessary to run a Cost Benefit Analysis on the matter. As you may have gathered, Pete and I have long since come to the conclusion that it's much easier to learn how long different items of fresh food keep and arrange for stowage in the darkest and coolest part of the boat. We buy food that is very perishable in small quantities and enjoy it for a day or two while it is really fresh— and that way such things are more of a treat. In fact the only times that we really hanker for a refrigerator is in the Tropics, and I'm not sure how much of that is due to the temptations of cold beer!

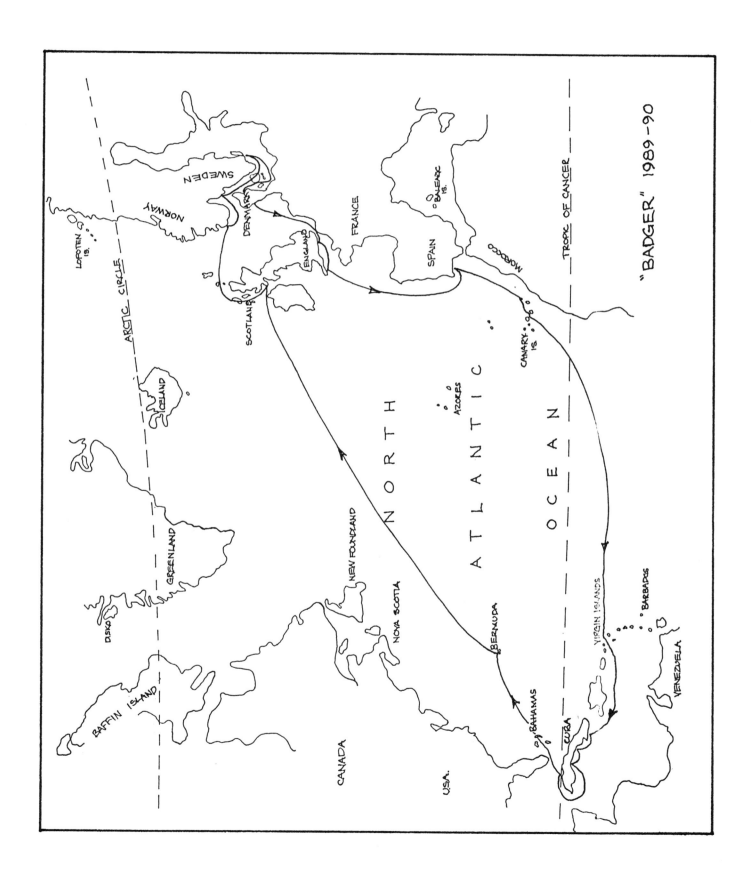

Chapter 13

The Inner Man

There seems to be an awful lot about food in this book. From this you might get the impression that I'm a foodie, but actually, the main reason is that food is a very important part of sailing life and in many ways our eating and cooking habits are the cornerstone of our philosophy. We first began truly to *live* as opposed to existing on the cheap, when we discovered how to eat well for very little money. From there it was a logical step to discovering how to live well for very little money.

Cooking on board boats has been written about many times and this is not meant to be another cookery book, but I feel that there is quite a lot to be said about the philosophy of cooking. The present trend seems to be convenience food, labour saving devices and time saving methods of cooking. However, all of this is a result of regarding cooking as a chore, something to get finished as quickly as possible, a tedious task. Personally, I don't regard it as that. I enjoy trying to make good food and I enjoy other people's pleasure (as well as my own) from eating good food. It is infinitely more rewarding to make a delicious meal from raw ingredients and ingenuity than from opening cans and has the advantage of being cheaper, too.

I suppose the epitome of making your own is probably bread making. There are few things that smell better than a loaf straight from the oven and there is something immensely satisfying about kneading the warm dough. There is no real mystery to bread making — keeping everything warm seems to solve most problems and with a bit of low cunning, that is not too difficult to do. In a warmish place, the dough likes to be put in a bowl inside a polythene bag and placed in a sunny spot out of the wind. In cooler places when you are using large amounts of dough, it can be snuggled up with a hot water bottle to help it rise, but I've made very successful bread up in Greenland, with the cabin temperature only in the upper 40's F, with no more extra bother than wrapping the bowl in a towel to keep it warm. The oven temperature is not

critical either — I've cooked many a loaf at 350° F with excellent results. In fact, it's not even necessary to have an oven as bread can be made in a frying pan or heavy based saucepan over a low heat. It can also be steamed in a pressure cooker and as so many people seem to be intrigued by this idea, I shall give directions.

Make the dough as normal and then put it in a tin, in the pressure cooker, on a trivet. When you are ready to cook, carefully pour in a pint of water (seawater is fine). If you prefer, you can put the water in first, but if it's rough, the tin may bash about a bit, which isn't so good for the bread. Loosely cover the dough with foil. Light the stove and put on the pressure cooker. Fit on its lid and put on the weight, lower the valve or do whatever is necessary to put it under pressure. If you put on the weight after steam has started to issue forth, the sudden increase in pressure may flatten the loaf. If the loaf hasn't risen very satisfactorily, heat up the water on a low flame and the bread will rise further. If it's OK, bring the cooker up to pressure in the usual way and cook for 25 minutes. Pressure can be reduced quickly if you wish. And that's all there is to it.

Cakes, too, are ridiculously easy to make in a pressure cooker, but for perfect results you want:

(a)   to steam the cake, without any weights, for fifteen minutes over a low heat, in order to let the raising agent do its thing before putting on the weight and bringing it up to pressure.

(b)   a cooker with an option of five pounds pressure to give the best results. (If you have one of the modern Ultra Prestige cookers, a set of weights such as the older models used, can bought from a hardware store and used with it).

They generally take about thirty-five to forty-five minutes to cook, depending on whether they are a light sponge or a more substantial offering. A good fruit cake will do wonders for morale on a rainy day and a perfectly satisfactory batch of scones can be turned out using the same technique. If you substitute liquids for solids in your cake baking, the result is very light. To do this, you use two-thirds of a cup of cooking oil for every cup of margarine/butter and half a cup of honey for every cup of sugar. The oil also keeps better than butter or margarine and is a lot cheaper than the former. By the way, for baking, it is well worth following the American custom of using a measuring cup, as scales will not work on a boat if she is moving noticeably.

Another unfailingly popular item on *Badger* is steamed puddings. These can be either sponge or suet (there is such a thing as vegetarian suet, by the way, which keeps very well) and Pete loves to eat them when it's cold. I make fairly substantial ones and they last several days, either hotted up again or eaten cold. With a pressure cooker, they are very easy to make and good belly timber after a day's sail.

The main consideration for those on a small income, is managing to cook good food without spending too much on fuel. The four main cooking fuels are gas, paraffin, diesel and alcohol.

Gas cookers are very popular for their familiarity, their instant heat and controllability. If you are considering going off voyaging, I assume that you have already considered the safety aspects of cooking with gas. Please don't underrate them; enough said. Most of the cookers provided on production boats are very shoddy, stove-enamelled, pressed steel cookers, designed for caravans. The oven doors burst open at inopportune moments and the gimballing does not take into account the different movements caused by pans on top or a casserole in the oven. Taylors™, Shipmate™, Optimus™, Plastimo™ and Force 10™ all make stainless steel cookers, specifically for boats, but like most things, you get what you pay for. Gas ovens are expensive to run, but in many places, we are told, gas is relatively cheap. However, when we took *Missee Lee* to France, we took a cylinder of Camping Gaz™, having been told that this was the thing to do. Cooking in our normal manner, the first cylinder lasted two weeks before having to be changed. We went to a dealer and were charged the equivalent of £8.20 for a refill. After that we used many more tins and were much more careful how we used the gas — impairing our quality of life. We found that we could buy it more cheaply in supermarkets, at about £6.80 a cylinder, but even so we were paying about £2.20 per week for cooking and *being careful with the fuel*. We had been told that paraffin is difficult to buy in France, but found that every supermarket sold it. The cost was outrageous at about 90p a litre, well over twice the British price, but we reckoned that it would still have been substantially cheaper to cook on paraffin than with gas, we could have used the cooker as and when we wanted to and would not have needed to worry about the gas running out at a place where there was no large supermarket to sell us a cut-price replacement.

Bottled gas tends to be no problem until you start voyaging off the beaten track and then you find life can get complicated. In many countries, you cannot simply swop the cylinders over, as the regulators have different threads and so you need to get the bottle refilled at a bottling plant. Having found out which town has a bottling plant, you sail there and lug the bottles ashore. Then you stop a bus and are informed that they are not allowed to carry gas cylinders, so you either smuggle them aboard, heavily disguised as a grip of laundry or you have to find a taxi. Not all taxi drivers are keen on gas bottles, either, but eventually you get one to drive you to the plant, which is on the outskirts of the town, in the interests of the good citizens' safety. They happily fill your bottles and at a reasonable cost and you get back in the taxi and return to town. On paying off the taxi you then do the reckoning on the actual cost of the gas you've just bought. From that day on you use the oven to store your pans. Incidentally, I have heard that in Sweden, they no longer allow the use of propane or butane gas on boats. While I doubt that they would prevent visiting yachts from using their own, it must add to the difficulty of getting gas cylinders refilled there. Let us hope that the trend does not spread to more 'Nanny' countries. In the meantime, fans of gas cookers would do well to lobby manufacturers to make bottled natural gas more widely available. Lighter than air, this is a much safer fuel than the other two. Perhaps you could persuade the manufacturers to use a standard bottle and thread, as well.

Paraffin is the traditional voyager's fuel. It is getting difficult to get in one or two places, but on the other hand, even ten gallons doesn't take up that much room and will keep you going for several months; on *Badger*, we use about half a gallon a week for cooking. When it's cheap it's worth stocking up, as the price varies tremendously from one penny per litre in Venezuela to £1 per litre in Iceland (and maybe further extremes either way). A half gallon per week would amount to about 80p per week at average British prices. A lot of people seem to think that paraffin cookers are slow, dirty and difficult. Having cooked on paraffin for a total of over ten years, I can only disagree. A pressure stove is as fast as gas and with clean fuel is perfectly soot free. There is an awful lot of drivel talked by otherwise intelligent people, about the "terrible flare-ups, with oily flames everywhere that you get when lighting paraffin cookers". Nearly all flare-ups are caused due to impatience and/or incompetence on the operator's part and have nothing to do with the design of the cooker. So long as sufficient methylated spirits/alcohol are used to pre-heat the burners, there is no reason at all for them to occur and this is easily organized by using one of the little wicks that Tilley make for pre-heating their lanterns. We keep ours in a jar of meths and simply clip it under the burner and light it. When it is just about to go out, you turn the burner on and Hey presto! — off it goes. It never fails, is quite foolproof and is perfectly safe at sea as the burning meths can't spill. The built-in, high-pressure pre-heating systems on certain Optimus stoves do appear to bung up after a while, probably due to low grade fuel, although I know one or two people who have had no problems at all. Talking of Optimus, I very strongly recommend fitting only their burners to pressure paraffin cookers. A lot of people will try to fob you off with Portuguese lookalikes, but they are very inferior and not much cheaper. The real thing have "Optimus" and "Sweden" on them. If you insist, your chandler will find them for you. We have recently come across a situation where flare-ups are caused for a different reason, which may be of interest to others. It occurred with a Shipmate stove whose installation involved a long pipe from tank to stove. After refilling the tank, the burners refused to work properly, 'panting' badly and flaring up. The solution we subsequently discovered, is to insert a valve, close to the cooker end of the line. The valve used is similar to the nipple fitted to the burner; the idea is to prevent the surge of pressure that occurs in a very long fuel line. However, if it were my boat, I should try to move the tank closer to the cooker — apart from anything else, if the line should split the paraffin would come out at pressure and make an unholy mess of the boat.

Taylors' stoves come with a cast iron simmering pad to put over the flame. With the burners turned low, you can simmer better than on any marine gas cooker that I've ever used and they are a feature which in my opinion, make the Taylors' stoves superior to any of the opposition. For safety's sake, the hot plates should live in the oven or beneath the cooker when not in use, to avoid the risk of them hurtling across the cabin. We always fill our cooker's tank via a filter funnel and actually have a filter in line between the main tank and its pump. This saves having to prick out the nipples, which means that they last longer. As they are not cheap and are a nuisance to change, it's worth taking the effort to do this. I prefer to top up the tank with a small amount every day, rather than to fill it when it's empty. This way you can usually avoid the situation of having to fill the tank in very rough weather, because you can skip the odd day that you feel there's a good chance of spilling paraffin. Incidentally, this brings me to another advantage of paraffin cookers over gas — they don't run out of fuel in the middle of cooking dinner.

The only real drawback of a paraffin cooker comes when you live with someone as parsimonious as Pete, who reckons that using unnecessary meths is a wicked extravagance and mutters darkly if you have the temerity to put on the kettle for an unscheduled cup of tea. In fact, alcohol can be very expensive and should be bought in quantity whenever it seems cheap. Chemists, by the way, usually sell it, but a hardware or painters' store is often a much better bet as they will often stock it in bulk. The other drawback of going to a chemist is that they are always on the lookout for alcoholics and subject you to the most intense and embarrassing scrutiny when you ask for a gallon of meths.

By the way, don't believe what you read about pressure paraffin cookers that can also use diesel — they are not quite what they seem. The type of diesel to which they refer is a grade sold only in countries that regularly have severe winters, where diesel is divided into two grades — light and heavy. The cookers use the light grade whereas the stuff you buy in most countries is heavy. If you are considering one of these cookers to reduce your fuel bill, forget about it, unless you intend to do most of your cruising in North America.

In fact diesel is a very cheap fuel, because even in places that are generally expensive, it rarely seems to be more than £1 per gallon and in countries with their own plentiful supply of oil, they just about give it away. Diesel cookers have all the benefits of an Aga type cooker — and all the drawbacks too. Once lit, they give off dry, cosy heat and always have an oven available. They simmer beautifully and often have room for three or four pans, as well as the oven. They can be left on twenty-four hours a day for warmth and constant hot water and are silent. However, they are giving off all this cosy heat in temperatures of 90°F and are as slow as a wet weekend when it comes to getting your pressure cooker to start cooking. We originally fitted a Dickinson™ Bristol range to *Badger* and I cooked on it for over five years. However, in the end I decided that it did not suit us because I use a pressure cooker a lot and because it was too far above the cabin sole to be a really effective heater. It was wonderful when we were sailing around higher latitudes, as the person on watch could stay nice and snug, the kettle was always full of hot water and wet gloves could be hung up over the stove. The boat was always dry and I could simmer things slowly instead of using the pressure cooker. If I had the room, I think that I would have kept the range and had a two burner Primus™ as well, but in reality, it just wasn't practical, If I used the pressure cooker less, we might well have kept it, so I feel that they are well worth considering. Yes, it was too hot in the Tropics, but I think any type of cooking makes the cabin too hot there, and I don't remember really resenting the heat from it then.

Cookers using alcohol/methylated spirits are much loved by the more officious coast guards of the world, who have never sailed, let alone on a small income. Alcohol cookers are purported to be safe, due to the facile argument that you can put out the flames with water and yet I'd be willing to put money on it that more fires have been caused by alcohol cookers than any other type. The reason for this is that, particularly with the unpressurised ones, the flame is both silent and on a sunny day, invisible. From what I've heard, the pressure ones are somewhat erratic and given to spurting neat, burning alcohol about at embarrassing moments. Add to this the fact that alcohol would work out to be an outrageously expensive cooking fuel in the quantities that you would require and that the cookers are slow and I think that you will probably come to the same conclusion as I have, that they are not worth considering for serious work.

Having decided on your fuel, you then have to decide on the particular brand of cooker. Pete and I are great believers in the principal of spending money up front while you have it (i.e., when you are working) for something that will then last indefinitely, rather than economizing initially for something that will have to be replaced out of one's voyaging income. Therefore, if we were buying, we would examine all the cookers carefully and go for the one built to the highest standards from best quality materials and also one for which spares would be available for the foreseeable future. A magnet would be of great assistance here; sometimes, what appears to be brass is in fact, plated and genuine stainless steel is non-magnetic. One of the advantages of choosing a paraffin cooker is that a lot of people prefer gas and so they are generally quite easy to obtain second-hand and in excellent condition.

The cost of fuel is particularly important, due to the fact that poor folk tend to cook food rather than just heat it up. For those of you who think that this is a good get out, I must point out that even doubling the fuel costs will be as nought compared with the savings in food costs that can be achieved from working a bit harder at the cooking of more demanding food. This increase in fuel costs will be dramatically reduced by the use of a pressure cooker. If, like us, you go the whole hog and cut out meat more or less entirely, you will then undoubtedly use a lot of pulses, which take forever to boil, but no more than twenty-five minutes (for the slowest of all) in a pressure cooker. If your small income is somewhat larger and you feel that you would be unhappy unless you can continue your carnivorous habits, you can still save a lot on your meat bill by cooking the cheaper cuts in your pressure cooker. Even the toughest meat is reduced to edible texture, especially with the judicious addition of a glass of wine — a point worth knowing anyway, as in many countries when you come to buy a piece of meat, you won't have the foggiest idea of from whereabouts on the animal it came. Pressure cookers are also good for pot-roasts, which means that for those who like such things, roast meat can be served up at the cost of far less fuel than would be the case if the oven were used. Deep-fried chunks of potato make an acceptable substitute for roast ones, by the way.

A lot of people are wary or even downright scared of pressure cookers, but if you are truly determined to get your cruising costs down, you should learn to make friends with them — they are the sailor's microwave — and generally quicker. In fact, they have recently been given a new lease on life by manufacturers who have got irritated at claims made by the microwave advertisers and they are being designed to be more "user friendly". If starting from scratch, I would try to buy a stainless steel one, not in the least because I have doubts about the long-term health effects of using aluminium pans. They are more expensive of course, but once again the high initial outlay will eventually pay for itself. You want to check that the cooker uses 15 lbs. pressure — a lot of Continental ones use only 10 lbs., which makes them slower. Prestige have been making pressure cookers for decades and still probably make the best, with the advantages that spares are

readily available in many different countries and that they will service it for you, or replace the lower part should you be daft enough to try cooking under pressure without any water. They also sell models with different weights, which produce better results when 'baking'.

Following the manufacturer's instructions should make the whole thing quite trouble free and with the new cookers' controlled pressure release knobs, reducing pressure is much more simple and no longer requires buckets of cold water or nerves of steel. Personally, I would be inclined to avoid the cookers with built-in timers, as sooner or later they will probably succumb to the marine environment and would be difficult to replace at a moment's notice. If I had room, I would seriously consider having two pressure cookers, so much do I use one. The record is five times in one meal, but I frequently use it twice and would be lost without one. Perhaps their greatest virtue is in really heavy weather, when you can fill it with chopped onion, garlic, vegetables, some beans, rice, curry spices and water, secure the lid and cook a gorgeous curry with no fear of spilling boiling food on the cook — or anyone else for that matter.

Cooking at sea is something of an art, but I feel that it can be made more straightforward if you organize the galley properly in the first place. If all that you need is to hand and if things are kept in the same place, then it will be a lot easier to prepare food because you won't be scrabbling in lockers trying to find what you want. Sharp knives are essential, as there is nothing worse than trying to cut up an onion with a blunt knife as it slides backwards and forwards over the counter, but they should be kept in their own rack and not in a cutlery drawer where they are a menace to fingers. Pans should be broad-based and deep so that they keep their contents and don't tip over — even if you have a gimballed cooker, you may want to put the pan down on the counter. Yet again, it is worth investing in the best you can buy. The pans that we have on board were given to us as wedding presents in 1975. They are enamelled and have lasted very well. Cooking popcorn in them makes them almost non-stick, but you can still use wire wool in them if needs be. I never use metal instruments in them — I can't stand the noise — which might explain how they've lasted so well. That they are good quality is sheer fluke — when I chose them I knew nothing at all about cooking and decided on these particular pans because they were pretty! The enamel started to lift on the kettle after ten years and I think that was because we left the whistle on when it was not in use. The frying pan had to go in 1984, because the enamel had come away from the middle — that was due to *Sheila's* Optimus cooker not having a simmering pad and compounded by our cooking on a single, "roarer" burner paraffin stove for a year, while we were finishing *Badger*: the heat was concentrated in a small part of the pan. If I were to choose again, I would go for taller pans because I don't have a gimballed cooker and the smallest one can't be used if we are heeling much. I wouldn't generally go for cast-iron because my wrists aren't strong enough to lift one up with only one hand, although I do have a cast-iron frying pan, but otherwise I should think that when enamelled, they must be the best; however you'd want particularly secure stowage for them. Yet again, it's worth buying the best you can afford; they will last much longer and produce better results — on the other hand, I think that on a boat, copper pans are open to debate.

With decent pots and pans and with everything organized, cooking at sea is enjoyable and I am perfectly happy in my galley pottering about, with the boat sailing well and the sun shining down. We enjoy our food at the best of times and it is a well-worn cliché that sailing gives you an appetite. I'm a slow cook and it takes me the best part of an hour to cook our main meal, but so what? We've got all the time in the world at sea, so why bother saving it? Even in harbour we are rarely rushed and I find cooking satisfying and therapeutic. However, that said, I will confess to keeping the odd tin on board, so that there is an alternative to baked beans on toast, when we've come back late or I really don't want to cook. Fortunately, on a small income, 60 pence 'wasted' on a tin means 60 pence less to spend on treats so the temptation to take short cuts is not great.

Talking of treats, I think every boat should have a 'treats locker' — probably most do. This locker, carefully chosen to be generally out of sight, contains little luxuries that you can't normally afford to buy. Thoughtful friends and relatives often give such things as tinned fruit cakes and jars of Keiller™ marmalade and these are lovingly stowed away. Then again, you might find a shop selling off cheap, something you can't usually afford to buy, or you might be given some money for a birthday which can be spent on treats. Then on 'half-way day' or a similar occasion, the cook rummages through the locker and pulls out one or more of these delights with which to celebrate. One of the very nice things about voyaging on a small income is that everything that is not a necessity is therefore a treat, so you in fact enjoy far more treats than the more wealthy sailor who has ample funds and can buy anything that takes his fancy; all of which actually adds to our quality of life.

The 'treats locker' also comes into its own when entertaining people on board, because it provides another excuse for having something special. When we first started cutting meat out of our own meals, I used to be embarrassed about inviting people round to dinner, but eventually decided that (a) they were meant to be coming to see *us* and (b) it would be a much-appreciated night off for the cook anyway. I also stopped mentioning the fact that the food was vegetarian and I'm sure that people often didn't notice. Nowadays, when it actually seems to be rather fashionable to be vegetarian, it's no problem anyway. In places where food is particularly expensive or where cooking makes the cabin unbearably hot for guests, we tend to invite people round for drinks and 'tapas'. The latter is an idea we've stolen from the Spanish bars where they put out little bowls of nibbles to have with your drinks. What I do is invariably make a huge bowl of popcorn and then things like sardine paté, lentil, mushroom and walnut paté, hummus, etc. and put out lots of bread or crackers for people to load up with the various spreads. In Venezuela, crackers were ridiculously cheap at £1 for a huge tin and salted peanuts were quite inexpensive so that we bought a dozen tins of each for the 'treats locker'; in Spain we bought 'chorizo' (a hard, spiced sausage that keeps for ages); in Portugal almonds, in Morocco olives, and in St. Martin tinned paté, all of which were stowed away and brought out at a later date for tapas. This type of food is also useful for the times when you want to invite a load of people round and have a party. An added advantage is that the leftovers make a luxurious lunch the next day.

UNLESS YOU ARE WALKING AROUND IN
A LIQUORICE ALLSORT COLOURED OILSKIN

Chapter 14

The Outer Man

Clothes are as much of a necessity to the poor as to the wealthy. However, it is quite unnecessary to spend much money on them. Many people like to make their own, but they can be obtained even more cheaply from charity shops, thrift shops, jumble sales and second-hand ('nearly new') shops and in the case of the first three, there is the added advantage of knowing that your money is going to a good cause, rather than lining the pockets of some bloated plutocrat. Devoted relatives are a good (often too good) source of home knitted sweaters and socks for cooler climates. Indeed, most of us have an embarrassment of clothes rather than a paucity and have problems deciding where to stow them.

On many boats, there are only one or two small hanging lockers and so the majority of clothes are usually kept folded. On *Badger* we have far too many clothes (well, you can't throw them away until they're worn out, can you?) many of which live under the double bunk when unsuitable for the present climate. What should be the hanging locker is actually pretty full of foremast and I have given up trying to hang anything there and made it over to ropes and fenders. As there generally won't be room to hang everything up, it is well worth while learning to fold clothes properly. In this way, they not only take up less room, but actually come out of the locker looking as though they have been pressed. With trousers, the idea is to put the inside and outside seams together, thus obtaining a knife edge crease front and back. With shirts, they should be unbuttoned and the collars pulled up. About mid-point on the reinforcement of the shoulder where it joins the sleeve, is the place where the crease of the sleeve ends. Join shoulder to shoulder at this place, with the back inside and the fronts outside. Smooth the sleeves down one side then fold in two with the sleeves in the middle. In two again and the shirt will stay smooth and pressed until needed. Incidentally, it is less effective to fold shirts up in the way that they are done when you buy them because the collars tend to get crushed.

You may think that all this is somewhat bourgeois, but as we are judged by our appearance like it or not, it's worth bowing to popular prejudice. After all, we can't have everything our own way. As well, it's not much more effort to fold clothes carefully than to stuff them in a locker and it's quite amusing to watch people's incredulous expressions when you casually observe that you haven't done any ironing in the last ten years. It's bad enough having to endure the sobriquet of boat bums, without gratuitously adding to our bad press, so I replace the buttons and mend the tears. In many countries — particularly the more so-called primitive ones — a reasonable smartness of dress is the standard set by the native inhabitants and it is an insult to these people to look as though you just came off a rubbish heap. Second-hand clothes don't have to look second-hand.

In order to look reasonably respectable however, it's worth doing some homework on different materials so that you needn't spend your time slaving away to keep things tidy. A lot of cottons and most silk have to be ironed and should be avoided, except for tee-shirts and simply cut clothes that will fold well. The exception is cheesecloth the appearance of which is actually spoilt by ironing. Man made fibres crease far less badly, don't shrink, don't wear out as fast and don't fade so quickly; they can also be unpleasant to wear. However, polyester and cotton mixtures are good for blouses, tee-shirts and trousers, as they last for ages, but the cotton helps them to 'breathe'. Good quality polyester/cotton is as comfortable to wear as cotton. In particular, we have found that cotton tee-shirts tend to deteriorate rapidly in the Tropics while the poly/cotton ones last much longer. Man-made materials also dry a lot more quickly than natural ones. For warmth wool takes a lot of beating — 3,000,000 sheep can't be wrong — although I have found acrylic very good and modern fibre-pile clothing is meant to be excellent; it's also very expensive and hasn't found its way into the second-hand shops yet, so we don't have any, alas. Both wool and acrylic seem to last forever, the exception being Shetland wool, which usually goes through at the elbows pretty quickly. Talking of warmth, although denim jeans are very popular, they are not at all warm at sea, corduroys are better, particularly heavy ones, but they're all dreadful when they get wet. Track suit pants and sweatshirts are very good sailing gear because they are nice and roomy so that you can easily move in them and not being skin tight, they trap a layer of air next to your skin. Once again, it's worth buying them of a mixed fabric because heavy cotton sweatshirts and trousers take a lot of drying. I have also discovered that it's worth trying to buy decent quality because the cheap ones soon wear through. One fairly recent fashion with which I've become enamoured are leggings (stretch trousers), which are wonderfully comfortable to wear in temperate climes, although not warm enough when it's cold. As to colour, we try to avoid white because it's too much like hard work keeping it that way. Sooner or later anything white seems to end up grey or yellow and all the stains show. For that reason, patterned material is often to be preferred, but in fact both of us have largely self-colour clothes, probably because we have rather conservative tastes.

Washing generally has to be done by hand, as those of us who are paupers cannot really afford a launderette. As very few people seem to hand wash these days, it might not be out of place to say a few things about it.

I have found that liquid detergents are far superior to powders. Not only do they not need to be dissolved and therefore work well in cold water, but they seem to rinse out a lot better. A substantial washing bowl — about five gallons capacity — is of very great assistance because it enables the clothes to be sloshed about without the water going everywhere. Buckets are useful for rinsing, but not for washing.

When I'm doing a pile of laundry, I first mix a capful of detergent with a pint or two of water to make a concentrated solution. I then wet all the tea towels with this and then wring them out and put them to one side — effectively giving them a short soak. Then I take a half inch paint brush that I keep for this purpose and use it to dab neat detergent on any obvious stains. It's powerful enough to remove most stains, including blood, but tends to be defeated by red wine. I then add the rest of the gallon to what's left in the bowl and then wash in the normal manner. Sheets, tea towels and trousers all tend to get a bit grimy if they are not scrubbed regularly and I use a six inch brush with stiff, man-made bristles. The clothes usually end up at least as clean as they do from the laundrette and often cleaner. The detergent only really needs to be rinsed out once, but as much water as possible should be wrung out of the clothes before rinsing. Wringing out clothes is a problem, although my friend Lesley on *Cameleon* has a mangle on board, which does a pretty thorough job, with Chris manning the handle. Not having room for such a luxury, I have developed one or

two techniques instead, such as doubling clothes around the guard rail or mainsheet horse (traveler), in order to get a fixed point to wring against, which is very effective. For the sake of the record, I usually use about six gallons of water to do a fortnight's washing.

The best place for getting the laundry dry is, of course, a hot climate where one wears very few clothes. The worst place is a cool climate where one wears more. There is very little justice in this life. On the other hand, you don't sweat as much in a cool place, so you can wear your clothes longer and when there are only two of you, you don't notice one another's pong. Therefore, you can have a shower and change before going ashore where you are likely to meet people, but otherwise not worry over much and keep the amount of dirty clothes to a minimum. If you don't let the washing build up too much, it isn't too awful a chore, but in my opinion, having to do the laundry by hand in small quantities of cold water is the worst thing about the sailing life, especially on cold, windy days. Rubber gloves help in these conditions, by keeping the icy wind from evaporating the water on your hands. By the way, don't be tempted to use salt water, whatever Bernard Moitessier might say. You need so much fresh water to clear out every trace of salt, that you might as well have used fresh in the first place and the salt crystals do not shake out with the wind — at least not before the clothes have worn themselves out with flapping. Clothes with salt in them will never dry properly.

Shoes are always a bit of a problem on a boat because they take up so much room. In hot climates, Pete and I used to wear thick-soled flip-flops a lot because they are cheap and don't object to getting wet. They have recently been taken up by trendies and are sold at outrageous cost under the name of 'slaps', while we paid 60p for ours in Venezuela (for the deluxe version) and Woolworths have them at a reasonable price. However, the problem with them is that your feet get filthy and they are lethal on smooth, wet surfaces, such as the floors in fish markets. Sand shoes are also very good and very cheap 'sur le continent', but when worn regularly can cause one's heels to crack and I have found they bruise my big toes if I walk far in them! Deck shoes can be worn with or without socks, depending on the temperature, which makes them very useful. They can be expensive, but if you keep a weather eye out you can sometimes pick them up very reasonably in sales. Incidentally, good quality ones can be re-soled and furbished up in the USA. Trainers are an excellent alternative and 'last year's model' can occasionally be a bargain in the sales. If we are dressing up at all (for those occasional dinners with the local consul!), I like to have a pair of good shoes to go with a dress. However, they don't get worn much and the pair I bought in 1987 (in a sale) are still as good as new.

For sailing we prefer bare feet and generally only wear deck shoes if it happens to be both cold and dry. Bare feet have an even better grip and don't wear out. If it's so cold that we need socks, we often wear seaboots when we are out on deck, but if we are doing a lot of hand-steering, we tend to get fed up of clumping around in boots. We usually buy ours from a farmers' shop or similar establishment; yachting wellies are a dreadful price, don't last very well and don't seem to be much more non-slip. Besides, we promised Skipper, when he pulled us off the beach, that we would never wear yellow wellies (he hated yachties in yellow wellies; I'm glad to say that we were innocent of them anyway at the time). Due to the fact that on *Badger* we hardly ever need to go on deck, we find slippers are good footwear in cold weather (one more advantage to sailing with junk rig) and so have much less need to consider the non-skid property of various types of footwear. I think that the virtues of computer engineered tread on various designer deck shoes are somewhat overrated. Bare wood is safe in virtually any type of shoe and shiny, wet fibreglass equally lethal.

The Designers have recently had a go at oilskins and you are now nobody worth considering unless you are walking around in a Liquorice Allsort coloured oilskin, with built in lifejacket, clanking safety harness, fifteen pockets and reflective tape for falling overboard with. Having worked up to the dizzy heights of Henri Lloyd Offshore (circa 1982, i.e. incorporating warm lining and storm cuffs) we've come to the conclusion that a lot of the business is a complete nonsense. To keep warm wear thermal underwear and sweaters. To keep dry and protected from the wind you want a waterproof jacket and trousers. If your boat is sensibly sorted out you will not be up to your waist in water, so chest high oilies are not necessary. However, if you need to go on the foredeck, you will certainly need them. I see that they are now made with a large gusset in the bib, which must make them easier to get in and out of, but I have many unpleasant recollections of struggling out of the wretched things, bursting for a pee, only to find when I stood up again that the straps had dangled in the bowl. Waist high trousers are also less of a pain to carry when you've gone ashore in the pouring rain, all kitted up, only to find that it turns into a hot, gloriously sunny day 20 minutes later. We both now have bottom of the range Guy Cotten™ trousers, as worn by fishermen. They are cheap and waterproof; they do not have Velcro® fastened storm cuffs and with long wellies, we've never needed them and they do not drag on the ground when we're walking along.

As to the jackets, if you are living on board they will tend to be worn ashore as often as at sea. If you want to look like a wally, that's fine, but I prefer something less obviously yachtie than the current oilskins "in a range of high-fashion colours". Pete's jacket is a fine, double-breasted, second-hand, heavy duty PVC job, which makes him look like a bucko mate, especially when worn with a sou'wester. Mine is made by Messrs Douglas Gill and is actually designed for someone of my height (most manufacturers' small women are 5-foot, 6-inches tall), apart from the sleeves, which were designed for a gorilla. It is made of a very soft material and folds down to a sufficiently small bundle that it will fit inside its own hood. It originally had storm cuffs, but they trapped the moisture inside, so that the sleeves stayed wet for days and so I cut them off. Water runs down my sleeve if I work over my head, but it also runs out again better than it used to. Until the poppers died, I fastened the sleeves with the pop-studs on the cuffs to keep the worst of the water at bay in that situation, but the sleeves now hang down so far that they keep the wind off my hands. We have found that all oilskins tend to get damp inside when you've been sitting out in the pouring rain for three or four hours — perhaps the situation is better when you are standing at a wheel and are a better shape for shedding water, but who wants to stand up to steer, anyway? I have also found that all sleeves seem to end up wet when the rain is tippling down; oilskins seem to dry out again more easily if they are not too heavy to begin with. We put on safety harnesses if we need them (which is pretty rarely) and can wear them in the Tropics without having to put on our "Ocean Conqueror" jacket first, thus leading to heat stroke. We do not wear lifejackets because when you are sailing a boat with self-steering and only two crew, you are likely to end up drowned anyway, if you fall overboard. For the same reason, we don't need light reflective tape to make us look like Christmas trees. Yellow oilskins are traditional and brighten up the atmosphere when you are surrounded by gray sea and sky.

As I mentioned earlier, at the end of the day you are much more likely to find that you have too many clothes rather than too few. You can take them back to the Oxfam shop, from time to time — a good throwing-out session is wonderful for morale — or chuck them overboard (if they are bio-degradable, of course) or limit yourself to a small selection and wear them out. Unfortunately, the only things we ever seem to wear out are trousers.

DIESEL CAN BE QUITE DIRTY

Chapter 15

A Load Of Hot Air

If you go voyaging rather than simply living aboard a yacht, it is more than likely that you will not want to spend all your time cruising in the Tropics. While there is a lot of pleasure to be had sailing there, eventually the extra challenge of higher latitudes becomes enticing. For us, sailing in the Tropics is like being on holiday, but we don't want to spend the rest of our lives on holiday, surrounded by other yachts. So we look at the globe and think of the lonely places where the daylight hours are endless and where sharing an anchorage with another yacht is cause for a get-together and yarning into the night and not a nuisance.

As far as I'm concerned however, there is no pleasure to be had in being cold and so I consider some form of dry heating (i.e. a heater with a chimney to vent away the moisture) as essential on a voyaging yacht. Reading such authors as Maurice Griffiths, it is apparent that 50 years ago, nearly all cruising boats had a little solid fuel stove on board — nowadays it's not easy to find a spare bit of bulkhead against which to put your heater. When and why this eminently sensible tradition died out, I wot not, but such is the case and should you be buying a boat, chances are that you'll have to fit a heater to her and to do that, you'll need to alter the accommodation. Nothing's ever easy.

As with selecting a cooker, you have first of all to decide on which fuel you want and then to decide who makes the heater of your choice. The fuels available are wood/coal, diesel, paraffin and gas, more or less in order of cheapness. However, with heaters there are the various levels of sophistication to be taken into account, too.

Probably the most efficient system, insofar as heating the boat quickly and in its entirety is concerned, is the blown-air type of system, such as is made by Webasto™. This system was developed for keeping the cabs of lorries warm in Sweden, where the cold no doubt, is a real problem. It has become very popular with yachtsmen because it is thermostatically controlled and ideal for the modern boat with split accommodation, where heating the after cabin would generally require another unit. The heater itself is usually fitted in a cockpit locker

and so there is no requirement for a bulkhead space on which to fit it. The air can be ducted through lockers to keep them dry and the whole boat can be effectively heated. However, there is unfortunately a high price to pay for all this. Firstly, the cost of the system and its installation are not to be sniffed at, after which there are other considerations to take into account. These systems are supposed to run on diesel and so they do; the drawback is that on ordinary marine diesel they can be quite dirty and put sooty marks all over the boat near their exhaust. In fact this is such a problem that friends of ours finally gave up and started to use paraffin and have been doing so ever since. Thus if you have installed one of these heaters so that you don't need to carry a variety of fuels, you will be more than a little irritated by this. Another drawback is that the fan required to shove all this warm air about, uses a lot more electricity than the manufacturers would have you believe, especially in an uninsulated boat, where the heater would be on a lot of the time and so you have the worry of flattening your batteries. A further drawback is that the units are undoubtedly rather noisy and the fact that they are often installed in cockpit lockers means that they are a nuisance to neighbours as well. Finally and most importantly, they are not particularly reliable — I have come across a lot of people who have had problems with them — and I can think of few things more likely to spoil your pleasure than to have your heater break down during your circumnavigation of Spitzbergen.

If however, you fancy the idea of diesel stoves, there are some excellent ones about, of which the Danish Refleks™ is possibly the best. We have one on **Badger**, which we installed when we sold the range and decided that we needed a heater that was not reliant on our ability to get wood or buy coal — both of which are exceedingly difficult to obtain in some parts of the world where you want a heater. As well, we don't intend to spend more than a few months at a time anywhere cold, so the cost of running a diesel stove is now acceptable. I like the Dickinson stoves from North America, but am less enamoured of the fact that they come with a 12v fan. I'm afraid that there is no way in which I could recommend the drip-feed stoves sold by a well-known British manufacturer of heaters and cookers. Maybe my acquaintance have been unlucky, but everyone I know who has had one of these stoves has had problems with it and several have had fires. One of the problems is that because the drip is effectively controlled by the pressure in the header tank, its rate varies with the fuel consumed and it will also start to drip faster when the diesel warms up and becomes thinner. Because it is a drip feed, it can fill the pan up to such a level that a slight movement of the boat can cause it to spill over. On the other hand, Reflekes, Dickinson and several other makes of stove use a type of carburetor with a float to keep the flow of fuel constant. However, even this is not always 100% safe. Our stove, for example, could spill diesel if heeled too far when turned up high because it then actually has a pool of oil in the combustion chamber. On its lowest setting, not enough oil is passing through the carburetor to spill. It is worth carefully examining your stove to find out what its safe operating parameters are. Good quality diesel heaters are not particularly cheap, but they are very well made, with little to go wrong and this is one of the many instances where paying money up front is cheaper in the long run. There are second-hand Reflekes' about in England, in fact, we've actually bought two, one for £65 (for *Badger*) and one for £60 (for *Missee Lee)*. The drawbacks? They can be tricky to light — firelighters often help, but an asbestos wick, dipped in meths and attached to the end of a long piece of wire is the best we've found up to now. Of course, diesel costs money, which wood need not — not a lot maybe, but it might be more than you would wish to spend on heating and diesel stoves do lack a certain aesthetic appeal compared with solid fuel. If buying from new, by the way (when you have some choice in the matter) it makes sense to buy the sort that can take a pan or a kettle on top. It also makes sense to install the heater's header tank in the accommodation where, in really cold weather, the diesel won't be too viscous to flow.

Good old paraffin is also to be considered. Here the major drawback is definitely that of cost. Even in a well insulated boat, you are going to be talking of using five gallons a week and if we were in England now, that would represent about 30% of our weekly income. However, if your small income is greater than our small income, you may fancy paraffin. Taylors turn out a super little paraffin heater that has been a favourite for many a year. They used to come with an optional hot-water tank, of about a gallon capacity, that fitted around the flue pipe above the heater, but I'm not sure if they still do this ("There's no demand, you know"). Force 10 also make a heater which uses paraffin and purports to use diesel, but as mentioned earlier, this is the lighter grade of diesel that is not sold in many places. The drawbacks of the paraffin heater are that they put out less heat, which might make them a little too small for your boat, they need fairly frequent pumping, which makes their use at night debatable and they are a little noisy. However, in an uninsured boat, the use of any non-solid fuel heater when you are asleep or off the boat is a risk not many of us would wish to take. Another point to consider is the cost of burners when they are being used twenty-four hours a day, seven days a week. The old type of free standing heater with the circular wick, is used by some people, but it gives off far too much condensation to be a realistic proposition. Having said which, I have heard of them being fitted with a flue pipe which leads outside.

If you use propane/butane gas (and in cold climates it's worth remembering that butane gas freezes at about the freezing point of water whereas propane can cope with lower temperatures) you might be tempted by a catalytic heater. Don't be. Catastrophic would be a more accurate name. They are the worst of all worlds, expensive to run, using dangerous fuel and giving off gallons of moisture. There are heaters now using gas, designed along similar lines to the Taylors unit and with a little ingenuity, you could make your own. Another point to consider is that some of the hot air systems mentioned above can now be used with bottled gas. Personally, I would be very reluctant to lead any more gas lines around the boat.

Finally we are back where we started, with the solid fuel stove and here I will say that I am hopelessly prejudiced by the fact that I love a "real" fire. To try to be dispassionate for a moment, solid fuel stoves are somewhat dirty (they make smoke and the ash-pan needs emptying), the fuel takes up a lot of room and a good quality unit is made of cast-iron and therefore heavy. However, having said that, the fuel can be free which means that in desperate times (and very expensive places) you could cook and keep warm for free. When we had a solid fuel stove in *Badger,* we found that we could usually heat for free by scavenging wood — boatyards are a very good source of supply, usually having lots of scrap about (but please don't use their wedges!). However, although wood is the cheapest fuel and burns hottest, it takes up the most room. Smokeless fuels are the cleanest, but make the most ash and take up quite a lot of room, a bag of smokeless fuel consisting of a lot of air. Anthracite is efficient and takes up the least space. Although solid fuel is dirty stuff, you can cope with the problem by pre-bagging it in (dare I say) plastic carrier bags so that each bag holds the right amount to top up the firebox. If your boat is dry, you could perhaps pre-bag it in paper sacks; it may be worth considering pre-bagging anthracite anyway, as this often comes in small pieces that fall through the grate as you shovel it in, but act as one when put on in a job lot. I am reliably informed that the king of coals is Welsh Steam Coal, but perhaps we should leave that for the steam engineers. We often used coal even when wood was readily available, because it gives off less heat and our Tor-Gem was extremely efficient. By the way, we have been staggered to find that coal can be exceedingly difficult to buy outside the UK. Indeed, in the USA, Canada and Iceland we found that it was effectively impossible to buy either smokeless fuel or coal. Wood, in the form of driftwood is usually available, however, but we had to resort to sawing up broken pallets when we were in Reykjavik. In fact, it was the difficulty of finding coal, together with the amount of space needed, that eventually persuaded us that a diesel heater would be more realistic for us. Had *Badger* had any depth of bilge in which we could have carried a plentiful supply of fuel, we would probably have stayed with our much-loved Tor-Gem. Our friends Ros and Tom, can carry half a ton on their Bristol Channel Pilot Cutter, and that is the sort of quantity that frees you from worrying too much about where next to bunker. Solid fuel stoves give off a lovely, dry heat and are generally so efficient that on a smallish, insulated boat like *Badger,* you will often have to open hatches. Because they need a draught, they create good ventilation in the boat and a well-designed one is safe and easy to keep ticking over for the night or when you are away for several hours. They can also be used to burn rubbish on ocean crossings and in countries where rubbish is simply dumped over the nearest cliff. Although they apparently burn at a lower temperature than proper rubbish incinerators, so that burning plastic produces polluting fumes, floating plastic isn't any better for the environment.

Lighting a solid fuel fire can do a lot to make you wonder about the supposed fire risks of a wooden boat. Francis B. Cooke writes in **Cruising Hints** that "the best method of lighting a coal fire is by means of a handful of cotton waste steeped in paraffin. This is far better than fooling about with damp wood and the **Daily Mail**". Most of us who have had solid fuel stoves have spent what seems to be an unconscionable amount of time fooling thusly and his advice is welcome. In fact, the cotton waste can be admirably replaced by a firelighter, a plentiful supply of which should be kept on board — again some other benighted countries do not have these for sale. They are useful in warmer climates, too, for starting beach bonfires. Incidentally, a solid fuel stove should be mounted with its door facing either forward or aft to reduce the chances of its opening inadvertently and tipping the contents on to the cabin sole. The final advantage of a bogey stove must be on the grounds of aesthetics; to quote FBC again: "the cheerful glow of the fire imparts to the little saloon an appearance of homeliness that is very comforting on a cold winter night" — make sure that the stove you buy has windows in the door.

Half the problem with keeping a boat warm lies in preventing the heat from escaping. On *Badger*, we lined the whole of the inside of the boat with half-inch cork (covered in wood veneer) to help stop warmth escaping and also to reduce condensation. It has worked very well. It was incredibly messy stuff to work with as it was composed of quite large fragments of cork which would come away from the edge of the sheet at the drop of a hat; if we were doing it again, we'd use polystyrene, especially as they now make a fire-retardant variety.

As well as cork and polystyrene, we have met people using fibreglass with apparently, satisfactory results. This must be particularly horrid to fit and I wonder whether it would absorb water, but its insulating

qualities are beyond dispute. In fibreglass boats, a lot of people use indoor/outdoor carpet to fairly good effect, although if *that* gets sodden, it goes pretty rank. The popular insulation for steel boats is spray-on foam above the waterline or all over the hull and decks. This takes a lot of work to smooth down and needs a substantial lining such as plywood to cover it up because you can't get it perfectly fair. An alternative that also seems popular with steel boat-builders is Rockwool™. Finally, in a traditional wooden boat, the conventional, horizontally run lining of battening below the deck level keeps an air gap between the topsides and the interior and works surprisingly well, if properly done. The coach roof sides present more of a problem. I have heard of an ingenious idea for the deckhead whereby it had been doubled and made into separate hinge down sections. In each of these were stored several charts, kept flat and they were thus out of the way as well as providing insulation.

As with so many things, it is a case of assessing your individual needs and what is suitable for your boat — then "you pays your money and you takes your choice". However, should you decide that cold climates are not for you, it is worth remembering that an interesting spin-off of having insulation is that as well as having a boat that is snug in cool climates, you also have a boat that is cooler in hot ones; several people have commented on this when they've come aboard *Badger* in the Tropics.

Although insulation is a great thing in the Tropics, it is also essential to have a way of scooping draughts of air below. Any decent boat is going to be fitted with at least some Dorade ventilators, but these are insufficient on their own. When it is really hot, you need a forced draught and one way of doing this is by using a wind scoop. These are now actually being manufactured and sold through chandlers, but it is not beyond the wit of most people to make one themselves. The general principle is to have a rectangular back and two right-angled triangular sides, with the short side at the bottom, the hypotenuses at the front and the third side sewn to one long side of the rectangular piece of cloth, using a light fabric such as spinnaker nylon. At the top is fitted a spreader, made of doweling or some such and above that is usually sewn a shallow triangle of stouter fabric, with an eyelet to which is tied the securing line. Commercially made wind scoops usually have a batten across the lower end of the rectangle and eyelets at the front corners of the sides, the idea being that you wedge the batten across the after end of the hatch, tie the two corners to the forward end and tie the top to the boom or forestay, or whatever. The drawback of this system is that you have to take the damn' thing down each time it rains — which seems to be about ten times a night in most of the Caribbean. What we have done on *Badger*, is to take out the batten and put in two extra eyelets at the other two corners. We have screwed down little brass saddles at all four corners of the hatch and to put up the wind scoop, we close the hatch, tie the four corners to the saddles, tie the top up to the foresail and then open the hatch at 180°. Then, when we have a shower of rain, we can simply shut the hatch. Should the squall be accompanied by an excessive amount of wind, it is no big deal to untie the top of the scoop and drop it on deck. This system also has the advantage that it can be used sideways, should you happen to have the problem of a tidal stream placing you athwart the wind or if you are tied up alongside; it also stops the scoop flapping about in fluky breezes.

Whilst on the subject of ventilation, we've found that our two forward facing, opening scuttles are excellent for a through draught and we also like the ones in the galley and heads. The other six are very rarely opened and although on the few occasions that we've been alongside in a hot place we have really appreciated them, we have never opened them since we were alongside in the Hemingway Marina near Havana. This is because we left them open one day when we were there, visiting the city. It hadn't rained during the whole time we had been in Cuba, but on that day, a front came through and by the time we returned from Havana, the rain had poured in the open scuttles and all over our books in the shelves below. They also leaked on one occasion when we were knocked down and the water pressure forced out the neoprene gaskets with which they were fitted. After those two experiences, we have come to regard them as more of a liability than an asset. To be fair, the only reason we fitted these six opening ones in the first place was because they were offered to us for £1 each.

Badger has four opening hatches — one is over the double bunk, one is over the saloon table and one is in the bridge deck. The fourth one is a *Jester* type, pram hood opening which is secured against intruders, cold or excessive weather by a plastic astrodome. When we are on board, the bubble is hardly ever put over the hatch and sits forward of it, making a good protective cover for the compass. The pram hood, another brilliant idea of 'Blondie' Hasler's, is a marvelous extractor and since we fitted it in the autumn of 1990 we have found the boat stays much fresher when it's cold and raining and we are sailing along, battened down. The pram hood is three-quarters of a hemisphere and it is turned so that its opening is to leeward. Even in a gale of wind it has never let any water in, apart from one or two drops when a wave crashes against it. One can keep lookout from under it and even going to windward it can be turned so that you can just see ahead and only need to put it down for the occasional glance over the weather deck. Now that we have it, we wonder how we ever lived without it.

We don't have a conventional sliding companionway and washboards because we didn't like the idea of weakening the back of the cabin and washboards drive me dotty. Also, in our experience, sliding hatches do seem to have a tendency to leak and we have much more privacy than with a conventional companionway. A fixed scuttle at the after end of the cabin allows one to look out. The hatch over our bunk and the after hatch are hinged at the forward end. The one over the saloon table is hinged at the after end and when opened at an angle of 45°, makes such an effective wind scoop that the other one is rarely needed.

Our Dorade boxes are situated so that there is one over the heads and one over the galley. We used to have two over the sleeping cabin on the foredeck, but every now and then they got inundated and leaked over the double berth. In the end, we sealed off the baffle and changed the cowls round so that they are directly over the hole through the deck. When we go to sea we put covers over and seal them off. The ones in the heads and galley cannot be shut off and we have occasionally had a dollop of water down them in heavy weather, but it can't do any real harm in either place (unlike over the bunk) and I don't think it would be a good idea to be able completely to seal the boat. Besides, we lead the cable for the water generator down one and that for the log down the other. We have used cast brass cowls, which look very smart on the principal that they should last the life of the boat, which is more than can be said for plastic — they were also very reasonably priced at the time, which may also have had something to do with it. By the way, we had spun brass cowls on *Sheila* and were very disappointed with the strength of this form of manufacture.

As well as the above methods of ventilation, we have a bronze mushroom ventilator over the after deck, another one over the cooker and a Plastimo solar ventilator on the forehatch. This latter is a flat baffle type similar to the Tannoy™ and gives some ventilation even when the little fan isn't running. However, it is also fitted with a solar charged battery so that it can run 24 hours a day when there is a surplus of sunshine. Although it works very well and we believe it to be the best of its type, we have discovered that although it may be weatherproof, it most certainly is not wave-proof and has to be covered with a plastic bag if there's any risk of heavy weather. I think on a coachroof it would probably not leak, but in spite of its advantages, it was a mistake to fit it on the forehatch.

Fusty smelling boats are very unpleasant and unfortunately living on board, you can get used to your boat's own particular miasma so that you don't notice it any more. Whenever we've been away I leap on board, nose twitching to see if I can detect a musty or stale odour, but am glad to say that, to me at least, *Badger* always smells quite fresh. Good ventilation will prevent frowstiness, which can be particularly bad on boats that are also permanent homes. Fresh air circulating down below is also good for the boat, preventing mildew and even rot (and don't forget that even fibreglass boats have structural woodwork) as well as keeping your possessions dry. As with anchors, we work on the belief that you can't have too much of this particular good thing — as long as it lets in air and not water. It is not at all difficult to improve poor ventilation on any boat and it adds immensely to your quality of life to live in a dry boat that is rarely too hot or too cold, but is, in fact, a comfortable home.

(Right) *Badger's Dorade box includes mounts for the running light and a clear top for letting light in below.*

(Below) *Badger's heater at the aft end of the settees and just forward of the mainmast. Jay R. Benford photo.*

(Below right) *Annie looking out of Badger's Jester pram hood. Jay R. Benford photo.*

THE WORKHORSE

Chapter 16

The Workhorse

Your yacht's tender will probably be the most abused and least cared for item of equipment that you have aboard and it is difficult to comprehend what a hard life it has, until you have cruised actively for an extended period. The reason for this abuse is that dinghies are used virtually every day when you are not actually on passage and they are used hard. As well as acting as a taxi, carrying you to and fro, they are dragged up beaches, left tied up alongside barnacle covered walls, used to ferry cargo, to paint the parent ship and to carry out the kedge. Many dinghies are subjected to having fish and shellfish, both dead and alive, thrown into them, they get covered in mud and sometimes oil, the sun shines on them day after day, they fill with rain water and are subjected to the unwelcome attentions of local children. Sooner or later they will be capsized in the surf and at least once, they will be towed under because their owners are too lazy to pull them aboard. The reason that the poor things tend to be so badly cared for, is simply because they are needed so often that you can rarely give them the couple of days' rest needed for maintenance.

Choosing the right dinghy for a voyaging yacht is a real headache, with all sorts of contradictory requirements. It has to be a good load carrier and easy to stow, it has to be light enough to carry up a beach, but robust enough to leave tied to a wall. It has to row well, but it needs to be stable. Most people buying a dinghy these days opt for an inflatable. I am told that the reason for this is so that they can be stowed in cockpit lockers, but in practice, the majority of yachtsmen seem to tow the things behind them, hitched up on to the yacht's stern in a vulgarly suggestive manner. Having owned an inflatable myself, for a mercifully brief period, I can attest to the fact that they are an infernal nuisance to inflate and deflate and assume that most other people feel the same — hence the popularity of towing a type of dinghy manifestly unsuited to towing. In anything of a breeze, the average "rubber duck" will perform a series of increasingly alarming evolutions at the end of its string, threatening to pull off the towing eye and eventually culminating in a 180° capsize, so that a vacuum is formed between the surface of the sea and the bottom of the dinghy causing incredible drag. Hence hitching it half way up the stern. Some people try to stow them on deck, but unfortunately the average modern boat was not designed with this eventuality in mind and so there is no suitable place to

stow a dinghy. This means that the unhappy helmsman has to spend his time peering over and around it, bearing a more than passing resemblance to a short man in a cinema, who finds himself sitting behind a stout and be-hatted woman.

In favour of inflatables, it must be said that even the most lubberly of people can bring one alongside a boat without damage, due to the fact that the whole craft is one great fender. They are also extremely good, if wet, load carriers, they are stable and they make good swimming platforms. A good quality inflatable, such as an Avon™, will last for years, with the minimum of maintenance and the use of a 12 volt inflater will encourage you to deflate and stow it rather than tow it. If your boat has nowhere that you can stow a solid dinghy and still see where you're going, I suppose that they are the only alternative to a folding boat.

However, inflatables have several important drawbacks, especially to those on a small income. On odds, I think that the most serious of these is that there is a lot of demand for them and a disturbingly high percentage of yachtsmen are quite happy to buy an inflatable that they have good reason to believe could be stolen. As a new inflatable is a costly item, at best it would be a very real inconvenience to have to replace it and at worst of course, it could be exceedingly difficult to replace one that has been pinched, as they are not always easy to buy at a moment's notice. The risk of theft should not be underestimated and is not confined simply of one or two countries. There are a number of well authenticated stories of yachts seen with half a dozen or so inflatables stacked on deck or of people who have had their tender disappear off the stern of their boat while they are asleep, as happened to our friends Paul and Janette one night in Falmouth. It is bad enough to have to fork out a lot of money on a dinghy in the first place, without having to worry about having to replace it before its allotted span.

Another drawback of inflatables is that they are absolute pigs to row. To a certain extent this can be overcome by paddling them, canoe style, as long as there are two people and you don't mind getting wet behinds, but if you are on your own there is no alternative but to try and row. Fitting wooden floorboards helps a lot, by making the craft more rigid. Incidentally, fitting floorboards also makes the boat easier to get in and out of without getting a welly full of water and enables you to put things down in the dinghy with a little more chance of them staying in place. However, having to fit floorboards each time you assemble the thing, is a powerful disincentive to using them and if you buy the type that has them fitted permanently, it becomes more difficult to stow. For many people, both problems are solved by fitting an outboard and towing the dinghy when under way. The latter I have already mentioned, but for those of us on a small income, the outboard engine is not a satisfactory solution. Once again there is the risk of theft, which again raises the matter of initial cost. Running costs are also to be considered, although in all fairness not even I would suggest that a two horsepower, four-stroke would cost a lot to run. Still, pennies make pounds and they are undeniably an unnecessary expense. It is an idea to put away temptation by choosing a dinghy to which an outboard cannot be easily fitted and give yourself the opportunity to enjoy the healthy and pleasant pastime of rowing.

The worst drawback of an inflatable and yet probably the least obvious, is that it is extremely difficult to use one to row out a kedge in a strong breeze. As already mentioned, they are not particularly good to row at the best of times, but against any wind and sea and dragging an anchor line through the water, the job becomes nearly impossible. In this instance it is positively dangerous to attempt to use the outboard motor and in some cases you may just have to give up the idea altogether — not a happy thought.

Talking of kedging, it is a hazardous and unseamanlike procedure to stand up in a dinghy and chuck the anchor overboard. Apart from anything else, you are quite likely to capsize and anyway, while you're fooling around standing up, picking up the anchor and giving it the old heave-ho, you will have been blown almost back to your ship. A much better system is to dangle the anchor over the stern of the dinghy and hold it in place with a line running through the anchor shackle and back to a point near to the rower, where it can be secured with a slippery hitch. Then, when you have rowed the requisite distance, you simply undo the hitch and the anchor will drop over the stern, pulling its chain and rope behind. Needless to say, if you want the dinghy's transom to last for more than a season, it is necessary to have some sort of fairlead for this purpose. One idea is to line the rowing notch with brass or stainless steel, but a better idea is to fabricate a roller, which can be secured in place on the transom when required. It is an unnecessary refinement to have a roller that actually rolls. As an alternative to our slippery hitch, the roller could be fitted with a pin to go through the anchor shackle and a line can be attached to the pin and led back to the rowing position. Incidentally, the whole business of laying a kedge is much simplified if anchor and cable are placed in the dinghy in their entirety. The bitter end should be made fast in the dinghy, of course and then you can row out the correct distance and lower away the anchor. This method saves the difficulty of dragging rope

and chain through the water upwind — it is much easier to do so when returning to the parent vessel. Harsh experience forces me to suggest that you take an extra length of line with you, as you usually end up about five feet from your yacht with all the cable paid out. The roller is also useful when breaking out a recalcitrant anchor. In this case, the idea is to pull in the chain over the roller until it is up and down. Then move your weight aft in the dinghy and secure the chain so that it can't move. Once this is done, shift your weight as far forward as possible, which has the effect of raising the dinghy's stern several inches. This is likely to break out the anchor and much less dangerous than leaning over the side trying to get it up.

If I were to buy an inflatable dinghy, I think that I would be most tempted by the Tinker Tramp™, which has a permanent built-in floor, which makes it a little better to row. It can also be fitted with a sailing rig and a canopy and CO_2 cylinders, for use as a liferaft. This is by far the best way of getting a liferaft, as you know that it will work when you need it. One of these dinghies would cost of lot of money, however, and Pete and I have never felt that its virtues outweighed its drawbacks.

We have always had solid dinghies and are quite happy with them. Once again, the design is a compromise so that you usually end up with a little boat that does a lot of things surprisingly well, but doesn't excel at anything. For those with limited space, a quasi-solid dinghy can be provided by way of a folding boat, of which there are a great variety available. They range from a lethal practical joke to fine and attractive looking craft and thus need to be looked at carefully, before any decision is made.

For several years we had a design of Danny Greene's called *Two Bits*, with which we had a great deal of success. This is a nesting dinghy, the bow of four and a half feet and the stern of five feet, which is held together with three bolts and makes a nice, roomy nine and a half feet. It could be assembled and launched in a couple of minutes and sat happily on *Badger*'s foredeck. As the nested boat was no higher than the coachroof, it did not impede our view forward and, sitting over the forehatch, made an efficient dodger so that we could frequently open the forehatch when under way.

However, my better half decided that it was too much work to put the two halves together and when *Brock* was beginning to show the strain of his seven years use and abuse, we decided to try another design. The one we chose was Phil Bolger's *Tortoise*, from **Different Boats**, which has turned out to be a great success. It is two metres by one metre and made out of two sheets of plywood. We used very light — 4mm — plywood and glassed and epoxied it inside and out, using substantial fillets in all corners. The removable, longitudinal seat that Mr. Bolger recommends, we made permanent and as such, it also provides buoyancy. One of the many remarkable features of this little craft is that it has an after deck, which means that it can be launched over the side of the boat, stern first, without shipping any water. It is astonishingly stable, rows very adequately and is easy to pull back aboard. We have tried towing it for the sake of interest and she tows very well indeed, tracking beautifully. However because she is no trouble to haul aboard, we are rarely tempted to tow her. Apart from her low initial cost and the fact that she can be built in a little over 20 hours (we timed it), excluding painting, etc., what makes her appealing to small income voyagers is the fact that one cannot fit an outboard to her stern, because of the after deck. Mr. Bolger has designed a sailing rig for her — we may get round to making it one day. She is not likely to be coveted for her good looks — we christened her *Skip*, at the suggestion of a friend who thought that was what she looked like. But handsome is as handsome does and we reckon she will take a lot of beating.

The perfect tender would be a one piece stem dinghy, with two rowing positions and a sailing rig, with plenty of built in buoyancy. It would be fairly narrow in proportion to its length, but very stable and would easily carry four people. And, of course, it would stow without any problems at all, on the foredeck. Nick on *Wylo* had three dinghies at the last count, including a nice 12 foot pulling boat. He carries two of them on deck with the third in davits, finding this latter method perfectly satisfactory. While there is a lot to be said for a spare dinghy, you can get carried away by your own enthusiasm.

I am very fond of plywood dinghies and in spite of the fact that they need painting, I prefer them to fibreglass ones. The advantage of plywood dinghies are that they can be lightweight, they are cheap to build, easy to repair and individual. If you keep them light, they are easier to get on deck or to carry up a beach. If tied alongside a wall they are less likely than a heavier boat to self-destruct. Because they have such a hard existence, I think that it's unrealistic to expect a yacht's tender to have a very long life and so it seems unnecessary to use the best quality plywood to construct one. We built a perfectly satisfactory *Tortoise* for *Missee Lee* for under £25, using epoxy and glass, which can't be bad. Ease of repair is a great advantage. While a decent quality inflatable is difficult to damage there is always the risk of coral or, God forbid, of vandalism, and then repairs are rarely very satisfactory. A little plywood dinghy however, is easily patched and it is no big deal to put a whole new bottom on one. The reason I like their individuality is not only because I think it's nice to be able to recognize your own at the bottom of the steps, but also because potential thieves will appreciate the same thing and choose something less obvious. And if they do take a shine to your tender, it is some consolation that plywood is usually readily available and a replacement won't cost too much. You could even consider having a kit of parts on board — perhaps you could stow it under the bunk. I may be going overboard here, but I can think of at least two occasions when we have had fellow yachtsmen asking us if we knew of any dinghies for sale. How handy it would

have been if we could have knocked one up in a couple of days!

Ideally, the dinghy should never be towed, but human nature being what it is, you will probably be too lazy to lift it on board each time you go for an afternoon's sail. The towing point should be strongly attached and well down on the stem, to discourage water breaking over it. Mr. Bolger, who likes simple solutions, suggests drilling a hole through the bow transom of his little prams and tying a stopper knot at the end of the painter; the system works surprisingly well. It's always a good idea to have a spare painter between the yacht and the tender for towing. If it starts to breeze up, for heaven's sake heave-to and bring the beast aboard, otherwise it will ruin your entire sail.

Spare oars are essential — if you have a spare set, you won't lose your main ones. Again they should be very individual and/or carved with the boat's name in order to discourage theft. Fortunately, outboard motors are the preferred form of propulsion, nowadays. Oars also get a lot of abuse and a spare pair enables you to take the current pair out of service and do a proper varnish job on them. Good oars are expensive and deserve looking after.

Much as I like the appearance of those smart bronze rowlocks that fold down neatly out of the way when not required, I feel that the ever present thief makes them a poor idea. I'm sorry if I sound negative, carping on about thieves, but without a dinghy you are in dead lumber when cruising and they are very difficult to protect in many places, which is why I am trying to emphasize making them unattractive and awkward for potential thieves. If you take your rowlocks when leaving the dinghy, the casual thief or the person who borrows it to go somewhere, will move on to a boat that has its rowlocks in place. Few people can scull or enjoy doing it. The children of Spain unfortunately excel in this art and generally there is no way of discouraging them from using your dinghy for practice. However, on *Skip*, we fitted a socket for the rowlock instead of a sculling notch, which may help. The only consolation is that they at least play with your dinghy as a boat and don't use it as a trampoline, in the manner of their supposedly better educated peers in other countries. If children are a real nuisance, the only solution is to go ashore in shifts or sail to another anchorage.

A sailing rig in a dinghy is great fun to use and we often used to take *Brock* on picnics and exploring up creeks or round islands. Loaded with food, beer and firelighters, we have had many a happy day spent sailing along to a beach, gathering wood, lighting a fire, eating and drinking and then sailing back again. The rig should be easy to set up — no rigging, if possible and easily accessible, or you won't bother to use it. We haven't yet made one for *Skip* but have had a lot of fun rowing her about. For Pete and myself, picnics are one of Life's great joys and we indulge in Memorable Picnics in much the same way as Bill Tilman had Memorable Bathes, but I think ours are more fun.

Danny Greene Comments:

Two Bits was about 9½ feet long, 4 feet wide, and stowed in 5 feet of length. She served me well. Over the years, I experimented with various other dimensions, hull shapes and construction details. I tried boats up to 16 feet in length and with two and three nesting pieces. Some rowed beautifully, some sailed very well, some towed well, some were stable, some handled rough weather easily, some were light and compact to stow and some were very easy to build. None, however, combined these qualities in a way that satisfied me, until *Chameleon*.

Surely there are small boats that can outperform her in one or two areas, but I do not know of any that have these same all-round performance characteristics that make *Chameleon* an ideal tender for a cruising boat. She is, as well, a very attractive multi-purpose boat that can be easily transported by one or two people and stowed in a very small place. *Chameleon*'s two pieces can be assembled and disassembled in the water, so it is possible to launch and retrieve her one piece at a time. Each piece weighs approximately 50 pounds. There are built-in buoyancy chambers in the stern quarters and a foredeck locker that could be left sealed for buoyancy, fitted with a watertight hatch, or fitted with a "water-resistant" plywood hatch.

As a rowboat, *Chameleon* features two rowing positions, so she can be properly trimmed with one, two, or three people aboard. Oars of about 7½' length seem to work best. Safe capacity is about 500 pounds. For those interested in fitness rowing I have designed a sliding seat/outrigger option that is inexpensively built of plywood and allows use of 8½ to 9' oars.

Chameleon is built in the "stitch and glue" plywood/epoxy technique. The plywood panels are cut out from dimensions provided in the building plans (or from full-size patterns) and fastened together using copper wire and nylon fishing line. There is no strongback or building jig required; the hull is both self-supporting and movable during construction. Thus it can be worked on outdoors if desired, and moved inside (or covered with a tarp) at night or in inclement weather.

After the panels are assembled into the hull shape, a thickened epoxy fillet is applied to all the inside corners, followed by two layers of fiberglass cloth tape and epoxy resin. Then the outside corners are rounded and taped. Next the entire outside is sheathed in cloth and epoxy and the other construction details completed. Though *Chameleon* is intended for the amateur builder, she is not an extremely easy boat to build. The number of details involve in making the two-piece nesting dinghy make it nearly as much work as building two dinghies. Some previous boatbuilding experience, or some previous experience working with epoxy resin, would certainly be an asset. Yet, I think that a very handy builder, with some assistance (in the form of an experienced friend or some reference material on "stitch and glue" construction) could successfully build *Chameleon*.

Tools required to build the design include a table saw (or access to a table saw), electric sabre saw, electric grinder, drill hand saw, wire cutters, pliers, hammer, screwdriver and about six clamps (3" or 4"). The basic materials for the rowing version are 3 sheets of ¼" exterior (or marine) plywood, 3 gallons of epoxy resin, fiberglass tape and cloth, and two fairly clear spruce 2x4s, 12' long. The sailing version requires one additional sheet of ¼" plywood, another gallon of epoxy resin, and two more 12' spruce 2x4s. Costs and building time will certainly vary with the skills of the builder and the sources of materials. I would estimate the time and cost of building the rowing version of *Chameleon* at 80 to 100 hours. The sailing version would require an additional 30 to 40 hours.

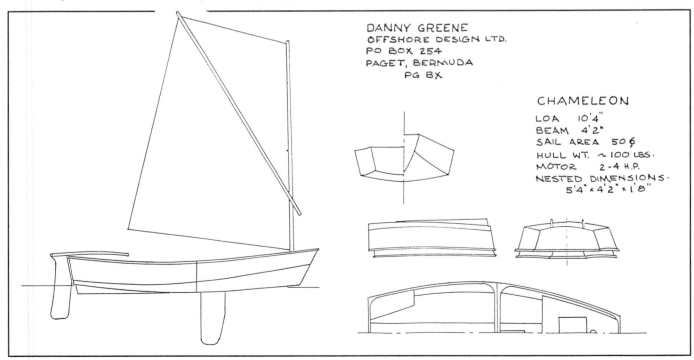

DANNY GREENE
OFFSHORE DESIGN LTD.
PO BOX 254
PAGET, BERMUDA
PG BX

CHAMELEON

LOA   10'4"
BEAM   4'2"
SAIL AREA   50 ₲
HULL WT. ~ 100 LBS.
MOTOR   2-4 H.P.
NESTED DIMENSIONS.
5'4" x 4'2" x 1'8"

Phil Bolger Comments:

Tortoise was going to be called *Sand Box* at first. I changed the name when she turned out to deserve more respect than that. I'd moored my cruiser *Resolution* for the winter up on the flats above Lobster Cove bridge in Gloucester, Massachusetts, and drew up this punt to get aboard her there. I figured it was so small that nobody would resent it lying on a public float; it would look so unobtrusive that vandals might not think of vandalizing it; and it would cost so little that it wouldn't break my heart if they did. It was supposed to be of the right proportions to rest my weight on when I had to walk over saltwater ice, pushing it ahead of me.

It'd have made a cat laugh to see me designing it, because I kept trying to get more curves into it, profile sheer and sweep to the sides. Every curve made it more expensive, or bulkier, or took away capacity, so I kept ending up with straight lines as the only reasonable way to do it. The bottom was rockered to stiffen the plywood so it could be walked on without having to add framing and to bring the ends up clear of (smooth) water with a fair load.

To make it easy to clean and as light as possible to carry on my shoulder, I made the straddle seat removable. I meant to have this filled with foam, for use as a lifeboat, but this never got done.

The decked-over stern was an afterthought to use up some of the leftover plywood. The idea is that the punt can be launched dangling on end from its painter without shipping any water. The first trial was done that way, from a wharf 16 feet above the water in low-water springs. Since then, it has been launched many times off the cruiser's deck; it always ends up right-side-up and dry. The afterdeck also stiffens the sides and gives a little reserve of bouyancy for, say, laying out a heavy kedge anchor, as I have done in her.

I had all the framing put on the outside, where it won't trap dirt and where it gives some protection to the plywood.

This was meant to be a disposable boat if there ever was one — shop-grade plywood construction (though I'm beginning to think that this may be less apt to rot than exterior grade), no priming, and only one coat of paint. But it grew on me. It rowed quite well if I kept the stroke short and gentle. It towed in docile fashion at eight knots (as fast as the cruiser would go). I could swing around in it, and even stand up, without feeling very insecure. It carried two sizable men and their heavy gear without protest. I could throw the oars and the seat up on the cruiser's deck and snake the punt up after me without a second thought.

When Harold Payson saw the design, he was unexpectedly taken with it and built half a dozen of them in the process of working out the fastest way to do it. He figured he could make wages at $85 each (1979). I can remember when that would buy quite a lot of skiff, but since the U.S. government took a lesson from the late Roman emperors in debasing the coinage, it's rumored

there's an Act of Congress prohibiting anyone from selling a boat that cheaply.

He asked me to draw a sail plan for the boat, with the idea that children might have a good time sailing it. The removable seat came in handy for this because the whole one-meter-by-two-meter space could be left clear to sprawl around in. I put the rig to one side to help with this. I don't remember why I felt she had to have her daggerboard in an inside case instead of just dropped through a couple of battens blocked off the outside. Perhaps I didn't want to make the boat that much wider. She feels almost like a real boat under sail, quite lively in a fresh breeze. You don't get anywhere to speak of, of course, but that's not a drawback as long as it is time, not distance, that needs killing.

The catch is that whereas the unpainted, but usable, rowing hull costs $85, including about $30 in materials, the finished and rigged sailing version costs $350, suggesting that it'd be smart to invest in more hull if you're going to buy the rig components.

The first time I tried pushing *Tortoise* over the ice I stepped in a hole and both my boots filled with water. I fell on my stomach on the afterdeck, and it supported me and the ice water nicely. I spent the rest of the day trying to dry out the boots with the Shipmate.

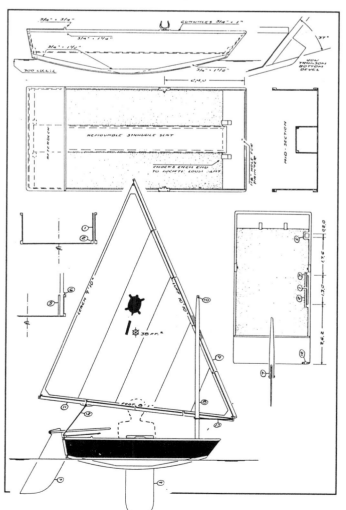

YOU CAN'T HAVE TOO MANY ANCHORS

Chapter 17

You Can't Have Too Many Anchors

One thing that never ceases to amaze me is the number of people who begrudge forking out for a decent anchor. They will cheerfully go out and pay a fortune for the latest electronic gadget, clothe themselves in the most fashionable designer oilskins and spend every night of their fortnight's holiday in a marina, never questioning the amount spent. However, ask them to shell out for a good anchor and they will throw up their hands in horror at the cost. This is doubly surprising when you realize that anchors rarely go wrong or wear out and that good ground tackle means that you can anchor with peace of mind and so will not need to rely so much on marinas in the first place.

Some time ago, we were talking to a couple in Falmouth who were about to go off. They had worked hard on their boat and spent money where needed, to ensure that she was seaworthy and would not let them down and had bought quite a few electronic navigation aids and safety equipment. They asked us what else we thought they needed.

"How many anchors do you have?" we asked.

"Well, the boat came with one, but we thought that going off cruising we ought to get another one," was the reply. Then they said that on their 35-foot yacht they had a 35-pound CQR™ and a 25-pound Danforth™ that they had just bought. We urged them to buy another CQR or Bruce™, not only in case they lost the one that they had, but also because they might well need three anchors at some time. We also pointed out that neither of their anchors would hold particularly well in weed or rock and that a fisherman would be useful. After thinking the matter over, they decided to stick with what they had — after all, they had the extra weight to consider.

I think that they made a mistake, but it's a very common one. The long and short of it is that sooner or later you will be in a situation where you would give all the money that you possess for a decent anchor. When the wind has suddenly shifted and you find that you are on a lee shore, believe me, you will bless every penny you spent on ground tackle. From personal experience, Pete and I have come to the conclusion that you can't have too many anchors and that you want the right gear for the job. The following stories are part of the reason for our way of thinking; they may make you agree with us.

In 1983, on *Badger*'s first transatlantic crossing, we were in Santa Cruz in La Palma in the Canary Islands. We were waiting for the wind to sort itself out — for reasons only it understood, it was staying stubbornly south westerly. The place was becoming a bit of a bottleneck, with so many boats waiting for a fair breeze before they would set off and the anchorage was overcrowded. Local boats were moored fore and aft, so visiting yachts anchored the same way. The wind had a tendency to come from different directions, due to the way in which it got deflected off the surrounding countryside and we had our two 15-kilo Bruce anchors out forward, our 7.5 kilo 'baby Bruce' wedged into some rocks on the harbour wall and a long line of 10mm nylon to a point ashore. We were therefore held at four corners, as were most of the other yachts at the back of the fleet.

One day it decided to blow and went about it in no half hearted manner. Those boats who had wind speed indicators at the top of the mast said that the needle locked at 65 knots for quite long periods. The wind came down the harbour, knocking the front row of boats over and then it would bounce off the town and come back attacking the next row. Hitting the nearby volcano, it would rebound back down the harbour, without losing any of its velocity and send the back row flying. It was just like watching a line of dominoes. Before very long, boats were starting to slide sideways as their anchors dragged, fouling another boat's and setting that one going. At the back row, we were in a very vulnerable position because there was no way we could sail out through the maze of boats and we had no engine at that time. Even if we had, the web of anchor warps would have made it very tricky, anyway. Astern of us was a stone wall and there was another to port. To starboard was *Calidris*, 30 tons of ferro ketch. We took out another line and fastened it to a local mooring and tried not to think about the bad holding close in.

Eventually the stern line of another boat tripped *Calidris'* bower anchor and she started to drag down on us. She had three anchors out and had one in reserve. She stopped alongside, fenders out and leaning with gentle force against us. Obviously our gear couldn't hold both of us for long and we discussed how best to get their remaining anchor out and then realized that they had used up all their chain on their other anchors. In our lazarette, we had a spare 100-foot length of chain, which we have in case we lose the bower anchor and chain and so we passed it to them, hand over hand and they shackled it to their fourth anchor. Pete then rowed our dinghy off in the direction they wished to lay the anchor. Attached to *Brock* was *Calidris'* dinghy with the crew rowing mightily, the idea being that Pete's continued rowing would allow the dinghies to hold station while the anchor was dropped. The wind was so strong that they had to catch hold of other boats' anchor lines in the gusts, to stop them losing all that they had gained, but eventually the anchor was dropped and after a good deal of work, Keith and Viv managed to haul themselves off *Badger* and sit out the rest of the gale in relative peace. Had we not had that chain, we could well both have been in trouble. If they had only had two anchors — indeed had any of us only had two anchors, we would have been in a lot of trouble.

When we next went to England in 1985, we decided that we ought to get a decent fisherman anchor, the one we had being inadequate. We have always lusted after an American anchor made by Paul Luke and designed by Herreshoff, which instead of breaking down into two pieces, in the conventional manner, comes apart into three, thus taking up far less room. They have enormous flukes, making them a good anchor in mud, but of course they come into their own in rock or in weed, where no other anchor will hold. Being cast, they are strong enough to take the loads that this type of anchorage will often impose. They cost a vast amount of money and for a long time remained a dream anchor.

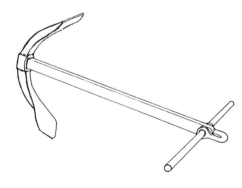

Three-part Luke Anchor

However, we noticed in the adverts that Plastimo were making and selling an anchor whose arms would fold back along its shank, thus once again reducing the space necessary to store it. They made them in a variety of sizes and we decided that the 20 kilo would best suit our needs — not so much that it's the ideal size, but it's about as big an anchor as I can lug about. Accordingly we sent off our cheque to one of the large mail order companies and sat back to await its arrival. About a week before we were due to set off, we received a letter from the company saying that they were out of stock and would send us an anchor when they had received the next consignment. Unfortunately we couldn't wait, as we had neaped ourselves for the winter and so could only leave on certain tides. Accordingly we set off, reckoning to have the anchor sent on. At Crinan, in Scotland, we saw the identical anchor in the chandlers — and in stock, of course, but cash flow being what it was, we couldn't buy it because the other people still had our money and might not have refunded it just because we had found an anchor elsewhere. We carried on without our fisherman, carefully avoiding areas of kelp, which is spreading on Scotland's west coast.

One day found us anchored in North Raasay, a beautiful anchorage near to Skye. A couple of other boats were sharing it with us as we waited for yet another depression to go on its way; one was a 26 foot, twin keel cruising boat, the other an ex Royal National Lifesaving Institute Watson lifeboat. The little twin keeler, *Sea Nome* had dragged the previous day, but sat happily on the only bit of flat ground until the tide returned, causing her owner to bless twin keels. The following day it was our turn.

We had appeared to hold perfectly well the previous day when it had blown pretty hard and *Sea Nome* had dragged, but seeing them had us sufficiently concerned to put out our 'baby Bruce' as well. The wind having dropped, we went to spend the afternoon with the crew of *Sea Nome* and were on board when it started to blow again. It was quite a squall and we decided to go back to *Badger* as soon as it subsided. Imagine our horror, therefore, when glancing out of the window, we saw her suddenly turn broadside on to the wind and drift down the harbour. Pete was in *Brock* in a flash, but *Badger* had hit the beach before he could get to her. It happened so quickly, that even if we had been aboard, we could have done nothing to prevent it. From where I was, *Badger* was apparently crashing against the wall of a mussel bed (a built-up area especially made to encourage mussels to grow), which was rock and barnacles. A few moments later, Keith and I rowed over to *Badger* to see what we could do. Fortunately, she had come to a stop literally six inches away from the wall and the beach was not too rocky, the larger boulders having been used to build the mussel bed. The tide was ebbing, but every wave made her lift and fall. We decided to lay out anchors to pull her off as the tide came back, which was desperately hard work, but would probably work if we could manage it. However, as we were discussing the situation, Dorte called from *Sea Nome* and Keith went back to see what she wanted. Apparently the skipper of the lifeboat had seen our predicament and called up on the VHF to see if he could assist. We don't have one, but *Sea Nome* had and Dorte relayed the message — Skipper would pull us off on his winch, just what lifeboats were designed for. He was lying to two, one-hundredweight anchors and wasn't going anywhere. He bent together every line and piece of string on his boat, even to the flag halliards and floated down a fender. We then attached all our nylon anchor warps and mooring warps and then added the 100 metres of 10 mm nylon that we carry 'just in case' and found that we had just enough to reach from one boat to the other.

In the fullness of time, although it was still blowing a steady Force 7, Skipper pulled us off — a piece of consummate seamanship, when you consider that the 10 mm nylon was doing most of the work; it was like playing a large salmon on a rod. He bade us tie to his stern for the remainder of the night and told us that it was the worst summer gale that he could remember, having lived in that part of the world for over 50 years. He too, had dragged his anchor, a 45-pound CQR and had had to re-anchor on his RNLI fisherman. He'd never dragged there before, but on pulling up his anchor had noticed kelp entangled around it.

I'm not saying that if we had had that fisherman we wouldn't have dragged, although I think it's very unlikely. But if it had been on board, we would have been using it, especially after *Sea Nome* had dragged, because we then suspected that there might be kelp about. We sailed to the nearest boatyard and hauled out to do repairs (fortunately, there was only slight damage) and my parents forwarded our letters. Included was our cheque returned by the mail order company, with a note explaining that they could no longer obtain the Plastimo folding anchor. We sailed to Crinan and bought the one that they had. We found that we used it a lot, in Scotland, Sweden, Norway and the Mediterranean and never regretted purchasing it. Since then we have been lucky enough to find a second-hand 65-pound Luke anchor. Although I can't lift it any distance assembled, I can take it forward in pieces and put it together on the foredeck, if necessary.

For people voyaging on a small income, anchors work out as cheap insurance. They also give very real peace of mind, adding immensely to the pleasure of lying at anchor. With decent anchors down you can sleep at night and even consider leaving the boat somewhere sheltered for a time. Most of us can't afford insurance, but even if we could, it would be no substitute because good anchors may save not only your boat, but also your life and no amount of insurance will buy that back. On *Badger,* we have a 35-pound CQR, two 15 kilo Bruces, one 7.5 kilo Bruce and the 65-pound Luke, which I have mentioned. Excuse the combination of metric and imperial, but that's how they are sold. The rest of this chapter is also mixed, but if you're going voyaging you'll have to become 'bilingual' in the two systems, so this is a good place to start.

The CQR and one of the Bruces live on the foredeck, ready for immediate use. For several years we just had the Bruce by itself, but we put the second anchor there in order to encourage ourselves to use two when in doubt. The easier it is to use, the more likely we are to put it out when we think about it. Like taking in or shaking out a reef, the time to lay out a second anchor is the moment you wonder whether you should. (Again, in Scotland, had we been anchored to two decent sized anchors, we might not have dragged.) The Bruce is No 1 bower and lives in the bow roller. It is shackled to 100 feet of 3/8" chain, which in turn is spliced to 50 metres of 16 mm nylon multiplait. The CQR, No 2 bower, lives in chocks on deck and is shackled to 40 feet of chain, which is spliced to another 50 metres of nylon multiplait. By having a substantial length of chain on No 2 bower, it becomes a genuine alternative anchor rather than a second best, so that should the wind change, a good anchor and gear will be holding us. The weight of chain from No 1 stops us wandering around too much. Since we fitted the second anchor, we have found we use it a lot. Both cables share the same locker and do not seem inclined to get entangled. The extra weight in the bow is noticeable, *Badger* is wetter since we put the CQR in place, but we feel it's a small price to pay for the convenience of being able to put out a second anchor with the minimum of fuss.

The 7.5 kilo Bruce lives in the lazarette and it has its own cable — 3 fathoms of 5/16" chain, which is spliced onto 100 metres of 10 mm nylon. As such, it is simply a kedge and its purpose in life is to pull us off when we run aground or to kedge us out of a tight corner. The rope and chain are on a reel and we can put the handle of the deckbrush through the middle to assist it to run out. It is kept on deck when cruising in areas where we may be using it frequently.

The Luke lives in the lazarette and its cable consists of 20 feet of chain (which was meant to be 3/8", but looks more like 7/16"), which is spliced to 50 metres of 16 mm nylon and lives under the galley floorboards. If we are in an area where there is a lot of kelp, we can unshackle the Bruce and put the Luke on the bow roller.

The fifth anchor, another 15 kilo Bruce, lives in the bowels of the lazarette. Its real function in life is to replace the No 1 bower, should we lose that and accordingly, there is a spare 100 feet length of chain. Carrying the spare anchor and chain is very reassuring — you never know when you might need it and for that matter, you might be able to help someone else out, too. However, now that we have the Luke, we feel that it's less necessary.

You will no doubt have noticed that we carry quite a lot of chain on *Badger*. Originally, we decided to keep weight out of the bows and just anchor on a 15 kilo Bruce, 40 feet of chain and then warp. However, we soon got fed up of *Badger* walking all over the place at anchor and went back to using mainly chain. Apart from the catenary effect which is due to its weight, another advantage of chain over rope is that it is unlikely to chafe through on rock or coral, thus removing one of the worries of anchoring in that type of bottom. Anchor chain does not wear out at the same rate as rope either and when the galvanizing wears off, it can be re-galvanized at surprisingly low cost. Indeed, instead of going to the yacht chandlers and buying their expensive chain, you could consider buying ungalvanized chain and have it done yourself — as long as you don't need it calibrated for your windlass. However, you should always buy tested chain. The galvanizer needs to have a spinner so that the chain's links don't stick together, but it is not that difficult to find one in an industrial area.

We feel we now have adequate anchor tackle for most situations on *Badger*, although God forbid that we ever have to try riding out a hurricane. However, a point worth making is that it is very hard work to handle it in bad conditions, when several anchors are being brought into use and we would not like to have to deal with heavier gear. This is another reason why we feel that *Badger* is as large a vessel as we wish to own and part of the appeal of smaller yachts.

On another occasion when we lay in Santa Cruz de la Palma, a 70 footer tried to elbow its way in among the smaller yachts in the more protected part of the harbour. In all honesty, there wasn't room for anything larger than us anyway and after a while we realized that he had only put out two anchors (this time we had three out). As soon as the wind changed, he moved sideways, fouling our stern anchor and actually threatening to hit the stern of our neighbours, who were ashore. While we let out *Lily's* stern line, Trevor on 30 foot *Salvation Jane* went to see if he could help the large boat, as there seemed to be only one person on board. It turned out that he was the owner and his professional skipper and crew had gone off to town. No, they didn't have any more anchors, just the two that were out and yes, one of them was just on rope, because they only had one length of chain. In the end, Trevor dug out his spare anchor and lent it to the yacht, to protect us all.

If yacht insurers could vet the situation, I'm sure that they would give reductions on yachts with good ground tackle because such vessels would be much less likely to damage either themselves or others by dragging their anchor. For ourselves, we feel that anchors and chain are good value for money, especially when you consider that in certain situations, they are the only thing preventing your boat from destruction and in every situation, you sleep better at night knowing that the chances are that you'll wake up in the same place as you went to bed.

The cost of the different types of anchor varies considerably and you tend to get what you pay for. The basic fisherman is generally the cheapest, but for general use (rather than in weed or rock) you need a very heavy one to hold well in sand or mud — Mr. Hiscock recommends about three times the weight of your normal patent anchor. As well, they ought to have large flukes and those made of steel rod, flattened out at the end, are not going to do much good in mud. If you are on a very tight budget and feel that a patent anchor is beyond your pocket, it would probably be worth buying some of these anchors and getting someone to weld on larger flukes. The anchors could then be re-galvanized and should be pretty effective. Fishermen's co-ops are often a good source of heavy fisherman anchors. It is possible to have a fisherman made up to your own design — both Claud Worth in **Yacht Cruising** and Herreshoff have drawn designs which can be obtained quite easily.

Assuming that we are talking of boats in the 25 to 35 foot range, the next cheapest type of anchor tends to be the Danforth™ and copies of that design. I believe that it's always worth buying the pukka job and wondered where a Danforth could be bought in the UK. I was pleased to discover that Sowester market an anchor called a Meon, which is made under license to the Danforth design. The major drawbacks of a Danforth/Meon anchor are that they are awkward to handle, having a tendency to trap fingers; they can get jammed with large pebbles and the stock is more vulnerable to bending than other designs. Although a variety of tests have shown this type of anchor to hold as well, or better than the Bruce or CQR in sand, other tests have indicated that when it comes down to brute strength, for example in rock or coral, the Bruce and CQR are significantly stronger, a point worth bearing in mind. On the plus side, they are reasonably priced, easy to stow and generally reliable.

Up to 15 kilos/35-pounds, Bruce and CQR anchors jostle for position on price. After 15 kilos, Bruce anchors suddenly become more expensive. The point on a CQR is arguably an advantage in a hard bottom. The advantages of a Bruce are that it has no moving parts and is generally reliable in all bottoms (with the exception of kelp!). We like to have a variety of anchors available because sometimes anchor A refuses to set for some reason, where anchor B may. When we were cruising around Mallorca, we found that the Bruce suddenly started to drag in a number of anchorages and the CQR wasn't too happy. We hadn't bought the Luke at this time, but found our Plastimo anchor would work. The bottom causing the problem was dense, short, thin-stranded weed over sand. We took the Bruce off and shackled the fisherman on. In other anchorages with a different bottom, the fisherman wouldn't hold and we had to use the CQR. The charts weren't clear as to what the holding was likely to be so we often put down both anchors and were fairly sure that one or other of them would hold.

Before leaving the subject of anchors, let me reiterate that while holding power is very important, the main consideration is brute strength. The difference between various anchors was well illustrated in a test carried out by an organization in the USA called Boat/US, in conjunction with **Cruising World** Magazine. It was to test tensile strength and the tests were conducted on a machine under controlled laboratory conditions intended to simulate what happens when an anchor that's hooked or wedged in rock or coral is overloaded. Here is an extract from the report:

Anchor Tested	Maximum load sustained	Results
25-pound Luke	9,000-pounds	Bottom of shank began to bend at 3,000-pounds shank-to-fluke angle finally reached 90°
27-pound Danforth P-1500 (deepset plow)	5,700-pounds	Tensile failure occurred when the swivel bushing parted from plow neck
33-pound Bruce	18,500-pounds	Shank began to bend at 10,000-pounds, twisted and bent more at maximum 20,000-pounds load.
35-pound Harbor Fast Simpson Lawrence	8,150-pounds	Shank-to-stock pivot pin rotated and tore through the eye of the shank.
35-pound CQR	13,250-pounds	Shank bent and twisted to 90°.
14-pound Fortress Aluminum alloy	4,650-pounds	Failure of the stock, anchor sheared into four separate parts.
20-pound Danforth H-1500 (hi-tensile fluke)	5,250-pounds	Shank strap (which prevents shank from impinging on crown plate) failed in tension, then crown broke.
24-pound Danforth S-1600	1,500-pounds	Both flukes bent, one tore apart near weld point to crown plate.
25-pound Danforth T-4000 (deepset hi-tensile fluke)	2,600-pounds	Welds holding crown plate sheared off, anchor opened to a full 180°

For the sake of the record, the 25-pound Luke would be considered a suitable anchor for a 20 footer; Danforth recommend the 27-pound P-1500 and their 20-pound Hi-tensile for a 50 footer; Bruce consider that 33-pound would be suitable for a maximum of 40 feet; Simpson Lawrence recommend their 35-pound Harbourfast for a maximum of 36 feet and their 35-pound CQR for 40 feet; Fortress say that their 14-pound anchor will be suitable for a 45-footer. These are working anchor weights, not storm anchors and assume that there will only be the minimum of chain with the anchor. For storm anchors, again with the minimum of chain, most manufacturers recommend going one size up; for example, Fortress reckon their 14-pound anchor would be a suitable storm anchor for a 35-foot yacht. The working load of best quality 3/8" anchor chain is about 5,400-pounds One's anchor should be stronger. Look at the results and make your own decision.

A lot has been written about anchoring with the correct scope and the marking of anchor chain. I don't intend to add anything to the theory; however, in practice we find that all 100 feet of chain goes out, if there is enough room to swing and try to anchor on at least 4 to 1 and preferably 5 to 1. In shallow water, because we have the full amount out, our scope is greater and in really deep water, you can get away with 3 to 1 in normal conditions.

A lot of Americans anchor on rope, with little or no chain at the end, a practice which appears to be crossing the Atlantic. The trouble with this method of anchoring is that it is really rather anti-social, as in a good breeze and shallow water the recommended scope is 12 to 1, which means that the boat takes up a lot of swinging room. If the cost of chain is really beyond your budget, I would strongly recommend making use of a 'Chum'. This is a heavy weight let down on a length of rope so that it stops just above the sea bed. The original 'Chum' was a trade-marked item made in Scotland, I think , and you can still see advertisements for it in the back of old copies of the Clyde Cruising Club cruising guide. They were designed to suit a variety of boats and weights could be added or subtracted in the form of discs, which were called 'biscuits'. Alas, latter day chandlers seem to have lost their capacity for devising charming names. The weight makes for a good catenary and helps stop the boat sailing round her anchor. A good source for such a weight would be a coal merchant whose 56-pound weights are occasionally condemned by the Weights and Measure chappies. Indeed, such a weight is a good idea even for a boat with chain, as anything that helps keep you anchored in one spot when the wind gets up, must be worth having.

One of the drawbacks of chain is the snatching at anchor when it's blowing hard and shock loads hit the chain. These are less noticeable with a heavy boat, that responds slowly to the gusts of wind, but are quite uncomfortable on a lighter boat, to say nothing of the fact that the noise tends to keep sleep at bay. We have overcome this difficulty by using a nylon snubber, which we made up several years ago. We spliced a large soft eye, protected with plastic tubing, in one end of a 6-foot length of 16 mm multiplait. Then we put a length of heavy duty polythene tubing over the rope and spliced a chain hook to the other end. Chain hooks aren't that easy to buy and usually need to be sent off for galvanizing, anyway. However, one or two chandlers have started to sell them already galvanized or alternatively, one could be made from a flat plate of stainless steel with a slot cut into it to fit around the links of the chain. Having made up the snubber, we use it by attaching the hook to the chain, dropping the eye over a bollard and then letting off some more chain until the nylon takes the load. The chain stays on the bow roller and the nylon leads over it, protected by the anti-chafe hosing. We usually let off a couple of feet or so of chain and in really windy conditions, I have seen the nylon stretch so far that the chain is nearly straight. The snatching has been totally eliminated, but the boat is still held to her chain by the mooring bitts. The snubber lives aft, either behind the backrest or in the lazarette and being easy to use, gets used.

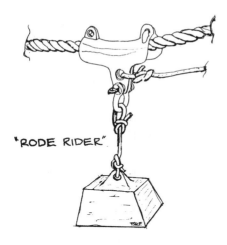

"RODE RIDER"

Some time ago we removed our conventional, lever operated windlass from the foredeck, finding it 'lo-speed' rather than otherwise and awkward to use, positioned as it was just forward of the foremast. We once took it to bits to service it and were more than a little disconcerted to find that its main component was a bicycle chain. Considering the number of yachtsmen who insist on using their windlass gypsy as a mooring bitt, one can only be amazed at how few end up in disaster when all that is between them and eternity is a length of bicycle chain. The practice of anchoring by the windlass is very common, people pointing out, quite correctly that they are strongly secured to the foredeck, while forgetting that the unit itself

is not designed to withstand the loads of a vessel at anchor. We have seen a Moyle Marine designed anchor windlass, a serious piece of equipment, twisted apart from being used for anchoring, and no windlasses are designed for this purpose. It was reassuring to notice on the box of our present device, a Simpson Lawrence Anchorman™, a note reminding new owners that it was "unwise and unseamanlike" to anchor by the windlass. Unfortunately, most owners never get to read the box, buying the windlass with the yacht. I assume that windlasses get used for securing the anchor cable, due to the lack of heavy cleats suitable for chain, or samson posts on many modern boats. Our foredeck contains two bollards — generally one is used for the chain and the other for the snubber and two smaller cleats, which are useful for dock lines, a tripping line, etc. Our windlass is on the foremast and is very effective there as the man operating it can really crank away.

Having your anchoring equipment properly sorted and easy to handle encourages you to anchor. With a lighter boat, the gear does not need to be too heavy and the effort involved is less than a lot of people seem to believe. Admittedly, if you anchor in 100 feet of water, you will be fit for nothing by the time you've hauled in your anchor and chain and Pete reckons that 50 feet is as much as he would wish to anchor in, but most anchoring situations are nothing like that. Sailing in and dropping the hook where you intended to, is a very satisfying manoeuvre and considerably less effort than rummaging for warps and fenders and then bringing the boat alongside another (very expensive) vessel.

Another very satisfactory manoeuvre is that of kedging the boat. All too frequently, we carry out this operation to pull us into deeper water when we stood on a little too long on one tack, but on occasion we use it to get out of a crowded anchorage. For this operation, we use the 'baby' Bruce, which is easy to get at and light to handle. If we need two or three separate pulls to get out, we simply drop the bower with the minimum of chain to stop ourselves, what time the 'baby' is rowed out again. For all these nice operations, accessibility is what makes you do it the proper way rather than reaching for the starter button/cord. And having practiced doing things the old way, when the engine lets you down, you are quite happy using an alternative method.

We can never understand people who would rather use marinas than lie at anchor; marinas are noisy places — all those clanking halliards — and often dusty and dirty; uninvited people can come aboard more easily and even more to the point, so can such potential troublemakers as rats and roaches. I think that many yachtsmen's reluctance to anchor stems from the fact that they are not happy about anchoring, simply because they haven't had much practice and acquired confidence in their ground tackle. The rewards of learning this skill are many; not least is the satisfaction of discovering a beautiful and sheltered anchorage and having it all to yourself.

Badger's CQR stowed on deck. Also
note dinghy chocks, mast boot, cleats,
mooring bitt, bow roller, stanchions,
fairlead blocks and hatch ventilator.

A GENERATOR THAT CAN EITHER BE
SLUNG FROM THE STERN RAIL

Chapter 18

More Trouble Than It's Worth?

Before we moved onto *Badger*, we had spent five contented years living on boats without any electricity at all and had never seen any reason to change. However a combination of factors altered this situation so that now, for better or worse, we too are part of the 20th century.

The event that made us consider having electricity was the legalizing of the tri-colour masthead navigation lantern. This struck us as an excellent idea, because while we are cautious of relying on a ship even having a lookout in the first place, we felt that if they did have one, a tri-colour lantern gave them a fighting chance of seeing us, whereas navigation lights three or four feet above the water, out on the ocean where no-one is expecting to see a yacht, are a snare and a delusion. Then modern technology brought about a proliferation of alternative energy sources such as solar panels, wind and water generators, etc. However, the overriding pressure came when, studying the Collision Regulations (COLREGS), we realized that it was now a necessity to carry lamps that could be seen at a distance of one mile. Previously that paragraph had always contained a phrase along the lines of 'where possible' at the end, which of course, meant that if you only had small oil lamps, it was not expected that you would be seen from a mile away. Oil navigation lanterns that can be seen from over a mile away are in existence, but we have never seen any for sale.

The reason that this alteration had such an effect on us was because it meant that with oil lamps only, we would be in breach of the COLREGS and therefore would *per se, be held responsible in case of an accident, even if it were not our fault*. If we carried insurance it would have made no difference, because if you are in breach of the Collision Regulations, your insurers might not shell out anyway, and quite rightly. Therefore, we decided that we ought to have legal lights. We seriously considered using

pressure paraffin lanterns in order to achieve the correct brightness, but other considerations apart, felt that the cost of the paraffin that these lamps consumed would discourage us from using them. Of course, once we had started to consider electric lights, other arguments in their favour made their voices heard. For example, wouldn't it be pretty daft to have to go on deck to rig navigation lanterns on a boat that was designed to ensure that we didn't have to go on deck for any other reason? And so it was decided that we would fit a tri-colour lantern. (We didn't require any other navigation lights at that time, because we had no engine).

To do this, we needed a battery and to power that we needed some sort of generator. After looking at what was available (this was in 1982), we chose the Aquair™ wind and water turbine as being most suitable for our needs. This is a generator that can either be slung from a stern rail, or equivalent, and has a line and rotator attached to it, utilizing the boat's speed through the water or be hoisted in the rigging with a windmill attached and utilize the wind to charge the battery. The whole rigmarole, lamp, battery and generator ended up costing us about £400 (three and a half percent of the boat's total cost)—just to have a legal navigation lamp.

Since then, of course, we have fitted the engine and so have had to fit other navigation lamps. Fortuitously for us, as we were fitting the engine the COLREG people decided that an all-round white light for steaming would be as acceptable as two lamps covering three hundred and sixty degrees for vessels of our size; this was particularly helpful for us because we could not have fitted a steaming lamp above boom height due to the parrels running all round the mast, without removing the masts and setting in a new cable and we have no stern rail on which to mount a stern lantern. We solved the problem by fitting a tri-colour with an all-round white light. (In fact, we have fitted two, as one of them mysteriously broke off the top of the mast one day, leaving only the bare bulb showing and us illegal once again.) This also means that we use less electricity when well offshore, as we can burn the ten watt white light —yes, it is illegal, but on the other hand, it is probably obvious to a lookout on a ship who is not expecting to see a yacht in the middle of nowhere. We switch on the tri-colour as soon as the watchkeeper can clearly see the ship's sidelights.

The Aquair has proved to be an excellent piece of kit. However, there are two problems with it. The first is that it takes a quarter of an hour or so to change from one mode to the other and the second is that it needs a gust of twenty knots to get it started, when hung in the rigging. (This type of generator is now into its second generation and apparently the new Aquair starts in a much lighter breeze and charges at twice the rate of the one we have.) This meant that we had problems keeping the battery charged when we were daysailing, being too slothful to change from one mode to the other, or in areas of light breezes. The net result of this was that we had a flat battery at rather too frequent intervals. Incidentally, we use a deep-cycle battery, which is ideal for this type of situation because it can tolerate being completely discharged, but generally speaking, they are not the most suitable for boats because they do not like to be charged at the high amps associated with an engine alternator. The charging device on our engine, a generator which gives about five amps at maximum would not hurt it, but in fact it's neither use nor ornament and anyway, in an average year we probably only use our engine for fifty hours.

The next step in this sorry saga was when we decided that the best way to get over the problem would be to have two generators and so when we went back to England, we bought a Rutland wind generator, and Pete made a framework for it so that we could hoist it up at anchor. This generator was second generation, started in the lightest of breezes and generally charged at one to two amps, the average wind speed being astonishingly low. As our towing generator gives us a steady one and one half to two amps, our battery remained fairly healthy, except in periods of prolonged calm, when we had to watch our consumption very carefully.

After a while, Pete got fed up with hoisting and lowering the Rutland, every time we moved and we also came to dislike the amount of room it took up down below. Pete has a bit of an obsession about being able to get the sails up and clear out of an anchorage at a moment's notice and felt that the generator compromised this. While we were visiting a friend in Norway, he happened to mention that he was interested in wind generators and before either he or I quite grasped it, Helge was the proud owner of a Rutland — complete with framework for hanging it in the rigging. By the time we got back to England, we had a flat battery again.

The next decision, and by now you will realize that alternative energy can be very expensive, was to buy a solar panel. I don't like solar panels, but I have to admit that you don't need to do much to them if you accept that they will only be working at low efficiency levels. We fitted it on the centre deck immediately abaft the saloon hatch and it isn't too intrusive and doesn't generally get walked on. It is rated at thirty watts and we do actually get an amp out of it for a large part of the time, in spite of the fact that numerous things can and do cast shadows on it. Because our demands our very low, it is adequate for in harbour and a good back-up to the Aquair at sea. In truth, we wait impatiently for the day when someone creates a solar panel the same size as ours, which is indestructible and of such high output that we can mount it in place of the present one, ignore it and do away with the Aquair, which can be a nuisance.

Of course, having installed electricity, we now run the radio-cassette player off it and the echo sounder and have fitted an extractor fan for the engine compartment, cabin lights, and an electric log, to say nothing of the little Sony™ multi-band radio and a socket for the search light, soldering iron, etc.

From the above, it would appear that the major problem with electricity lies in generating it in the first place. Until recently most yachtsmen relied on their engine for this, but if you don't use your engine very often I can think of few things worse than having to put up with its noise and smell for the sake of getting the amps — apart from having to put up with the noise and smell from someone else's engine, that is. Add to this the fact that unless you have a very small engine with a large alternator, you will be doing it no good at all, running it without any real load and it becomes even more of a nuisance. The situation can be improved by fitting a rheostat. Most alternators start charging at about thirty-five amps, but then drop the charge right down when they sense that the batteries are fairly healthy, so that you have to run the engine for ages to top them right up. A rheostat allows you to control the rate at which the alternator is charging, so that you can charge the batteries more quickly. The more sophisticated devices that automatically cut down when the battery reaches its full potential sound like a wonderful idea. However, they don't seem to be up to being used full-time, as several of my friends and acquaintances will attest.

Petrol generators are also a popular method of charging batteries and again a very antisocial way of doing so. However, recent improvements in small generators have made them much more acceptable to one's neighbours. It is now possible to buy four-stroke generators with sound-proofed boxes, which ensures that those downwind of you do not have to put up with the unpleasant noise and stink of a two-stroke. These small generators are apparently much more efficient when used by way of a 220/240-volt battery charger, rather than on their twelve volt system because they are really designed around the 240-volt function, so I am told. The cost benefit analysis on a petrol generator is quite complicated. Not particularly cheap initially (for the neighbour-friendly version) one also has to consider their life expectancy, how much money will need to be spent on spares and of course, the cost of the petrol itself. It is also necessary to consider safe storage of the fuel, in a locker that drains overboard and the fact that the salt air probably will do no good at all to the construction of the generator and that you will need to drain out every drop of petrol, if it is to be stored below.

A lot of yachtsmen use and are very happy with solar panels. These are particularly popular in the Tropics where there is an abundance of strong sunshine and on multihulls, where there is an abundance of clear deck space. However, it should be remembered that the cells are linked up in series and that a shadow across one will affect them all. It is also worth mentioning they won't be much use during a winter in England, for example. I am bound to say that I don't reckon much to them on aesthetic grounds, either and feel that they are pretty dangerous when scattered around the deck. A chap we met in Venezuela was buying translucent units that he could incorporate into his hatches, which struck me as a good idea, but although we have looked for these since, we have not been able to source them. The great advantages of solar panels, as compared with the opposition is that there is very little to go wrong with them apart from the protective surface getting damaged and if you are prepared for them to function at a low level of efficiency, once installed they need no further attention. I must say that I strongly disapprove of units attached to the stern rail which one can tilt towards the sun. Quite apart from the fact that they look hideous and are an infernal nuisance at anchor, they are both vulnerable and dangerous at sea. To lurch against the sharp corner of one of these could give you at least a very nasty bruise and at worst could knock somebody's eye out. Far too many yachtsmen seem to forget that the basic *raison d'etre* of a sailing boat is that it works at sea and concentrate so much on ensuring that they have 'all the comforts of shore-life' that they compromise its ability as a cruising vessel.

Wind generators range from the paltry little devices that are fobbed off on unsuspecting yachtsmen and reluctantly trickle out a quarter amp or so, to the mega devices seen in the Caribbean which knock out fifteen amps in a Force 6 and are used for running freezers. The former probably are better than nothing for preventing your battery from going flat and something in between the two extremes will suit most sailors. As mentioned above, we have had experience of both the Ampair/Aquair™ and Rutland generators. The former are the more expensive, but do appear to be better built than the Rutland — on the other hand, there are hundreds of happy yachtsmen using Rutland units. I haven't yet met anyone who has had either make break down, so in the long run, Time Will Tell. Neither gear is cheap, but on the other hand, money up front now is usually saved in the future. Many people mount their wind generators permanently, either on a pole or the mizzen mast. Pete and I are not keen on the idea because in strong winds, we like to be able to reduce our

boat's windage as far as possible. Another drawback of a rigidly mounted wind generator is that they tend to reverberate through the boat and can be very noisy. We also think that they do nothing for the appearance of a boat at the best of times, but particularly so when mounted on a galvanized pole on the stern. You may think I go on about aesthetics rather too much, but don't forget that quality of life is a part of our philosophy and having a good-looking boat enhances this. Our Aquair came with a device for slinging it in the rigging, but we had to make one for the Rutland, which is designed for fixed mounting. It worked perfectly well and didn't look too bad — they seem less noticeable when hoisted than on a pole. Incidentally, some of the huge two-bladed devices used for belting out lots of amps can be quite noisy and are again, rather anti-social — it is well worth seeing one in action before buying.

Electricity can also be generated by using a water turbine. As already mentioned, we have found the Aquair very efficient and a friend of ours who has a second generation one found that it put out far more electricity than he needed so that he could have lights on all over the place. To haul in one of these can be an exercise fraught with peril and frustration. We were told that this can be overcome by buying a large plastic funnel and splitting it along its length. To haul in the rotator, you put the funnel over the line leading to the rotator with its mouth facing aft and allow it to run down to the end. It then stops the rotator and the whole lot can be hauled in, in a civilized manner. When we tried it the funnel simply disappeared. Perhaps we did something wrong. The only method we have found effective is to heave-to and stop the boat before pulling it in, which is unpleasant to contemplate when the wind is getting up.

We have found to our cost that towing generators and Walker logs do not get along at all well. In a decent beam wind, if the log line is to windward of the generator, it can get blown over the generator line and the most appalling snarl-up is the result. Even worse is the fact that the log line usually snaps at the cost of a new rotator and line. However, towing a generator gives you electricity so that you can use an electric log. In desperation we decided to do this and bought a Stowe log with a towing rotator. This isn't as loopy as it sounds, because this rotator is on thirty feet of wire and the lines go nowhere near one another. We chose this type because we didn't want to make a hole in the bottom of the boat and it was also quite reasonably priced. Pete likes the speedo, too and although we were initially very dubious about the whole thing and had some problems with the connections, eventually we got everything to run and have generally been very happy with it. The only insoluble problem we have is that it over-reads enormously when we are running the engine and someone stands on the engine box. Don't ask me why. We wonder glumly how long it will last, having little faith in any electronic equipment and have kept a Walker log, in case. We did however, exchange our lovely Excelsior™ that we were given for a wedding present, for the far less aesthetic Knotmaster™, because we could no longer afford the rotators for the former. We were delighted to discover that it went to a good home.

Water pressure may also be used to charge batteries by way of a shaft alternator. Various people produce them to fit to your boat or you can design and build one yourself, if you understand the principles. Some people say that you can't use them with an hydraulic gearbox, others say you can, but I haven't yet met anyone with a *functioning* shaft alternator who has an hydraulic gearbox. In fact most shaft alternators never seem to get far beyond the design stage. The principle behind them is that you utilize the spinning of the propeller to charge the battery. Their drawbacks are that they can be noisy, they can create a lot of wear and tear on the propeller shaft and its ancillaries, and that they create a lot of drag — they're not going to produce much if you only have a dinky little two-bladed prop. In favour of the system, you are using something that is already on the boat and don't need extra pieces of equipment dangling about, getting in the way and needing a home when not in use.

At the end of the day it comes down, yet again, to 'you pays your money and you takes your choice'. I firmly believe in going for quality here, as the gear you select will get a lot of use and abuse — if you're going to have electricity you need to get full value out of the equipment on which you have spent so much money, time and effort. We chose to go for electricity on the principle of spending the money when we had it, i.e., when working, rather than going for the high running costs of pressure lanterns. (Remember it all started from the nav. light) I can't say that we are a hundred percent convinced that it was worth it.

Because we live on our yacht all the time, the details of our boat are in many ways as important as the major aspects. For example, I refuse to spend the rest of my life camping out and using sleeping bags on our bunk. Quite apart from anything else, they are exceedingly difficult to wash. Instead we use a duvet or continental quilt, which to my mind were invented for boat use. They make the bed very simple to make, the cover in polyester and cotton, is easy to wash and dry and the sleeping cabin looks bright and cheerful. Equally, when it comes to illuminating the boat at night, I think that it's as important to have a pleasant atmosphere as it is to have effective lighting.

As mentioned, we have always used oil lamps on our boats and been delighted with them. We use the standard type of gimballed oil lamp, with a one inch wick and have two of them positioned so that we each have a lamp behind and above us for reading. A lot of people seem to think that they are no use for reading, but after over 15 years of living with oil lamps — and both of us are avid readers — we still have A-1 vision. Anyway, the latest thinking seems to be that one's eyes benefit from having to work. It is important to position the lamps properly and also to keep the lamp glasses clean, but the

essential thing to do is to trim the wick correctly. In **Cruising Under Sail**, Eric Hiscock says that you should trim the wick concave, unless it is a narrow one, but I have found that with a one inch wick trimmed concave or even straight, the flame will produce horns when it is turned up high. The way I trim them is to cut them to a shallow point — the angle at the top being about a hundred twenty degrees, and then snip off the top so that the shape is more or less convex. That way, the wick can be turned up to produce a flame about an inch high which is quite adequate to read by.

Another advantage of oil lamps is that they are excellent for use when sailing. Because they are less bright than an incandescent bulb and burn with a yellow flame rather than the bright blue-white light of a fluorescent lamp, they are much less damaging to one's night vision. When coastal sailing, we always leave the lamp over the chart table turned down low. This means that we can pop down below to read the chart at any time, without spoiling our night sight and it also dimly illuminates the whole cabin for making a brew, etc. If the other person is off watch and asleep, the lamp doesn't disturb them because, not being on the deckhead, it is hidden by the lee cloth. For some reason, I always find it reassuring to have a light on in the cabin at night, when we are at sea. We think an oil lamp is greatly superior to the much vaunted red chart light, not in the least because it emphasizes the magenta teardrop indicating a lit navigation mark, whereas the red light, being at the same end of the spectrum tends to disguise them.

On any serious cruising boat, oil lamps are an essential back-up to electric lamps. On *Badger*, we have one in the heads, one at the after end of the galley, one between the galley and saloon and one between the saloon and the chart table.

After fitting *Badger* with our generators, we decided that it would make better financial sense to use electric lamps instead of oil, as we use about half a gallon of paraffin a week, in a place where the nights are long. Originally, after talking to various people, we fitted a couple of fluorescent strip lights on the deckhead. However, I dislike the light they give out and find that lighting from above does not make for a pleasant atmosphere. We then bought a couple of quartz halogen spotlights, which we fitted at the same place as the oil lamps, behind where we sit. These are good for reading and could be bounced off the cabin side for general illumination. We discovered, however, that the bulbs are expensive and have a short life and that when we were reading on watch, they were far too bright and ruined our night vision. Accordingly we replaced the bulbs with the standard five watt type and decided to keep them solely for reading by at sea.

When we were back in England for a while, we decided that if the idea of using lights was because we had a surplus of electricity, then we didn't need to use lamps that are particularly efficient in their use of electricity and could instead have incandescent bulbs, which are much more aesthetically acceptable. This being the case, we decided to use incandescent lighting in the saloon, while keeping fluorescent lamps in the galley. After cooking, they are switched off and don't have to be tolerated any longer. We also fitted small electric lights in the sleeping cabin, heads and lazarette, all of which have been very useful. We found that the main problem in selecting electric lamps was finding lamps that could be situated on the bulkheads rather than on the deckhead. Finding lamps that we could live with anyway, was a problem, a lot of those available are really quite nasty. Eventually, however, we found everything that we wanted in Davey's catalogue and the brass lamps, with their ground glass shades actually enhance the appearance of the saloon.

We still have oil lamps in the saloon, galley and heads and use them quite often, if it's a little cool or if we want a mellow atmosphere, or if the battery is not as healthy as it might be, but I really wish that the COLREGS people had permitted us still to use oil navigation lamps and not caused us so much trouble.

Greenland 1991. I am at the helm, smiling with relief after we'd negotiated some very unpleasant brash ice. The water now seems almost ice-free! We are motoring to keep the speed down with the sails sheeted hard in. Note bubble fitted to keep the warmth in. Also solar panel mounted forward of the mast. The boat hook is not in its chock. Pete has been using it to fend off lumps of ice.

THE ENGINE TO FIT THE SPACE

Chapter 19

The Iron Tops'l

Reading the average sail test in a yachting magazine, I always find it disconcerting that the performance under power is considered before the performance under sail and that the boat is rarely handled under sail in close quarters. Listening to other yachtsmen, I am still surprised at how many of them will endlessly discuss their engine and yet how few of them seem interested in their sails; how many of them will consider putting in a new engine and how few will consider a brand new suit of sails from a top quality loft. Sailing along the coast, we are continually amazed at the number of sailing yachts that are motoring when there is sufficient breeze to sail and the rot has truly set in when one realizes how many people on an ocean crossing will start the engine as soon as the boat speed drops below three to four knots — "We need to charge the batteries anyway" — and then tell everybody what a fast passage they made. I suppose that there's nothing wrong with any of the above, but it seems to me that more and more yachts are actually used as motorsailers, and fewer and fewer as sailing or even as auxiliary vessels.

It is debatable as to whether the voyaging boat needs an engine at all. For the many people who make a passage from one place to another and then stay there several weeks or months before making a passage to another distant destination, I should be inclined to think that an engine would be more trouble than it's worth and would simply take up valuable storage space. For those who enjoy cruising around once they arrive at their destination, an engine is likely to be of rather more use. As for charging up the battery, there are actually much more efficient ways of doing so — and with devices that don't generally need a battery to get them going in the first place.

Even if you feel that you want some sort of auxiliary power, an engine is not the only choice. Alternative methods of propulsion worth consideration are oars or a sweep or yuloh. The simplest method of all, when using oars, it to get into your dinghy and tie a line

from it to the yacht's bows. Once you have way on, it takes surprisingly little effort to pull even quite a sizable vessel through the water at half a knot or so, in a flat calm. Of course the yacht can have her own oars, although this is a small boat option. However, they work quite well as long as the boat has reasonably low topsides and the oars are correctly balanced so that you are not having to lift their weight out of the water for each new stroke. It is much more efficacious, generally, to stand up to them and row forward fisherman style, rather than sitting and pulling like an Oxford blue.

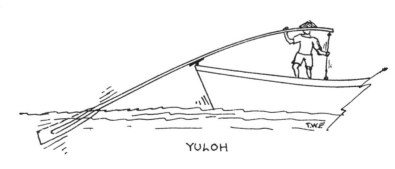

YULOH

When the boat is too heavy for a pair of oars, a sweep sculled over the stern is the next option. Using just one oar in a rowlock makes most boats go round in circles and you need so much helm to counteract this, that the rudder acts like a brake. If you can put the oar nearer amidships, this will be alleviated, but wouldn't be possible on many boats. Sculling over the stern should propel you at about one knot or so, which is better than nothing and can get you into an anchorage for the night. Again freeboard should not be too high. However, the problem of high freeboard can be overcome and the Chinese did this on their high-sterned junks, by using a bent oar known as a yuloh. Being Chinese, they also managed to make the oar more efficient by curving it in such a way that it was self-feathering and self-aligning, so that all the oarsman did was to push it from side to side, twitching a piece of rope at each stroke so that the yuloh automatically swung round to provide propulsion at each stroke. We attempted to make a yuloh, without much success, because we didn't have the right information on how to make one. I think our pointed stern meant that we were in the wrong position in relation to the blade to begin with. We have since seen several articles on yulohs, but have never done any more about one.

Yawl boats are the simplest way of providing propulsion using an engine. What you have here is a fairly substantial tender with an outboard motor on it. You bring it alongside the mother ship and tie the two together securely. Then you use the motor on the yawl boat and the rudder of the mother ship in combination. Gary and Beryl on *Alice Alakwe* used this system with a two horsepower motor to move their 45-footer around in a confined harbour or anchorage. Unfortunately, this idea has many drawbacks, not the least of which is that for small boats with small dinghies, a slight popple is enough to make the operation fraught with peril. Exponents of the idea point to the Maine schooners and marvel at how the owners of these ships are such purists that they won't sully their vessels with engines, but instead use a yawl boat. Alas, in reality, the overriding reason for the use of a yawl boat is that the U. S. Coast Guard regulations for the carrying of paying passengers are much less stringent on purely sailing vessels than on auxiliary craft. It is an idea worth keeping in mind though, because in a flat sea a yacht can make use of the idea. However, if you do own an outboard, a much better idea would be if you could fit it to the parent ship. Even a couple of horsepower is the difference between stop and go and might get you into an anchorage for the night when it's flat calm. One of the many advantages of having a smaller and lighter boat is that you need far less wind to make her move, so that she is much more rarely becalmed than her heavier sister. When she eventually is becalmed, you need much less power to make her move anyway.

Before you make the final decision as to whether or not to have an engine, it is worth considering the maintenance. An unreliable engine is worse than useless, it's not even particularly good ballast and there are so many things to go wrong with one. They are not such a big safety aid as people would have you believe. Far more boats have been lost from relying on an engine that let them down than from not having an engine in the first place. We can all quote the loss of the *Teddy* and others, but every week the lifeboats are going out to bring in yachts disabled through loss of the engine. How often have we read the scenario of sudden emergency, start engine, jib sheet round prop, now a real disaster. If you don't have an engine, you should have more sense than to sail into

bottlenecks or cut corners and if you do have one, you should always be ready for its sudden failure. The most reliable engine in the world can be put out of action by dirty fuel, an air lock or a plastic bag — good sails and rigging can't really let you down. Again, even if the whole machine is functioning properly, a flat battery can scupper you. Once again a small boat will come into its own here because she only needs a small engine and a small engine can be hand-started. With all the blather that there is about safety, this is a safety feature I rarely see mentioned.

Personally, I loathe oil and grease and dislike having to deal with engines. Fortunately, Pete will take on this onerous task, but even he approaches a recalcitrant engine with less than enthusiasm. If you feel as I do about all the gunge that is inevitably associated with engines, you will either have to conquer your revulsion, sign on an engineer, budget a vast amount of money for someone else to look at the thing or go without. As we are assuming voyaging on a small income and as the damn' thing won't be used that often anyway, the cost benefit analysis on paying for an engineer is easily done. If you would like an engine, someone is going to have to learn to look after it.

However, if the boat you own doesn't have an engine, it should be no reason to put you off going voyaging. Neither *Sheila* nor *Stormalong* had an engine and we didn't fit one to *Badger* at first. We sailed *Stormalong* at weekends for a season around England's Morecambe Bay and took a three week holiday across to the Isle of Man and down to the Scillies without an engine — and got back to work on time. We then sailed her across the Atlantic and back. In *Sheila* we did coastal sailing around England and south west Ireland. Before fitting an engine to *Badger*, we sailed up to the west coast of Scotland and spent a summer in the Outer Hebrides. We then sailed down to the Canaries and across to the British Virgin Islands, which we explored fairly thoroughly. From there we sailed up to the Chesapeake Bay in the States, where we fitted her engine. Several years later, when we were in Venezuela, the valves burnt out. We were just about ready to leave and couldn't be bothered with all the trouble of getting the engine fixed, so we sailed back to the United Kingdom via the Dominican Republic, the Turks and Caicos, the Bahamas, Bermuda and the Azores and never really missed it.

Because of this, we learned how to handle our boats under sail and, knowing that there was nothing we could do about calms, grew from tolerating them to actually enjoying them — with the exception of the wind dying away in the evening when we were still a couple of miles from our destination. I'm afraid that I have never been able to be philosophical about that. We came to fit an engine to *Badger* to extend our cruising potential, such as the passage down the Intracoastal Waterway and to help manoeuvering out of a crowded anchorage, of which there are so many nowadays. We enjoy kedging out and still practice it on occasion, even though it's no longer necessary, but we have had the situation of kedging ourselves into a good spot to sail off and having someone anchor right on top of us before we could do so. However, due to the fact that it actually costs money to run the engine, we avoid using it and we actually get more pleasure from handling the boat under sail, in the knowledge that we are doing it out of choice rather than necessity. There are several diehard sailors around who still sail engineless craft such as Tim and Pauline Carr on *Curlew*, Lin and Larry Pardey on *Taleisin*, Peter Tangvald and others. These are the truly sporting sailors and have my fullest respect.

When the cost of miles covered has to be counted, few of us will switch on the engine to save time ("for what?", one asks). As with so many aspects of voyaging on a small income, this economy actually leads to more enjoyment and greater satisfaction. Any fool can steer a boat downwind across the ocean — the test of handling a boat is in sailing in and out of anchorages and because this is where the skill lies, this is also where the most fun is. Neither of us is that keen on steering, but when it comes to entering a harbour or sailing a tricky course among the skerries, we both enjoy it so much that we have to take it in turns to ensure fairness. Even more fun is sailing out, with the added challenge of making sure that you get away on the correct tack.

When we came to fit an engine to *Badger*, we discussed in detail what sort to get. We really fancied an outboard motor, but with a pointed stern, were not sure how to fit one without ruining *Badger*'s appearance. We then looked at saildrives and decided that this was the best way to go — they are ideal for a flat bottomed boat. Taking into consideration the amount of useful stowage in the lazarette and putting that against the number of times we would actually use the engine, we decided that the engine would have to fit the space available and not vice versa. We had built *Badger* in such a way that an engine could be fitted at a later date either by ourselves or a subsequent owner, utilizing the area for storage in the meantime. In fact, this space was known as the 'engine box', because that is what it looked like. In the end, we decided to go for a Volvo Penta 7.5 hp petrol saildrive, the reasons being that we could afford it, it had sufficient power for an auxiliary, it fitted the space and, with due respect to Volvo, because the power head is actually a Honda four-stroke motor. We wanted a four-stroke for reasons of quietness and economy and knowing the price of Volvo spares, were relieved to find that we could use Honda instead. A friend of ours described the engine as "where the land of the midnight sun meets the land of the rising sun" and, on the whole, it has been a success.

Diesel engines are the usual choice in a voyaging yacht and there are many things to be said in their favour, most of which have been said, *ad nauseam*, in the yachting press. Used and maintained correctly, they are reliable and economical and the fuel is both relatively cheap and universally available. On the other hand they are noisy, smelly and tend to vibrate a lot, all of which make

motoring unpleasant, but is true, to a greater or lesser extent, about any engine. However, a point that should be made about a diesel engine on a voyaging yacht, and a point that tends to get overlooked, is that to be reliable diesel engines need to be used and used under load. The weekend sailor will probably give his engine a good run going from the marina and another one coming back, each time he uses the boat. The voyager, on the other hand, may have no reason to use the engine from one month's end to the next. A diesel engine suffers more damage and wear from starting, running under insufficient loads and from running cold than it does from pushing the boat at high revolutions for hour after hour. Modern engines only have a small volume of oil in the sump, which has to do a lot of work and on a voyaging boat, will often hardly have got warmed up before the engine is shut down. Petrol engines seem to be able to rest for long periods of time and still start without problem. Some of these problems can be alleviated by fitting an air-cooled diesel engine. Although you will have to suffer from extra noise, such a unit will probably last longer than a water-cooled one, because it will not have salt-water going through it (freshwater-cooled engines are only available in larger sizes). The absence of a cooling system will reduce its weight or allow you to choose a more heavily built alternative, which should have a longer life expectancy. You will also be eliminating all the associated problems of a water cooling system.

For many years, yachts were sailed quite happily without diesel engines and some petrol engines went on for ever. Pete and I both think that a diesel engine should be well down on the list of priorities. Of course, if we were to buy a boat that was fitted with a reliable diesel, we wouldn't hesitate about keeping it; on the other hand, I do think that people tend to dismiss the alternative, a petrol engine, out of hand muttering about safety and so I feel that perhaps it would be appropriate to point out some of the virtues of this type of engine.

For a start they are considerably cheaper, smaller and lighter than diesel units and more easy for the amateur to maintain. Admittedly, the fuel is substantially more expensive, which would appear to go against our usual philosophy of spending in order to save in the long run. However, if you are going to buy a diesel engine, you have to weigh its initially higher cost and its life expectancy against the fuel you will be saving. If you buy a diesel, you will find that the heavy, slow-running engines such as Sabb or Lister will last the longest. However, their weight, size and initial cost are all great. The more modern, lightweight and cheaper diesels only have a life expectancy of ten years before requiring a major overhaul. I think that you can reckon on a well-kept petrol engine lasting the same time. However, even if the diesel engine lasts twice as long as the petrol one and neither of them needs any money spending on it, you'll still have to motor a hell of a lot to make up the difference in cost out of fuel savings. In reality of course, both engines will need money spending on them and the diesel will tend to cost much more each time than will the petrol one. A new injector costs substantially more than most of the spares that are routinely required for a petrol engine and needs a skilled man and the right equipment to fit it.

Petrol engines also have a bad press about their starting problems. *Badger's* engine has electronic ignition and a hand pull start and rarely gives us any problems. I'm sure that most of the difficulties to which people refer, have been associated with damp, which does not need to be a real problem with careful installation and modern materials. In older boats, the engine was often situated under the cockpit sole and had rain and seawater over it at regular intervals. Even if that is the only place for it, judicious use of plywood, sealants, epoxy resin and glass cloth should enable you to give it a dry berth.

As to the safety aspect of a petrol engine, this is a very valid concern, but it is also surrounded with a lot of incredibly woolly-minded thinking. I am staggered at the number of people who tell us that they wouldn't have a petrol engine on their boat, for love nor money and yet keep outboard motors and cans of petrol in cockpit lockers that drain into the bilge, to say nothing of having a small generator stored below. Added to this, they cheerfully use propane or butane gas, turning it on before striking the match, without a second thought. Both petrol and gas are dangerous, if used carelessly, but there is no need to be careless. On *Badger*, we keep our petrol in five gallon tanks, as used for outboard motors, in deck lockers. When we want to start the engine, we connect the fuel line to the tank and pull the starter cord. When we have finished using it, we disconnect the fuel line and run it dry, thus having petrol down below only while running the engine. This system has two incidental advantages. It makes starting the engine slightly inconvenient, which discourages us from using it and it ensures that the engine gets run for a reasonable length of time (it takes about ten minutes to use up the fuel in the line), so that it gets thoroughly warmed up.

Our friend, Nick Skeates, is really the man to talk to about value for money, when it comes to a petrol engine. When he was building *Wylo II*, he used to have a van for getting around in and carrying gear. It was pretty old and clapped out and in fact a friend of his who had the same model, passed on his old one to Nick when it was ready for the scrap yard. "Use it for spares", he said. When he was getting towards the end of building the boat, Nick decided that it would be a good idea to have an engine in her and his eye rested on his van. 'Just the job', he thought and set about marinizing the engine and installed it in *Wylo II*, where it has functioned perfectly. He stripped down the engine from his friend's van and then started to work out what to take in the way of spares. In the end he put the lot aboard. This is voyaging on a micro income at its best — not only does Nick have a perfectly good engine, but he has already had more than his fair share of use out of it, has spares to the year dot and the satisfaction of knowing that when it does finally give up the ghost, it will owe him nothing. A new diesel engine would probably have cost more than the entire boat.

Outboard motors are also a very underrated way of fitting auxiliary power. At the thought of an outboard, most people imagine brackets on the stern, an unsightly and vulnerable engine and cavitation problems. However, with a bit of lateral thinking, the outboard can become more or less an inboard, but with the advantage that you can take it to the engineer and not the other way round, when it needs major work doing on it. Some production boats have this type of arrangement and one of the best can be found in those built by the British firm of Hunter Boats, in Essex. They use a Honda 4-stroke, so arranged that when out of use it lives in a cockpit locker, out of the elements, with the hole through which it fits plugged by a flush fitting plate. When the engine is required, the plate is removed and the engine lowered by a block and tackle system and ready to go. The fuel line can be left connected to the petrol tank, which lives in the same locker and electric start can be fitted if you want to go the whole hog.

We have met two cruising boats which have made use of similar arrangements. Danny Greene on *Brazen* uses a 10 hp, 4-stroke motor, which is mounted at the after end of the cockpit on his 34 foot steel boat. On *Salvation Jane*, Trevor went a stage further in lateral thinking and bought a paraffin fueled outboard motor on the principle that paraffin is generally cheaper than petrol. Both of them not only find the motors more than satisfactory, but can see no reason for changing their systems. When the time comes for us to replace *Badger's* engine, we would seriously consider an outboard in a well ourselves — after all, it's almost what we have at the moment.

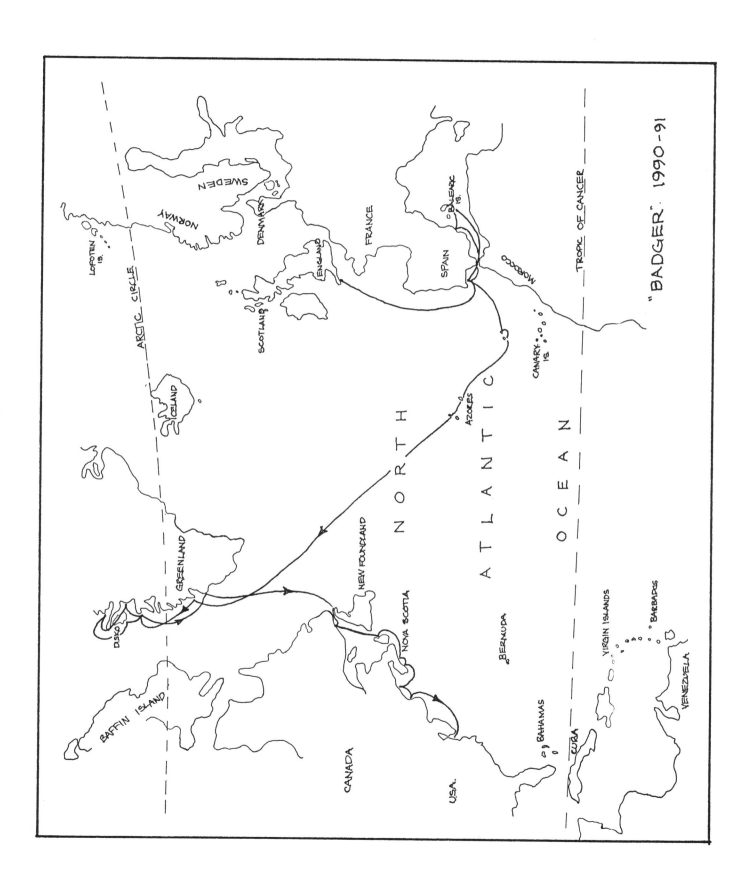

"BADGER". 1990-91

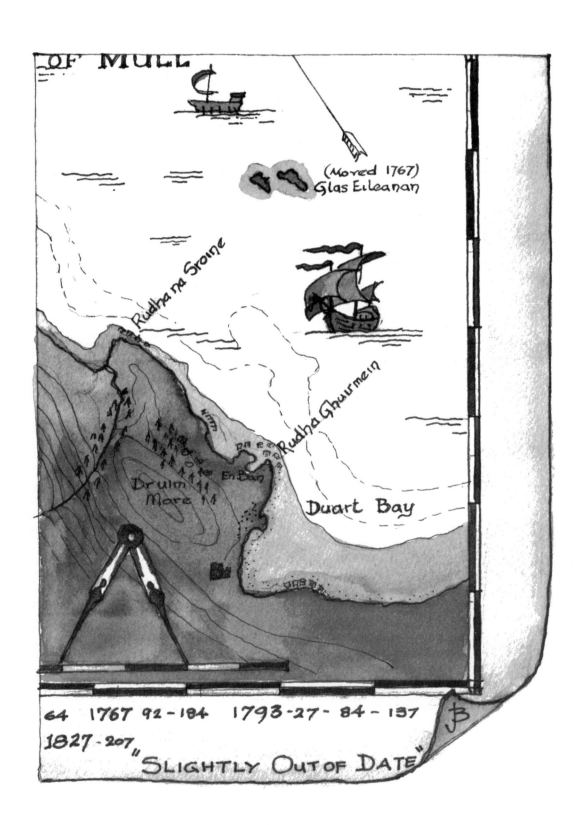

Chapter 20

Finding Your Way

Having got together a suitable boat, the wherewithal to live for a while and a destination in mind, the next stage in planning a voyage is generally to get together the necessary charts. For those of us on a small income this raises something of a problem, because charts are anything but cheap. Frank Wightman navigated from South Africa with the absolute minimum. He writes in **The Wind is Free**: "When we left South Africa we had been able to get only one chart. This took us to a point five hundred miles from Cape San Roque. From there we should have to navigate on an old atlas. We had tried to get charts in St Helena, but failed. There they told us we should almost certainly get them at Ascension. There were not charts at Ascension. We took our troubles to the Americans, and they let us have one of their aircraft charts. This was a lot better than having to navigate by atlas, but, being for aircraft, all coastal information that is so useful to ships was omitted. And all the distances marked on it were those of a straight line between points: the distance as a plane would fly it. All the same, we were glad to get it." With the aid of these charts and using a box sextant, Frank Wightman managed to make perfect landfalls at all his destinations. Admittedly, most of us are not of the same calibre, but his is the perfect example of what can be done, given sufficient determination. These days we are generally a lot better off, insofar as charts are readily available; but with very little spare cash, charts still represent a large capital outlay.

The best economy can be made by ensuring, when you are buying new charts, that you don't buy unnecessary ones. To plan which charts to buy it is well worth using a Chart Catalogue. These are published by the Admiralty and cost an arm and a leg; however, your friendly neighborhood chandler might be prevailed upon to sell you last year's (or an even older) copy, for a modest sum, and that will do perfectly well for your purposes. Studying the catalogue will show you for which areas an excessive number of charts has been produced, that is to say where

one stretch of coast is covered by several charts of various scales. For most requirements, the small scale general chart and large scale charts showing harbours and coastal detail are all that are required. The catalogue indicates which charts are in imperial measurements and which in metric, which will also affect your decisions.

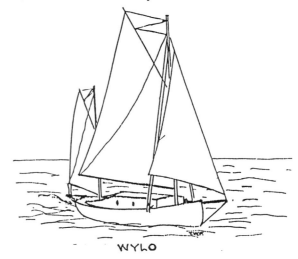

WYLO

Some time ago, I read a comment in **Practical Boat Owner** along the lines of "Only a crass fool would put out to sea with out-of-date charts!" While I realize what the writer was getting at and I appreciate that the magazine feels that it ought to encourage sailors to be prudent, my own feeling is that only a crass fool would trust that his chart is up to date. Having up-to-date charts on board can easily lead to a false sense of security. 'After all', you think, 'it's brand new and I know that I can rely on it.' However, what you have forgotten is that as soon as you leave the chart agent, the chart is effectively out of date. Of course, we all know that we are meant to correct them but even supposing that we actually had all the Notices to Mariners forwarded to us, our charts would still be slightly out of date. However, the main problem is that the assumption that a new chart is an up-to-date chart, is only valid when cruising in certain areas anyway. In a lot of places, even the most up-to-date chart is unreliable due to the fact that the country in question either does not concern itself with hydrography or if it does, refuses to let the rest of the world know its discoveries. Having accepted all the above, one will therefore work on the assumption that all charts may be incorrect and should be treated with caution. This being the case, we can then happily navigate on old and definitely out of date charts, which, considering that we really have no choice is all to the good. Comfort yourself with the reflection that the rocks don't change (unless they happen to be volcanic, or coral, or ...). One does occasionally find surprises such as we came across in Denmark when the water shown on our 1950's chart turned out to be reclaimed land, but this all adds to the interest of cruising. We were once sailing with a friend in Scotland and he was somewhat taken aback at the age of several of our charts. It was with great satisfaction, studying our chart of the Sound of Mull, that we noticed a castle marked on it as a correction — and brought it to John's attention.

When we set off for the Caribbean in *Stormalong*, we provided ourselves with the necessary charts for the voyage. At that time, 1975, they cost 75 pence each. The last time we looked at chart prices in England was 1989, by which time the cost had increased to £7.60, a tenfold increase far in excess of inflation. What they cost now, I hate to think. We have been told that this price increase is due to the decrease in size of both the Royal and Merchant Navies. Apparently, in the days when there were lots of ships about, the Hydrographer would engrave his charts and run off several thousand, one for each of HM's ships and the rest for the chart agents to sell to the merchant fleets. However, with far less demand for charts, there are fewer printed and so the cost has had to increase. The real purpose for which the Hydrographer exists was dramatically brought home by the complete re-drawing of the Falklands charts after the 1982 Conflict. Although charts are now far more expensive than they used to be, fifteen years ago we would have found it difficult to buy or borrow charts for the voyage. Now it is a different story, with people doing the milk run by the hundred every year and then coming back and selling their boats, lock, stock and barrel, before returning to 'normal life'. Thus, although we generally cannot afford to get new charts, it is much easier to get hold of second-hand ones.

There are, in fact, certain advantages in obtaining older charts. Quite apart from the fact that a lot of us do not yet " think metric", the imperial charts show a wealth of details that is sadly lacking in their metric equivalent and of importance to the small boat sailor. It is no exaggeration to say that a small-scale imperial chart will show more topographical detail than a large-scale metric one. As a friend of ours, Peggy, would say: "metric charts don't have a single *Conspic* on them!" The added details of the old charts make coastal navigation easier and the exploration of rivers, creeks and coves much more fun.

However, even more to the point, should you be missing the large-scale chart for the area, judicious use of a magnifying glass will often supply the necessary information from the small-scale chart — bearing in mind, of course, that any man-made harbour will probably have been altered. Metric charts were re-engraved for the sake of clarity and they are undoubtedly less cluttered than the old imperial ones. On the other hand, it is arguable whether people who cannot manage to cope with all the detail ought to be navigating in the first place. Imperial charts are also much more aesthetically pleasing and given the choice between a brand new metric chart and a twenty year old imperial, I would generally take the latter, except in the case of a chart of an artificial harbour.

One of the major drawbacks of old charts is that the lights may have changed. For reasons best known to themselves, Trinity House and their equivalent in many other countries, take a delight in altering the frequencies and characteristics of their lights and seem unable to leave well alone. This was brought home to us on one of the rare occasions when we were sailing with an up-to-date almanac and found ourselves somewhat confused that the light that we could see was not at all what it should be — in fact the characteristics had been changed in the five months since the Almanac had been published. When we were sailing in northern Norway, an area with a profusion of islands, lights and withies, we found that our 1925 charts were accurate in every detail, except for the actual harbours themselves, where some changes had been made and also the odd road bridge connecting islands together. Our friend, Helge, told us that fishermen teach the frequencies of the local lights to their sons so that they know them by heart when they come to skipper their own boat. Trinity House please take note. However, the problems of inaccurate light information can be overcome with a fairly low outlay of cash, by buying an up-to-date Admiralty List of Lights, which should prove fairly, though by no means entirely, reliable. If you are full of energy, you could even correct your charts accordingly.

There are several ways of obtaining second-hand charts. The most expensive would be to advertise for them — knowing that somebody wants their charts will immediately raise the asking price. After that, the shops which sell second-hand boat gear are a good bet, although last time we asked for them in Bacon's in Annapolis, they said that they didn't sell second-hand charts any more, because they tended to be out of date! If you are a member of a yacht club, that may turn up someone who has the charts you want, either to buy or to borrow and a postcard in the local chandlers may produce results. We have obtained many of our charts from swopping with other cruising people. It's sometimes a good idea to swop your duplicates for anything that they have, even if you don't necessarily want it yourself, as you may well be able to trade it further down the line. Even if you don't you can always decide to go there after all. Other sailors will often sell you charts, too; it used to be one pound per chart, but inflation has reared its ugly head here, as well. If you have the opportunity to buy charts for somewhere you definitely want to go, you'll probably pay what is being asked, but by being selective, you can buy a minimum. It's worth keeping your swops separate for ease of trading.

I've met several people who have been given charts from ships. They have gone aboard to check their chronometers or some other excuse and then come back with a load of charts. I've never had the nerve to do it and there is now an ugly rumour that the Owners have a deal whereby they return their charts to the agents, who amend and replace them by the folio, so that every chart has to be accounted for. I always feel that it's a shame that chart agents can't sell obsolete charts at a knockdown price with a 'Government Health Warning' on them.

Having got your hotchpotch collection of charts together, it is well worth while organizing them in a logical fashion. Apart from making life easier when you are navigating, there is the added advantage that when you are considering whether or not to buy a new chart, you will easily be able to check whether you have it or whether what you have already will do. We keep our charts in folios, using the second-hand canvas covers that you can buy at most large chart agents. These are also quite easy to make being simply a piece of canvas, hemmed all round, with tapes along the edges, top and bottom and slightly more than twice the size of a folded Admiralty chart. To use them you place your folio of charts on one half, fold the cover in two and tie the tapes together. Apart from being easier to sort and store, keeping charts in folios extends their life by protecting them. We group our charts into categories that suit us e.g. Baltic, Atlantic Islands, etc. and store them in the appropriate folio. For an index, we use a chart catalogue (needless to say, ours is very out of date) and with a highlighter pen, we show which charts we have. We then indicate on the pages of the catalogue to which folio the charts belong and then number the charts in each folio, in accordance with the order in which they are listed in the catalogue. However, if there is a gap in the sequence of charts, because we are missing a few, we number the next chart as though we had all the missing ones so that new ones can easily be fitted into place as we obtain them. We also have a special folio that we keep for swops, which are obtained when you buy a job lot or get a better edition of the same chart.

One thing that we discovered the hard way is that should you be in the desperate straits of needing to buy new charts, it is not enough to take with you only the names and numbers of the charts you require, culled from your catalogue. We did this once and because our numbers were so out of date, we ended up buying two charts which effectively duplicated two that we had. Next time, we would make sure that we took our chart catalogue along, as this would show just what areas were covered. One of the few advantages of buying new charts is that the nice man at the chart agents can often be persuaded to wrap up what you buy in generous quantities of cancelled charts, thus giving you several freebies. The same applies when your order them, although they use fewer charts; at least, that is the case with Dubois Phillips in Liverpool. They employ a bloke there whose knowledge is encyclopaedic and knows not only all the up-to-date numbers, but also the old ones so that when you ask for 1422 he will say, "Oh no, you don't want that one, it was cancelled five years ago, you want 5462 now".

In recent years a new innovation has come to the aid of the impecunious voyager. This is the emergence of the cruising guide for yachtsmen, frequently a weighty tome full of sketch plans and valuable information. Unlike the Admiralty Pilots, they are aimed at the person in a yacht and are therefore far less off-putting and far more useful. Yachtsmen's guides tend to be quite expensive — until, that is, you compare them with the cost of — an Admiralty Pilot or reckon up the cost of the charts you would otherwise need to buy. We have found that if you have a small scale chart of the area, the guide will provide all the rest of the information that you need. They invariably have a disclaimer saying that they should not be used for navigation, but this more for the avoidance of litigation than an indication that their charts are unreliable. Anyway, most people navigate by eye and by bearings and not by measuring distances to the nearest yard or so. Knowing that many of them are amateur publications, one will treat them with additional caution and keep an eye on the echo sounder, but they are more than adequate. I have to admit that we once navigated a fair section of the Chesapeake Bay using a table mat, for lack of any other chart, and found it adequate. Just. These guides do tend to cover only the more popular places, of course and in that way may encourage overcrowding, but they are undoubtedly a great aid to be welcomed.

I would however, suggest that if possible, you ask other yachtsmen if they have used them and what they think of them. We have been caught out twice, once by a certain guide on Norway which seems a bit of a rip-off because it only covers a small area and has little advantage over the Admiralty Pilot and once by a guide to Venezuela, which almost cost us our boat due to one instance of appalling inaccuracy. Unfortunately, a lot of the Venezuelan guide is founded on hearsay. However, there are precious few charts for Venezuela, so this guide is better than nothing, but please be very careful entering the anchorage on Tortuga — the reef extends two-thirds of the way across the entrance and you need to keep to the *starboard* side of the channel, going in. I believe that an alternative cruising guide to Venezuela is now available.

By the way, any guides or charts of Spain and Portugal need to be treated with more than ordinary care as both races are prodigious builders of harbours and are continually altering and extending them, so that they are never the same on two consecutive visits.

One of the very few drawbacks of voyaging on a small income is that you never dare to get rid of any charts or Pilots that you are likely to need again. This means that you need a lot of storage for them, something which is rarely allowed for on production boats. On *Badger,* we have six feet of bookshelves for Pilots which is nowhere near enough so that quite a few are stowed under the saloon sole; we also have a locker, about two feet six inches high, under the chart table for charts, which is not enough for what we have and several folios live in the lazarette, under the afterdeck. Pilot books are very bulky and allowance has to be made for the fact that the new style Pilots and Air Sight Reduction tables are rather on the tall side. By the way, a very useful publication that all hard-up voyagers should have on board is a slim volume called **Cook's Tables**. A desk-top publication, it provides the necessary tables for the sun until the year dot, using an ingenious set of corrections. We bought a copy several years ago for £1 and would strongly recommend it.

The stowage of charts under the chart table is a satisfactory arrangement because it is often difficult to find any other large, flat place in which to put them. It is useful to have a small drawer directly under the table, in which to stow ready-use charts. A number of people use a lift-up lid, but it is more convenient to have a fold down flap instead, as whenever you want to lift up the lid you can guarantee that, for some obscure reason there will be either a heavy object or a container of liquid on top. The chart table itself should be a permanent one if at all possible. Get rid of other things, if needs be; on a voyaging yacht the chart table is used a lot. On passage it is a good thing if the chart can be left out all the time and it is almost a necessity when daysailing. The table should be at least half size, but preferably full size, as by Sod's law, the most difficult and testing pilotage will take place on the crease of the chart. A full-size chart table is useful for many other things, too, such as a place for booze and snacks for a party, building models or putting the Christmas tree on. It is popular to have an athwartships chart table with a seat, but on *Badger*, we have one running fore and aft which we stand up to. We use the galley strap when on the port tack and have all the space where we would otherwise put our knees for putting our charts; we are well pleased with the arrangement.

Because one of the great delights of this way of life is the planning of future voyages, there's a lot to be said for being able to carry a large stock of accessible charts, so that you can get them out easily and study them. Many a happy hour can be spent picking out anchorages and deciding what islands to visit — whether you actually go there or not is quite irrelevant; plans are made to be changed — that's a part of the freedom.

We spent two months in Palma Mallorca in 1990 and 1991. We used long stern lines to the dock and dinghied ashore. This saved us worrying about the self-steering being damaged and about uninvited visitors. It also gave us more privacy, but some of our friends objected!

(Above) *Greenland 1991. After five days of wind, calms, fog and rain the weather changed for the better to help me celebrate my birthday. This anchorage is at the mouth of Pakitsoq off the Vaigat. We explored it that morning, as far as we could.*

(Right) ***Badger*** *anchored in nine feet in Cayo Anclitas, southern Cuba. Clear water crawling with langostine, hundreds of sandy cays and not another yacht in sight. Note **Badger's** clear, uncluttered decks and the Rutland generator in the 'rigging'.*

BUY FOOD IN BULK BECAUSE IT
WORKS OUT CHEAPER THAT WAY

Chapter 21

A Penny Saved Is A Penny Earned

One of the most infuriating things about reading cruising books is the authors' coyness about money. You know that they are trundling around the world living an interesting life and enjoying themselves, but they refuse to tell you how they finance it — with the exception of those who don't have any to begin with. I have therefore decided to attempt to redress the balance by explaining how Pete and I find the wherewithal to go voyaging. This is not only to appease your curiosity, but much more importantly, because the way that we fund our cruising is the cornerstone of our whole philosophy.

To begin with, we always remember that the object of the exercise is to go voyaging. It isn't just to live on a boat, or just to visit other countries, or just to sail in different waters or even just to enjoy 'the way of a ship upon the sea'. It is a combination of all these things and more as well. We've always tried never to allow ourselves to get sidetracked from this main aim and when we've not actually been voyaging, we've been working towards getting away again.

Because our particular aim is to make voyages in our own boat, there is no way in which we want to sail from A to B, find work and then, when we have enough money, go on to somewhere else. That isn't cruising, that is leading an almost normal lifestyle, but simply changing your base from time to time and living on a boat. You go out to work every day, or whatever, then take a holiday and sail somewhere and then go back to work. It suits a lot of people — we've done it ourselves, but it isn't what we want to do. What is more, it is getting increasingly difficult to find jobs, not in the least because in many places there isn't enough work for the locals, let alone for itinerant sailors;

as well, there is every chance that in the place you really want to visit, there won't be work available at all. Voyaging to us, is about miles under sail, about passage-making, about travelling and seeing new places and then planning more voyages. To do what we want to do in a single lifetime is difficult enough, to do it when constantly harassed by the necessity to find work is impossible. Therefore, as we had no private means and no expectations, we decided that we would organize the work that we did to give us the most freedom that we could manage, on the principle that money = freedom.

"Work is the curse of the sailing classes", is one of my favourite themes. Going to work gets in the way of going sailing and so we want to do the minimum work necessary to provide us with the money we need. Neither Pete nor I have ever earned particularly good wages on the occasions that we have worked and yet, since we've been together, well over fifteen years now, we've managed to get in a fair bit of cruising. We are now also in the happy position of being able to voyage indefinitely, all things being equal, on an income that we have organized for ourselves. That sounds quite impressive, but it really isn't that difficult to do if you want to do it enough. The Chinese have a saying to the effect that "there are two parts to wealth — acquiring money and keeping money". We have taken this to heart.

To obtain the necessary wealth to go voyaging, the first thing that you have to do is decide how important it is to you to go voyaging because quite simply, this will affect how much money you will need — if you want to go voyaging more than anything else, you will be content with very little money while you're doing it. You then need to work out the minimum amount of money on which you can live and the best way to do this is when you are actually working. This way a lot of costs are constant and you will be able more easily to separate fixed costs from variable ones. Once you start voyaging, prices will vary a lot and make the whole thing more complicated. There are many advantages in living the same way when you are working as when you are cruising, by which I mean that you live as far as possible on a similar income, living on the boat, spending your money as you would when cruising. We always tried to do this and the idea behind it is that we were working solely for our freedom and therefore, any money spent on non-essentials meant that we had to work that little bit longer to gain our liberty again. Admittedly, we would buy ourselves more treats on the 'After all, we are working' principle, but they were bought in the full awareness of their being non-essentials and a step back from freedom. You need some compensations for going to work, but must never lose sight of what you are working for, otherwise before very long you will be out at work in order to afford to go out to work. Don't laugh — a lot of people do it. Think of the number of professional women who spend nearly all their salary on nannies, smart clothes and a decent motor car. If they are actually enjoying being out at work and doing what they want to do, then of course that's fine, but a lot of them have lost sight of their original objective, which was to get some more money in order 'to improve their standard of living'.

At first it is hard work and you always have to remind yourself of why you are living so frugally. You have to learn the theory of Cost Benefit Analysis and apply it to everything that you buy. What this means is learning to look at money in quite a new way. You don't say, 'It's only 30 quid', you say: 'If I invested that 30 quid, that would bring me another £3 a year forever and ever', which doesn't seem much to write home about, until you start to think how relatively few times £3 you need to live on. With this way of looking at things, 'a penny saved is a penny earned' was never more true. Don't forget you want to go voyaging — you don't want to work for the rest of your life. When you are out shopping, look at everything and ask yourself, 'Do I really need that?' If you're not sure, put off buying it until next week and then ask yourself the same question. Even in the small details of day to day life, the same applies. You love broccoli, but sprouts are cheaper; your jeans have worn through — try a jumble sale or second-hand shop before buying new and if you must buy new ones, at least get them in a sale. You usually go out for dinner on your birthday — buy yourself your favourite food, cook it at home, have two bottles of wine and it will still be cheaper — and you don't have to stagger home. One of the biggest savings is doing without a motor car. My mother always used to tell me, 'Oh, it's all right for you, you don't need one', but that's because we learned to live without one. When we were working, if we needed to travel any distance, we'd either use public transport or hire a car; otherwise it was Shanks' pony. You'd be astonished how much money you save. It isn't easy at first and it is easy to be negative about it all, but once you see that money invested and the income starting to come in, you suddenly begin to realize what it's all about. After a while, you will start to thrive on the challenge and enjoy the way in which choices have become simplified.

It took us a total of ten years to pile away enough to live on — with quite a lot of cruising thrown in. When we had to go back to England, due to family illness, we went out to work and salted some more away, otherwise we'd have carried on voyaging, very happily, on an income of £25 per week. After selling *Missee Lee* we had a little more to invest and then we went and did some more work for our friend, Steve, in the US, out of which earnings we also saved a fair bit. However, we continue to live and run the boat on £25 pounds per week and the extra money is invested and the income from it re-invested. This not only gives us a hedge against inflation, allowing us an increase in our allowance when we need it, but also means that we have sufficient capital to buy expensive pieces of equipment such as a new engine, without having either to reduce the money on which we live or go out to work.

Obviously, it's not that easy to put away say, £12,000 in a couple of years and you may not want to wait until you have enough saved up to go voyaging on a small income, but you can still make use of the idea. Let's assume that you have managed to save £5000. If you invest it in a fixed income investment at ten percent it will give you £500 per annum or say, £10 per week. You decide that there is no way you can live on £10 per week; however, look at the other options available. You can decide that you need £1000 per annum to live on or say £20 per week and go off cruising for five years, after which you will have no money and have to work again, back at square one. You can invest say £3000 giving you an income of £300 per annum or £6 per week and with £2000 cash, go off for two and one half years, as the money will be eked out by that constant £6 per week. At the end of two years, that £3000 will still be there. Or you can invest your £5000 and find some work while you're cruising to top up your £10 in the knowledge that after five years, you will still have £5000 capital and £10 per week. You will also have the security of the capital behind you in case of emergency and the knowledge that even with only £10 per week, you will never be destitute. Add to this the fact that if you are lucky enough to find well-paid work that you quite enjoy, you could well be able to invest your surplus, as well as not touching your fixed income — remember the idea of living to the same standard when you're working? — and in just two or three months, you will have added substantially to your capital. Now you may have enough to give you £15 per week, which is getting a lot nearer to your goal.

As far as possible, we have worked on the principle of never spending capital on normal living expenses. When we started cruising in *Badger* in 1983, we had £15 per week. It wasn't really enough, but we managed and at least we were off voyaging. And, as we weren't desperate for work, we found it quite easily, with a bit of help from our friends. Had we really needed it, I'll bet we wouldn't have found it. Because the £15 per week wasn't really enough, we lived on a bit more money — about £20 and saved all that we could. We worked in the Caribbean and then for a friend in the States, who paid us our best wages ever — $7.00 per hour and this was when £ 1= $1.20. At the end of about six months work, we had an engine in *Badger* and she had been given a mini re-fit including polyurethane painted topsides, polyurethane finished brightwork and top quality antifouling along with a new radio receiver and tape recorder. We had made her a new suit of sails and we had an income of £25 per week. We earned enough for all this in four month's full-time work and five or six month's part-time work, spread over a period of time in which we also sailed up from the Virgin Islands to the States and then returned via the Intracoastal waterway. From then on, we were effectively independent.

I believe that the important thing is to have a fixed income so that you know that in five year's time, you will still be sailing on £X per annum and can plan accordingly. We have found that gilt-edged Government stocks suit us best, as they are fixed interest. OK, so it's irritating to hear that you could be getting fifteen per cent when you're only getting ten per cent, but you've got enough to live on — why be greedy and anyway in five years you might be winning. Because we know our income is fixed, we don't need to worry what's happening to interest rates in the United Kingdom and can concentrate on voyaging.

Inflation is more of a worry and so, for that matter are exchange rates. The latter can be controlled to a certain extent by choosing the countries in which you cruise with care and if a place seem too expensive, you can always go somewhere else. In fact, we find that we live on our stores in expensive places and stock up in cheaper ones and have no real problems.

The best way of dealing with the worry of inflation is to endeavour to have a bit of surplus income that is re-invested. This can be done in several ways, separately or together. Say that you want to have £30 per week to live on. To do this, you would need £1,565 per annum. You've acquired what you think is the right capital to achieve this and if, for the sake of argument, you decided to invest it in Government stocks, you'd go to the Post Office, get some of their forms, fill them in and send off the cheque. After several days, they send you the bond certificates and you work out what you are actually going to get. It comes to £1,650 per annum. Now if you stick to your £30 per week, you will now have a surplus of £90 to re-invest. If you re-invest your surplus over £1,560 every year, you will soon be having a fair bit of extra money that you can start to draw on, when you need to increase to say, £32 per week.

Another way of getting a surplus is when you are changing money. If there are actually two hundred and twenty ickeys to the £, you pretend that there are two hundred and give yourself six thousand per week, thus winning about £3 every week. This too, can be saved and re-invested at the end of the year.

A third way to end up with extra money is by working the 'topping-up' method. To do this, you look in your purse at the end of the week and see what you have left. Then you take enough money to 'top-up' what's left to your allowance of £30. This can often result in quite large savings over a period of time.

Finally and our favourite method of saving money, is to make a long passage at sea — just think, three or four weeks at sea and you've saved yourself £100.

Obviously, we don't stick strictly to a weekly budget. When we are stocking up for a voyage, or if we see some exceptionally good bargains, we will buy them and adjust our allowance for the rest of the year accordingly. After a major stock-up, it may well mean that we actually only draw out £15 per week but have enough food on board that we don't require any more money.

Apart from the obvious advantages of living on income rather than off capital, there are one or two less obvious. For example, if you do as we do and buy your stocks through the Post Office, you in fact have a very liquid investment. If you need a substantial amount of money, you simply fill in one of the forms (of which you would have a stock on board) and send it off to them requesting them to sell x amount of stocks. The money will be in your bank account within a week of their receiving your instructions. This is, therefore, a form of self-insurance where instead of paying a premium, you live off the income. Admittedly, if you write off somebody's boat, you probably won't have enough to cover that (once again a smaller, lighter boat makes sense), but you will have enough to cover most eventualities, from damaging either your vessel or someone else's to medical expenses. Even if you should lose your boat, you will not be destitute and can go somewhere and start again. In fact, you might even have enough money to build another small boat and still have some left over for the first voyage.

We used to carry our money in travellers' cheques, but got somewhat disillusioned with them. Quite apart from the fact that you pay commission both when you buy and when you sell, the money is not earning any interest when it is sitting in your safe place aboard, as travellers' cheques. Also you need to take a passport ashore each time you use them, they are easily lost or stolen and complicated to sort out if that happens, a surprising number of banks don't like them and using these cheques forces you to change £50 when you only really wanted £30.

We went to our bank manager and asked him for a Barclaycard (Visa seems truly international). We then said that our present account was a deposit account (paying us interest) and that we would like to arrange it so that the Barclaycard people sent our account straight to him in order that he would immediately pay it from our deposit account. He couldn't think of any reason to refuse and so agreed to do it. We have used this system since 1985 and found it excellent. We never pay bank charges and we never pay interest on the money that we get out. The one and a half per cent charged by Barclaycard on a cash advance is cheaper than the commission on travellers' cheques, we get out the amount that we want and we often get the use of the money for several weeks before our account is debited. The Barclaycard itself is useful for paying larger bills in shops or for mail or telephone ordering anything that we need. Should we lose it, we have the emergency number to ring and until we get a new one, we can always use the old-fashioned system of asking our bank in England to forward a draft to a local bank.

I know that all this seems incredibly mean and penny-pinching and you are probably wondering how anyone can enjoy living in such a way. But it does work and we thoroughly enjoy living as we do. We get a lot of pleasure in seeing how far we can make our money go, in buying all the treats in different countries that we can't buy in other places and because we can live on so little, we are in fact wealthy. Poverty is having insufficient money to buy the basic necessities and comforts of life. Wealth is having more money than you need to live on at your chosen standard. We generally save some money every year, therefore we must be wealthy. Because we have chosen how much money we live on, we don't have any right to complain if we can't afford anything, so therefore it must be a case of we *won't* afford it, which is something entirely different. We live at a good standard and we never feel that we are missing out. Our boat has all that she requires and because we bought the best when we could earn the money, it doesn't keep wearing out or need replacing. We have more clothes than we know what to do with. I buy food in bulk, because it works out cheaper that way and so we generally have at least a year's supply of food on board. We can invite people round for the evening if we feel sociable — if not, we have our books for entertainment. We can visit any country we want to, as long as it has access to the sea and stay as long as its bureaucracy will allow us. We own what we have and we don't owe anybody anything. I wouldn't swop places with anyone.

(On this and previous page) **Badger** *visiting in St. Petersburg, Florida, February, 1992. Many of the details of the deck layout, dinghy stowage, and rigging can be seen. Jay R. Benford photos.*

SOONER OR LATER YOU MAY
WELL LOSE YOUR BOAT

Chapter 22

Peace Of Mind?

Once upon a time, no-one who went voyaging in a small yacht would even have considered taking out insurance. Eric Hiscock's **Voyaging Under Sail** (now updated and combined with **Cruising Under Sail**), carried by all serious cruising people, didn't even mention it and the great man himself was not insured for his excellent voyages. Nowadays, with more and more people making ocean crossings, a different type of person is taking to cruising and these people are concerned to protect their investment. Their insistence on being insured is such that the rest of us begin to question our own judgment when we gaily set off without any insurance other than our own wits, luck and money. For those of us voyaging on a small income, the cost of insurance alone will be enough to discourage us from taking it out. I have been told by a very respected yacht insurer that if you can't afford to insure your vessel, you can't afford to go cruising, but in my opinion that is a load of cobblers.

However, as is so often the case when one is unable to afford something, this apparently negative factor can turn out actually to be a positive asset, when one comes to look at aspects of taking out insurance that are not often discussed.

For a start, let's take the question of cost. To insure even a production fibreglass sloop (such as the insurers will have heard of) just to go the western Mediterranean will cost the best part of a couple of hundred pounds. This represents a large proportion of a small income. If you wish to venture slightly further afield to such adventurous places as the Azores, the cost will skyrocket. I can say this with some authority by the way, because I have spent some time in a job that involved me in arranging insurance for various yachtsmen. The majority of companies that insure yachts at a competitive premium, do so by avoiding anything at all risky. Although it is

possible to get insurance for just about anyone to go anywhere, in whatever way they choose, you'll have to dig even more deeply into your pockets for the privilege.

Putting the cost aside — perhaps your doting and worried parents offer to pay for insurance — a study of what is involved when insuring your boat will make you begin to wonder from where the Underwriters get their statistics and ideas. In a nutshell, it is much cheaper and easier for an absolute tyro to insure a boat to sail back and forth across the Dover Straits than it is for an experienced yachtsman to insure himself and one crew for a voyage to the Azores and back. Policies tend to be full of warranties and the breaching of any of these on any one occasion will make the whole contract null and void. Some people respond to this with the remark of "If they find out", but as the whole system is supposed to be based on mutual trust, I think that one should intend to act honourably in these things. Even before they consider taking on your vessel, the insurers will start to influence your decisions and therefore, your freedom. They would have thrown up their hands in horror at *Trekka* and would undoubtedly have laughed *Moonraker* out of court and yet both of these wonderful little ships did more than creditable voyages and looked after their crews extremely well. Underwriters have peculiar likes and dislikes. They detest wooden boats "of a certain age" and many won't touch ferro-cement. They insist on you having expensive surveys carried out and yet, even when the surveyor says that your boat is as good as new, they will put loadings against her because of her age. Underwriters have an absolute phobia about two people going sailing together. In many cases, for an open water passage (as they describe it), they insist that a third experienced hand is taken on the voyage. As far as we're concerned, taking a third person, with one or two exceptions, on a long crossing would destroy a lot of our pleasure. I've recently heard that the Underwriters are now more lenient towards a couple sailing from the United Kingdom to the Caribbean, but I fear that on checking the small print, you would discover that they would insist on you being a part of that awful ARC affair.

Having told you what type of boat you are permitted to sail and whom to take with you, the insurers will then start hedging their bets by telling you at what time of the year you must sail and how far you may go. Thus you can set off on a gale warning on 20th of August and be fully covered, while if you leave a week later, in settled weather, you may have voided your insurance due to the warranty saying that you must be across Biscay by the 31st. (Although insurance companies pay lip service to the principle that those that they insure must sail their vessels as though they were uninsured, in fact they seem happy to shell out for people who are incompetent and to quibble about paying out for misfortune.) In short, your insurance may actually force you to leave before you are fully ready or on a dubious forecast, because you are being pushed by the provisions of the policy. On arriving at your destination, you may then find on checking the small print, that you need to be based at a marina. I have had insurers demand that the boat spend every night at a marina while cruising in places such as northern Spain, Portugal or Norway, where compliance would be manifestly impossible. Had the owners of the boats accepted the policy, they would have discovered that the whole agreement had been made void due to the fact that they were in breach of the warranty. When I pointed this out to my clients they, without exception, changed their plans.

Thus, when you actually come to consider taking out insurance for ocean voyaging, you discover that, far from giving you peace of mind, you have a constant niggling worry that you may not be keeping within the bounds of your agreement with the Underwriters. You meet another boat and decide it would be fun to cruise in company with them and find you are not covered. Your crew goes ill, or changes his mind. A minor problem delays you from leaving by your artificial deadline. You decide that you'd rather go to the Azores than to northern Spain and have to try and alter your cover from a noisy public phone in France. In short, all of the freedom for which you have worked so hard is swept away at a stroke by the Underwriters — a sort of lurking Bogeyman whose one aim seems to be to frustrate your plans and poison your dreams.

So, what do we do about it?

Once again, the whole issue is covered to a large extent by adopting a somewhat different philosophy from what is considered to be the norm. The first thing that you have to accept is that sooner or later, you may well lose your boat. It happens to all sorts of sailors, regardless of experience and pretending that it can't happen to you is burying your head in the sand and also stacking up the odds against your fighting back, if the worst does happen. Therefore, the first thing to do is to ask yourself what would happen if you lost your boat. Will you be destitute? Will your life savings be scattered around you? Is there anything at all for you to fall back on? Not to put too fine a point on it, you have to be able to afford to lose your boat.

When we set off in *Stormalong*, she had cost us a couple of years of (very) part-time work and about £1,500. We had about £400 in our pockets and that was it. Had we lost her, we'd have lost the boat, but we could have borrowed money for a flight home and soon recovered our investment with a few month's work. Most of our possessions were not on the boat, but in fact dispersed around our families. On the other hand, *Badger* is entirely our home and all that we own is on her. She cost £11,000 and would not be easy to replace. However, we have to all intents and purposes, insured her because by following another part of our philosophy, we have accumulated capital and live off the interest from this. Thus in the event of our losing our ship, we have enough money to get back to the United Kingdom or wherever, and either build or buy another boat. Not a *Badger*, of course, but at least a boat. In fact, we'd probably have enough left over on which to go off again, albeit at a very modest level. So instead of forking out several hundreds of pounds a year to the insurers, we are actually getting income from our insurance fund. What is more, this is effectively a multi-purpose insurance, because should we be ill, we have a fair bit of money behind us to pay hospital bills. If you have a boat that you can't realistically afford to lose, there are only two alternatives: you insure her and take all the drawbacks that come with that or you sell her for something cheaper and, probably smaller, invest the difference and go and enjoy your freedom.

The fatal flaw in the above argument is third party liability insurance, although I do feel that we ought to be responsible for our own actions rather than taking out insurance in case we are careless. However, it would be nice to be able to go to the Underwriters and, showing a spotless record, get third party liability insurance, at a reasonable cost, as with a motor car. Unfortunately it doesn't quite work like that. Most insurers won't give it at all and even if you can get it, it will only be marginally cheaper than full insurance.

However, even this worry can be overcome by thinking the matter through and dealing with it rationally. For a start, the most dangerous situations arise from coming alongside and entering a marina. However, our philosophy already deals with this because we don't do either of these things anyway, as a general rule. If you keep away from other people's boats, its damn' difficult to do them any harm. Crowded anchorages may seem like another place of peril, but again other factors generally make you avoid these. Because you are not insured, you will try to be very careful to ensure that you are not boxed in lest bad weather should spring up and prevent your exit. As well, if you feel that the crowded anchorage is otherwise a safe one, you can bring yourself into its centre in perfect safety, kedging in and thus always under one hundred per cent control. This will take a lot longer, of course, which is why most people wouldn't even consider it. Finally, having anchored, you will know that you're not going anywhere you shouldn't, because you have plenty of decent anchors on board.

Again, if you have a smallish boat of moderate displacement, there is much less risk of doing third party damage anyway. She will be a lot more manoeuverable than a larger vessel and may be able to wriggle out of a tight corner. If you've completely bungled it, she will at least be easier to stop and do less damage to your unfortunate victim. As well, because you do all the work on your own boat, you may well be able to do any repairs needed yourself and a fellow cruising yachtsman should appreciate when an accident is an accident and accept your offer gracefully. There is always, of course, the spectre of the completely unreasonable person whose boat has been damaged by yours in spite of all your best efforts and this has been something that we've just had to live with. Recently, however, there has been a development to remove this worry. A German insurance company, called Pantaenius has opened an office in Plymouth and they offer third-party only insurance to yachtsmen. This is world-wide cover and, moreover, is very modestly priced. In 1992, I was quoted £40 for *Badger*; the quote being based on the unusual criterion of sail area. This seems odd, as a heavy, under-canvassed vessel could do a lot more damage that a light over-canvassed one. However, far be it from me to quibble with *anyone* who offers moderately priced, third-party cover. I have recently met a number of yachtsmen using this company and have heard good reports. I believe that they will also insure against total loss and third-party, all other risks being carried by the owner, but of course, this would be appreciably more expensive. Pantaenius offer the usual range of insurance, as well as the above, but unfortunately, as with most other brokers, they too insist on more than two people aboard for offshore passages. Perhaps as more voyaging couples take up their third-party only cover, they will come to realize how many hundreds of boats make trouble-free, happy, long-distance passages with only two people on board, and be prepared to consider offering them full insurance cover on sensible terms. However, I think that most of us who wish to voyage wherever we please and on our own terms accept the fact that we carry our own insurance and live perfectly happily with that knowledge.

If you sail without insurance, you are constantly aware of this fact and this makes you a better seaman. You know when you are going into a dead-end and plan an escape. You know that your engine might let you down and so you leave the sails ready to hoist and have the anchor ready to let go; you *always* use an anchor lamp and are blessed by your fellow sailors entering the anchorage at night; you hoist an anchor ball during the day, knowing that without it you are in breach of the Collision Regulations and therefore haven't got a leg to stand on should a motor boat come into you at twenty knots and slice you in two, because he will be held the innocent party.

The use of anchor lamps and anchor balls has often caused us to be involved in heated discussions. Americans in particular, have a bee in their bonnet about a thing called a designated anchorage. Now these do in fact exist in inland waters in the USA, but there is nothing in the COLREGS about them that I have ever seen. Rule 5011 is quite clear that, when at anchor, all vessels must show an anchor ball during the day and an anchor lamp at night and that is an end to it. In 1985, the Virgin Islands got a bit of a dusting from Hurricane Klaus. In St. Thomas, a cruise liner was entering and got into difficulties; while sorting herself out, she wiped out a number of yachts anchored in her lee. The courts held that the master was not responsible, because he couldn't have known that the yachts were at anchor, as *they were not showing the correct signals.* And yet the yachts were anchored where yachts are always anchored — perhaps in a designated anchorage?. It's no real effort to do the correct thing and may some time save you a heavy bill or allow you to claim against an offending vessel. Anyway, I think it's rather fun playing at being a real ship. Of course, the same applies to showing the correct navigation lamps: being uninsured means that self-interest will make you turn on your steaming lamps as soon as your start the engine, but nothing looks more lubberly than a yacht steaming under a tricolour lantern, quite apart from the danger that can arise from the fact that you know you're steaming and the other chap thinks that you're sailing and you both act accordingly.

At the end of the day, it's a personal decision and depends on how much sense of security insurance will give you. However, I think that perhaps you should ask yourself if it's worth all the sacrifices and whether you want to wait until you can afford it. Freedom is never very safe. If you need so much security — are you doing the right thing by yourself in going voyaging in the first place? Insurance won't give you your life back — sailing can be risky — but that's part of its appeal.

Finally don't forget that there is some consolation in knowing that if you are doing your voyaging on an income, this assumes that you have enough capital behind you to get another boat. She may not be your dream boat or anywhere near it, but at least you'll have something to sail and somewhere to live and with any sort of luck, you'll only use part of your capital to buy her, so that you'll still be better off than a lot of people who are dreaming of 'going off', but waiting until they can 'afford it'.

AN OUNCE OF PREVENTION IS
BETTER THAN A POUND OF CURE

Chapter 23

Self Security

There is probably more hot-air talked about safety than any other aspect of sailing. The yachting magazines are obsessed with it, chandlers try to sell it and Yachtmasters interminably witter on about it. Somewhere along the line it has been forgotten that the sport is *meant* to have a certain element of risk — that's what makes it a sport rather than a pastime; we are rapidly approaching the stage where it is considered foolhardy in the extreme to undertake any enterprise that could possibly put you in danger.

In matter of fact, sailing is a pretty safe occupation: as long as you have a half decent boat, she will look after you in most situations and also, the speed at which the whole operation is carried out tends to give you plenty of time to think things through. However, accidents do happen and boats fail to arrive at their destination, so that the risks entailed should be born in mind by anyone who wishes to achieve their allotted span.

In many cases, potential voyagers are as worried about health as they are about safety and have nightmares about a burst appendix in mid-ocean, but as with so many worries, rational consideration will make you realize how low the chances really are. This is not merely an anodyne statement — Pete will be the first to agree that I am one of the world's great worriers, but I do not consider my health to be something to worry about in our way of life. Most people in our society are surprisingly unfit and it is one of the many pleasant aspects of the voyaging life that one becomes increasingly healthy. Pete and I both enjoy the rudest of health and the only times we ever suffer from colds, is when we come ashore for any length of time. I believe that our largely vegetarian diet has at least something to do with this, but I'm sure that the fact that our lives are satisfying and under our own control has even more to do with it. We do a lot of walking, having no land transport and enjoy a fair amount of fresh air — although

in cold places, even when sailing, you might be surprised at how much time is spent below. No doubt the exercise we receive is good for us — standing up to cook in a boat that is underway knocks aerobics into a cocked hat — and we have a good rowing machine, in the form of a dinghy.

Assuming that you are in generally good shape, with no heart condition, bronchitis or similar complaint, I believe that you can more or less forget any worries about illness. Most illnesses are acquired by contact with others, so that the risks of being seriously ill at sea are lessened by this factor. As well, an appointment with your doctor will pay off here; if you explain to her what it is that you are intending to do, she will be only too happy to prescribe a small but satisfactory medicine chest for you — and probably ask if there are any spare berths. Antibiotics are an essential, so that if you are seriously ill, it can be controlled until you arrive at your destination — in many cases it may well be cured. In **Daughters of the Wind**, David Lewis quotes the case of a climber on Mount Everest who had acute appendicitis, which he kept under control for a considerable time with antibiotics. However, if you want them to continue to work like a miracle, only take them if there is no alternative. Powerful painkillers are worth having in case of broken limbs — our doctor very wisely gave us some tablets for this purpose. He pointed out that although they take slightly longer to work, which may be harrowing at the time, there is no risk of jabbing a needle in the wrong place — or worse still, breaking it and it also means that should you be searched by Customs officials, there won't be any embarrassment about having a syringe and powerful drugs on board, with the consequent suspicion of drug abuse. We also carry medicines against diarrhoea (never used), chest infection, etc. and antihistamine, largely due to my strong reaction to insect bites; I rarely take them, but sometimes they have been useful. Obviously this is not the place to go into the matter in any detail and a qualified doctor, preferably one who is a sailor, is the person to see.

Accidents are less easy to legislate for, but planning and common sense can help a lot. You should ensure that you're unlikely to be thrown about down below, by fitting lots of handholds and using a galley/chart table strap. Broken limbs are really pretty unlikely until you are getting to the age of worrying about brittle bones, but the risk of this is reduced by good handholds above and below decks and by avoiding the necessity of going on deck in rough weather. You should have a first-aid book on board and ideally, at least one person should have a working knowledge of first-aid — you can tell the other clot how to bind up your sprained wrist — and your first-aid kit should have the usual triangular sling, etc. Inflatable splints are a good idea for the real worrier, but if push come to shove, you can always use an oar. To be quite honest, the things that we use most are sticking plasters and we have found the metre strips of Elastoplast™, which can be cut to the correct size the best. Plasters made from cloth seem to stick a lot better than the plastic ones like Band-aid™. Butterfly sutures — sticking plaster designed to span a deep cut and hold the edges together, are worth having aboard as they substitute for stitches, a gruesome task to perform or to have performed upon oneself. One thing that I would consider essential is antibiotic powder. We've used this on several occasions in the Tropics on cuts that we felt could go septic and have never had any problems at all, including the time that Pete got fairly severe coral cuts. However, as with all antibiotics, this should be used with great discretion. The only other things we've ever had to use are pain-killers for headaches and so on.

The only time either of us has been ill while underway happened while we were on passage from Iceland to Norway; I developed a rash of blisters all over the left hand side of my back which was followed by excruciating stabbing pains. I worried myself into a virtual decline, convinced that I had skin cancer, AIDS and anything else that came to mind. In fact it turned out that I had shingles. The nice Norwegian doctor told me that there was nothing he could do about it, the illness must run its course, but he could prescribe some pain killers. As we had those, I declined gracefully. If you enjoy good health anyway, I can see no reason why going to sea should suddenly change you into a chronic invalid. I think that it should also be remembered that before we had inoculations against the various terrifying illnesses that we no longer risk, people contracted these diseases and survived. Even taking the worst case, with our present opportunities for excellent nutrition, we are probably a lot healthier than our forbears and should we be unlucky enough to be struck down with an illness, there is every chance that we would recover, even without the use of the drugs we have on board. Don't worry about it — you're more likely to be knocked down by a bus — and one of the points about having some capital behind you is to cover that sort of emergency. Incidentally, our medical costs while we have been voyaging have totaled £5 to date, the fee to the Norwegian doctor. We have our teeth checked in England, but in the last ten years, I doubt that we've had three fillings replaced between us. We generally don't eat sweets or desserts, which may have something to do with it.

If you still feel concerned about being lumbered with an horrendous hospital bill, due to some dire and sudden illness, you may wish to consider catastrophe insurance. Our friend Danny Greene, an American living in Bermuda, has this and the idea is that he foots any hospital bill up to $10,000, after which the insurers pay. This might be something worth following up, but I'm not sure whether any British companies would do it because unlike the US, we do have free medical care in the UK which would cover any catastrophe.

Voyaging on a small income, you will find yourself beset by people trying to make you spend money on safety, but in reality it is not something you can buy, it's an attitude of mind. Take man-overboard equipment, for example. This is the favourite obsession of them all, but nobody ever seems to remember that in a large number of cases, boats are only sailed by two people. "Post one crew member to watch the victim", goes the advice "and don't let them lose sight of the person in the water. Another crew member must lower the sails while a third person starts the engine and prepares to motor back." How you do all that when you have been left by yourself, no-one ever mentions. Particularly when voyaging, you should be aware that *if you fall overboard you're dead*. Chances are that the boat will be self-steering, the other person will be down below, maybe even asleep; it will probably be minutes and possibly hours before they realize that you've gone. It might well be blowing and with poor visibility. With many boats, the rig will be tied down with vangs and preventers, which will make it difficult to retrace the course straight away. Singlehanded, the person attempting to do the rescue will have an appalling job trying to get you back on board, even assuming that by some miracle they do get back to you. Man overboard ladders and sugar scoop sterns sound fine, but in a big sea and with a madly rolling vessel, you'd need a great deal of courage even to approach the stern, which would be threatening to knock your brains out on every wave. The moral is: DON'T FALL OVERBOARD. An ounce of prevention is better than a pound of cure. Good guardrails will stop you from going over and the lines should be checked frequently; leading control lines back to the hatch will mean that you don't need to go on deck anyway; a reliable and powerful self-steering gear will look after steering in heavy weather while you can be safe down below. If you have to go on deck, you should know where all the handholds are and a good safety harness should be worn at night or in heavy weather. The rope to the clip should be fairly short, so that if you do slip and slide under the guard rails, you will not actually end up in the water— that way you may be able to haul yourself back up, or at least give the side of the boat some welly so that the person below will hear the noise and come up to see what's wrong. Incidentally, in rough conditions, you are much more stable sitting down or on hands and knees and should scramble about the deck, forgetting about being *homo erectus* for the time being.

Many people say that you ought to wear a lifejacket in a dinghy and this is undoubtedly very good advice. However, for cruising people, it is not very realistic because if you have rowed ashore to go shopping or exploring, you will not want to lug a lifejacket around with you and if you leave it in the dinghy, it's likely to get nicked. Ensuring that the dinghy is unsinkable is a reasonable precaution and after that, like falling overboard, it's a case of being aware of the danger and using common sense. In all honesty, there is no real peril in overloading a dinghy with people who can swim, when you are in a tideless area with warm water and in daylight. In bad weather at night, with cold sea and strong tides, when everyone is bundled up in oilskins, it's a different story and most people are perfectly capable of assessing the risks for themselves. Wearing lifejackets, in fact, can often make you much more clumsy and therefore more likely to get yourself into trouble. I think too, that such devices can lead to a false sense of security— it's a fat lot of comfort to know that your head is being supported at the correct angle above the water while you perish from exposure.

Safety does not need to cost a lot of money. Good ground tackle is not really expensive, especially as a percentage of the overall cost of your yacht, and may save your life. Maintenance takes more time than money, but makes for a much safer vessel. 'Eternal vigilance' just takes effort.

Everyone knows that fatigue leads to mistakes and mistakes may lead to danger. However, this is an aspect of safety that can be approached in different ways. Admittedly, an electronic navigator does not get tired, but it would be much better to spend more time in devising ways of saving the crew's energies instead of spending money on devices to help them when they are already tired out.

A self-steering gear is a marvelous piece of safety equipment and they can be built quite inexpensively from designs in books such as Bill Belcher's **Yacht Wind-Vane Steering**. When considering self-steering as safety equipment, I think it becomes self-explanatory as to why I would suggest a mechanical, wind-vane gear rather than an electric auto pilot. However, it is worth mentioning the smaller electric auto pilots are not very reliable, when used for long distance voyaging. Yes, I know that they take them in short-handed, round-the-world races, but most boats have several back-ups on board and anyway, they're talking of one race not dozens of passages over many years. As well as the spectre of unreliability, very few auto pilots work really well down wind and especially not in heavy weather — just when you want it to work. And, of course, there is the usual worry about flattening the batteries. If you can afford the extra outlay and envisage doing a lot of motoring, maybe it would be worth having one, but if you

can only afford to buy (or build) one type, I would suggest that a wind-vane would prove a better bet.

This piece of equipment will not only save you from the physically tiring work of steering, but will allow for both people on board to get sufficient sleep, as it can be steering while one person makes breakfast and the other sleeps, for example. Another happy talent of a self-steering gear is that it steers with great accuracy and doesn't suffer from lapses in concentration, so that as long as you have done your bit, checking that the wind hasn't shifted and altering the self-steering if it does, (ideally, its control lines should be led to the hatchway) you will know what course has been steered, which will assist you with your navigation. Your self-steering will never fall asleep on watch. It is also useful when coastal sailing because it will "hold the helm" while you carry on with pilotage, double checking a doubtful light, taking a fix and allowing the other person a few hour's sleep. Moreover, while the self-steering concentrates on the helm it frees you to keep a better look-out. Standing in the hatchway you can take a slow and careful three hundred and sixty degree look around the horizon — there will be no risk of a ship sneaking up behind you in your blind-spot, as you huddle in the corner of the cockpit. For most of the watch too, you can sit below and read a book, write letters or contemplate the infinite, warm and dry. Therefore you are rested and alert and in far better shape to cope with any emergency. Because of all this, you will enjoy your passages far more, which mightn't have a lot to do with safety, but has a lot to do with the fact that enjoying yourself is what it's all meant to be about.

Making your little ship easy to handle is another thing that can be done at the expense of time and thought rather than money. As already mentioned, this will help you to stay on board, but it will also stop you from getting exhausted. The motion of any small boat — and by small boat I mean anything under 80 feet or so — in heavy weather is extremely tiring. If you have to add to this wrestling with sails and ropes, then you are increasing the risk of exhaustion. It's not only heavy weather that can cause fatigue, however, fluky wind conditions with calms and squalls, or wind coming from all over the place can mean a lot of sail drill which will soon start wearing you out. To add insult to injury, when the wind does finally settle down, you may be too weary to care and continue jogging along with too little canvas. We have found that the ease of making sail is one of the great advantages of the junk rig, particularly when going to windward, when an undercanvassed boat in a lumpy sea will get nowhere and be diabolically uncomfortable.

Your boat should be properly sorted out down below. It costs very little to arrange for proper stowage for everything and a boat that stays tidy in heavy weather adds greatly to morale; bolts or turnbuttons are fairly cheap, the latter can be made out of wood, in fact, and will keep doors and drawers shut. Sinks should be deep enough that they don't spill water onto the floor and if they are fitted with seacocks, these should be easy to get at so that you can shut them off to stop the drains gurgling. Another source of annoyance is clinking bottles and other rattles and thumps. Again, such minor nuisances can prevent you from sleeping and so become, in fact, a real problem. The heads should be in a place that is comfortable at sea, otherwise the female part of the crew will suffer unnecessary privations and even the risk of injury. It is easy to fit extra handholds and here I would say that pillars are better than handles; they suit all heights and can be used with an arm hooked around them, leaving the hands free. The table should be well supported so that people can lean or even lurch against it. Good leecloths ensure a comfortable and safe night's sleep. A galley/chart table strap leaves hands free and makes work more relaxing. There should be at least one 'downhill' seat for the person on watch to be able to sit in comfort. Light switches should be within reach of the smallest person on board, regardless of the angle of heel. Hatches and windows should be waterproof - cold and damp people function very poorly — and don't have much fun. Oilskins should be easy to get at and there should be a safety harness attachment point on deck, accessible from down below.

When you have sorted out the physical aspects of the boat, safety can be courted in other ways. A lookout should be kept at all times and if you have self-steering and somewhere comfortable to sit, there should be no reason for both of you to be asleep. On the other hand, three days of difficult steering could exhaust you both and if there is nowhere comfortable from where you can keep watch while the other person sleeps, you will start thinking of excuses not to bother. It's not essential to sit in the cockpit continually gazing into the dark when you're in the middle of the ocean, but you should have a good look round at least every quarter of an hour, which also means that you can keep an eye on the course and check that you have the right amount of sail up. The chances of getting run down are slight, but they exist — we've had several near misses where we've had to alter course to avoid a ship in the middle of the ocean. As well, the boat is sailed much more efficiently when there is always someone on watch and it's satisfying to know that she is sailing at her best.

A hotly debated safety item is the liferaft. If you're voyaging on a small income, you can't really afford one — the initial cost is bad enough, but the cost of servicing them is the killer. If you carry crew other than your spouse, this is a cost that will have to be faced, but in this book we are not talking about that situation. If you don't have them serviced, they are, once more, a false sense of security. On *Badger*, we have a collision bulkhead forward. This in fact, is the bulkhead abaft the chain locker and is watertight. Access to the chain locker can be gained through two watertight hatches and an incidental advantage is that the chain locker can be fitted with a drain hole so that we don't need to bother about stopping up the hawse pipe. All of our bulkheads are bonded to the hull,

making for watertight joints; the entrances between the saloon and the sleeping cabin and between the saloon and the lazarette can be fitted with washboards so that if we are holed, we can isolate the section in question while attempting to seal the hole by nailing on a plywood patch (an advantage of hard-chine, wooden construction), maybe even able to use underwater epoxy to seal it. We kept the lower washboard, forward, permanently in place while sailing among the ice in Greenland and often ship it on long passages as an extra precaution. The wooden hull and its "cork", insulation have a fair amount of natural buoyancy and we feel that we should be able to survive most hits. Humphrey Barton reckoned that a well-built boat should be able to hit a solid object at five knots, without seriously damaging herself, and for that reason suggested that this was a sensible speed at which to make offshore passages — a point worth considering. It should be remembered however, that in the majority of cases where a boat founders, the cause was not collision, but the failure of a through-hull fitting. I suppose that what I'm saying is that, with a large amount of expenditure in thought, a medium amount of expenditure in effort and a little expenditure in money, a lot can be done to try to ensure that you will never have to abandon your yacht in the first place.

When all our efforts have failed, when we are standing on the top of the cabin with the water around our knees, then I suppose that we will take to the dinghy. We will try to be consoled by the knowledge that we are taking to a life*boat* rather than a life*raft*, which will mean that we have a chance of doing something positive to find land rather than having to drift about in the hope that someone will pass by and rescue us. We will make sure that we have put in something for a sail and a compass. We will take a space blanket and jerricans of water. We will take sunburn lotion and fish hooks and if we have time, I will take jars of honey and peanut butter— lots of calories and not too much protein, which utilizes water in being broken down. This time we will wear our lifejackets and try and take spare clothes to keep us warm and prevent chafe. We will have a flare gun, but we won't have an emergency transmitter because, like Eric Hiscock and Bill Tilman, we believe that having made the choice to go sailing offshore for our own pleasure, we should look after ourselves and have no right to ask anyone else to expend vast resources and risk their lives, in order to rescue us from what is effectively our own folly. We would expect another ship to stop and assist us, for that is the way of the sea, but we would not wish to institute an expensive air-sea rescue operation on our behalf. Quite honestly, unless we were near the coast or in a shipping line, I wouldn't expect to survive. And therefore, until that terrible moment, we will spend our efforts, resources and ingenuity in keeping *Badger* afloat, because with her lies our best chance of staying alive, because she is the best lifeboat we could have.

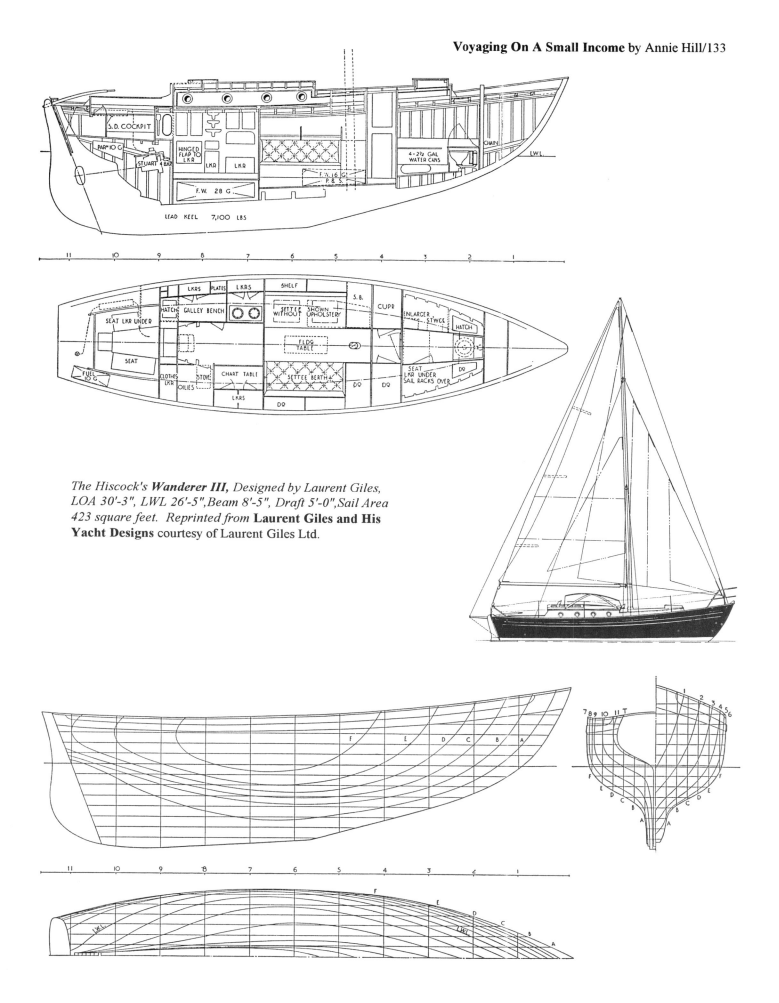

The Hiscock's **Wanderer III,** *Designed by Laurent Giles,
LOA 30'-3", LWL 26'-5",Beam 8'-5", Draft 5'-0",Sail Area
423 square feet. Reprinted from* **Laurent Giles and His
Yacht Designs** courtesy of Laurent Giles Ltd.

Chapter 24

Landfall

What a splendid book that was — it's a pity to finish it and yet I couldn't help reading it as fast as I could to see what would happen next. Daft really. It's another of those books that I would never have bought from looking at the cover or reading the publisher's blurb. It's amazing how many of the swops we get are such good books. It's a bit different from *Stormalong* days when we would take over all our Penguins and end up with Westerns. All those wealthy sailors have certainly improved the quality of the swops. It must be quite something to go into a book shop and buy a score or so of *new* books — still, we get the benefits. That last lot has jammed up the shelves again, they were glad to get rid of them without swopping at all. Finishing this one now was a bit of good timing, because I think it might be an idea to put the boards up in the companionway and sit in the hatch to keep a lookout, now we're approaching land.

I suppose we've done quite well arriving at this time. We might have to heave-to until daylight, but shouldn't have long to wait. In fact, it would be worth popping a couple of reefs in each sail and slowing down — I'll do that now. Typical to have a fair wind now, when for so many days we couldn't lay the course. And all those sail changes — thank God for junk rig! I can't imagine what sort of state we'd be in now if we'd been changing jibs and reefing and unreefing slab reefs every five minutes. Hmmm, even with those two reefs in we must be doing four knots. Still, I'm not sure exactly how far we have to go yet, and it's not that long until it will start getting light. I suppose if we had a brand new chart, we could sail straight in, but then, knowing what these people are like, they'll have been altering the harbour anyway. Like when we arrived in Santa Cruz at two in the morning to find out that they'd extended the mole. It was a good thing that the harbour was well lit. I suppose though, come to think of it, we wouldn't have gone in otherwise — hardly any of the yachts would have had an anchor lamp up probably, and it

spoils a good passage to conclude it by sailing into a fellow yachtie.

Considering all the headwinds and some fairly strong ones, too, I suppose that this has been a pretty good passage. I've really enjoyed it, in spite of the weather. I imagine that the self-steering has more than a little to do with that — it's nice to be able just to pop my head out of the hatch every quarter of an hour to see how things are getting on and not having to sit and shiver in the cockpit, steering and cold and bored. People like the Pyes and the Hiscocks were real heroes. I wonder if I would voyage without self-steering. I know Pete would. What, with doing the sail handling from the hatch and never having to steer, we lead a positively cosseted existence. So much for the healthy, outdoor life. Let's see — on watch for twelve hours a day — look out four times an hour, that's forty-eight times at say, two minutes per lookout, which is being generous — ninety-six minutes or an hour and a half in total. I'd probably get more fresh air walking to the bus stop to go to work! I think one of the things that I really like about self-steering is being able to eat dinner together. Eating in shifts always seems uncivilized somehow and it's a shame to go to all the trouble of cooking vegetables to perfection and then have to keep them warm. We've certainly eaten well on this passage — hardly anything went bad and I reckon that we've at least a week's stock of fresh stuff left. At least that means we don't have to rush ashore to go shopping, as soon as we've dropped the hook. We should be able to buy all sorts of treats here; everything is so cheap, from all accounts, with lots of choice. Didn't the crew from the *Kittiwake* say that the market is really excellent here? I wonder if they'll be in harbour, they may have moved on by now but I should imagine it's odds on that there'll be at least one boat we know.

What a beautiful night it is now! And there's Orion and his faithful hound still in pursuit of the Bull with his red eye glowing. Nice to see them so big and clear again — I remember how peeved I was last time we were in England, when I realized that I couldn't always see them. The wind is dying away a little now — all to the good really, so long as it doesn't go calm. I hate having to motor the last few miles, it spoils the whole passage somehow and it's such fun to *sail* into a new harbour. I should pick up the lighthouse — or at least its loom — soon. Then I'll check it against the one on the List. It's a silly little game to play — I've no idea what I'd do if they didn't match — we know perfectly well where we are. I suppose that I'd just curse the List and the Locals for changing their navigation aids without so much as a by-your-leave.

Funny to say that we know perfectly well where we are. I suppose if we weren't used to taking sights, we'd have said that there's been no sun for a week and yet the sextant shades make the disc of the sun stand out quite clearly, even with the overcast. Now, when we don't need clear blue skies, the cloud has disappeared, of course. Still, it will be nice if it's fine in harbour — it's not a lot of fun lugging back shopping in the pouring rain and I've got quite a bit of laundry to do, which will need to dry. God, how I hate doing the washing! Although I'm bound to say it's been less of a chore since they invented liquid detergents — at least you don't need to rinse everything out a dozen times. We could do with some water too, it's been too rough to collect rain from the decks; One thing about a bit of a rough passage is that it makes me appreciate *Badger* all the more. We really have got her sorted out now, what with her good basic design and all the little improvements we've made over the years. That booze locker has been marvellous and yet I've never seen anyone put bottles in what is effectively a drawer before — or read about it either. I ought to send the idea to **Practical Boat Owner**. I'll bet I have a few bruises around my behind from the galley strap, though! Remember that time we were having spag bol and just as I was carrying the plate to the table, the boat lurched and it all slid off, some on the floor and some into the open cassette drawer! Just as well the floor was clean — I've kept the drawer shut since then, too. I shouldn't have made the sauce so wet: with the wooden plates, the food normally stays in place. I wonder what sort of plates the manufacturers of those non-slip mats reckon you use. I can just see it now, the boat heels, the plate stays put and the food slides off! I can't see that a gimballed table is any better — the food would be going up and down and anyway, you'd either eat it at chest height or knee height.

Hello — is that a ship's light over there? I do believe it is. I can guess that we're going to the same place, but I'd like to know where she's coming from, on that course. I can't remember the last time we saw a ship, but we did see that yacht a week or so ago. I wonder if they were keeping lookout and saw us? It's strange that, although we've seen plenty of yachts, we've never met a yacht in mid-ocean and stopped for a chat like you read about. I suppose that the ones that we do see might be

trying to call us up on VHF. Probably think that we're antisocial and don't want to speak! You'd think that it might cross their minds that not everyone has a radio. Mind you, that woman on *Fairwinds*, that forty-five footer, took the biscuit. "Oh yes, you have to have VHF in the Caribbean, now". "Whatever for? When did this happen?" we asked, all of a panic. "Oh it's absolutely essential. You can't book a table without one — the restaurants don't use telephones any more!" Well, that was a relief — hardly something to worry us.

I suppose that those people are the epitome of what Pete calls Consumer Yachting, really. They had all the right gear, whether it was the latest electronics, the underwater video or the trendy yachtie clothes. But that boat wasn't sorted out at all. Let's see, we've seen them in 4, no 5 different places and in each one they were getting something fixed. Oh, and wasn't she cross when she found that there was no laundrette available? She must never have hand-washed in her life. Then they had all those crew problems and yet the crew seemed nice enough and so are they. I suppose that even a boat of that size is a very small space when you can't really get away from one another. It's a shame to think how long and hard they have worked to get their dream boat and sail away and now, I don't think that they are really enjoying it, that much. They've made their life too complicated and I think that in many ways they have too much money. Whatever they want they can buy, they eat out all the time, stay in marinas and take a taxi to the biggest and best supermarket and yet they never seem to have *fun*. Maybe 40 years at work destroyed their ability to do that. We'll never be rich, that's for sure, but we certainly know how to have a lot of fun.

The wind seems to be quite warm. If it weren't for the direction, I'd think it was blowing off the land. It will be off the land, when we turn the bottom corner of the island, and my poor, deprived olfactory senses will be in for a treat. I don't think there's anything quite like that sensation of smelling a new country — especially in a hot climate, with the much heavier scents borne on the warm breeze. On the other hand, I remember the smell of the wind when it blows over the gorse on the south coast of England and the blossom, bathed in the sunshine, smells just like coconut. How lovely England is in the summer and how much more I have come to appreciate it from being able to compare it with other places, so many of which are very beautiful themselves. Those hedges of blue hydrangea in the Azores and the wonderful, shaggy palms of the Caribbean. The colours of the water in the Bahamas, almost unreal so that you would not believe them if you saw them in a travel brochure. The superbly clear air in the Arctic with blue, blue sky that seems to stretch upwards for miles, while further south, it seems quite close to you. The loch sides of Scotland, covered in purple heather; the marshlands of the Carolinas, blue and gold; the pure white of Iceland's glaciers, the splendid orange cliffs of the Algarve and then Laguna Grande of three colours and a hundred shades. The perfect blue of the sea and sky, the dark green mangroves and burnt green cactus where the iguanas scuttered and the reds, oranges and ochres of its desert landscape and crumbling hills. That is still one of my outstanding memories. We must go back — and yet I'm almost afraid to, in case memory surpasses reality.

How strange to be approaching a new land and to be thinking of ones already seen. And yet in many ways I don't like to speculate too much on what a place will be like, because I enjoy discovering it for myself, without too many preconceptions. I suppose that's why I always find it annoying when people tell me what places I must go and see and where the best anchorages are. I know that they are trying to help and are generously passing on knowledge which is often useful, but I close my ears to their descriptions and leave it to Pete to remember the information that we will be pleased to have, once we arrive. It's just as well he has more sense! I feel the same about yachtsmen's guides in some ways — I'm glad that we have them, but they can spoil the sense of adventure. It must have been so wonderful in the early days of ocean voyaging, the fifties say, when cruising yachts were a rarity, but on the other hand, we now have self-steering and polyester ropes and boats that don't leak and, for that matter, we have officials who know what to do with us and lots more information to make life easier for us. I suppose, in fact, we can have the best of both worlds, because if we want to explore, we simply turn off the beaten track and suddenly find ourselves in a place with no yachts at all and have to start working a bit harder. Maybe that's the great appeal of high latitudes, although Mr. John found a Pacific island that had never been visited by a yacht before. Which one, I wonder? Wise man to keep it a secret.

Quick look round and a cup of tea, I think. Earl Grey or Assam? It's nice and warm tonight — Earl Grey. To eat or not to eat, that is the question. How on earth do these people with their 'snack boxes' keep from getting obese? One of the advantages of poverty is that we can't afford to fill our lockers full of mini-Mars bars and packets of crisps. Some boats must eat their way across the Atlantic, "snacking heavily" through the watches. I suppose that's why they have labour intensive boats — to burn off the calories. They must have high dental charges, too. Oh, go on, it's the last night, I'll have some of those almonds I've got put by — they'll only go to waste. Fat chance of that, but I might as well have some before they get eaten as tapas by other ravenous yachties, once we're in harbour. Tea's brewed, back to the hatch. How nice not to have to put a jacket on. I can never decide at what stage the rain becomes strong enough to make it worth putting on a jacket. Invariably if I just shove my head out and it's raining, I'll find we've wandered off course or I think I see a ship's light or decide to put a reef in or shake one out. If I put my jacket on, everything will be fine and I'll be back under the pram hood before I even get damp. The amount of mental effort I put into being lazy must say something.

What was that? Yes, definitely the loom of the light. One elephant, two elephants, three elephants, four elephants, five elephants ... two flashes every five seconds. Put down tea (see, it always happens when it's inconvenient) and pick up Light List. Well, blow me — they're both the same, we're nearly there now, it's only a low powered one and not very tall either. It may be imagination, but I think the sky is beginning to lighten — surely the stars aren't so bright now? The wind's really easing now, we'll have those reefs shaken out before we reach that light, if I'm not mistaken. Then I'll wake Pete and he can start making navigating noises. We should be in in time for breakfast — and we have some eggs left, too. How splendid — we'll have the whole day. We'll be able to clear in and sort ourselves out at our leisure and then we can go ashore and explore. How I love long passages, they make our landfall even more exciting. What an idiot I am, I'm getting butterflies in my tummy just thinking about all that we'll be doing today. And then, there's a full night in bed to look forward to, as well. How can anyone appreciate the luxury of eight hours' sleep who has never kept watch and watch about? I love a night watch like tonight's though, with *Badger* sailing so well, the stars shining and the air so balmy. Wonderful. Wonderful boat, wonderful night, wonderful passage, wonderful life.

EGGS REFRIGERATED ! NO SEÑOR

Appendix I
Preparing And Storing Food For A Voyage

The basic rule for keeping any food in good condition is to store it in a cool, dark place. If you're cruising in the Tropics, it is obviously impossible to fulfill these desiderata, but it's worth keeping these requirements in mind when deciding where to stow things. As far as possible, food should be kept below the waterline and in dark lockers; however, if this can't be achieved a lot of things will still keep perfectly well.

Tins

While plenty has been written about the care of tins for voyaging in small boats, perhaps reiteration would not come amiss. As soon as a tin gets damp it will shed its label and start to rust. Now, while it's easy enough to recognize a tin of bully beef, ham or sardines by its shape, most of the rest look very similar to one another and 'taking potluck' may well end up being rather more exciting than one's guests had anticipated. The old favourite, which seems to work perfectly well, is to mark the tin distinctly or make a note of its code and write it down in your stock book along with a description of the contents, then remove its label and varnish it — rather safer than taking off the label first. This will protect the tins quite adequately, providing that they can't move about too much and chafe one another. We don't bother doing this on *Badger*, (she said with nauseating smugness), because we're not really troubled with damp lockers. It is however, worth removing labels on tins you buy in a lot of places anyway, due to the ever present risk of the ubiquitous cockroach, who unfortunately is rather fond of paper. Tins take up a vast amount of room and one idea which I believe is worth consideration is to leave the tins of fruit on the shelves. Many people like to buy in cans of fruit for desserts, but it strikes me that instead of using up all that space, it would be far more sensible to have fresh fruit, which also has the advantages of having no added sugar, being better for you, cheaper and nicer to eat.

A recent alternative to tins that is becoming easier to obtain is a variety of vacuum wrapped products, in aluminium foil containers. For voyagers on a small income they are the type of thing that is really only of academic interest, but on the other hand, they are worth knowing about in case you see any that take your fancy and want to buy it in as a treat. They come in a variety of products and I have seen such things as chili con carne, sweet-and-sour-pork, pies with puff pastry, hot dog sausages and also a number of fish-in-sauce meals in these containers. Most of them can be boiled in water, but those with pastry obviously need an oven. They are lighter and more compact than tins and, having tried one or two, they seem to taste better and have the type of food that you expect with frozen rather than tinned products. However, as I mentioned above, they are not cheap and I am including them largely for the sake of interest.

Tetrabriks

Another long-life wrapping that is becoming increasingly popular is that of Tetrabrik cartons such as orange juice is sold in. These containers are also good for voyagers, being lightweight and easy to store. We have bought milk, orange juice, tomato puree and wine in this type of container and found them all quite successful. However, they do need to be carefully stowed as if they can slide about, they are likely to chafe and the contents will be damaged. They are not bio-degradable, either, because there is a layer of plastic sandwiched between the cardboard and the metal foil.

Preserving meat

If you like to eat meat, it is quite feasible to can it yourself in good quality jars such as Kilner make. The ones with the metal lids should be used, not those with glass lids. A good quality pressure cooker must be used and it is essential that it works at 15 pounds pressure. A new gasket and safety valve should be fitted before doing any processing. It is a long process, needing about 45 minutes for a 16 oz. jar of meat and you need to take a lot of care when doing the job, because if the meat is not processed properly, with a perfect vacuum, you would have an excellent breeding ground for botulism — a lethal bacteria. North American farmers and backwoods people do a lot of their own canning and sell wonderful pressure canners as well as having a fair bit of literature about the subject. Although people also can their own fish, it does seem rather a risky business and I think you'd need a canner with a fitted pressure gauge to feel really confident of it. I wouldn't risk it, personally.

Meat can also be preserved by brining. A rule of thumb, going back to days of yore is that you fill your container — I would suggest an ice cream tub or something similar — with water and then add sufficient salt until the brine will float a potato. The meat is then cut into suitable sized pieces and immersed in the brine. A cover should be put over the lot, weighted down to keep the meat under the brine and then the whole lot is left alone for several days. I would top up the tub with brine before putting the lid on. The books say that the meat should be kept at no higher temperature than 50 °F, but a friend of mine brined down meat in the Tropics with great success and it kept for quite a few weeks; none had gone off by the time he finished it, but I can't say how long it would have kept. It's the method that was extensively used in the days of Nelson, and although many complaints were made about the quality of the meat, the actual method of preservation seemed to work all right.

Salting can also be used for keeping bacon. Ideally, if you like bacon, you should buy a whole piece cured in the old-fashioned way, such as can be bought in Spain and Portugal. This can be hung up somewhere (so that it will keep dry) and you slice bits off as you need it. Unfortunately, it's not particularly cheap and only a windfall or bacon addiction would give sufficient reason for small income voyagers to buy it. However, if you get an offer of cheap bacon that is already cut up, it's worth putting by in salt. I have done this on several occasions and found it quite successful. I normally use a flattish plastic container and put a layer of salt on the bottom and then put one layer of bacon strips on this. Then another layer of salt and then another layer of bacon, until all the bacon is in the box, covered with salt. Kept as cool as possible, it will last for several weeks. Ideally, only preserving salt should be used, but I've used the stuff with added ingredients, so that 'when it rains it pours' and never had anything dreadful happen. Modern curing methods, with water injected into the bacon, reduce the successfulness of this method, because the bacon is really too wet. I have also salted down bacon from tins, which usually have between 15 to 20 strips in them, which is too much even for us to eat at one sitting and found it quite satisfactory. Before using it, you thoroughly rinse it in fresh water to get rid of the excess salt. Of course, as far as health goes, all the additives in bacon and all the salt as well, can't be a particularly good thing, but cooking bacon does smell marvellous. For all these preserving techniques, I would recommend reading **Putting Food By** written by Ruth Hertzberg, Beatrice Vaughan and Janet Greene, an American publication that I have seen for sale in British book shops.

Crackers, etc.

We always like to have some sort of crackers on board as a change from bread or for when we don't have any. These are rarely in moisture-proof packs, but keep well in polythene containers or biscuit tins, which an extra coat of paint or varnish will make reasonably rust-proof. We had Ryvita on *Stormalong* and like everything else, it got damp. However, we found that it could be made quite delicious by popping it onto the toaster for a few seconds and crisping it up. This turned out to have a secondary advantage because the little maggots, whose existence had hitherto gone undetected, objected strongly to the intense heat and wriggled out of their hole, whence they could be flicked off. It's surprising what you can get used to.

We are very partial to curry and like to have poppadoms with it. I have found the ones produced by the ladies of India, you know, the ones with the red writing and the child's face on the packet — the ones they sell in health food shops — keep extremely well in those tins that one buys Danish cookies in. Somebody you know will always get one of these tins in at Christmas and will give it to you when they've eaten all the bikkies. In fact, you could ask for

one or two tins for a present and eat them yourself. I don't know quite how many poppadoms a tin will hold, I'd estimate at least 100, so two tins will keep you going. You need to get them when you can, because not every country is lucky enough to have a large community of curry eaters, so therefore you can't buy the poppadoms. The same applies to curry spices, by the way, they can be difficult to get hold of. It's best to buy them whole. I should say and then crush or grind them, but *I* don't because my wrists just don't seem to be up to it, although I do give them a cursory going over with the pestle and mortar and the curries still taste fine. Root ginger is a problem, too, but keeps very well if you buy big lumps of it and keep it in your coolest spot. It can last astonishingly well; some I bought in St Maarten in early January, for about $1 a pound was only just finished by the time we arrived in Scotland in early June. Just scrape of the dry bit where you last cut it and cut some more off. When all else fails, you can use dried.

Flour

Once you leave a cool climate, keeping whole meal flour for more than a couple of months is impossible because it either goes stale or rancid. If you actually buy it in a hot climate, it always seems to develop beasties. If you want to use whole meal flour all the time, there is only one solution and that is to buy a grinder and grind your own. White flour, of course keeps for ever. However, the main reason that I carp on about whole meal everything is that it tastes better. It's also better for you because it's high in fibre and as well, in a vegetarian diet, whole grains are an essential source of protein. Pete and I have never really been able to get enthusiastic about sacks of wheat berries and grinding our own, so we muddle along somewhat ineffectually, buying brown flour where we can. The best thing, we've decided, is to carry plenty of whole meal crackers (such as Ryvita) and to buy brown bread once brown flour becomes a problem. Unfortunately the crackers are often expensive and the bread occasionally is and so, as I say, we muddle along.

Rice, Pasta, etc.

Pete and I prefer brown rice, which again is worth buying carefully due to the risk of wildlife. Whatever you do, don't trust plastic or cellophane bags to protect any of your food from either wildlife or damp. As I mentioned elsewhere, polythene appears to be porous and if it is actually immersed in water, will allow it to penetrate. Cellophane doesn't seem much better. The beasties that stow away have amazingly efficient choppers and will make short work of both types of wrapper. This is a nuisance for pasta, as the pre-packed stuff would otherwise keep quite well. If you are free from unwanted guests and have a dry boat, the pasta will last for ages in the wrapping in which it comes. We've often eaten spaghetti that has doubled the Atlantic; it has kept dry in its home behind the backrests in the saloon. Otherwise, pasta will have to go into good quality polythene containers. If you're wealthy, Tupperware is probably the best, but if you're wealthy, you're probably not reading this. However, if anybody is wanting to buy you something, you can always suggest some Tupperware. Our best source of really excellent containers was Glasplies in Southport (near Liverpool) who had incredibly robust plastic buckets with immovable lids which they sold me for about 20p each. They were designed to keep horrid chemicals in, so have done a good job of keeping interlopers out. They also do a pretty good job of keeping me out too, as the lids take about 5 minutes to ease off and they are therefore used for bulk storage. Ice cream containers and Kraft margarine containers used to be good but seem to come with much flimsier lids, now. The trouble is that we don't buy either, so we have to keep a weather eye out for them. Rubbermaid® products, made in the USA are excellent if you can get them; they are also a bit pricey.

Butter and Margarine

Susan Hiscock wrote about putting butter into clean glass jars and covering the top with a layer of salt, in order to keep it and I'm sure that the idea would work well. Butter can also be bought in tins and this is also a satisfactory way of keeping it. Salted should be chosen, where possible, because it will keep better when opened than will unsalted. We bought some in Venezuela, probably EEC surplus, for a mere 30 pence per 14 ounces; it was very good and kept extremely well. In fact I found a stray tin 2 years after we had bought it and it was still in perfect condition. Gibraltar is another good place to buy it and the cheapest is sold by Moreno's, under their own name. All too often, however, we can't afford butter and have to make do with margarine. Both hard and soft margarine keep quite well, but the soft is the easiest as it generally comes in cartons. The hard stuff, wrapped in grease proof paper needs either to be stacked so that nothing can squash it when it gets warm, or put in plastic boxes for the same reason. I wouldn't recommend buying 2 kg containers by the way, unless you do a lot of baking, because it usually goes mouldy before you can finish it. I normally buy 250g or 500g containers of sunflower margarine which stack well and it doesn't taste as bad as the other types. I've kept it for several months and it seemed to be OK, although sometimes there was a little mould on the top which needed scraping off. (French stuff is better packed, with a sheet of grease proof paper between the margarine and the plastic lid.) Margarine is generally full of E numbers and preservatives and the 'best before' dates are very conservative, as you would imagine.

Milk

Dried, skimmed milk (e.g. 'Marvel'™) keeps well, is good in tea and coffee, but is quite bulky. Mixed to put on your muesli it is quite palatable. *Dried, skimmed milk, with added vegetable fat* (e.g. 'Five Pints'™) keeps about 18 months and is compact, but doesn't mix well in near boiling tea or coffee and doesn't taste too good on the muesli. *Dried whole milk* cannot be sold in EEC countries but is available in such places as the Canaries (still officially a 'deprived' country) and the Caribbean. This is usually in vacuum packed bags and keeps excellently, tastes good on the muesli, is not too expensive, but really needs to be mixed with cold water before adding to tea or coffee. The 'best before' date is very conservative. *Long-life* (UHT) whole milk has a strange taste that not many people care for and goes off quite quickly when opened. Long-life skimmed milk has much less of the strange taste (which I assume is caused by the cream) and keeps better after opening. Both types can be bought in either plastic bottles (difficult to dispose of) or Tetrabriks (which squash flat, when emptied) and the price varies immensely. The 'best before' date is conservative. *Tinned, evaporated* milk can be diluted with water and used as fresh, but has a taste to it that not everyone likes. *Tinned, condensed* milk is only any good for people who like sweet drinks.

Incidentally, in the USA, you cannot buy either simple, pasteurized milk (it all has added vitamins and is homogenized, for a start) and the only preserved milk is tinned, evaporated. In Canada the situation is slightly better because the 'Marvel' type of dried milk is available.

Eggs

You can Vaseline™ them or grease them to keep the air away from the yolks; you can put them one at a time in boiling water for 10 seconds each in order to put a thin lining of sealed albumen around the shell; you can varnish them. However, what I do is to put them in plastic egg boxes and turn the boxes through 180° every week. The egg boxes made by Carver will hold the largest eggs, worth bearing in mind because many places don't sell them conveniently graded into sizes.) I drilled 1/4 inch holes in each hemisphere, because otherwise the boxes trap condensation which in turn causes mould to grow on the egg shells; this eventually penetrates through to the egg making it quite inedible. The boxes are turned in order to keep the yolk suspended in the egg; if it lies against the shell, it comes in contact with the air and then goes bad. The eggs keep for ages — at least six weeks, BUT MAKE SURE THAT THEY HAVE NOT BEEN REFRIGERATED. As the eggs, well ... mature, the white slowly changes from clear, through yellowish to greenish. Eggs soon become a bit stale for eating boiled, but can be scrambled with garlic or made into Spanish omelettes when well past their prime. They can be fried, with plenty of pepper, too, but once the yolk gets on a bit, it breaks as soon as it makes contact with the pan. When they reach this sort of age, I would recommend fried egg sandwiches with lots of tomato ketchup. We usually find that with Annie's Patent Method eggs last very satisfactorily. In some places it's difficult to buy eggs that aren't already bad. The worst places that we've come across have been the supermarkets in Roadtown, British Virgin Islands and the south west of Ireland, where stock rotation meant picking up the glasses of Guinness one at a time, in order to top them up as the head settled.

Cheese

Due to the fact that Pete doesn't care for cheese, I have not had as much experience with keeping this as I would like. Because it's also quite expensive these days, I suspect that we wouldn't eat much of it anyway. What I have found to last well is, of all things, the pre-wrapped packs of cheese that you buy in the supermarket. They are vacuum packed and so the air cannot get in to start mold, (although some of them seem to have better vacuums than others). They do leach oil a bit, which makes them look a bit off-putting, but if you let the cheese breathe for an hour or so after opening them, they taste fine. I have heard that wrapping cheese in a vinegar soaked cloth works, but it didn't seem to on the one occasion I tried it — maybe I didn't use enough vinegar. You will also find that cheeses sealed with wax will keep, but once you break into them they go off as quickly as any other, so stick to small ones.

Yoghurt

I love yoghurt and would eat it every day and live to be a hundred, but unfortunately it needs milk and as you will have guessed, milk is often expensive and hard to come by. If you can afford it you can either make your own with a yoghurt maker (non-electric ones are available); or by heating the milk to the correct temperature and putting it in a Thermos; or by obtaining some Keffir, which is a sort of super yoghurt culture, which does not need extra heat. You may be able to get it in a good health food shop and a few yachts have it on board. As it grows with use, they will probably have some spare to pass on. It will die, though, without regular doses of milk, although can go 'hungry' for several weeks first.

Drying food

When I was in the States in 1984, I had access to an electric food dryer, a sort of very cool oven with racks for the pieces of food and tried drying a variety of different foods. In all honesty, I can't say that I was impressed with the results. I have also tried drying vegetables and fruit on frames covered in fly screen and these have been equally disappointing. Bearing in mind the nutritional losses when drying food, I can't honestly say that it's worth the effort.

That being said, however, I have had success with mushrooms and small chili peppers. The mushrooms I cut into thin slices and dried them out on a baking sheet set on the fiddles of the cooker, with the hot plate very low. This was when I had the range; even with the door open, the oven was too hot and tended to cook them. With my Taylor's cooker, I could probably put slices in the warming oven to dry. When they had cooled completely, I packed them in glass jars and they kept well having a slightly stronger flavour than when fresh and being a more than welcome addition to the galley supplies. Small chili peppers can be strung up by their stalks and hung up in a reasonably dry spot in the boat, where they will eventually shrivel up and dry out. Be careful though, some of them get increasingly hot as they dry out. For lazy people, they can be bought in Portuguese markets already strung into little necklaces. If you get too many without stalks, salt them down, sliced longitudinally into halves or quarters with at least 4 parts of salt to 1 of peppers by weight.

I have known several people successfully dry fish — gutting, beheading and splitting them and then hanging them in the rigging (if you have such a thing). You have to be careful to bring them in before the dew falls or in showers of rain. Personally, I don't think it's worth it. I have also eaten dried reindeer meat, which was effectively freeze-dried, by being hung up to dry in temperatures that were well below zero. It was quite delicious. However, the French couple who had dried the meat had spent a winter in Hudson Bay to achieve this end, which I think is beyond the ambitions of most of us. We ate it before we were out of the Labrador current because we felt it mightn't last too well in warmer climates.

Bananas can also be successfully sun-dried, splitting them lengthwise and turning them over. They go brown and chewy and are a nice thing to have on watch.

Bottling Fruit

With most fruit you're as well eating it fresh. If you have a load of cheap or free fruit though, you may want to try bottling it. I suggest using Kilner jars and if you don't want to find all your efforts wasted, it's usually worth using new lids. I have found that the new style Kilner jar, with the glass lids and plastic rings are much less effective than the old-fashioned ones with metal lids. The metal lids do rust though, and it's worth putting Vaseline on them to reduce the chances of this happening. The jars should be packed carefully to ensure that there is no air trapped in them when you pour in the (hot) water. Having filled them with fruit, top up with water to within an inch of the lip; they can be processed in your pressure cooker, using a couple of pints of boiling water. With a 15 pound weight, a 16 ounce jar would normally take about 10 minutes. Alternatively, they can be done without the weight, and then you should fill the pressure cooker with sufficient water to come up to the necks of the jars, clamp the lid on the pan and cook for 30 — 40 minutes. In this case you must not use sea water, because it will boil at a lower temperature than fresh water and not be hot enough to kill off the bacteria. You need to use the trivet in the bottom of the pan in either case. It is not necessary to add sugar when bottling fruit, although it helps to preserve the colour. Honey can be substituted if you wish, giving a more unusual flavour; if following a recipe you need half a teaspoon of honey for every one teaspoon of sugar, as it is twice as sweet. Honey is also easier to store than sugar.

Appendix II

Preparing And Storing Fruit For A Voyage

The first rule is if possible, NEVER BUY ANYTHING THAT HAS BEEN REFRIGERATED. I don't know why, but refrigeration seems to destroy the will to survive in fruit and vegetables and once they have been refrigerated, they go downhill fast. In some places, such as the Virgin Islands, it's hard to buy anything that hasn't been refrigerated and half of it seems to have been actually frozen. In such a case it's worth seriously considering sailing to another place to stock up. Otherwise, you are best to concentrate only on such robust characters as oranges, onions and cabbage and forget most of the others.

The second rule is to *check over everything as you bring it on board.* You are checking for insects and their eggs, as not only are such visitors unpleasant, but you can't afford to feed them as well as yourselves. If you've brought produce in boxes, there is the added risk of rats or mice. People we know who have had rats on board have said that they are almost impossible to get rid of before substantial damage has been done.

Generally speaking, the objective seems to be to keep fruit and vegetables dry and, as far as is possible, in the dark. There are one or two exceptions to this. Quite a few things object to being packed too densely and this also has to be taken into account. Ideally, one would wrap certain fruit in tissue, but that seems a bit expensive and prone to disaster, should the tissue get damp. Root vegetables seem to appreciate having a bit of dirt on them, the rest should be clean. Nearly all fruit and vegetables should be washed in about 1/2 a gallon of fresh water to which a tablespoon or so of household bleach has been added — the bleach kills off any moulds on the skin. For exceptions to this rule, see below. They should then be dried, either with a clean cloth or out in the sun and then stacked away carefully. Personally, I'm not that keen on the nets so beloved of aspiring voyagers. Quite apart from being an unsightly nuisance, the fruit and vegetables often get damaged skins from the thin string, are susceptible to chafe and bruising as the nets swing about and are in the light. Of course, one would ideally have a vegetable and fruit locker made out of slatted wood, with adjustable slatted shelves, for stacking everything one layer deep. However, I'm assuming that you have to make do with what you have. A deep locker makes quite a good bin for long term supplies and they are best supplemented with the little plastic baskets about 18" x 12" x 6" that you can buy in hardware stores and the like. Wicker baskets are also very good except for the fact that they are ideal nesting material for a variety of insects. Softer fruits and vegetables do not take kindly to having heavy weights on

them, so one has to be judicious, with onions at the bottom say, and tomatoes at the top. The little baskets make picking over easier than a deep locker. PICKING OVER IS ESSENTIAL, as just one bad potato can affect a dozen within a few days, so that all dubious ones must be removed straight away. Recommended times for doing this job are given below, but obviously as the stuff gets a bit older, or if it's of inferior quality, you need to check it more often. It's a bit of a bore to put it mildly, but is makes you feel virtuous, like so many boring things. Also when people ask, 'but what do you *do* at sea?' you can answer: 'I pick over my fruit and vegetables', which is a guaranteed conversation stopper because no-one likes to ask why. Finally, just remember that fresh food is much nicer than tinned food, as well as being generally cheaper.

I'm not sure how the vitamin C content stands up. Studies I've read on fresh food imply that once picked, fruit and vegetables lose vitamin C at a catastrophic rate, so that a week old cabbage had hardly any left. As this ruined all my carefully nurtured ideas and prejudices, I decided that it must be wrong. However, Scurvy is a very real threat — I've met people who have suffered from the first signs of it, due to eating a wholly tinned diet. Pete and I never seem to have had any signs of it; we have never taken vitamin supplements, but have always carried fresh food, from which I would conclude that the fresh stuff retains enough vitamin C to keep Scurvy at bay. Vitamin C is destroyed by heat, water and air. Only tinned tomatoes and fruit juice retain vitamin C (don't ask me why). Pressure cook or steam your vegetables for the minimum of time, so that you don't lose the vitamins in the cooking water and don't cut them up until you need them. If you're still worried, take vitamin pills and anyway, have them on board in case you can't get hold of any fresh produce and it's too cold to sprout your own.

The following does not attempt to be an exhaustive list of fruit. However, there should be sufficient different ones for you to be able to judge fairly accurately how long the strange object that you're buying will keep. Keeping times will of course vary, depending on how hot your hot climate is, how cool the cool one, what is the sea temperature, how good is the ventilation and how low down on the boat things are stored. It's also worth bearing in mind that one side of the boat may get more sunshine than the other, or that you will be predominantly on one tack and stow your fresh stuff accordingly. If you look after your fresh food carefully, you may be pleasantly surprised as to what you can carry for a passage.

Apples

These keep quite well as a general rule. Avoid bruised fruit; the best apples for keeping are hard ones such as Granny Smith's; bleach wash and dry; hard apples can be stacked quite deep; *pick over weekly*. In *cool* climates they will keep *all winter*, up to *8 weeks* in the Summer. In *hot* climates, they will probably have been refrigerated; if not, *2 - 3 weeks*.

Apricots

These will keep fairly well if bought when firm, in which case they will never develop their full flavour, of course. Avoid bruised fruit; bleach wash and dry; stack no more than three deep; *pick over daily*. Usually rather expensive in *cool* climates, but they will keep up to *2 weeks*. In *hot* climates up to *1 week*. A good source of vitamin A.

Bananas

If you buy them at various stages of ripeness, the theory is that they will ripen gradually and give you a steady supply. PICK OVER VERY CAREFULLY FOR COCKIES AND OTHER NASTIES; if you only have small quantities, separate them, bleach wash and sun dry; can keep up to *4 weeks,* but in *cool* climates it is difficult to buy green ones. In a *hot* climate they usually take about a *week* to ripen and will then last *2 days*. If they all ripen at once, peel them and split them in two then sun dry them and eat like figs and dates. They go brown and sticky by the way and don't look anything like the commercially dried ones.

Berries

Apart from cranberries, which keep for months, these won't keep more than *2 days*. Eat them and enjoy them when you buy them. If you come across loads of free ones, bottle them in water — sugar really isn't necessary. (See Appendix I).

Cherries

If bought under ripe these will keep for a few days. Again bleach wash and dry carefully. They should keep for *a week,* less when it's *hot.* You can also bottle them in the same way as Berries.

Currants

If bought under ripe, they probably won't ripen very successfully. Generally treat as berries. If very firm bleach wash, shake dry by tossing them in a clean cloth. There are usually one or two bad ones that you miss so they'll probably only keep for *2 or 3 days* in any climate.

Dates and figs

These can both be successfully sun dried. I don't know about fresh dates, but fresh figs will only keep for *2 - 3 days* in a *hot* climate - a little longer in a *cool* one.

Gooseberries

Being harder and less sweet, these will keep better than most berries. Bleach wash and dry; stack in small boxes; pick over every *2 days*. *Cool* climates only, would last *1 week*. These could also be bottled, sweetened with honey or made into a very pleasant jam that turns a tasteful shade of pink.

Grapes

Buy as firm as possible. Bleach wash and hang up to dry in the sun. This is one fruit that I would recommend hanging up; drape bunches over a line stretched across the fo'c'sle or some such place, where it's a little cooler. In *cool* climates small grapes might last up to *2 weeks*, although the only way you're likely to be able to afford any is if someone gives you them from their greenhouse! In *hot* climates, maybe *4 days*.

Grapefruit

The best grapefruit I have ever eaten we bought in Venezuela. They looked dreadful with green and badly marked skins, but were as sweet as oranges and we ate them for dessert. Not long after, we bought some in the Dominican Republic. These were so sour that we couldn't eat them so I bottled them in a honey syrup. They still tasted awful and we didn't eat them at all, in the end. We approached grapefruit cautiously for a long time, after that.

They keep well. Bleach wash and dry; they can be stacked quite deep; *pick over* every *2 days*. In a *cool* climate, they are usually too expensive, but if you found some at a reasonable price, they would last up to *2 months*. In *hot* climates, *2 - 3 weeks*.

Kiwi fruit

These keep quite well. If you're lucky you could get *10 days* out of them when it's pretty *cool* and they are sometimes quite cheap, but in a *hot* climate, I'd recommend eating them within *3 days* of purchase.

Lemons

Lemons are the best anti-scorbutic around, with the exception of strawberries; they are not particularly edible raw, unlike strawberries. Make fresh lemonade from them or put hefty slices in your gin and tonic, or rum and tonic for that matter and then suck the lemon down to its skin at the end of each glass. That way you don't waste any alcohol either! Of course, you can squeeze lemons into all sorts of things when you're cooking or over pancakes and fish.

Buy firm ones of any size. Bleach wash and then hang them up by threading some strong twine through the nipples (ouch!) and pulling it taut between two points; ensure that they don't touch one another or swing into anything else. In *cool* climates, *2+ months*, in *hot* climates, *1+ month*. If stacked rather than hung up, *pick over every 3 days*; they will keep about half the time.

Limes

The reason that we poor English sailors are called 'Limeys' is because of the lime-juice that the Board of Trade insisted each British ship must carry. Indeed, I believe that they have a duty to provide it, if it is requested by any registered vessel, but I fear that I am probably wrong. Unfortunately it was all done in error due to some fool of a clerk reading 'Lime' for 'Lemon', because limes are nowhere near as well loaded with vitamin C as lemons. However, squeezed into equal parts of rum and water, they make an excellent pre-prandial snorter and are a palatable way of taking in the fairly generous amounts of vitamin C that they do have. Treat and store as lemons.

Mangoes

Sometimes when under ripe, fruit like mangoes may take 3 or 4 days to ripen. In which case they will keep *3 or 4 days*. Usually you will need to eat them immediately. They are, by the way, an excellent source of vitamin A.

Melon

Watermelon are too big to try and keep because once ripe, you'll need to eat the whole thing and the space could be better utilized. The little round melons with the orange flesh which come under a variety of names are, in my opinion, the most delicious. Buy under ripe, bleach wash thoroughly as they are quite susceptible to mould and dry. Stack one layer deep. In *hot* climates, *1 week*, in *cool* climates a *fortnight*. The trouble with buying them too under ripe in a cool climate is that they may never ripen. Anyway, they are usually far too expensive for small income voyagers. Honeydew and similar rugby football shaped melons will last about the same. Less subject to mould, but with an inferior flavour.

Nectarines

A cross between plums and peaches, nectarines seem to keep more like plums. Even in England they are often quite cheap when bought in mid-summer. If bought under ripe, you will never get the full flavour of them. However, it's worth doing for a passage. Bleach wash and dry. Stack up to 3 deep until ripe, after that one deep. *Pick over daily* - if you've obtained a large quantity, they'll go ripe pretty quickly and you may need to check them more often - moving the ripe ones to the top. Also turn each one daily, because if they rest on one spot, that area will soon go bad. A bore, but they do taste lovely. In a *hot* climate, *3 - 6 days,* in a *cool* climate, *4 - 14 days,* assuming that they are not very ripe when bought.

Oranges

These are one of the best voyaging fruit. They keep well and are high in vitamin C. I've kept them for 2 months sailing between Canada and Norway, but have never had enough to last longer. Thin skinned ones seem to keep slightly better than thick skinned ones; in the countries where they are grown, green-skinned ones often have superior keeping qualities. They are susceptible to mould so it is important to bleach wash and dry thoroughly. Stack up to 4 deep (any more and the bottom ones may get squashed). *Pick over every 3 days* for the first couple of weeks, *every other day* as they start to deteriorate; *every other day* in *hot* climates. Good quality ones will keep *3 - 4 weeks* in a *hot* climate. In a *cool* climate, they will last up to (and maybe beyond) *2 months*.

Passion fruit

I can't honestly say how well these last, as I've never tried to keep them. I know that they will keep *4 days* in a hot climate, because they lasted that long in Venezuela. We ate them in that time so they would probably have kept longer. They would be worth experimenting with if cheap (Pete isn't fond of them, so we didn't). I can't imagine ever being able to afford them in a cool climate.

Pawpaw/papaya

These would only be bought by poor sailors in a hot climate. They are delicious and sometimes free so worth trying to keep. Obtained under ripe, they will last up to *1 week*; even ripe ones will last *2 days* in the *Tropics.* Probably worth bleach washing if you're going to keep them more than a couple of days. Can only be stacked when very firm. Another use for your limes.

Peaches

They can be surprisingly cheap in England in mid-summer and very cheap in other countries. Again, if you buy under ripe, they will not develop their full flavour, but will keep better. Bleach wash, especially the furry ones you'll buy in hot places. Stack no more than 2 deep. *Pick over daily* - and also turn every day, for the same reason as nectarines, which incidentally, seem to keep rather better.

In a hot climate they will last 3 days, a little longer if bought under ripe. In a cool climate, 1 week, maybe even 10 days if you're lucky.

Pears

Soft pears don't keep more than a couple of days, whatever the climate. Hard pears, treat as apples, they should last *2 - 3 weeks* in a *cool* climate, probably even more if they are very hard. In a *hot* climate, they have probably been refrigerated and will only keep *3 - 4 days*.

Persimmon/Sharon fruit

If you've never come across these, they look rather like large tomatoes, with a big leaf on top. They are eaten when they are very ripe and the skin is almost translucent, otherwise they are inedible. In *cool* climates they are expensive, but often sold under ripe in which case you might buy yourself some for a treat and they will last about *1 week*. In *hot* climates, if bought under ripe, they should last *3 - 4 days*. Bleach wash first and inspect under the leaves for cockies, etc.

Pineapple

These are usually too expensive to buy in cool climates, unless over ripe in which case they will last about 2 days. In *hot* places, they are often very cheap. Bleach wash carefully, they are susceptible to mould and sluice the leaves out thoroughly to get rid of hitch-hikers. Sun dry. Stack 2 or 3 deep and examine daily. They should keep at least *1 week*, maybe more if bought well under ripe. They are ready to eat when one of the leaves pulls out easily.

Plums

If bought too under ripe, these will never ripen, so you'll have to chuck them out. Buy slightly under ripe. Bleach wash and dry, stack up to 3 deep, *pick over daily.* They will last *4 - 10 days* in a *cool* climate and *2 days* or so in a *hot* climate. If you get offered a load from somebody's garden, bottle like berries or make into jam (1 lb. of fruit to 1 lb. of sugar).

Pomegranate

These are ideal fruit for eating on a tedious watch, when the self-steering is doing the work, but you have to sit up keeping a continuous lookout. Using a pin, you can pick out one seed at a time and while away the hours. I've never tried keeping them in a hot climate, but in a *cool* climate, they will keep *2 - 3 weeks,* if well-ventilated. Bleach wash certainly, in a *hot* climate, as the tips would make an ideal nest for nasties. I would guess at *1 week to 10 days*, with care.

Rhubarb

I can't imagine anyone wanting to stock up on this, but if you fancy some, it will keep *1 week* in a *cool* climate. If you're given loads of it, bottle it in sweetened water, as with berries.

Tangerines, satsumas, clementines and mandarins

As with other citrus, these make good voyaging fruit. They also present you with one of life's little challenges as you attempt to peel them in one. I distrust people who mock your efforts — I'll bet it's only because they can never manage it. Clementines are the most difficult, because of their thin skins. However, they do seem less susceptible to mould than the thick-skinned satsumas. They can be incredibly cheap — about 10p a kilo in Mallorca in season. Bleach wash. Stack 3 or 4 deep. *Pick over every 3 days.* In *cool* climates they will keep up to *4 weeks* for thin-skinned, hard clementines, *10 days to a fortnight* for satsumas. In *hot* climates, from *3 to 10 days*, depending on the variety.

Moving on board while you are building has absolutely nothing to recommend it. Some lockers had sanding dust in their corners a year after launching!

Appendix III

Preparing And Storing Vegetables For A Voyage

This section is on vegetables. Before reading this, I suggest that you read the introduction to **Appendix II**, if you haven't done so, which mentions such things as washing, insects, etc.

Our basics are onions, garlic, carrots, cabbage, potatoes and green peppers, if we can get them cheaply enough. With that lot, you can't go too far wrong.

Artichokes (globe)

Definitely not recommended for small income voyagers as if they're cheap they are also likely to have all sorts of beasties about them, they take up a lot of room and are poor nutrition. They are also delicious, so I'd probably succumb to temptation and worry myself into a decline in case I'd brought anything on board with them. They will keep *a week or so* in a *cool* climate and *2 or 3 days* in a *hot* one. You cannot bleach wash them because they will trap the moisture and go bad, so if you store them, don't say you weren't warned.

Artichokes (Jerusalem)

I've never eaten them, so I don't know, but I'd guess they'd keep like carrots or better.

Asparagus

Chance would be a fine thing - I can't imagine ever being given the opportunity of having so much asparagus that I'd need to worry about storing it. I'd estimate about *3 days*, but I'm only including it for completeness.

Aubergines

Like all squashes, aubergines will keep for several days. If the stalk will come way without being cut, remove it. Bleach wash, don't stack more than 2 deep. *Pick over every 3 days.* Good ones will keep *1 week* in a *hot* climate, even *2 weeks* in a *cool* one.

Avocadoes

In Venezuela, I kid you not, they grow avocadoes as big as footballs. Try splitting one of those in two and filling it with a few prawns for a starter. The way to consume these is as **Guacamole**, which is mashed avocado mixed with finely chopped onion, tomatoes and chili peppers (as hot as you want) with some lime juice added to it. Piled on crackers it is heavenly and huge as they are,

it's a full meal. To be honest, they weren't particularly cheap, even there, but we ate them anyway. When you buy normal sized ones, bleach wash and dry carefully. Pack no more than 2 deep and *pick over daily* to find the ripe ones. Bought unripe, even in the *Tropics* they will keep for *3 or 4 days* and in a *cool* climate, *a week* or more. There are dozens of lovely ways to eat avocadoes, but de-stoned with mayonnaise or French dressing takes some beating.

Bean sprouts

You will probably grow your own anyway, but in a hot climate eat the *same day* and in a *cool* climate, within *3 days*.

Beetroots

I can't get terribly enthusiastic about these, but in some places they are cheap and you may like them anyway. Bleach wash and examine the stalks carefully. Sun dry. Stack 3 or 4 deep. *Pick over every 5 days.* Some we bought in the Bahamas, which would be considered a *hot* climate, lasted *10 days*, before I pickled them (which is the only way I enjoy them). In a *cool* climate, I'd expect them to last *3 - 4 weeks*. If you like beetroots, or are given some and have to eat them, you may wish to cook them as **Borsch**, a Russian soup, which consists of 2 large onions, 2 large carrots, 2 stalks of celery, 4 ozs cabbage, 2 tbs. olive oil, 1 3/4 pints of water, 8 oz can of tomatoes, 1 lb.cooked beetroot, some soured cream or yogurt and some dill. Fry all the raw vegetables in the oil. Peel the beetroot, which will give you very red hands and cut them into dice. Add them with the water to the vegetables and season. Simmer it for 3 or 4 minutes and then mash it up a bit to thicken it. Pour the cream or yogurt into each bowl of soup and sprinkle with dill.

For a **Beetroot** soup which won't use up half your stocks, use an onion, a large potato, a potato, a pound of cooked beetroot, 2 pints of water and some lemon juice. Fry the diced onion and potato and add the cooked, diced beetroot. Add the water and cook until the potatoes are soft. Mash it all up and season with salt, pepper and lemon juice.

When cooking beetroot, by the way, don't cut off the tops or peel them, as they will then bleed all over the place. Cook them and then remove tops and skin.

Broad beans

These seem to be a *cool* climate crop. They only keep *4 or 5 days* anyway, so are not a good provisioning vegetable, as well as taking up so much space for the amount you get from them. However, they are very good eating and cheap in season. Try them cold in a French dressing.

Broccoli

The king of brassicas! Sadly this does not keep more than *a couple of days* unless you are in a very cold climate.

Brussels sprouts

In a *cool* climate these will keep about *1 week*, in perfect conditions. In a *hot* climate they won't keep at all and will best be eaten the *same day*. By the way, it's quite unnecessary to throw half of them away as most people do; all you're trying to do is to get rid of the dirty leaves on the outside. If you take the time to peel them off one at a time and then trim the stalk, instead of the other way round as most people do, you'll end up eating a much larger proportion of what you've bought.

Cabbage

What would we do without cabbage? We use it in coleslaw with carrots, mayonnaise and maybe yogurt for a salad and fry it and steam it for a vegetable. Its leaves can be stuffed or chunks of it can be put in stews. It's cheap and readily available and keeps well. The ones that keep best seem to be the hard and densely packed white or light green ones. The leafy ones have a better flavour and also more iron. However, they also act as a haven for wildlife too, if you're not careful. Assuming you buy the white ones: don't wash them because the leaves will trap the water and go bad. Remove any bad leaves; stack them wherever you have room. Cabbages are a nuisance if you are trying to keep several because unless it's quite cold, they will start to go bad and if it is cold the outer leaves start to yellow. The best way to use them is to take a few leaves off each one for every meal — that way you can slowly whittle the base of the stalk away as you remove the leaves. They generally go bad from the base, so you should be able to keep one step ahead. If you have half a dozen cabbages, it can be quite an operation. In this way they will keep *2 - 3 weeks* for good ones in a *hot* climate and *2 - 3+ months* in a *cool* one, depending on how cold it is.

Carrots

Another good standby, these are not easy to keep well if they've been cleaned as thoroughly as most of them are these days or are thin. If possible, buy them with some earth on, it seems to stop them from drying out, and look for fairly long ones about an inch in diameter at the stalk. Too big and they'll rot, too small and they dry out.

Keeping them in polythene just makes them sweat and rot. *Pick them over weekly* in *cool* climates, where if you've chosen well they should last *a month* (up to *3 months* in *cold* places). Pick them *over every other day* in *hot* climates, where they may last *2 weeks,* or more with luck. As soon as you see any rot on them, isolate them and eat them soon. Even cutting it out doesn't seem to work very well. Cutting off the root end does seem to help reduce the chances of carrots going bad.

Cauliflower

Alas, these don't keep so well either. *Cool* climate fare, you may get a week out of them but I'd reckon on *3 days*. If it's cool enough, keep them in polythene, but not if they start to sweat. When they're a bit past it they make an excellent soup with the addition of a potato or two and an onion. Milk is added towards the end and plenty of black pepper and a grating of nutmeg finish it off.

Celeriac

This also seems to be *cool* climate food. Being a solid root vegetable, don't wash the dirt off, but examine it carefully. It keeps well, *at least 3 weeks* I should think, although I've never tried to keep it more than a week. If you could buy it in a *hot* climate, I would reckon a *week*, maybe even 10 days, if kept dry and well ventilated.

Celery

This doesn't keep so well, although it does quite like a polythene bag, if it's not too hot. Its flavour can be obtained by using celery seed. In a *cool* climate it will keep *2 weeks*, but be a bit limp. In a *hot* climate, it's probably refrigerated and would last about *3 days.*

Chicory

This is quite good *hot* climate salad stuff, but tends to be a bit pricey. It will keep for *up to a week* and may benefit from being loosely wrapped in polythene. In a *cool* climate, it would keep about 3 weeks, but unfortunately a lot of leaves will have dried out by then, so I'd suggest *10 days* and in a plastic bag.

Chinese Leaves/Bok Choy

The first are a sort of cross between a lettuce and a cabbage and the bok choy is the same sort of shape but with a wide white rib and a dark green edge to the leaf. To keep them, you will have to avoid ones with their tips cut off, as they will start to rot from that point. Don't wash them but check very carefully. As with a cabbage, eat away at the outside leaves, one at a time. If it's not too hot, they might like a loose plastic bag. *5 days* in a *hot* climate and *10 days* in a *cool* one.

Courgettes

These lovely miniature marrows do not keep too well, unfortunately. Bleach wash and dry. Stack 2 or 3 deep. *Pick over daily. 3 days* in a *hot* climate, 5 at best. *A week* in a *cool* one, maybe a fortnight with really firm, fresh ones.

Cucumber

These don't keep so well when it's hot ... *Hot* climates *3 days, cool* climates often more than *a week*. Beware of those bought in the USA (and maybe elsewhere), which often have waxed skins. I'm not too happy about eating the wax and I rather like cucumber skin.

Fennel

This is quite good, as long as you buy firm roots. As it's rarely cheap, I've not often kept it, but I've found that fennel is one of the few vegetables that can be kept by using a polythene bag loosely wrapped round it, to prevent it from drying out. The bag must not be sealed, otherwise it will sweat and in a hot place, you must keep a careful eye on it and take it out of the bag if this starts happening. If you wash it, water will get trapped, so check it over carefully, especially in warmer places. Stack as deep as you wish — although I can't believe that you'll take that much on board. *Pick over weekly, more often* when it's *hot*. It should keep in hot climates *a week, cool* climates *a fortnight*

French beans

I think that these are the nicest of all 'pod' beans, but they don't keep at all well. Bleach wash and dry thoroughly. Shallow stack. *Pick over every other day.* I've managed *4 days* in *hot* climates, in *cool* climates you'd be lucky to do much better than a *week* at best, because if kept in plastic they sweat and rot and in paper or loose they dry out.

Garlic

This is the great favorite of many cruising people and rightly so. As well as being such a useful seasoning anyway, it comes into its own with aging eggs. Undoubtedly the best way to keep it is on the ropes of garlic that you can buy occasionally. The bulbs with big cloves keep better because they take that much longer to dry out than little cloves - they are also easier to deal with. If you buy loose bulbs, I have found the best way to keep them is by separating them into cloves and storing them in a little woven basket. That way they don't seem to trap moisture and go mouldy. Stack as deep as you like. Pick over *weekly*. In *hot* climates it should keep for at least *1 month* and in *cool* climates *3+ months*, so I have found it worth stocking up when I find good quality stuff. It doesn't seem to like light, by the way, and will start to sprout, (except for the ropes, which are obviously dried with much more care).

By the way, I never bother with a garlic crusher. I usually simply chop it up very finely or if making a spread, crush it with the blade of a knife.

Kohlrabi

Deal with as for turnip; actually they taste about the same - far less exciting than they sound.

Leeks

We both love leeks, as a vegetable, mixed with beans in a sauce or in leek and potato soup. However, they don't keep at all well and soon dry out. I've never seen them in a hot climate, except refrigerated. In a *cool* climate they will keep from *4 - 7 days* at best, just loose with your other vegetables.

Lettuce

The only ones worth buying for voyaging are hard, hearty ones such as Webbs, Iceberg or Batavia. You mustn't wash them until you come to eat them and then only the leaves you've picked off, otherwise trapped water will rot them in short order. They can keep astonishingly well, if you pick off the leaves one at a time, like cabbages. DON'T CUT LETTUCE, otherwise they will rot from where they have been cut at an amazing rate. In a *cool* climate, you can keep them in an unsealed polythene bag for *2 - 3 weeks* as long as you eat some every day and eat them concurrently, picking off the leaves as mentioned. I have actually managed to keep them *10 days* in the *Tropics* which should be enough from market to market, but in a hot climate, you can't put them in plastic or they'll just sweat and rot. Nutritionally lousy, I worry about them simply because they are so nice to crunch. If at all expensive, they're not worth it. The greatest fun of keeping them comes from the fact that everyone thinks that you must refrigerate lettuce and it's nice to prove them wrong. The loose-leafed ones don't keep well at all and usually have no crunch either, but they do have some iron, which I suppose is worth something.

Mange-tout peas

These can occasionally be bought for a very reasonable cost, but don't keep at all well. They have a large surface area and dry out quickly. In a *cool* climate, they may last *4 or 5 days*, but in a *hot* climate, *2 days* would probably be the maximum.

Marrow

Even when I had an oven, I never really knew what to do with these things. Although I love them, I've never found stuffed vegetables a great success, apart from cabbage leaves, because when I do them, they always fall to bits and then there seems to be either a lot of waste or too much stuffing. Also they are not particularly filling for hearty appetites like ours. Like all squash (apart from aubergines and courgettes) marrow are rather dull, in my opinion. However, they are often incredibly cheap in *cool* places and will keep for *2 - 3 weeks*. Bleach wash, as they are susceptible to mould and stack them 3 or 4 deep, if you have so many; then do with them whatever you do with them.

Mushrooms

Fresh mushrooms are not long-term supplies. Even in a *cool* climate you'd be lucky to get a *week* out of them. Your chances of keeping them are improved immensely if you keep them away from plastic, which makes them sweat and rot. If you put them in a shallow container in the coolest part of your boat, they'll keep longest. Sometimes you will find them for sale very cheaply and want to make use of them. You will be pleased to hear that this is possible as they dry very satisfactorily. What you do is to wipe the dirt off them, slice them into 1/8" slices or even thinner and then dry them. This can be done on a baking sheet in the coolest of ovens — you don't want to cook them. In fact on a baking sheet on the top of the stove in which the oven is lit is probably better. You can dry them spread out in the sun, if it's calm — otherwise they will blow away. Or you can string them up in the cabin by using a fine needle and thread through each piece. They dry very quickly and are definitely worth the effort as they keep well in air-tight glass jars and tend to be a luxury for voyagers on a small income. To use them you simply drop them into what you're cooking. If it's something like an omelet, just soak them in a little warm water for a quarter of an hour.

Olives

I'm fairly sure that these are fruit rather than vegetables, but then so are tomatoes. We have found them to be inexpensive in Spain and Portugal and dirt cheap in Morocco. Unfortunately Pete, who has odd tastes, does not care for olives, so they are definitely an indulgence bought just for me (and friends who come round for drinks). Although the pundits reckon that without preservatives, they should only be kept in a cool place, I managed to keep some for *3 months*, during which time we were always in a *hot* climate. I bought them in Morocco and a friend of mine had put the fear of god in me about some dreadful debilitating disease I could get from eating food which has been handled by grubby hands. My own standards of hygiene are far from 'squeaky-clean', but I took what he said to heart, as the Moroccans definitely had grubby hands. On buying the olives, I drained them and then poured boiling water over them (as Robin had told me), which presumably killed off whatever was there. That done I made a very strong brine solution (the old test of floating the potato would probably be suitable) and then filled litre jars with olives, as full as possible. I then topped them up with the brine and they kept perfectly well until we finished them at Christmas in Grenada, 3 months later. Some French people I met had apparently processed their own from scratch, but my French wasn't quite up to working out the details of precisely in what state they had bought them. They had used the same sort of brine solution. The Moroccans, by the way, have about 10 different ways of preparing their olives, from plain with stones, to exotic spiced and stuffed. They display them in huge bowls, about a metre across and scoop them into bags for you. I must admit, with all the flies about, they didn't look too hygienic, but you've got to eat a peck of dirt before you die (-'but not all at one sitting!', I hear Robin say). Incidentally, olives go dark and soggy when they are getting past it and taste unpleasant, so I don't think one is likely to eat them when they've gone off (bad ones can give you food poisoning).

Onions

The absolute staple of our existence — I fry onions while I'm deciding what to eat — well, just about, anyway. The number of days in which an onion hasn't played its part must be few and far between. They keep extremely well as long as you look after them in the right way. The first thing is to ensure that you stock up with the correct ones. Medium ones are slightly better than large ones, but the most important thing is to try to avoid buying 'twins'. These are the onions that, when you have taken the first layer or two off, are actually two together. If you are uncertain as to whether the ones you fancy may be like this, buy a few and examine them. They trap moisture where they are joined together and invariably go bad quickly. Moisture is what makes onions go bad and grow shoots, so don't wash them either. The way to avoid them being damp is to peel off the brown skins to allow the onions to 'breathe'. After a number of weeks, the top skin will slowly start to dry out and go brown and when it does, it must then be peeled off again. In the fullness of time you will discover that the onions get smaller and smaller, but they will keep and very few will go bad. In *hot* climates, this should be done to them as soon as they are brought on board, because it will also ensure that any wildlife gets chucked out with the skins. Stack as deep as you like and *pick over weekly*, more often as the voyage progresses. They should keep *3 weeks to a month*, a little longer in the unlikely event that you managed to get top quality. In *cool* climates, they can be stacked deep and *picked over every week* for the odd rogue. If they do shoot, cut them off and eat them, don't let them continue to grow shoots. They should easily last *2 - 3 months*, I have kept them for 4 months when sailing in cold waters and they weren't a brilliant batch to start with. They need to have ventilation; keep them dry. Although they are almost universally available, it's nice to know they keep.

Parsnips

As carrots.

Peas

Fresh peas are always a delight but don't keep more than *3 or 4 days*. Eat them within a few days and enjoy the treat.

Peppers

Oddly enough, I have found that these keep very well indeed, treated with care. By the way, beware of the ones which you buy in the USA and possibly other countries, which have waxed skins. Personally, I wouldn't wish to eat the wax and one ought to be aware of it. With untreated peppers, the best way I have found of looking after them starts with selecting ones with stalks on. When you bring them back to the boat, bleach wash them and dry them.

Then thread them together by the stalks and hang them up. Don't use a needle and thread, because this causes the stalks to split. Instead, take a half hitch around each of the stalks and this way they don't slide along and touch one another when the boat heels. If they do happen to touch one another, they will go bad at the point of contact. In a *hot* climate, *examine daily*, in a *cool* climate, *every other day*. As time goes by they will go red and then slowly shrivel up, but I have managed to keep them over *5 weeks* on a Trade Wind crossing, when it was pretty *hot*. They were past eating raw after 4 or 5 days and after 3 weeks they looked pretty sad, but were fine to cook with.

Potatoes

For the person who eats a traditional British diet, potatoes must present something of a problem. Quite apart from any difficulties attendant upon keeping them, they are somewhat bulky and people like Pete and myself are perfectly capable of eating 1 1/2 pounds of potatoes between us. Even assuming that you scrub them and don't waste half of them in peel, this is still a lot of potatoes. Therefore, my first suggestion to potato aficionados would be to develop a taste for pasta and rice. However, potatoes are good food and I certainly would feel deprived if I was told that I could never eat one again. They are best bought with some dirt still on them. Often, if you buy them by the 56 lb. sack they will not be scrubbed. If they are very muddy, it's worth washing the bulk of it off, but a certain amount of soil does seem to stop them from wrinkling up. For the sake of interest, 25 kilos/56 lb., eked out by rice and pasta, would feed Pete and me for 4 months.

Stack fairly deep, although I wouldn't recommend using a sack because it makes picking over so difficult. Keep in the dark, so that they don't turn green. In *cool* climates, *pick over weekly*. Good potatoes will keep from *1 to 4+ months*, depending on the time of the year and whether they are new or old. Very new potatoes don't keep so well. In *hot* climates, where they should keep *2 or 3 weeks, pick over at least once a week*, because one bad potato will quickly set off the others. Also, there are few things more revolting to get hold of than a rotten potato; quite apart from the nauseating texture, they smell appalling — once the skin has ruptured. Rotten carrots are pretty awful, too.

Where potatoes are difficult to buy, there are often other starchy tubers to act as alternatives. My own experience with these has made me opt for rice or pasta instead, but they are worth a try. Eddoes chip and mash quite well, but need peeling, which is an unpleasant job as they are very starchy and become slimy to the touch when immersed in water. I'm afraid I wasn't impressed with yams, but don't let me stop you.

Pumpkin

These are essentially another big squash. My comments on water melons would apply — where would you find room for half a dozen pumpkins and how on earth could you eat your way through them? Personally, I think that the nicest way to eat them is in pumpkin soup; I also like pumpkin pie, but when one considers all the other ingredients that have gone into it, I sometimes wonder whether the pumpkin is necessary at all. I don't regard them as passage making vegetables although they do keep well in anything other than a broiling climate.

Red cabbage

This is another of those vegetables where I'm never quite sure what to do with it. I love pickled red cabbage, but we don't eat many pickles and it's nice cooked for a change or in a salad with sultanas and walnuts. It keeps *like white cabbage* and one or two might add some variety.

Runner beans

See french beans. Runner beans might last slightly longer, being bulkier, but are prone to getting rather coarse and fibrous.

Spinach

As you might imagine spinach doesn't keep that well. In a *hot* climate I'd recommend eating it the *same day*. In a *cool* climate, wash it and shake it pretty dry and then pack it loosely in a plastic bag. Kept as cool as possible, it should last *3 or 4 days*. Tinned spinach, when mixed with flour (ideally pea flour), finely chopped ginger, a finely chopped green chili pepper, garam masala and garlic and made into a thick paste can be formed into balls and deep fried to make **'koftas'**. These are a delicious Indian dish, which you eat with yogurt and they go very well with a curry meal.

Swede

Treat as for turnip.

Sweet potatoes

These seem to be becoming increasingly popular, although I prefer my potatoes unsweetened. Should you develop a taste for them, they are often available where more conventional potatoes are somewhat of a delicacy and can be used as an alternative. I would store them in much the same way too, and they keep quite well with a modicum of care.

Tomatoes

These are another thing that keep surprisingly well. The first time we were in the Bahamas, we were told about the wholesale market in Nassau. Fruit and vegetables · are generally extremely expensive in the Bahamas, but the good ladies in the (covered) wholesale market by the bridge, will sell you a 'mixed box' of vegetables and fruit too, if you're lucky. When we went, they didn't have enough fruit in, but sold us a box of vegetables for US $6, if my memory serves me. Amongst other things, this box contained 2 large cabbages, each worth about $2, potatoes, beetroot, all sorts of other things and 45 tomatoes. Yes 45, to this day I remember carefully washing them and then lining them up on deck to dry and there were 45. What's more, the majority of them were green. We sailed off for Bermuda, which took 3 weeks and we had fresh tomatoes all the way. I have also bought them in the Canaries before crossing the Atlantic and had them last 3 weeks. So, I will say here that, if bought green, tomatoes will last at least *weeks* in a *hot* climate and 4 weeks in a *cool* one. Of course, don't stack them once they start to ripen and pick over daily to separate the ripe ones from the rest. Thus tomatoes also, can be good voyaging fare. High in vitamin C, too.

Turnip

More of a *cool* climate root, turnip keeps very well indeed. Their major drawback is that they are not something that most people would enjoy every day, so that I would imagine that supply could easily exceed demand. In some countries, such as the USA, both turnip and swedes have waxed skins and I wouldn't recommend eating this, although the food processors say it's quite safe. Generally I'd wash the worst of the dirt off, but not clean them too thoroughly. *Pick over once a week* and they will keep a *couple of months*. In *hot* climates, I've never tried to keep them, but I would expect them to last a *fortnight*, as long as they haven't been refrigerated.

The advantage of a stand-up chart table is the amount of stowage underneath — especially when the table is full (Admiralty chart) size. The drawers and bookshelves can also be seen.

Appendix IV

Badger
Designed by Jay R. Benford

Benford Design Group
P. O. Box 447
St. Michaels, Maryland 21663-0447 USA
(410) 745-3235

Although there has been plenty about *Badger* in the text of this book, I felt that an appendix would be of interest. The question is not only why is *Badger* a good yacht, but specifically, why is she a good yacht for voyaging on a small income?

To me, one of *Badger*'s greatest attractions is that she is actually designed for a couple. Most boats of her size have at least 6 berths and therefore the rest of the accommodation has to be built in around them. On many boats that are used for voyaging, the quarter berths are used for storage. However, on *Badger*, one can gain access to the space under the cockpit rather more easily and so this area can be used for much more efficient stowage.

Badger is designed to have a large and usable galley, a necessity on any serious voyaging yacht. She has a pleasant saloon with room for bookshelves and a double cabin. The heads is large enough so that you can close the door and have a shower. She has a full-width/raised-deck cabin from cockpit to forward cabin, which gives a great sense of spaciousness and is much stronger, structurally, than a conventional coach-roof. There is room for a heating stove. The dory hull gives a wide flat floor, which allows for the accommodation to be pushed further to the sides of the boat without you having to stand on the sides of the hull. She is comfortable to live on both while at sea and in harbour.

Plywood is a simple, quick and strong material with which to build. By shopping around carefully it can be bought for a very reasonable outlay and if you are building while working, it is possible to buy a little at a time. If you are using epoxy, it is not necessary to choose the best quality marine ply - well made exterior will be very satisfactory. When epoxy is used, you don't need expensive fastenings, which tends to make up for the initial cost of the glue. Glued construction has the advantage that it doesn't leak, a great advantage for any boat. The yacht is of moderate displacement, meaning that the initial building costs are also moderate. An advantage of plywood that is rarely mentioned is that it is very easy to repair because the damaged area can be cut out and a new piece or pieces scarfed in.

On deck, *Badger* is simple and uncluttered with a small footwell aft, clear centre deck and a sunken foredeck which keeps spray away from the cockpit area and allows a solid dinghy to be carried without impeding the helmsman's view. She has plenty of hatches for ventilation. The deck boxes abaft the back of the cabin allow petrol to be stored safely and provide a home for the tails from the sheets and halliards. They also make very comfortable seats. The rudder is hung outboard, for ease of maintenance.

The junk rig is possibly the best short-handed cruising rig ever devised. It is also very cheap to build and to maintain. It allows more room below decks and is uncluttered above decks.

Badger can be built simply and for very little money. Sheathed in cloth and epoxy she is easy to maintain and can be kept up to standard at very little expense — an essential prerequisite for a boat that is sailed on a small income.

———————

The following are the designer's drawings and comments about *Badger* and some of the other similar Benford dory designs of varying sizes.

———————

As a young yacht designer, twenty-five years ago, I did the first versions of what became a whole range of our sailing dory designs. My goals in doing the original design work are very similar to what led Annie and Pete Hill to choose our 34' Sailing Dory design to build their voyager, *Badger*. I wanted to create the type of boat that provided the most useful and capable cruiser on a very small budget. Since the prospective client for the first design ideas was myself, I could be completely ruthless in pursuit of anything that would simplify and boats and hold their costs down.

Over the ensuing years we've sold plans for several hundred of these sailing dory designs. A number of them have made ocean passages, and they have all told us how much they liked the boat's design and how capable they turned out to be at sea.

The construction scheme that I originally devised has been carried out throughout the whole line of designs. The planking is sheets of plywood glued and fastened to the bulkheads and furniture in the boat, which becomes the structural framing needed to keep her in shape.

Floor timbers span from chine to chine to take the load from the keel bolts. To this is bolted the cast lead or concrete and scrap metal keel, depending on the version. This sub-assembly can be bolted on just prior to completion and launching, so that the boat can be set noticeably lower in the shop to make access to the work easier.

The longitudinal framing consists of the clamp and chine logs, plus the raised deck and/or house framing. There are no ribs to contend with, nor any deck beams, except for a temporary framework while the deck layers of plywood are being glued together.

The simple, straight lines of these hull forms mean extremely easy lofting work. A professional shop can loft one of these in a matter of a few hours. The straight line shape also means that there are very few instances of having to fit curved pieces to the hull during outfitting. Thus, the joiner and outfit work goes much faster than with a round bilge hull form.

The first of the larger 36-footers, *Donna*, was built in under thirteen months by a shoemaker in Alberta. He had never built a boat before, and didn't have any other boatbuilders in the area (1,200 miles from the coast) he could visit for counsel and advice.

Professional boatbuilders tell us they can build these boats in even less time, indicating again that these certainly are the most boat for the money invested.

Can the dories be built in other materials? Yes, with some qualifications. We've done an alternate construction for one of them for building or several layers of timber laminated to a similar thickness as the plywood. We've also done aluminum versions for the 36 and 37½-footers. The aluminum makes for a vessel of about the same structural weight. Cored fiberglass is another way to build them, and we've done scantlings for the 36 and 37½-footers for this method.

We've also done a steel version of the 36 as a power fishing vessel, but the weight gain was so much that there was not much leeway for ballasting the boat if she were to be a sailing vessel and still float anywhere close to her designed waterline. My personal choice would still be for the plywood construction.

Several of these dory designs have alternative rigs already drawn for them. The Hills are persuasive advocates of the junk, or lug rig. On the 34' and larger dories there is enough stability to carry the weight of these rigs, which typically weigh more and have this weight at a height that raises the center of gravity a bit.

We did an inclining test on *Badger* when they visited us and confirmed that she had positive stability to

about at least 125° heel, even with her loaded with all their worldly possessions and with the heavier junk rig. As they have proven, this has made for a very capable voyager.

Many people who know dories only as rather tender open rowing boats are surprised at how stable these sailing versions are with the outside ballast added.

Pounding is something that is rarely experienced when sailing these dories. Even though they are flat bottomed, they present a v-shape to the water when heeled and this makes a more graceful entry into the waves. The only report I've had of one of them pounding was when the *Donna* was coming in across a breaking bar on the Oregon coast — under power. Thus, she was upright, and it was only reasonable to assume that there would be a brief period of pounding during the crossing of the bar.

Donna, the first of the 36-footers, was rerigged from the original gaff ketch to a taller Marconi ketch rig after several ocean passages. The rationale was that the taller rig would make it easier to catch the lighter Pacific trade winds. This rig, added at considerable expense, did indeed make for better ocean sailing performance. If this is truly a concern, I'd opt for the taller cutter rig initially.

As Annie has well outlined the many advantages of the junk rig in her book, I will only mention that the gaff rigged sails also benefit from having the weight of the spar aloft to help bring the sail down, a safety factor in some situations....

26' Raised Deck Cutter
Design Number 274
1988

This design is capable of doing the sort of voyaging that the *Badger* does. She has comfortable accommodations for a couple to cruise aboard. What she won't have is the sort of extended stores and long-term supplies carrying ability that makes the larger *Badger* work so well. She was designed with full foam floatation, intending to be the sort of boat that would float even if filled with water. The concern with this for a voyager is that the floatation is filling a lot of valuable locker spaces, and, if I was doing one for myself, I would bypass the foam floatation in favor of having more stowage space. She will take the ground gracefully when drying out on a tidal cycle, sitting upright on her twin keels and skeg on level bottoms. This can make exploring the shallows and back-waters more relaxing, knowing you won't have to spend a tidal cycle laying well over.

30' Sailing Dory
Design Number 32
1967

There are three versions of this design, shown on the following pages. The gaff ketch has a small aft cabin, providing separation for guests or kids. For a voyaging version, I would suggest that the interior of the Marconi sloop, with a chart table like the gaff sloop in place of the inside helm, would be the best choice. It is a slightly smaller version of what is in *Badger* and has similar practical separation of the spaces.

The ketch shows the lead ballast fin keel. The Marconi sloop shows the concrete and scrap metal ballasted fin keel. The gaff sloop has a long keel and either lead or concrete and scrap metal for ballast.

The indicated displacement is in coastal cruising use. For voyaging, I would assume that she would get loaded down a fair bit, like *Badger*, with the stores and supplies needed for such service. Fortunately, these dories take this loading gracefully, not unlike their predecessors the working dories which set out light and returned carrying tons of fish.

32' Sailing Dory *Shoestring*
Design Number 36
1968

The 32-footer was built and named *Shoestring* by one of the first of her builders. We so liked the name and

the thought that she could be built on the proverbial shoestring that we adopted the name for the design.

As the narrowest of these dory design, this boat is the most sensitive to weight aloft, and care needs to be taken that her stability is not compromised by putting too heavy a rig on her. Sail carrying power, and thus the ability to sail out of a close situation, is directly related to the stability of the boat. Anything that can be done to minimize or reduce weight aloft will aid the stability. All things being equal, transverse stability is directly related to waterline beam cubed. Thus, a beamier boat will have better ability to carry a heavier rig.

The ketch rig is shared with the 30-footer, as is the keel and general scantling drawings. An aluminum spar version of the 30-footer's sloop rig would be the best choice to give this boat the most stability.

A simple change in filling the berth flat all the way across the forward cabin will yield a nice double berth there and this is an alteration that I think would be an improvement, particularly with a sloop rig that would move the mast back to the aft end of the dining table and thus not breakup the head of the new double berth.

34' Sailing Dory *Badger*
Design Number 170
1978

The concept of this design was to use the basic interior accommodation plan that worked so well on the 34' Topsail Ketch *Sunrise,* evolved and improved on during the decade that I lived aboard her. I wanted to use it in one of our dory hull forms that would provide these very workable accommodations in a boat that could be built very economically. We'd done several sailing dory designs before this one and it benefited from improvements we would make for a better hull form, both for sailing characteristics and for stability.

The original cutter rig was done for building in an area where grown poles are available as spars. We worked out some simple hardware that could be made with modest equipment and this rig has worked out well on some sisterships.

There are two versions of how to build the deck, one with a trunk cabin and the other with a raised, flush deck like *Badger*. The latter makes the most sense to me and I would recommend it for anyone going voyaging. It adds to the room below and makes the deck layout more open and easier to work upon. It also adds to the stability in a knockdown by adding volume where it does the most good in shifting the center of buoyancy in the right direction.

As Pete and Annie have found, it is a layout that has worked out very well for them, as it did for me. For anyone wanting to do the sort of cruising that the Pete and Annie Hill are doing, this boat would be hard to beat. It's got room for a couple to live and cruise in comfort and yet is of a size that is affordable and manageable.

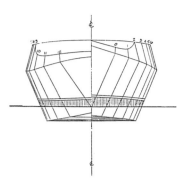

37½' Sailing Dory
Design Number 174
1978

This design is a slight variation on the 36-footer, with the stem tilted slightly more forward. The basic keel, bottom and structure are identical, using many of the drawings done for the 36-footer. The interiors are pretty much interchangeable, and some of the ideas from one can be used in the other size. The trick is to be sure the masts fall in areas that do not complicate the use of the interior space and that the reinforcing for the rigging structure is put in the right place. The raised deck version would again be my recommendation, for the same reasons mentioned about *Badger*, primarily more space and better stability.

Some alternatives to the layouts shown that would be practical would include the addition of a hard dodger or pilothouse to the forward end of the cockpit. If this was done with a version with an aft cockpit and quarter berths, the berths could be shifted aft and the pilothouse covering up this part of the accommodations. Note that the trunk cabin version has the same layout as the 36-footer, with the exception of having a double berth in the bow.

36' Sailing Dory *Donna*
Design Number 127
1975

This design has the same nice interior spaces as *Badger* with the addition of quarter berths aft. For a family of four to liveaboard, as has been done on one of the sisterships, this provides good separation of the sleeping spaces. I would put a double berth in the forward cabin, like *Badger*'s and as shown on the 37½, and have the saloon berths and quarter berths for sleeping in on a passage.

Several of these 36-footers have done a lot of ocean voyaging and the owners report that they have been very comfortable. They also report that the boats are good at making quick passages and will surf in some tradewind conditions.

Larger Dory Designs

As this book goes to press, we're starting work on a larger, 45' sailing dory motorsailer. We've also done design work on a concept for a 60-foot, three-masted junk schooner a couple decades ago. These are mentioned because there really should be no upper limit to the size of sailing dories that could be designed.

26' Cutter being rolled over. Roger Salmon photo.

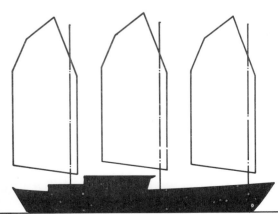

60' Dory — design idea.

Sailing Dory Particulars:

Size	26'	30'	32'	34'	36'	37½'
Length Overall	26'-0"	30'-0"	32'-0"	34'-0"	36'-0"	37'-6"
Length Datum Waterline	23'-1"	26'-0"	27'-0"	28'-0"	31'-0"	31'-0"
Beam	9'-9¾"	10'-0"	9'-0"	11'-0"	11'-0"	11'-0"
Draft	3'-0"	4'-0"	4'-0"	4'-6"	4'-6"	4'-6"
Freeboard: Forward	4'-6"	4'-6"	4'-2"	5'-0"	5'-0¾"	5'-2½"
Least	4'-4½"	2'-8¾"	2'-6¼"	2'-9"	3'-0¼"	3'-0¼"
Aft	3'-8½"	3'-3½"	3'-6½"	4'-0"	4'-2¾"	4'-9"
Displacement, Cruising Trim*	8,000	6,700	6,900	10,400	13,425	13,425
Displacement-Length Ratio	290	170	156	211	201	201
Ballast	2,600	2,680	2,760	4,160	5,350	5,350
Ballast Ratio	32.5%	40%	40%	40%	40%	40%
Sail Area, Square Feet	419	500	500	600	700	700/725
Sail Area-Displacement Ratio	16.76	22.5	22.1	20.15	19.83	19.83/20.54
Prismatic Coefficient	.614	.58	.60	.56	.63	.63
Pounds Per Inch Immersion	659			906	983	983
Auxiliary, Horsepower	9	9	9	18	27	27
Water, Gallons	40	25	25	100	110	110
Fuel, Gallons	25	25	25	40	55	55
Headroom	5'-3"/6'-1"	6'-1"	6'-1"	6'-3½"	6'-4"	6'-4"

*Caution: The displacement quoted here is for the boat in coastal cruising trim. That is, with the fuel and water tanks filled, the crew on board, as well as the crews' gear and stores in the lockers. This should not be confused with the "shipping weight" often quoted as "displacement" by some manufacturers. This should be taken into account when comparing figures and ratios between this and other designs. Also, loading down for voyaging and living aboard, as with the Hill's *Badger*, will add considerably to these figures, perhaps as much as 50%. Designs like *Badger* which load down gracefully and still sail well make a good choice for voyaging on a small income.

*Claus Oldag's **Penelope II** is a 30' Sailing Dory which cruises the Baltic. Manuela Scholz photos courtesy of Claus Oldag.*

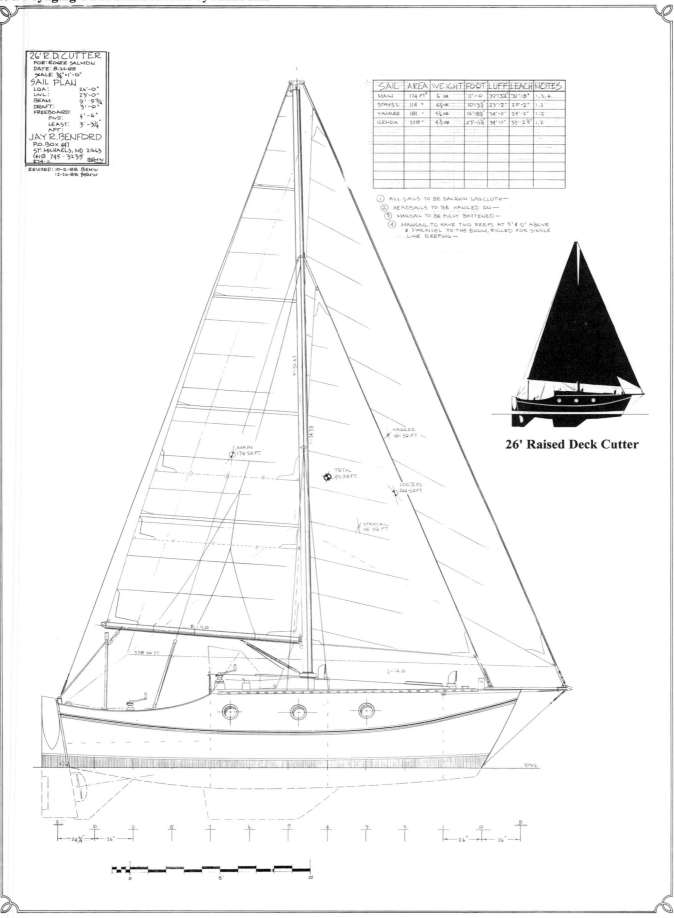

26' R.D. CUTTER
FOR: ROGER SALMON
DATE: 8-26-88
SCALE: ¾"=1'-0"
SAIL PLAN
LOA: 26'-0"
LWL: 23'-0"
BEAM: 9'-9¾"
DRAFT: 3'-0"
FREEBOARD:
   FWD: 4'-6"
   LEAST: 3'-3¼"
   AFT:
JAY R. BENFORD
P.O. BOX 447
ST. MICHAELS, MD 21663
(410) 745-3235
214-2
REVISED: 10-12-88 BEHW
         12-20-88 BEHW

SAIL	AREA	WEIGHT	FOOT	LUFF	LEACH	NOTES
MAIN	174 FT²	6 oz	11'-0	32'-3¼	31'-8"	1,3,4
STAYSL	114 "	4½ oz	10'-3½	23'-2"	20'-2"	1,2
YANKEE	181 "	4½ oz	16'-8½	34'-11"	24'-2"	1,2
GENOA	378 "	4½ oz	23'-11½	34'-11"	33'-2⅛	1,2

① ALL SAILS TO BE DACRON SAILCLOTH—
② HEADSAILS TO BE HANKED ON—
③ MAINSAIL TO BE FULLY BATTENED—
④ MAINSAIL TO HAVE TWO REEFS AT 5' & 9' ABOVE
   & PARALLEL TO THE BOOM, RIGGED FOR SINGLE
   LINE REEFING—

26' Raised Deck Cutter

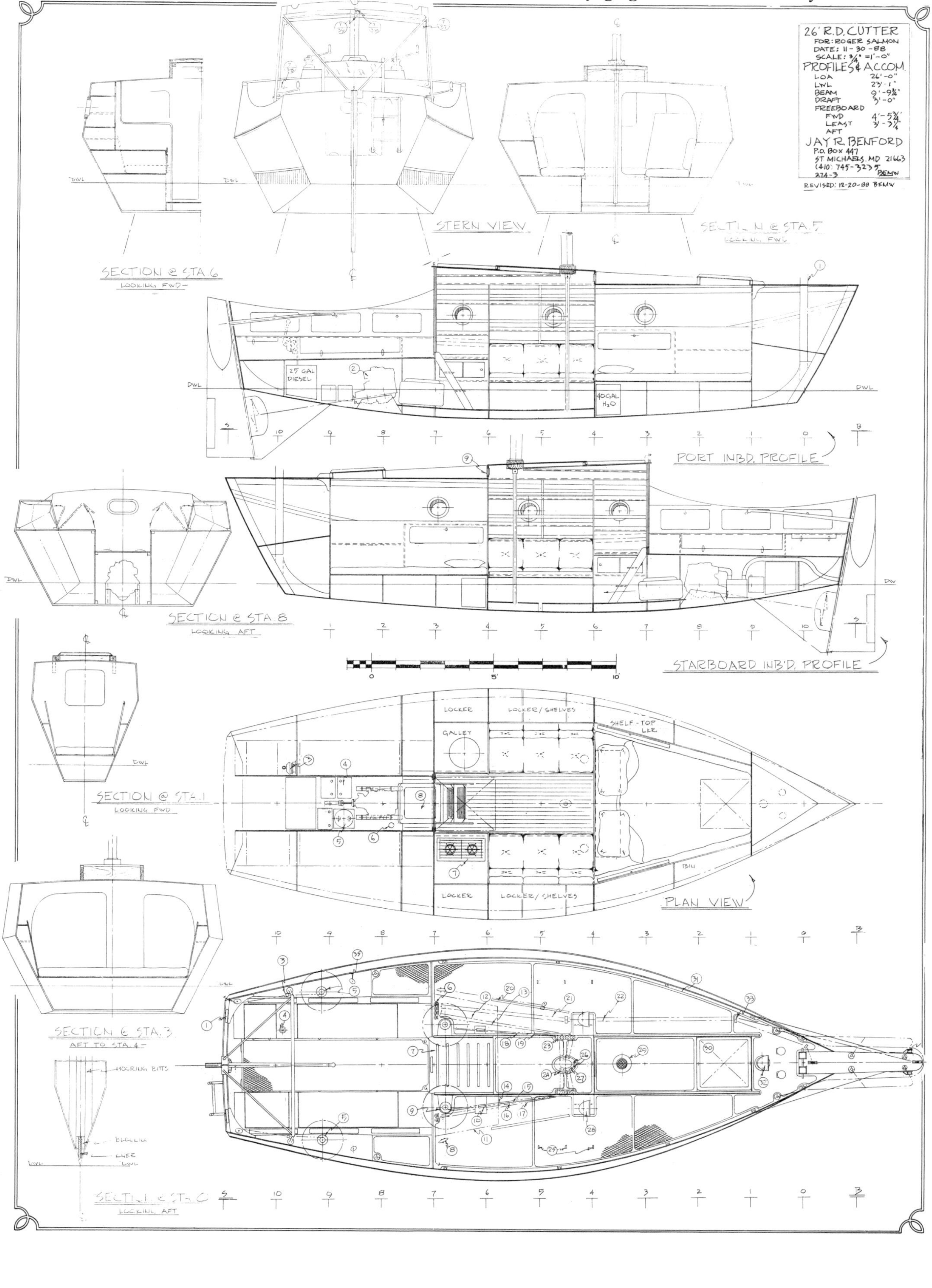

26' R.D. CUTTER
FOR: ROGER SALMON
DATE: 11-30-88
SCALE: 3/4" = 1'-0"
PROFILES & ACCOM.
LOA 26'-0"
LWL 23'-1"
BEAM 9'-9 3/4"
DRAFT 3'-0"
FREEBOARD
FWD 4'-5 3/4"
LEAST 3'-7 1/4"
AFT
JAY R. BENFORD
P.O. BOX 447
ST. MICHAELS, MD 21663
(410) 745-3235
274-3
BEMW
REVISED: 12-20-88 BEMW
SECTION @ STA. 6
LOOKING FWD
STERN VIEW
SECTION @ STA. 5
LOOKING FWD
25 GAL DIESEL
40 GAL H2O
PORT INBD. PROFILE
SECTION @ STA. 8
LOOKING AFT
STARBOARD INB'D. PROFILE
SECTION @ STA. 1
LOOKING FWD
LOCKER
LOCKER/SHELVES
GALLEY
SHELF-TOP LKR.
PLAN VIEW
SECTION @ STA. 3
AFT TO STA. 4
MOORING BITTS
SECTION @ STA. 0
LOOKING AFT
DWL

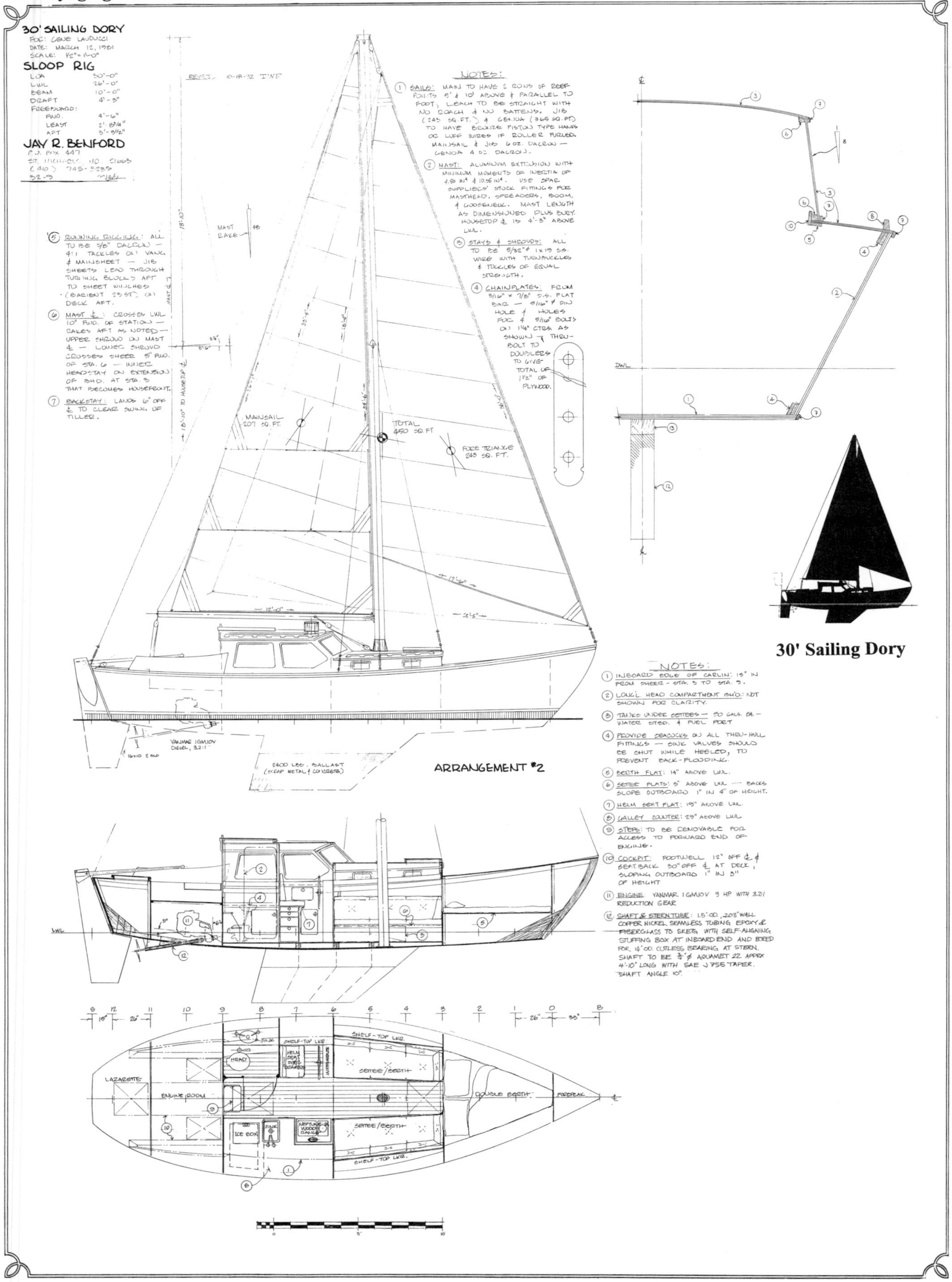

30' SAILING DORY
FOR: GENE LAUDUCCI
DATE: MARCH 12, 1981
SCALE: ½" = 1'-0"

SLOOP RIG

LOA	30'-0"
LWL	26'-0"
BEAM	10'-0"
DRAFT	4'-3"
FREEBOARD:	
FWD.	4'-6"
LEAST	2'-8¾"
AFT	3'-8½"

JAY R. BENFORD
P.O. BOX 447
ST. MICHAELS, MD. 21663
(410) 745-3235

NOTES:

① SAILS: MAIN TO HAVE 2 ROWS OF REEF POINTS 5' & 10' ABOVE & PARALLEL TO FOOT; LEACH TO BE STRAIGHT WITH NO ROACH & NO BATTENS. JIB (245 SQ. FT.) & GENOA (365 SQ. FT) TO HAVE BRONZE PISTON TYPE HANKS OR LUFF WIRES IF ROLLER FURLED. MAINSAIL & JIB 6 OZ. DACRON — GENOA 4 OZ DACRON.

② MAST: ALUMINUM EXTRUSION WITH MINIMUM MOMENTS OF INERTIA OF 4.91 IN⁴ & 10.56 IN⁴. USE SPAR SUPPLIERS' STOCK FITTING FOR MASTHEAD, SPREADERS, BOOM, & GOOSENECK. MAST LENGTH AS DIMENSIONED PLUS BURY. HOUSETOP & IS 4'-3" ABOVE LWL.

③ STAYS & SHROUDS: ALL TO BE 5/32"⌀ 1×19 S.S. WIRE WITH TURNBUCKLES & TOGGLES OF EQUAL STRENGTH.

④ CHAINPLATES: FROM 3/16" × 7/8" S.S. FLAT BAR — 3/16"⌀ PIN HOLE & HOLES FOR 5/16" BOLTS ON 1⅛" CTRS. AS SHOWN. THRU-BOLT TO DOUBLERS TO GIVE TOTAL OF 1½" OF PLYWOOD.

⑤ RUNNING RIGGING: ALL TO BE 3/8" DACRON — 4:1 TACKLES ON VANG & MAINSHEET — JIB SHEETS LEAD THROUGH TURNING BLOCKS AFT TO SHEET WINCHES (BARIENT 23 ST) ON DECK AFT.

⑥ MAST ℄: CROSSES LWL 10" FWD OF STATION — GALES AFT AS NOTED — UPPER SHROUD ON MAST ℄ — LOWER SHROUD CROSSES SHEER 5" FWD OF STA. 6 — INNER HEADSTAY ON EXTENSION OF BHD. AT STA. 3 THAT BECOMES HOUSEFRONT.

⑦ BACKSTAY: LANDS 6" OFF ℄ TO CLEAR SWING OF TILLER.

MAST RAKE: 4°

MAINSAIL 207 SQ. FT.
TOTAL 450 SQ FT
FORE TRIANGLE 243 SQ. FT.

YANMAR 1GM10V DIESEL, 3.2:1

8400 LBS. BALLAST (SCRAP METAL & CONCRETE)

ARRANGEMENT #2

30' Sailing Dory

NOTES:

① INBOARD EDGE OF CARLIN: 15" IN FROM SHEER — STA. 3 TO STA. 7.

② LOW'L HEAD COMPARTMENT BHD NOT SHOWN FOR CLARITY.

③ TANKS UNDER SETTEES — 20 GALS. EA. — WATER STBD. & FUEL PORT.

④ PROVIDE SEACOCKS ON ALL THRU-HULL FITTINGS — SINK VALVES SHOULD BE SHUT WHILE HEELED, TO PREVENT BACK-FLOODING.

⑤ BERTH FLAT: 14" ABOVE LWL.

⑥ SETTEE FLATS: 5" ABOVE LWL — BACKS SLOPE OUTBOARD 1" IN 4" OF HEIGHT.

⑦ HELM SEAT FLAT: 19" ABOVE LWL.

⑧ GALLEY COUNTER: 29" ABOVE LWL.

⑨ STEPS: TO BE REMOVABLE FOR ACCESS TO FORWARD END OF ENGINE.

⑩ COCKPIT: FOOTWELL 12" OFF ℄ & SEATBACK 30" OFF ℄ AT DECK, SLOPING OUTBOARD 1" IN 5" OF HEIGHT.

⑪ ENGINE: YANMAR 1GM10V 9 HP WITH 3.2:1 REDUCTION GEAR.

⑫ SHAFT & STERN TUBE: 1.5" OD, .203" WALL COPPER NICKEL SEAMLESS TUBING EPOXY & FIBERGLASS TO SKEG WITH SELF-ALIGNING STUFFING BOX AT INBOARD END AND BORED FOR 16"OD CUTLESS BEARING AT STERN. SHAFT TO BE ¾"⌀ AQUAMET 22 APPROX 4'-10" LONG WITH SAE J755 TAPER. SHAFT ANGLE 10°.

LAZARETTE
ENGINE ROOM
HEAD
HELM SEAT
OUTBOARD
SETTEE/BERTH
DOUBLE BERTH
FOREPEAK
SHELF-TOP LKR.
SETTEE/BERTH
ICE BOX

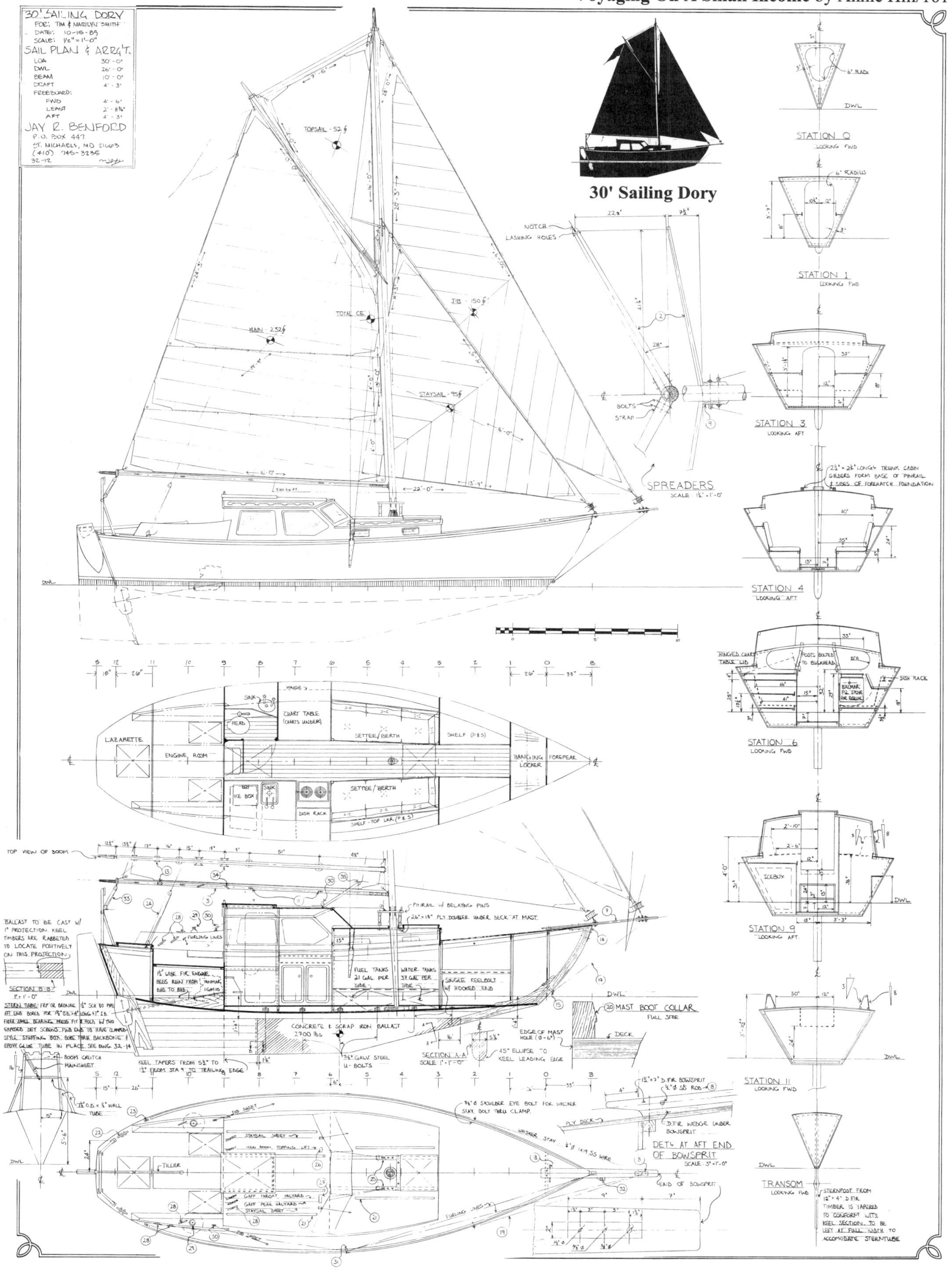

30' SAILING DORY
FOR: TIM & MARILYN SMITH
DATE: 10-18-89
SCALE: 1/2" = 1'-0"
SAIL PLAN & ARRGT.
LOA   30'-0"
DWL   26'-0"
BEAM   10'-0"
DRAFT   4'-3"
FREEBOARD:
   FWD   4'-6"
   LEAST   2'-8½"
   AFT   4'-3"
JAY R. BENFORD
P.O. BOX 447
ST. MICHAELS, MD 21663
(410) 745-3235
32-12

30' Sailing Dory

TOPSAIL - 52 □
TOTAL CE
MAIN - 252 □
JIB - 150 □
STAYSAIL - 95 □

SPREADERS
SCALE 1½" = 1'-0"

NOTCH
LASHING HOLES
BOLTS
STRAP

STATION 0 — LOOKING FWD
STATION 1 — LOOKING FWD
STATION 3 — LOOKING AFT
STATION 4 — LOOKING AFT
STATION 6 — LOOKING FWD
STATION 9 — LOOKING AFT
STATION 11 — LOOKING FWD
TRANSOM — LOOKING FWD

LAZARETTE
ENGINE ROOM
SINK
HEAD
CHART TABLE (CHARTS UNDER)
SETTEE/BERTH
SHELF (P&S)
HANGING LOCKER
FOREPEAK
ICE BOX
SINK
DISH RACK
SETTEE/BERTH
SHELF - TOP LKR (P&S)

TOP VIEW OF BOOM
PINRAIL W/ BELAYING PINS
FUEL TANKS
WATER TANKS
SINGLE KEELBOLT W/ HOOKED END
CONCRETE & SCRAP IRON BALLAST 2700 lbs
MAST BOOT COLLAR — FULL SIZE
EDGE OF MAST HOLE
DECK
BOOM CRUTCH
MAINSHEET

BALLAST TO BE CAST W/
1" PROTECTION KEEL
TIMBERS ARE RABBETED
TO LOCATE POSITIVELY
ON THIS PROJECTION

SECTION B-B
1" = 1'-0"

SECTION A-A
SCALE 1" = 1'-0"

45° ELLIPSE TO
KEEL LEADING EDGE

TILLER
STAYSAIL SHEET
MAIN BOOM TOPPING LIFT
GAFF THROAT HALYARD
GAFF PEAK HALYARD
STAYSAIL SHEET
FURLING LINES

DETL AT AFT END
OF BOWSPRIT
SCALE 3" = 1'-0"
END OF BOWSPRIT
D.FIR. WEDGE UNDER BOWSPRIT
HAWSER STAY

STERNPOST FROM
12" x 4" D.FIR
TIMBER IS TAPERED
TO CONFORM WITH
KEEL SECTION, TO BE
LEFT AT FULL WIDTH TO
ACCOMMODATE STERNTUBE

30' SAILING DORY

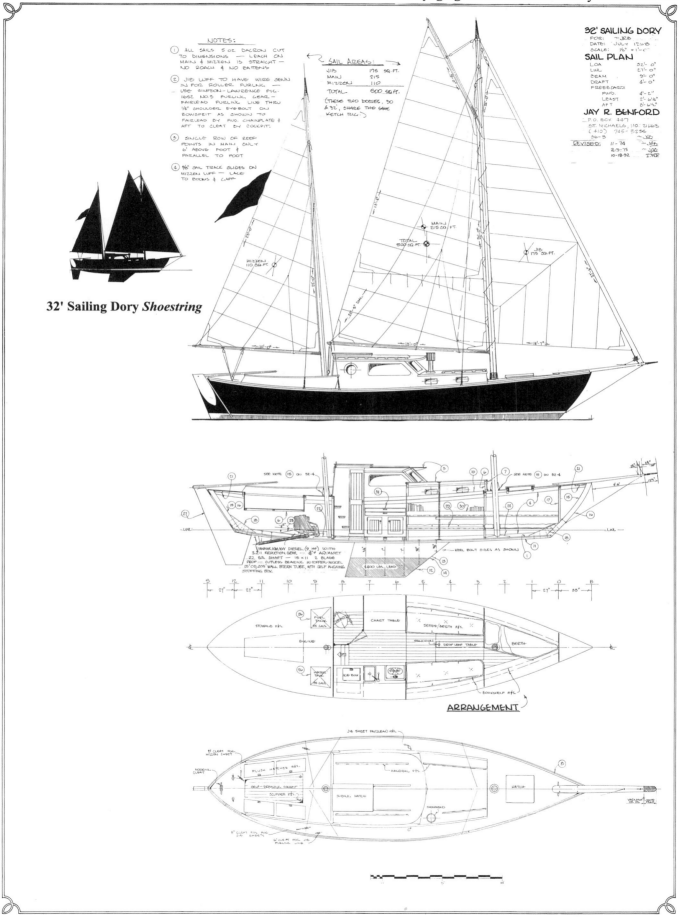

32' Sailing Dory *Shoestring*

ARRANGEMENT

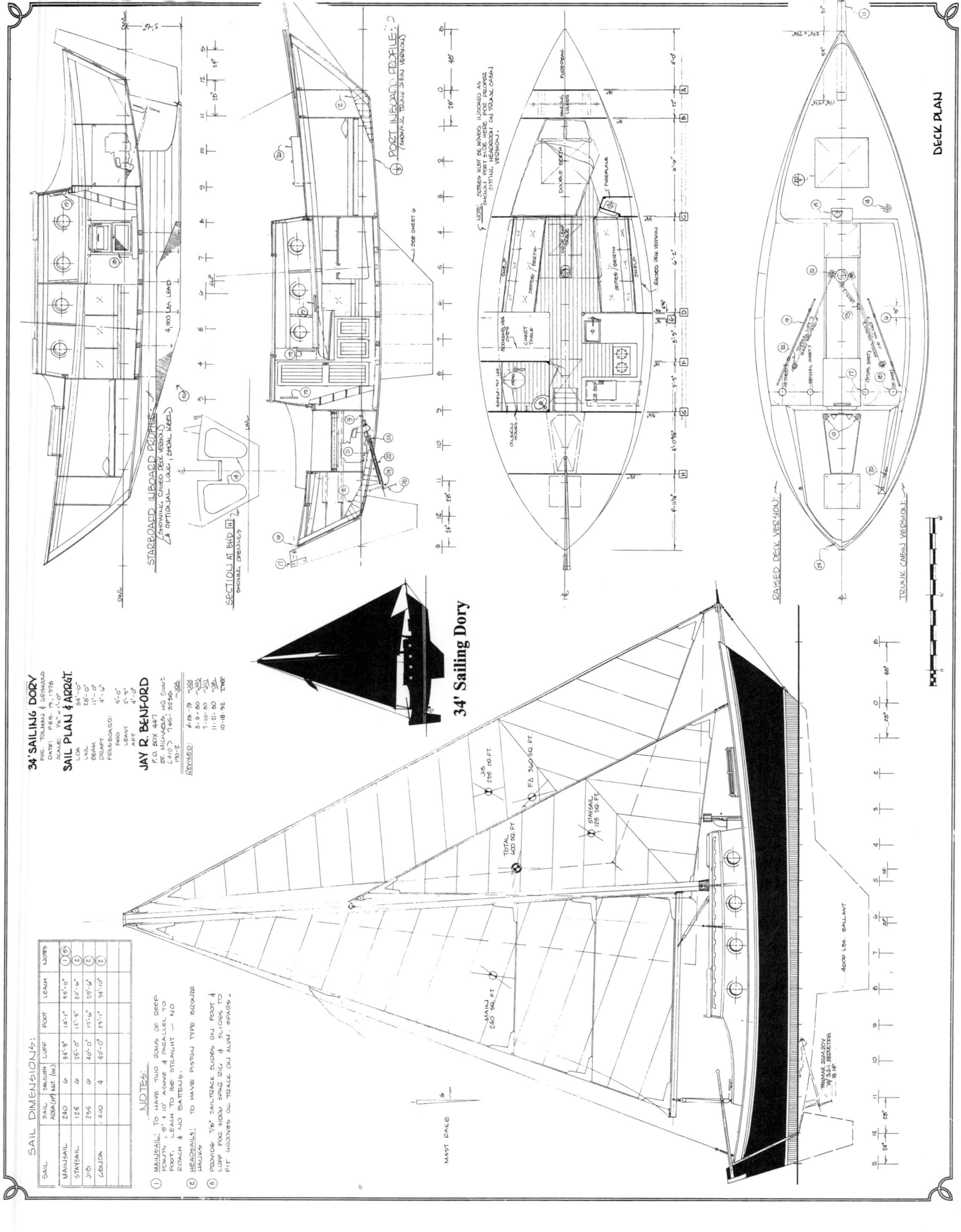

34' Sailing Dory

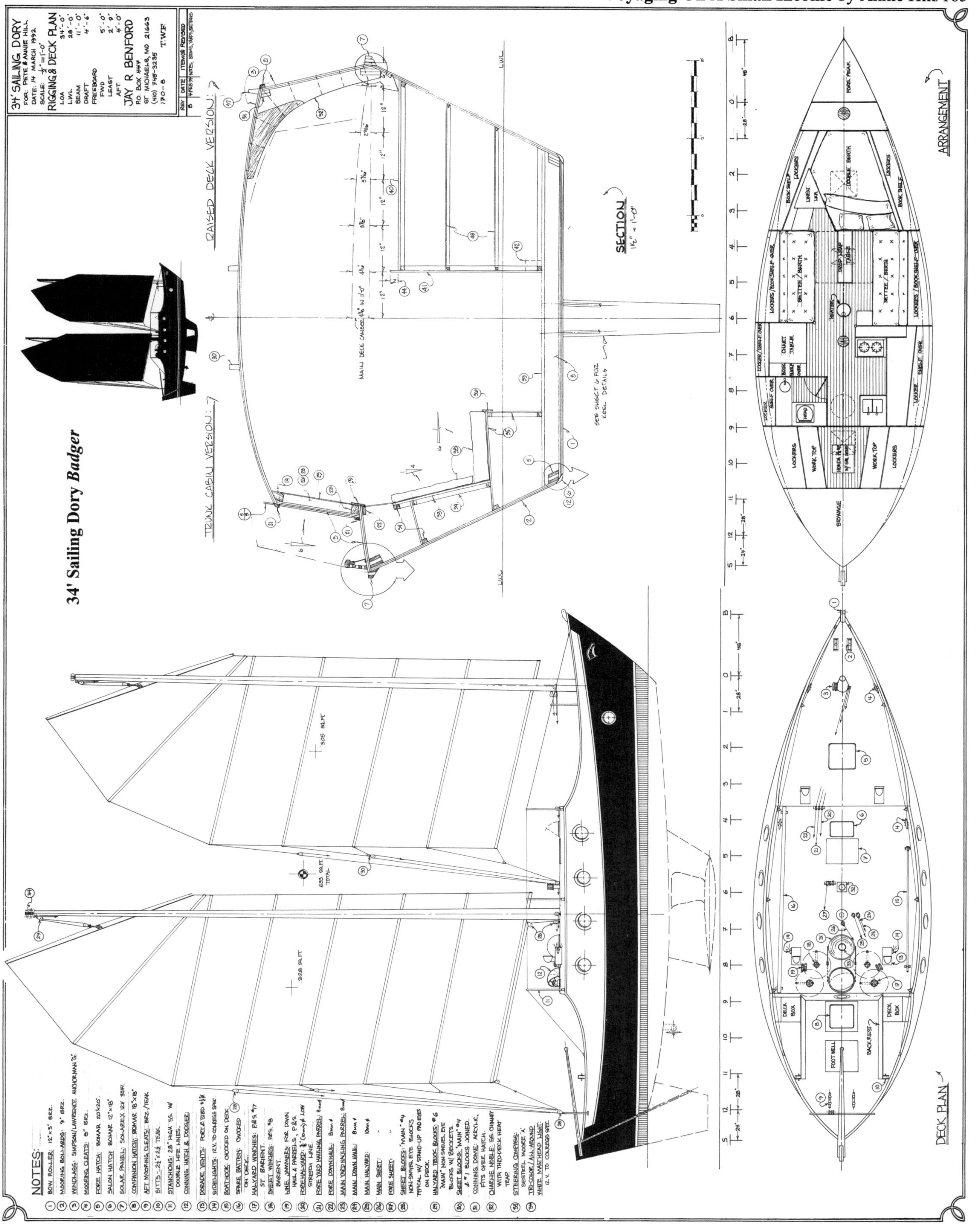

34' Sailing Dory *Badger*

RAISED DECK VERSION

TRUNK CABIN VERSION

SECTION
$1\frac{1}{2}" = 1'-0"$

SEE SHEET 9 FOR KEEL DETAILS

MAIN DECK CAMBER

ARRANGEMENT

DECK PLAN

Title block:

34' SAILING DORY
FOR: PETE & ANNIE HILL
DATE: 14 MARCH 1992
SCALE: $\frac{1}{2}" = 1'-0"$
RIGGING & DECK PLAN

L.O.A.	34'-0"
L.W.L.	28'-0"
BEAM	11'-0"
DRAFT	4'-6"
FREEBOARD	
FWD	5'-0"
LEAST	2'-9"
AFT	4'-0"

JAY R BENFORD
P.O. BOX 447
ST. MICHAELS, MD 21663
(410) 745-3235
170-6   T.W.P.

NOTES:

1. BOW ROLLER: 12"x5" SKEZ.
2. MOORING BOLLARDS: 9" SKEZ.
3. WINDLASS: SIMPSON/LAWRENCE ANCHORMAN 'G'.
4. MOORING CLEATS: 6" GEO.
5. FORE HATCH: BOMAR 201x205
6. SALON HATCH: BOMAR 12"x16"
7. SOLAR PANEL: SQ-APEX 122 50W.
8. COMPANION HATCH: BOMAR 18"x18"
9. AFT MOORING CLEATS: 8PZ./TEAK
10. BITTS - 2½"x24" TEAK
11. CONNING HATCH & DOGGED.
12. DORADE VENTS: PORT & STBD 1½
13. SIDELIGHTS: REV. TO COMPASS SPEC.
14. BOATHOOKS: CHOCKED ON DECK.
15. SPARE BATTEN: CHOCKED ON DECK.
16. HALYARD TERIDS BLOCKS: #6
17. SHEET WINCHES: RF5 #8
    ST. BAREIENT.
18. HALYARD WINCHES: RF5 #8
    ST. BAREIENT.
19. MAIN VANGS: FORE DOWN
    HAUL & PARREL-5, #5 P.&S.
20. FORE HALYARD: ¾ (-o----)½ LOW
    STRETCH LINE.
21. FORE VANG TAILING PARREL, 8mm.
22. FORE DOWNHAUL: 8mm
23. MAIN VANG/TAILING PARREL, 8mm
24. MAIN DOWN HAUL: 8mm #
25. MAIN HALYARD: 10mm #
26. FORE SHEET:
27. MAIN SHEET:
28. SHEET BLOCKS: 'MAIN' #4
    NON-SWIVEL EYE BACKS
    TYPICAL w/ STAND-UP PADEYES
29. SHEET BLOCKS: 'MAIN' #4
30. CONNING DOME: ACRYLIC,
    FITS OVER HATCH.
31. CHARLIE NOBLE: FOR CHIMNEY
    WITH THRO-DECK 'HEAT'
    TRAP
32. STEERING COMPASS:
    SESTREL, MOORE 'A'
33. TRI-COLOR/ANL-AROUND
    WHITE: MASTHEAD LIGHT
    Q.V. TO COMPASS SPEC

REV | DATE | ITEMS REVISED

(Above and below) *Bruce Talbot's 36'* **Windhover** *under construction in Vancouver, B.C., Canada. The simple, easily built shape of these designs is evident. Bruce Talbot photos.*

(Above and below) *Fred Schreiner's 36'* **Donna** *sailing off Friday Harbor, Washington, on her sea trials with her original rig. Jay R. Benford photos.*

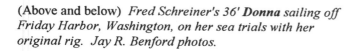

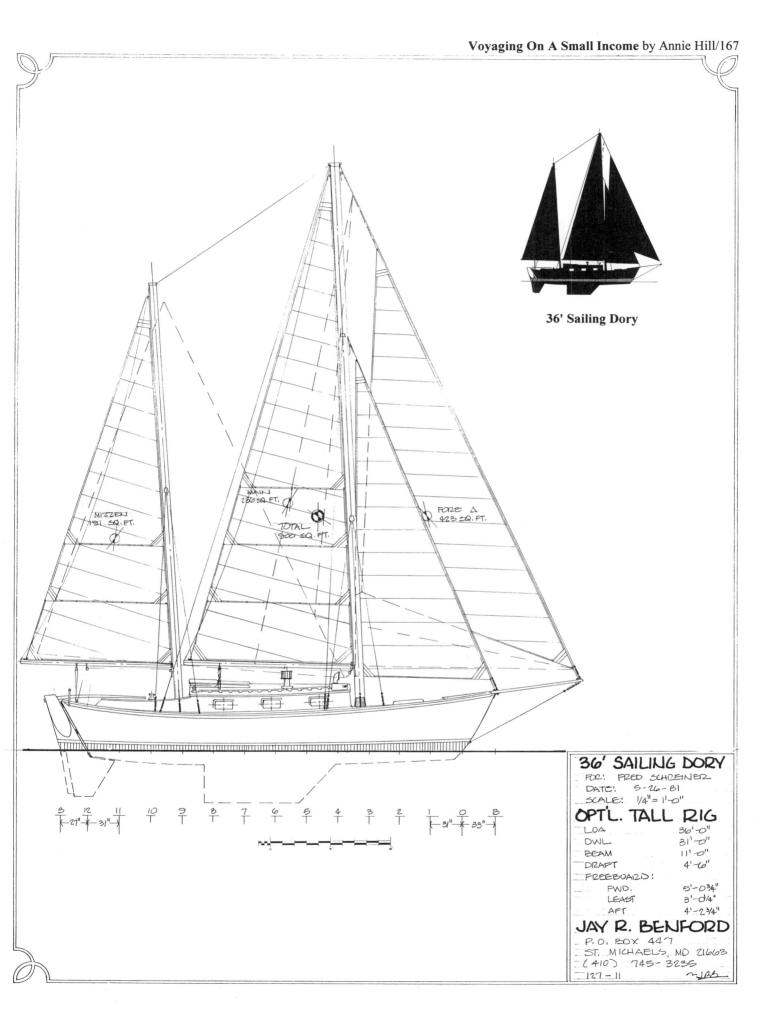

36' Sailing Dory

MIZZEN
151 SQ.FT.

MAIN
230 SQ.FT.

TOTAL
800 SQ.FT.

FORE Δ
423 SQ.FT.

8 12 11 10 9 8 7 6 5 4 3 2 1 0 B
⊢27"⊣ 31"   3"⊢ 33"

36' SAILING DORY
FOR: FRED SCHREINER
DATE: 5-26-81
SCALE: 1/4"=1'-0"

OPT'L. TALL RIG
LOA   36'-0"
DWL   31'-0"
BEAM   11'-0"
DRAFT   4'-6"
FREEBOARD:
   FWD.   5'-0¾"
   LEAST   3'-0¼"
   AFT   4'-2¾"

JAY R. BENFORD
P.O. BOX 447
ST. MICHAELS, MD 21663
(410) 745-3235
127-11

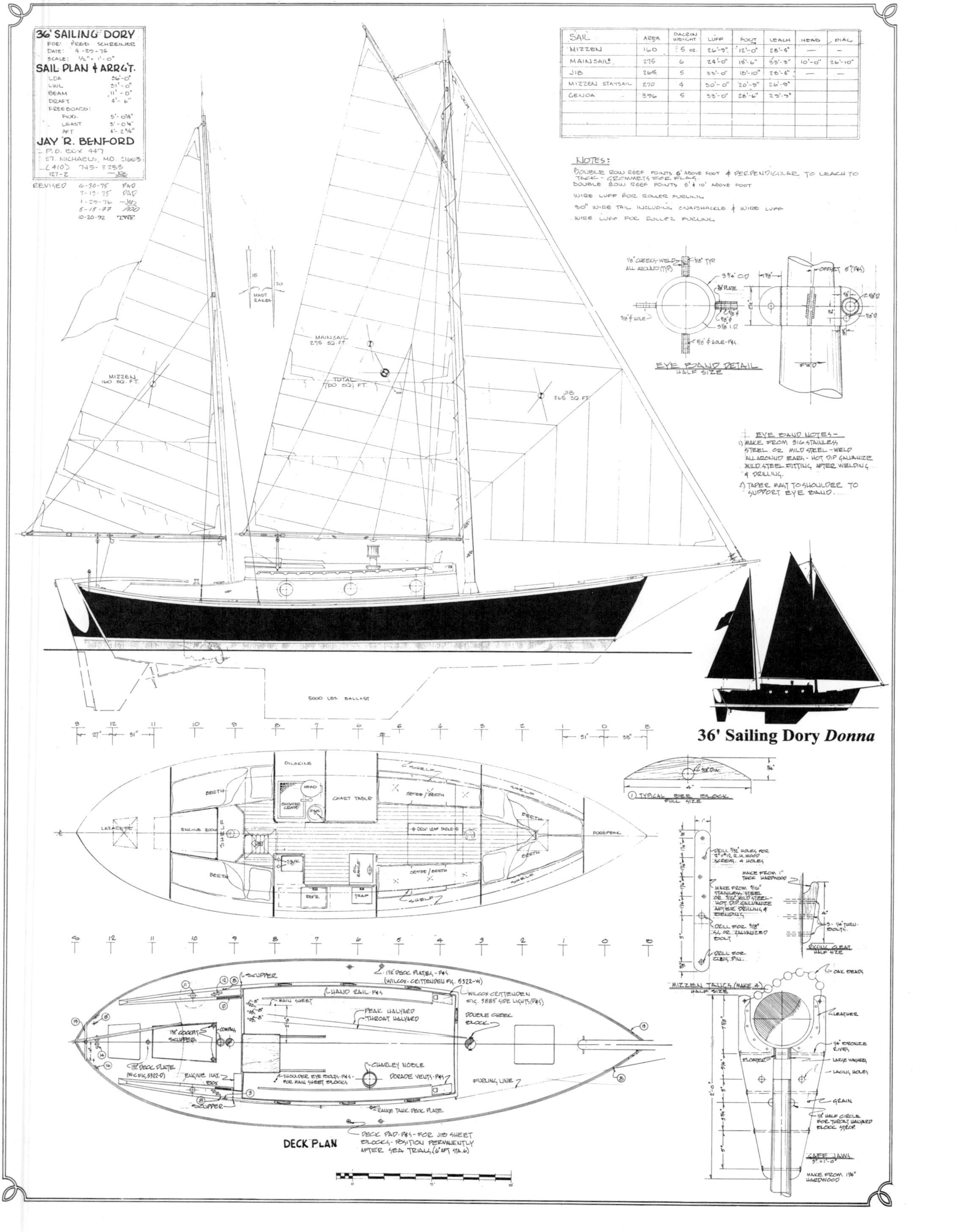

36' SAILING DORY
FOR: FRED SCHREINER
DATE: 4-25-76
SCALE: ⅛" = 1'-0"

SAIL PLAN & ARRG'T.
LOA .... 36'-0"
LWL .... 31'-0"
BEAM .... 11'-0"
DRAFT .... 4'-6"
FREEBOARD:
  FWD. .... 5'-0¾"
  LEAST .... 3'-0¾"
  AFT .... 4'-2¾"

JAY R. BENFORD
P.O. BOX 447
ST. MICHAELS, MD. 21663
(410) 745-3355

SAIL	AREA	DACRON WEIGHT	LUFF	FOOT	LEACH	HEAD	DIAG.
MIZZEN	160	5 oz.	26'-9"	12'-0"	28'-4"	—	—
MAINSAIL	275	6	24'-0"	15'-6"	33'-3"	10'-0"	26'-10"
JIB	265	5	33'-0"	15'-10"	28'-6"	—	—
MIZZEN STAYSAIL	270	4	30'-0"	20'-9"	26'-9"	—	—
GENOA	396	5	33'-0"	28'-6"	25'-5"	—	—

NOTES:
DOUBLE ROW REEF POINTS 6' ABOVE FOOT & PERPENDICULAR TO LEACH TO TACK - GROMMETS FOR FLAG
DOUBLE ROW REEF POINTS 5' & 10' ABOVE FOOT
WIRE LUFF FOR ROLLER FURLING
30" WIRE TAIL INCLUDING SNAPSHACKLE & WIRE LUFF
WIRE LUFF FOR ROLLER FURLING

EYE BAND DETAIL
HALF SIZE

EYE BAND NOTES —

MAINSAIL 275 SQ. FT.
MIZZEN 160 SQ. FT.
TOTAL 700 SQ. FT.
JIB 265 SQ. FT.

5000 LBS. BALLAST

36' Sailing Dory *Donna*

TYPICAL SIZE BLOCK
FULL SIZE

DECK PLAN

MIZZEN TANGS (MAKE 4)
HALF SIZE

GAFF JAWS

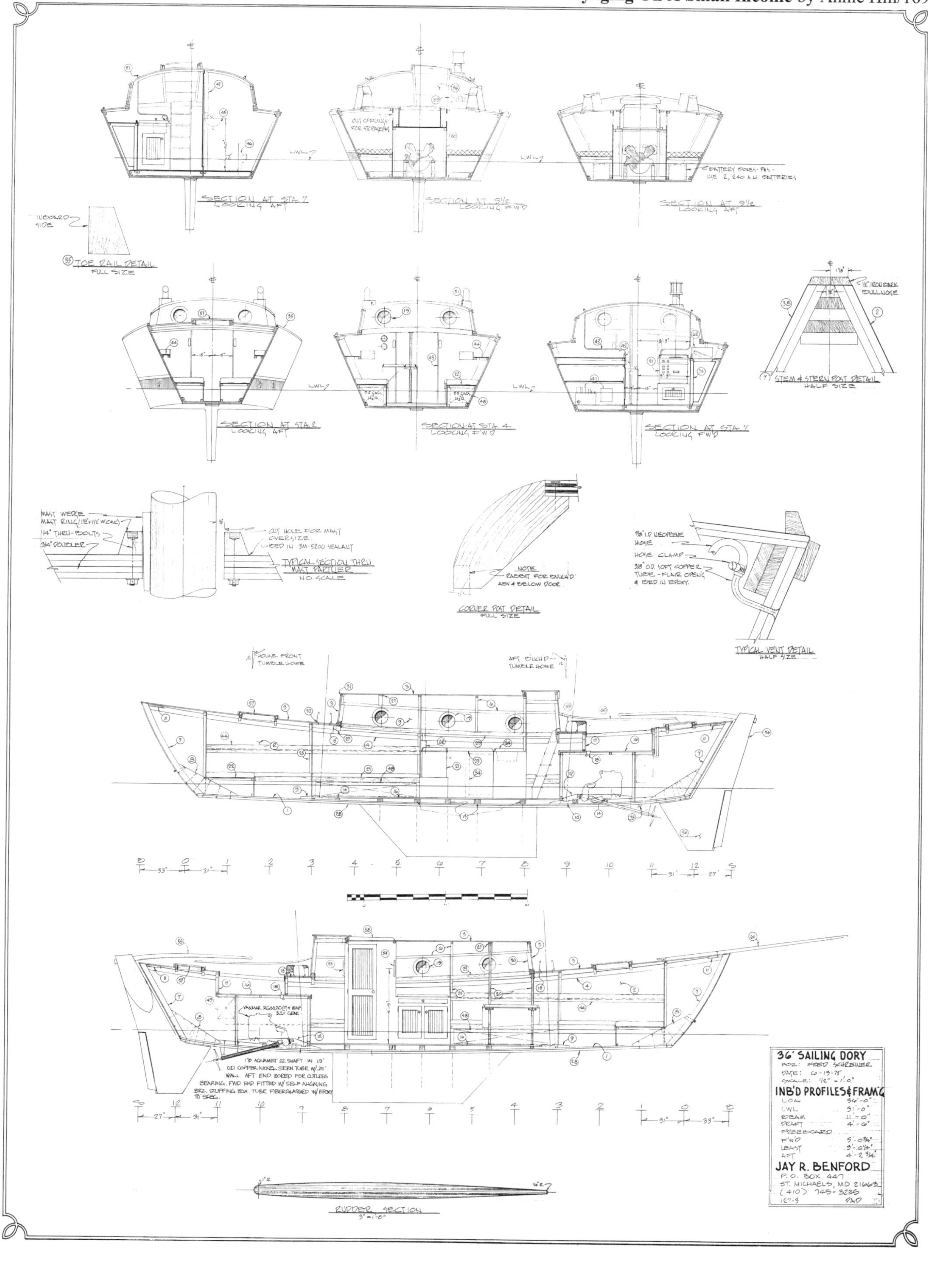
SECTION AT STA. 7
LOOKING AFT
SECTION AT 9½
LOOKING FWD
SECTION AT 9½
LOOKING AFT
CUT OPENINGS FOR STEERING
LWL
INBOARD SIDE
TOE RAIL DETAIL
FULL SIZE
SECTION AT STA. 2
LOOKING AFT
SECTION AT STA. 4
LOOKING FWD
LOOKING FWD
1⅛" IRONBARK BULLNOSE
STEM & STERN POST DETAIL
HALF SIZE
MAST WEDGE
MAST RING
1/4" THRU-BOLTS
3/4" DOUBLER
CUT HOLE FOR MAST OVERSIZE
BED IN 3M-5200 SEALANT
TYPICAL SECTION THRU MAST PARTNER
NO SCALE
NOTE
RABBET FOR BULKH'D ABV & BELOW DOOR
CORNER POST DETAIL
FULL SIZE
5/8" I.D. NEOPRENE HOSE
HOSE CLAMP
3/8" O.D. SOFT COPPER TUBE - FLAIR OPEN'G & BED IN EPOXY.
TYPICAL VENT DETAIL
HALF SIZE
HOUSE FRONT TUMBLEHOME
AFT BULKH'D TUMBLEHOME
1⅛ AQUAMET 22 SHAFT IN 1⅞" O.D. COPPER NICKEL STERN TUBE W/ .25" WALL. AFT END BORED FOR CUTLESS BEARING. FWD END FITTED W/ SELF ALIGNING BRZ. STUFFING BOX. TUBE FIBERGLASSED W/ EPOXY TO SKEG.
36' SAILING DORY
FOR: FRED SCHREIBER
DATE: 6-13-78
SCALE: 1/2" = 1'-0"
INB'D PROFILES & FRAM'G
LOA 36'-0"
LWL 31'-0"
BEAM 11'-0"
DRAFT 4'-6"
FREEBOARD
FWD 5'-0¾"
LEAST 3'-0¼"
AFT 4'-2¾"
JAY R. BENFORD
P.O. BOX 447
ST. MICHAELS, MD 21663
(410) 745-3235
RUDDER SECTION
3" = 1'-0"

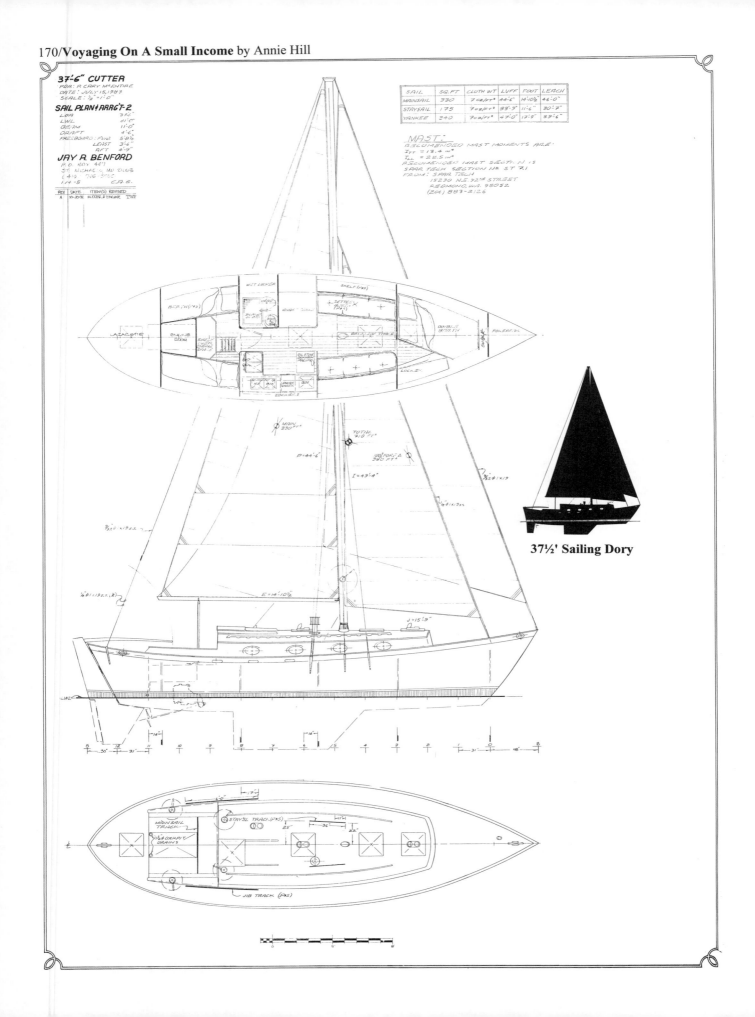

37'-6" CUTTER
FOR: P. CARY McENTIRE
DATE: JULY 15, 1983
SCALE: ⅜"=1'-0"

SAIL PLAN & ARR'G'T-2
LOA .... 37'6"
LWL .... 31'-0"
BEAM .... 11'-0"
DRAFT .... 4'-6"
FREEBOARD: FWD .... 5'-8¼"
LEAST .... 3'-6"
AFT .... 4'-9"

JAY R. BENFORD
P.O. BOX 447
ST. MICHAELS, MD 21663
(410) 745-3235
1/4-5   C.A.G.

REV	DATE	ITEM(S) REVISED	
A	10-20-91	RUDDER & ENGINE	TWF

SAIL	SQ.FT	CLOTH WT	LUFF	FOOT	LEACH
MAINSAIL	330	7 oz/ft²	44'-6"	14'-10½"	46'-0"
STAYSAIL	175	7 oz/ft²	33'-3"	11'-6"	30'-7"
YANKEE	240	7 oz/ft²	47'-0"	17'-9"	39'-6"

MAST:
RECOMENDED MAST MOMENTS ARE:
$I_{TT} = 13.4$ IN⁴
$I_{LL} = 28.5$ IN⁴
RECOMMENDED MAST SECTION IS
SPAR TECH SECTION № ST 7.1
FROM: SPAR TECH
15230 N.E. 92nd STREET
REDMOND, WA. 98052
(206) 883-2126

37½' Sailing Dory

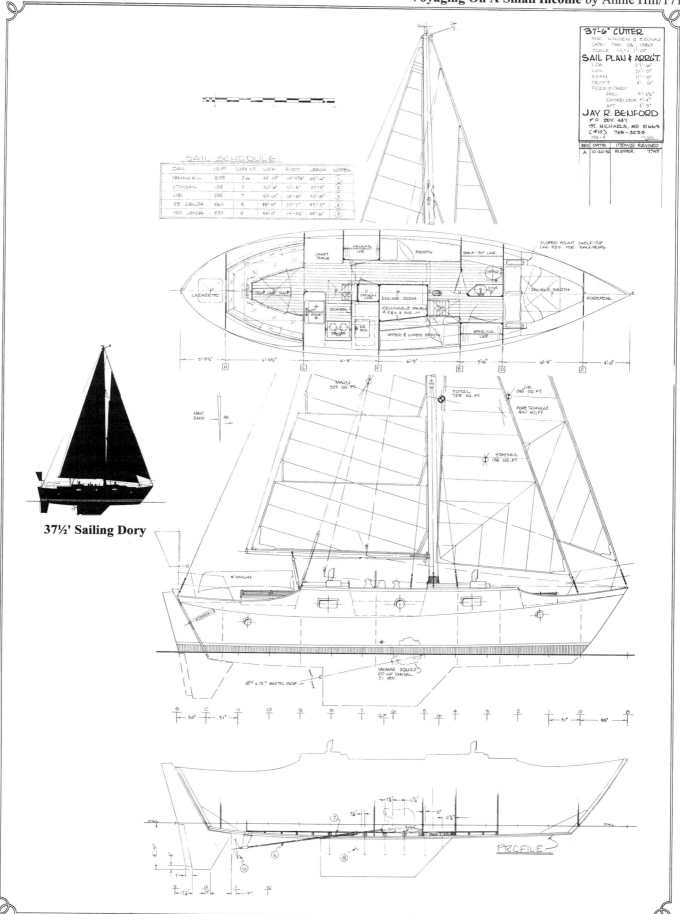

37½' Sailing Dory

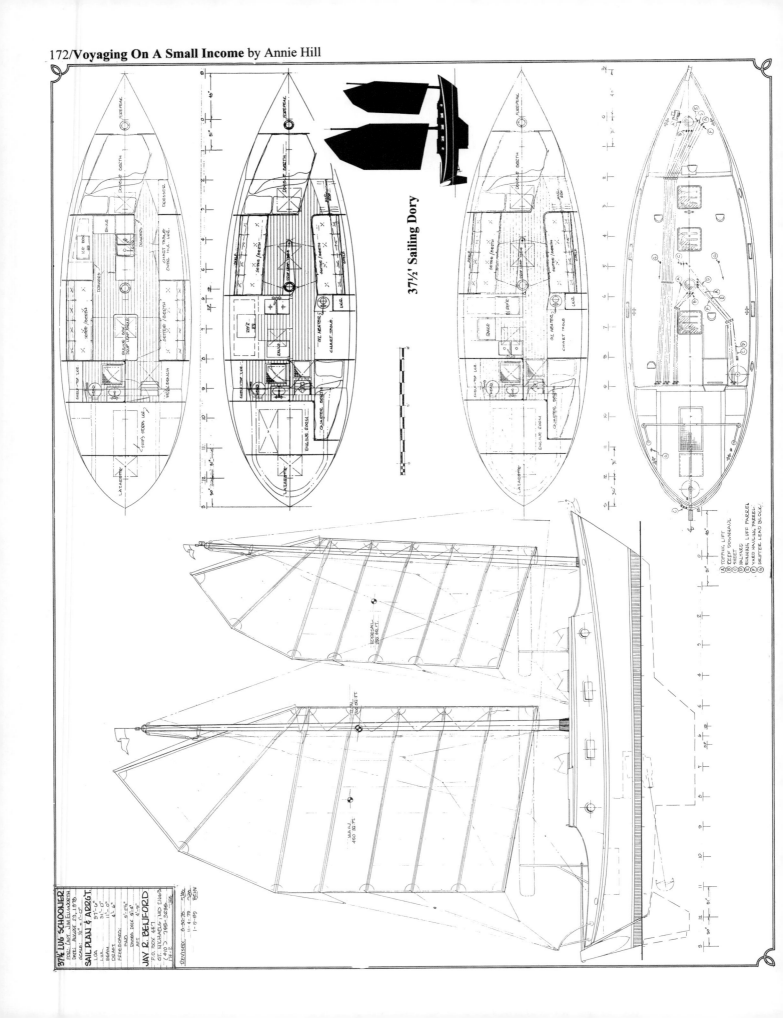

37½' Sailing Dory

Appendix V

Wylo II
Designed by Nick Skeates

With *Wylo II*, Nick Skeates designed a yacht specifically for voyaging with one or two people aboard and also wanted a vessel that could be built for a small capital outlay.

Wylo II has practical accommodation for a couple and a second double berth aft, but Nick did not fit one and uses this area for stores and spares. The forward cabin has headroom at the after end and with *Wylo II* being rather more full forward than *Badger*, there is room for a work bench and stowage for bicycles. When we met Nick, he was carrying a full size motorcycle in this cabin — wheels removed! The bulkheads are not structural and the accommodation is flexible, so long as the grab posts, marked with a small 'o' on the plans are retained, as these give structural support. The galley is smaller than *Badger*'s. The saloon is a pleasant area with room for books and there is a good size heads.

Wylo II has a full width cabin which Nick says is "logical from the point of view of strength, room on deck and room below." He is not fond of high latitude sailing but has fitted a stove in *Wylo II*. Although the double chines reduce the floor area to a certain extent, *Wylo II* still has a more spacious cabin than most other boats I have been aboard.

The boat is designed to be built of steel either with a centreboard version, which is how Nick built his own vessel or with a fixed keel. There is an option of a wing keel. The centreboard version has plywood decks, but the fixed keel version would be stiff enough to cope with the extra 500 lbs. that a steel deck would give. My personal preference would be to go for the wooden deck anyway, as being more pleasant to walk on and easier to maintain, long term than a steel deck. I would use epoxy and either sheath it with cloth or put on teak decks in accordance with the Gougeon Bros.' instructions. Steel is both cheap and strong. Nick has very simple accommodation on *Wylo II* and has found her easy to maintain inside and out. To achieve this happy state of affairs, it is essential to be able to examine the whole of the interior at regular intervals and to be able to get at it for routine maintenance. Steel is easy to repair, as long as one has access to welding materials.

On deck *Wylo II* is simple, with no cockpit at all, whereas the design shows a well. Nick's reason for this is that the self-steering generally does the work and the space aft can be better used for stowage. The dinghy can be carried in davits and there is room for one on the coachroof abaft the mast.

Wylo II is designed to have a gaff rig with a mast that will lower into a tabernacle and only overhang the boat a small way at either end. Nick's mast is actually a pole mast (without a yard for the topsail) because he was given the mast and didn't have the heart to shorten it. The headsails all have the same length luffs to make them interchangeable in case of one blowing out. The gaff is short and light. Sails are set, reefed or lowered, but not changed.

Wylo II is simple and should be cheap to build. There are several about being sailed very happily. They are stiff to windward and fast boats (runs of 190 miles a day have been recorded) when driven to their fullest potential. *Wylo II* has suffered her fair share of gales and storms and come through unscathed.

The design is also available with junk or Bermudian rig. A 35 ft. version is available, but Nick says and I agree with him, that the 32 ft. *Wylo II* is the better size.

Particulars:

LOA		32'-0"
LWL		28'-0"
Beam		10'-0"
Draft:	Centerboard Version	3'-3"/6'-3"
	Keel Version	4'-3"
	Wing Keel Version	3'-9"
Sail Area:	Gaff Cutter	660 Sq. Ft.
	Junk Rig	650 Sq. Ft.
Displacement		14,000 pounds
Prismatic Coefficient		0.53
Displacement/Length Ratio		285
Sail area/Displacement Ratio		18.2
Ballast ratio		39%

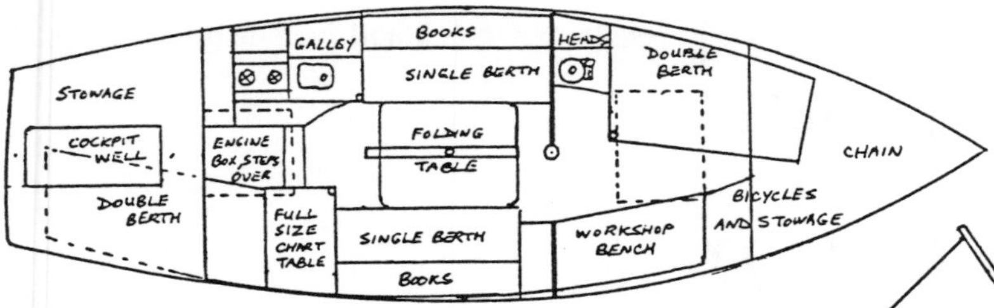

STOWAGE

GALLEY

BOOKS

SINGLE BERTH

HEADS

DOUBLE BERTH

COCKPIT WELL

ENGINE BOX STEPS OVER

FOLDING TABLE

CHAIN

DOUBLE BERTH

FULL SIZE CHART TABLE

SINGLE BERTH

WORKSHOP BENCH

BICYCLES AND STOWAGE

BOOKS

WYLO II

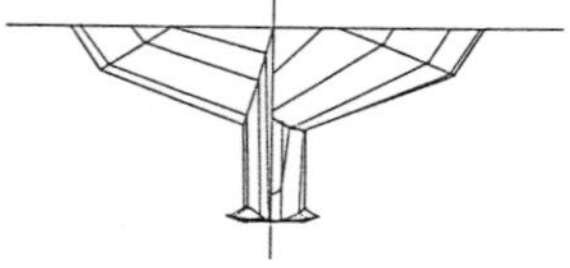

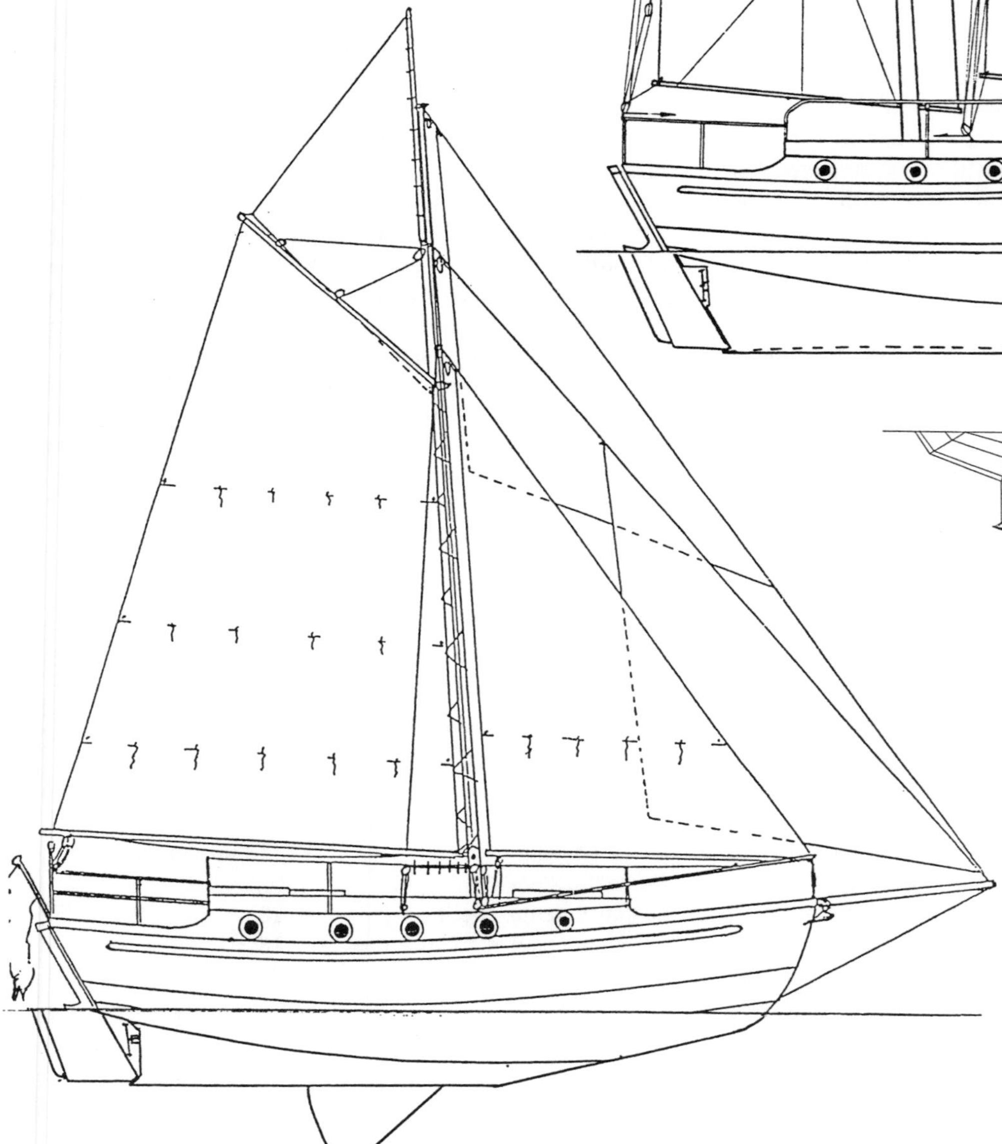

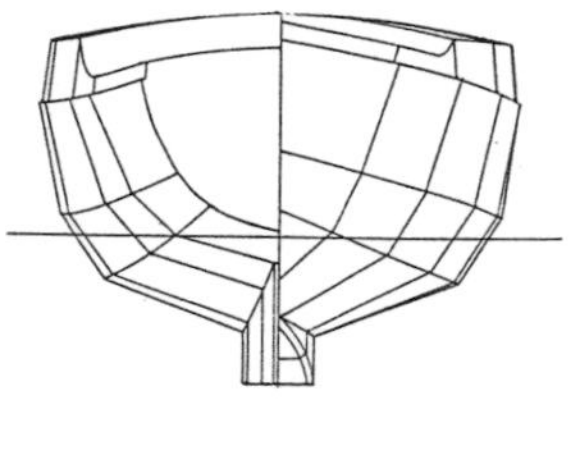

Appendix VI

Sources

In this appendix are contained books and addresses. The books and the other sources have often been mentioned in the text.

YACHT DESIGNS

This is a list of addresses of places where you can get designs for good voyaging yachts, yachts for amateur construction or specialist assistance with a cruising rig.

Jay R. Benford
P.O. Box 447
605 Talbot Street
St. Michaels, MD 21663 USA

Tel (410) 745-3235
Fax (410) 745-9743

Designer of *Badger*. Jay Benford has also designed many other boats from tiny dinghies to a 131 ft. sailing yacht. Designs sailing craft and power craft with the emphasis on cruising homes. A lot of his designs are for amateur construction.

Philip C. Bolger
29 Ferry Street
Gloucester, MA 01930 USA

Designer of *Tortoise*, our dinghy. Phil Bolger has also designed many other dinghies and a wide variety of cruising boats. He specializes in shoal draught and many of his boats are suitable for amateur construction.

Warwick Collins
23 Kingston Park
Lymington, Hants SO41 8ES UK

Tel 0590 79088
Fax 0590 72720

Designer of the tandem keel - a wing keel with a slot in it. We fitted one of these to *Badger* and have been very pleased with it. Warwick Collins also designs boats, but concentrates on fairly high performance craft.

Eventide Owners Association
David Wight, Plans Secretary
18 Mayland Close
Haybridge, Maldon
Essex GM9 7YR UK

This association sells plans, originally shown in Yachting Monthly. For amateur construction, they include *Mouette (Erik the Red)* and some Maurice Griffiths Designs; ranging from 13 to 31 feet.

Danny Greene
P.O. Box 245
Paget PBBX
Bermuda

Designer of *Two-Bits*, our last dinghy and of several other dinghies, nesting and otherwise.

Maurice Griffiths Plans
P G sheaf
"Orchards"
School Lane
Easton
Woodbridge, Suffolk IP13 0ES UK

Tel 0728 747427
Fax 0728 747663

Maurice Griffiths specializes in designing wholesome, comfortable, shoal draught cruising boats, strong enough to take whatever is thrown at them. His *Lone Gull II* has a reputation as one of the best designs of

its type. Send £2 for a catalogue (£5 overseas).

Nick Skeates
c/o 21 The Avenue
Brockham
Bletchworth, Surrey RH3 7EN UK

Designer of *Wylo II*

Sunbird Marine
373 Hunts Pond road
Titchfield
Fareham, Hants PO14 4PB UK

Tel 0329 42613

Designer of the Sunbird 32, a GRP cruising yacht with junk rig which they will build on request. They will also design a junk rig for existing yachts. Sunbird has a brokerage section, which specializes in second-hand yachts with junk or advanced cruising rigs.

James Wharram Designs
Greenbank Road
Devoran
Truro, Cornwall TR3 6PJ UK

Designer of *Stormalong*. Jim and his associates have also designed many other polynesian catamarans for amateur construction. Built to plan they are seaworthy, beautiful and romantic craft.

MANUFACTURERS OF YACHTING EQUIPMENT

This is a list of addresses of people who make equipment of products that may be needed when preparing a yacht for voyaging. References in the book itself, will often describe a product or where it's been used. I have used something form nearly all of the manufacturers mentioned and have generally been satisfied.

Ampair
P.O. Box 416
Poole, Dorset BH12 3LZ UK

Tel 0202 749994
Fax 0202 736653

Manufacturer of wind and water generators.

Davey and Company
4 Oak Industrial Park
Chelmsford Road
Great Dunmow
Essex CM6 1XN UK

Tel 0371 6361

Manufacturer and retailer of paint-on Latex, Wykeham-Martin furling gears, ventilators, lamps and a wide variety of top-quality traditional equipment.

Dickinson USA, Inc.
11324 Mukilteo Speedway
Lynnwood, WA 98037

Tel (206) 347-4028
     (800) 659-9768 US/Canada
     (206) 742-3699 Seattle
Fax (206) 347-8502

The Dickinson Manufacturing Co., Ltd.
#407 - 204 Cayer Street
Coquitlam, B.C.
Canada V3K 5B1

Tel (604) 525-6444
Fax (604) 525-6417

Manufacturer of diesel cookers and heaters.

Force 10 Marine Ltd.
23080 Hamilton Road
Richmond, B.C.
Canada V6V 1C9

Tel (604) 522-7741
Fax (604) 522-9608

Manufacturer of heaters and cookers fueled by paraffin or gas.

Guy Cotten (UK), Ltd.
Heathlands Road Industrial Estate
Liskeard, Cornwall PL14 4DH UK

Tel 0579 47115
Fax 0579 47119

Manufacturer of oilskins. Although they have branched out into "yachtie" gear, they still make basic, tough, long-lasting low-priced gear which is good value for the money.

International Paint, Ltd.
Yacht division
24-30 Canute Road
Southampton S09 3AS UK

Manufacturer of paints and finishes including UV resistant polyurethene varnish.

Interlux
2270 Morris Avenue
Union, NJ 07083 USA

Tel (800) INTRLUX

Manufacturer of paints and finishes including UV-resistant polyurethene varnish.

Plastimo UK, Ltd.
School Lane
Chandlers Ford Industrial Estate
Eastleigh, Hants UK

Tel 0703 262211
Fax 0703 266328

Manufacturer of a wide range of yachting equipment - moderately priced, reasonable quality, largely for production boats.

Refleks Olieovne A-S
Lrupvej 17
5750 Ringe
Denmark

Tel 09 67 12 68

Manufacturer of diesel stoves.

(Rutland) MARLEC Engineering Co., Ltd.
Unit K
Cavendish Courtyard
Sallow Road
Corby
Northamptonshire UK NN17 1DZ

Tel 0536 201588
Fax 0536 400211

Manufacturer of wind generators.

Shipmate Stoves UK
14 Hillview road
London NW7 1AJ UK

Tel 081 959 4203

Retailer of paraffin and gas fueled cookers and of paraffin and solid fuel heaters.

Shipmate Stove Division
Richmond Ring Company
P.O. Box 375
Souderton, PA 18964 USA

Tel (215) 855-2609

Manufacturer of paraffin and gas fueled cookers and of paraffin and solid fuel heaters.

Simpson-Lawrence
218/228 Edmiston Drive
Glasgow G51 2YT
Scotland

Tel 041 427 5331
Fax 041 427 5419

Manufacturer of windlasses, CQR anchors and other marine equipment.

Stowe Marine Equipment, Ltd.
Parklands Business Park
Forest Road
Denmead, Hants
UK P07 6XP

Tel 0705 241313
Fax 0705 261304

Manufacturer of electronic equipment including electric trailed logs.

Structural Polymer Systems, Ltd.
Cowes, Isle of Wight
UK PO31 7EU

Tel 0983 298451
Fax 0983 298453

Manufacturer of epoxy resins and associated products for bonding, laminating and fairing and also of UV resistant polyurethene varnish.

Sun Shower
Basic Designs, Inc.
Sausalito, CA 94965 USA

Manufacturer of "Sun Shower" - Portable shower.

Taylor Cookers and Heaters
Blakes of Gosport
Harbour Road
Gosport, Hants PO12 1BQ UK

Tel 0705 510045
Fax 0705 510481

As well as paraffin fueled cookers and heaters, Blakes also manufacture paints, seacocks and marine toilets.

Thetford (Aqua) Products, Ltd.
(Porta Potti)
Centrovell Industrial Estate
Caldwell Road
Nuneaton, Warwickshire
UK CV11 4UD

Tel 0203 341941

Manufacturer of portable toilets and associated products.

Thetford Corporation (Porta Potti)
P.O. Box 1285
Ann Arbor, MI 48106 USA

Manufacturer of portable toilets.

Tinker Tramp
Henshaw Inflatables, Ltd.
Bennetts Field Trading Estate
Wincanton, Somerset
UK BA9 9DT

Tel 0963 33267
Fax 0963 34578

Manufacturer of inflatable dinghies. Accessories include sailing rig, life raft canopy and CO2 cylinders to make for automatic inflation. The only life raft that can be sailed or used as a dinghy for the rest of the time.

Walker Logs
Thos Walker & Son, Ltd.
Bissell Street, Birmingham
UK B5 7HR

Tel 021 622 4475
Fax 021 622 4478

Manufacturer of mechanical towing logs - very reliable, every yacht should have one. Also make electric logs.

WEST System
Wessex Resins & Adhesives, Ltd.
189/193 Spring Road
Southampton, Hants
UK S02 7NY

Tel 0703 444744
Fax 0703 431792

Gougeon Brothers, Inc.
100 Patterson Avenue
P.O. Box X908
Bay City, MI 48707 USA

Tel (517) 684-7286
Fax (517) 684-1374

Manufacturer of epoxy resins and associated products for bonding, laminating and fairing. Also make UV resistant polyurethene varnishes.

The Yacht Leg Company
30 Crosier Road
Ickenham
Uxbridge, Middlesex
UK UB10 8RR

Tel 0895 39374

Manufacturer of custom-made, marine-grade aluminum yacht legs. The initial cost will soon be recouped by saving having to pay to be hauled out. Legs can also save you harbour dues and enable you to inspect damage straight away.

Pantaenius UK Ltd.
Yacht and General Insurance Brokers
11 Lynher Queen Anne's Battery
PLYMOUTH
Devon PL4 OLP
UK   Tel 0752 223656
           Fax 0752 223637

MAIL ORDER CHANDLERS

I have only dealt with the US ones while in that country, so cannot comment on their efficiency when sending gear abroad.

The British ones I have dealt with on several occasions while out of the country. When you suddenly need a piece of equipment, it is worth knowing that a letter, fax or telephone call can get you what you need. A credit card is of great assistance here. Check with your host country for its Customs requirements. Generally if the despatcher marks the parcel "Yacht in Transit" duty will be waived, but some places can be awkward.

BOAT/US
Boat Owners Association of the United States
880 South Pickett
Alexandria, VA 22304 USA

These sell at discount - a larger discount being offered to members. They also act as a sort of watchdog group on behalf of boat owners, calling members attention to new legislation, etc.

Cruisermart Discount Marine
36/37 Eastern Esplanade
Southend-on-Sea
Essex SS1 2ES UK

Tel 0702 460055
Fax 0702 461669

Discount chandlers. I have nearly always found them to be the cheapest in the UK and their service both in and out of the country has been first-class.

Defender Industries
P.O. Box 820, 255 Main Street
New Rochelle, NY 10802-0820 USA

Tel (914) 632-3001
    (800) 628-8225 US only
Fax (914) 632-6544

Well-stocked mail order chandlers. I mention them because this is the only source of which I know for Luke anchors.

Thomas Foulkes
8b Sansom Road
Leytonstone, London
UK E11 3HB

Tel 081 539 5627
Fax 081 556 7250

Discount chandlers. They carry a large stock and will look for things that they don't stock. We have had excellent service from them when ordering from without the country.

CHANDLER

West Country Chandlers
High Street
Falmouth, Cornwall UK

Most people voyaging to or from the UK can, or do go to Falmouth. This small chandlers is one of the best-stocked you'll find, with both the usual and traditional gear. If you want a wooden block, a heating stove, a dinghy, a chart, a barometer or spares for your Primus, chances are you'll find it here.

MISCELLANEOUS USEFUL ADDRESSES

Dubois-Phillips & McCallum, Ltd.
Admiralty Chart Agents
8a Rumford Place
Liverpool L3 9BY UK

Tel 051 236 2776

One of many Admiralty chart agents - I mention them because I have dealt with them both personally and by mail on several occasions and always found them helpful and completely satisfactory.

Junk (and advanced cruising) Rig Association
373 Hunts Pond Road
Titchfield
Fareham, Hants PO14 4PB UK

Tel 0329 42613

A world-wide association of those owning and/or interested in junk-rigged and advanced cruising rigged vessels. A twice-yearly newsletter recounts members' doings and discusses rigs. Very good value for £6 per annum.

National Savings Bank
Bonds & Stock Office
Blackpool, Lancs
UK FY3 9YP

Tel 0253 697333

This is the place from which 'gilt edged' Government stocks are bought and sold on behalf of people such as ourselves. They will provide more information if you contact them.

The Prestige Group PLC
1 City Road
Derby DE1 3RL UK

Manufacturer of pressure cookers.

Vega Instruments
74 Main Avenue
Bush Hill Park
Enfield, Middlesex UK

Compilers of "Cook's Sextant Tables", a long-term almanac which includes the dec of the Sun and 38 chosen stars, the GHA of Aries for every second of GMT, the SHA of the 38 stars and the Sun's GHA for every second of GMT until 2004 - and all for £1. Every yacht should have a copy.

BOOKS

This is divided into two sections - cruising yarns and textbooks/reference books. The cruising books are written by sailors who illustrate many of the topics I have mentioned in the book. It is by no means exhaustive and omits some books that all cruising people should read and re-read, such as those by Miles Smeeton. Such omissions are due to the fact that these sailors had a decent income, sailed with crew, had large vessels, etc., etc., and in no way reflect upon the cruises and voyages themselves.

The textbook/reference books are ones that I feel would be of interest to potential small income voyagers who, having managed to get through the book, would like to try out some of the ideas.

Cruising Yarns

Edward Allcard
Temptress **Returns**

A classic cruising story of a simple boat and the ups and downs of a voyage from New York back to England.

Commander R.D. Graham
Rough Passage

An account of a wonderful voyage in a 29 ft. yacht. Single-handed from UK to Newfoundland; a cruise in that area; an extremely rough passage to Bermuda and then back to the UK. He went for his health!

Maurice Griffiths
The Magic of the Swatchways
Swatchways and Little Ships
The First of the Tide
Round the Cabin Table

Most of the cruises in these books are from several hours to a couple of days. However, the author conveys the pleasure he derives from such simple cruises and the satisfaction of boat-handling in a manner that is truly inspirational.

John Guzzwell
Trekka **Round the World**

In a 21 ft. 6 in. boat that he built himself, John Guzzwell sailed competently around the world. A first-rate sailor, he makes it sound easy and rational.

Eric C. Hiscock
Wandering Under Sail
Around the World in *Wanderer III*
Beyond the West Horizon
Sou' West in *Wanderer IV*
Come Aboard
Two Yachts, Two Voyages

Let it never be forgotten that the Hiscocks were the first couple to circumnavigate or that they sailed 110,000 miles in *Wanderer III*, a yacht that many people these days would consider too small to cross the Atlantic. The large *Wanderer IV* only entered their lives when Eric was 60. They pioneered the way for the rest of us and showed us how to do it correctly, without drama and with pleasure; however, they were not small income voyagers, in the sense to which I refer!

Weston Martyr
The £200 Millionaire
The Southseaman

If you can read "The £200 Millionaire" without wishing, even for a moment, that you'd like to live like that, you must have no soul. **The Southseaman** is a good read and has a lovely description of going to sea for the sake of a long sail.

Bernard Moitessier
Sailing to the Reefs
Cape Horn - the Logical Route

The first is the best, when Moitessier didn't have two pennies to rub together but had a lot of fun. In the second he describes a splendid voyage which for a long time was considered the definitive work on Cape Horn sailing.

Harry Pidgeon
Around the World Single-Handed

The second man to circumnavigate single-handed. He built *Islander*

himself to a design from **Rudder** magazine and paid his way by giving magic lantern shows.

Peter Pye
The Sea is for Sailing
Red Mains' l
A Sail in a Forest
Backdoor to Brazil

Peter and Anne Pye are one of the very great partnerships. They sailed their 29 ft., gaff-rigged converted fishing boat, *Moonraker*, for many thousands of miles. They were not wealthy people, nor particularly robust, but enjoyed some cruises that would be unusual even by today's standards. Wonderful Books.

Donald Ridler
Erik the Red

If ever you feel that to go cruising you need to be wealthy, read this book. A completely unskilled carpenter, Donald Ridler built his boat out of scrap wood and used bed sheets for sails. With the absolute minimum of cash, he sailed across the Atlantic and back and had a whale of a time. "Go thou and do likewise."

Joshua Slocum
Sailing Alone Around the World

Another low-budget voyager, Slocum made best use of his opportunities. He rebuilt a near wreck and sailed forth. In spite of the replicas produced, *Spray* was far from ideal (she was not self-righting) and you need to read between the lines, fully to appreciate the skill of the sailor. Further readings will also reveal that this is a very funny book.

Erling Tambs
The Cruise of the *Teddy*

This is one of the most light-hearted accounts ever written. Erling Tambs, his wife and later, his baby son sailed half-way around the world before losing *Teddy* on the rocks. The boat leaked, they had very little money and they had a wonderful time.

Peter Tangvald
Sea Gypsy

Pete's greatest inspiration; Tangvald's comments regarding engines and marine toilets still merit serious consideration and from all accounts he still believes them. Another inspirational book.

H.W. Tilman
Mischief **in Patagonia**
Mischief **Among the Penguins**
Mischief **in Greenland**
Mostly *Mischief*
Mischief **Goes South**
In *Mischief's* **Wake**
Ice with Everything
Triumph and Tribulation

Bill Tilman took to sailing when he felt he was too old for the heights of the Himalayas. The idea was to sail to remote and unclimbed mountains, but eventually the voyages themselves were of great satisfaction. Tilman believed that any expedition that could not be organized on the back of an envelope was to complicated. He also believed that you should be totally self-reliant. His peers respected him immensely. He was an excellent and amusing writer and a great sailor; with *Mischief* he sailed over 125,000 miles, largely in high latitudes on which he was an authority.

James Wharram
Two Girls, Two Catamarans

Jim Wharram believed in polynesian catamarans as voyaging boats and so built one to try out his ideas. In the Caribbean he built an improved version to sail back. His unusual private life and his outspoken opinions have made him a lot of enemies. His designs have made him a lot of friends. His book is one of those that makes it all sound like something you'd like to do.

Frank Wightman
The Wind is Free
Wylo **Sails Again**

One of the great romantic sailors, his books are beautifully written. *Wylo* is the same design as *Islander* and, like Harry Pidgeon, Frank Wightman lived aboard her until his final illness, which implies something special about these boats.

Textbooks/reference books

Bill Belcher
Yacht Wind-Vane Steering

If you can't afford to buy a wind vane gear, don't worry, this book will tell you how to make one. The whole theory and practice is discussed and at the back are "recipes" for making your own. Worth having on board even if you have a production gear, in case it gets wrecked.

Jay R. Benford
Cruising Yachts

A variety of designs can be found in this book and such books help you to assemble your ideas about what you want out of a cruising yacht.

Philip C. Bolger
Different Boats

This is one of several books of designs by this author. Contains the plans of *Tortoise*, and if you've bought the book, Mr. Bolger reckons you've paid his royalty. There are also a number of other very interesting designs which provide food for thought.

Francis B. Cooke
Cruising Hints

Fifty years ago, people had to do things for themselves rather more than we do now. An interesting period piece with a lot of information that can be used today.

Rose Elliot
The Bean Book
Complete Vegetarian Cookbook

If you want to learn about cooking beans, you'll need the Bean Book. The second book has a lot of good recipes, many of which are inexpensive. I use both books a lot.

The Gougeon Brothers on Boat Construction

Although this book is about building with the WEST System®, it contains a wealth of information applicable to all glued wood construction. No-one should use epoxy without first reading this book.

Peter Harrison
Seabirds - an Identification Guide

Most of the time, when you are on the water, you will be able to see at least one bird. It is nice to know what they are, and interesting to know something of how they live.

H.G. Hasler and J.K. McLeod
Practical Junk Rig

The definitive work on Junk Rig for yachts. We used the information contained in this book to design *Badger*'s rig. It also contains all the information you would need to convert your existing boat to junk rig. Included are details for designing a *Jester*-type pram hood, which I can't recommend too highly. If you already own a junk-rigged yacht, you should still have this book for reference.

Ruth Hertzburg, Beatrice Vaughan and Janet Greene
Putting Food By

Although I don't go in for a great deal of bottling, etc., I find myself using this book quite a bit. It tells you about all sorts of techniques from air-drying right up to freezing and would be of use to most small income voyagers.

Eric C. Hiscock
Cruising Under Sail (Incorporating Voyaging Under Sail)

If you have only one textbook on board, it should be this one. From such basic skills as sailing off a mooring to the discussion of mid-ocean gales, it's all here, clearly presented and correct.

Claud Worth
Yacht Cruising

Hiscock's predecessor. Phil Bolger describes him as being "rarely outdated and never wrong," to which I can add nothing.

Appendix VII

Glossary

English	American
Aubergine	Egg Plant
Beetroot	Beet
Caravan	Trailer
Courgette	Zucchini
Fortnight	Two Weeks
Gas	Propane
Heads	Head
Jerricans	Jerry jugs
Jif	*Mr. Clean*
Junk rig	Chinese lug rig
Kilner jar	Mason jar
Meths/methylated spirits	Alcohol
Muesli	A mixture of cereals, nuts and dried fruit
Orbital sander	Vibrator sander
Paraffin	Kerosene
Petrol	Gasoline
Polystyrene	Styrofoam
Polythene	Polyethylene
Poppadums	Indian, large crispy bread discs - like tacos
Pulses	Legumes
Scuttle/port (hole)	Portlight
Skip	Dumpster
Sod's Law	Murphy's Law
Stugeron	Brand of anti-seasickness tablet
Two-pack	Two-part

For rope sizes, as a rule of thumb, 3mm = 1/8", 10mm = 3/8", 12m = 1/2", 18mm = 3/4", 25mm = 1"

1 imperial (UK) pint = 20 fl. oz's.   1 US pint = 16 fl. oz's.

1 imperial (UK) gallon = 160 fl. oz's.   1 US gallon = 128 fl. oz's.

1 ton in the text, is always 1 long ton, i.e.: 2240 pounds (1 metric ton = 2,205 pounds)

Appendix VIII

The £200 Millionaire
By Weston Martyr, 1932

My wife and I were sailing a hireling yacht through the waterways of Zeeland last summer, when one day a westerly gale drove us into the harbour of Dintelsas for shelter. A little green sloop, flying the Red Ensign, followed us into port. She was manned solely by one elderly gentleman, but we noted that he handled the boat with ease and skill. It was blowing hard, and the little yacht ran down the harbour at speed, but when abreast of us she luffed head to wind, her violently flapping sails were lowered with a run, and she brought up alongside us so gently that she would not have crushed an egg. We took her lines and made them fast, while her owner hung cork fenders over the side and proceeded to stow his sails. Urged by a look from my wife which said, 'he is old and all alone. Help him,' I offered to lend the lone mariner a hand. But he refused to be helped. Said he, 'Thank you, but please don't trouble. I like to do everything myself; it's part of the fun. But do come aboard if you will, and look round. You'll see there's nothing here that one man can't tackle easily.'

We went aboard and found the green sloop to be one of the cleverest little ships imaginable. It is difficult to describe her gear on deck and aloft without being technical; suffice it to say, therefore, that everything was very efficient and simple, and so designed that all sail could be set or lowered by the man at the helm without leaving the cockpit. The boat was 30 feet long by 9 feet wide, and my short wife, at any rate, could stand upright in her cabin. Her fore end was a storeroom, full of convenient lockers, shelves and a small but adequate water-closet. Abaft this came the cabin, an apartment 12 feet long, with a broad bunk along one side of it and a comfortable settee along the other. A table with hinged flaps stood in the middle, while in the four corners were a wardrobe, a desk, a pantry and a galley. Abaft all this was a motor, hidden beneath the cockpit floor. A clock ticked on one bulkhead, a rack full of books ran along the other, a tray of pipes lay on the table, and a copper kettle sang softly to itself on the little stove.

'What do you think of her?' said our host, descending the companion. 'Before you tell me, though, I must warn you I'm very house-proud. I've owned this boat for ten years, and I've been doing little things to her all the time. Improving her, *I* call it. It's great fun. For instance, I made this matchbox-holder for the galley last week. It sounds a trivial thing; but I wish I'd thought of it ten years ago, because during all that time I've had to use both hands whenever I struck a match.. Now I have only to use one hand, and you know all *that* implies in a small boat, especially if she's dancing about and you're trying to hold on and cook and light the Primus at one and the same moment. Then there was the fun of carving the holder out of a bit of wood I picked up, to say nothing of the pleasure it gives me to look at a useful thing I've made with my own hands. The carving brought out the grain of the wood nicely, don't you think? Now I'm going to make tea, and you must stay and have some with me.'

We did stay to tea. And we are glad we did. For one thing, it was a remarkably fine tea, and, for another, we listened to the most entertaining and thought-provoking discourse we have ever heard in our lives. That discourse, in fact, was so provocative of thought that it looks as if it were going to change the whole course of our lives for my wife and me. Said our host, 'I hope you will like this tea. It's brick tea, caravan tea. I got hold of it in Odessa, where it was really absurdly cheap. That's one of the advantages of this kind of life, I find. Cruising about all over Europe in my own boat, I can buy luxuries at the source, so to speak, at practically cost prices. There are four bottles of Burgundy, for example, stowed in the bilges under your feet, the remains of a dozen I bought at Cadaujac while cruising along the Garonne canal. I bought the lot for less than twenty shillings, and it's the sort of wine you pay a pound a bottle for in London. When I come across bargains like that it makes me wish this boat was a bit bigger. It's surprising what a lot of stuff I can stow away in her, but I really need more storage space. If I had room I would buy enough cigars, for instance, in this country where they are good and cheap, to last me over the winter. You see, I like the sun, and in two months I shall be going down the Rhone to spend the winter in the south of France, and the tobacco there is horrible and expensive.'

'Do you live aboard here all alone *always*?' exclaimed my wife, making her eyes very round.

'Most certainly,' replied our host. 'Now do try some of this Macassar redfish paste on your toast. I got it in Rotterdam from the purser of the Java Mail that arrived last week, so it's as fresh as it's possible to get it. It's really a shame to toast this bread, though. It's just the ordinary bread the bargees buy, but I find Dutch bread is the best in all Europe. Some French bread is good, but it won't keep as long as this stuff will. Sailing down the Danube a year or so ago I got some really excellent bread in Vienna, but it was a little sweet and not so good for a steady diet as this Dutch stuff. The *worst* bread I ever got was in Poland. I was cruising through the East German canals and I thought I would sail up the Vistula *via* Cracow, with the intention of putting the boat on the railway when I got to the head of the Vistula navigation at Myslowitz, shipping her across the few miles to the Klodnitz canal, and then cruising through Silesia and Brandenburg *via* Breslau down the Oder. It was a good and perfectly feasible plan, and I fancy it would have been interesting. But that horrible Polish bread defeated me completely. It was about all I could get to eat, and it seemed to consist entirely of straw and potatoes. So I turned back after passing Warsaw, and fled down the Vistula and the Bromberg canal and on by the Netze to Frankfurt. Do have some more tea.'

We had some more tea. It was a marvellous brew, as stimulating as good wine, and while we drank it our curiosity concerning our host and his extraordinary mode of life welled up within us, to drown at last our manners and overflow in a stream of questions.

'Do you really mean,' said we, 'that you live aboard here always? All the year round? And quite alone? And cruise to Odessa? And Warsaw? And how did you *get* to the Danube? And the Black Sea? And —? And —?' Thus we went on, while our host smiled at us—the kind of smile that told us we had made a new friend.

'I'll tell you,' he said, when we stopped at last for breath. 'you understand boats and this sort of life, I think, so you'll understand me. I've been living aboard this boat for ten years now, and I hope I shall never have to live anywhere else as long as I'm alive. It's a good life. It's the best kind of life a man can lead—or a woman either. It really is *life*, you see. Yes. And I think I ought to know. I shan't see sixty again, and I've seen a good deal of life—of different kinds. I'm a doctor, or was once. And I've worked very hard all my life trying to be a good doctor, but failing, I fear, on the whole. I married and we had five children, and it meant hard work bringing them up properly and educating them. But I worked and did it. Then I moved to London to try to make some money. That was the hardest work of all. Then the war came, and more

hard work in a base hospital. The war killed two of my sons—and my wife. And when it was all over I looked around, and I didn't like the look of the life I saw ahead of me. To go on working hard seemed the only thing left to do, but I found there was no zest left in my work any more. My daughters were married and my remaining son was doing well in a practice of his own. I found my children could get on very well without me. So there was no one left to work for, and I found I was very tired.

'I sold my practice and retired—to Harwich, where I was born. And there I soon found out that having nothing to do at all is even worse that working hard at something you've lost interest in. I did nothing for six months, and I think another six months of that would have been the death of me. By then I feel I should have been glad to die. But this little boat saved me. I began by hiring her from a local boatman for one weekend. We sailed up the Orwell to Ipswich and back again. The weather was fine, the Orwell is a lovely river, and I enjoyed my little sail. I enjoyed it so much, in fact, that I hired the boat again. I hired her for a week, and this time I left the boatman behind and sailed alone. Of course, I had sailed boats before. As a boy I got myself afloat in something or other whenever I had a chance, and my holidays as a young man were nearly all spent aboard yachts. So I found I could still handle a boat especially this little thing in those sheltered waters, and I remembered enough seamanship to keep myself out of trouble. I sailed to Pin Mill, and then up the Stour to Manningtree and Mistley. After that I grew bolder, and one fine day with a fair wind for the passage, I coasted along the Essex shore to Brightlingsea. I explored the Colne and its creeks, and the end of my week found me at West Mersea, so I had to write to the boatman and extend the time of hire. While I was about it I chartered the boat for a month. You see, I discovered I was happy, and I could not remember being happy for a very long while. The exercise and the fresh air and the plain food were all doing me good, too. I'd been getting flabby and running to fat, but the work on the boat very soon altered all that. I would turn into my bunk every night physically tired, knowing I would fall fast asleep at once, and looking forward to waking up again to another day of seeing after myself and the boat, and pottering about and enjoying my little adventures. The life, in fact, was making me young again—and I knew it. I would get up in the morning as soon as the light woke me and wash and shave and cook my breakfast. I used to stick pretty faithfully to coffee, bacon and eggs, and bread and marmalade in those first days, I remember. I was not much of a cook then, and I had yet to learn the pleasure one can get out of cooking a really good meal, not to mention eating it. Then I washed the breakfast things, cleaned up the cabin and washed down the deck. Housemaids' work? but there's not much of it needed to keep this small boat clean and tidy. And what little work there is soon became a labour of love. When I had made the boat all ship-shape I would sit in the cockpit and smoke, and look at her with great pride and contentment. I still do that. It gives me pleasure to see my home in perfect order and to feel that I've done it all myself. And I know, now, that if I paid someone else to do the work for me I should be depriving myself of a deal of the charm of life.

'When my morning chores were done, and if the weather was fine and I felt like moving on, I would heave up my anchor and make sail. During that first month I think I must have explored nearly all the rivers and creeks that run into the Thames Estuary. Most of them, as you probably know, are charming. If I wanted company I would bring up in the evening in one of the anchorages frequented by yachts, or alongside some Thames barges. There's a delightful freemasonry amongst sailors, whether yachtsman or bargees, and I'd generally find myself yarning and smoking with some congenial souls in my own or someone else's cabin until it was time to turn in. At other times I would let go my anchor for the night in some quiet creek, with never a human being within miles. I liked that best. I needed peace and quietness and I found them, to perfection, in those little lost Essex creeks.

'When the weather was bad, or the wind and tide did not serve, I would have a major clean-up, perhaps, or merely potter about, doing the little jobs of work a boat can always provide for you. Or I'd put my water-tank and a big basket in the dinghy and row to the nearest village to replenish my stores. One thing is certain, I never for a moment found time hanging heavily on my hands. There was always something to occupy me and always something interesting to see or to do. The life suited me and I throve on it, body and mind. And the way I threw off the years and turned into a boy again was perfectly amazing.

'My month was up almost before I knew it, and when it did get time to go back to Harwich and all *that* meant, I simply could not bear the thought of it. To think of returning to the sort of life I'd been leading on shore was as dreadful as the prospect of having to serve a life sentence in prison. I did not like the thought of it but there did not seem to be anything else I could do. You see, I've not got very much money. I had just enough to allow me to live, very simply, and even the expense of hiring this boat was really more than I could afford. What I wanted to do, of course, was to go on living aboard here, but, to my sorrow, that seemed quite impossible.

'Then, one night, I sat down in this cabin and thought the thing out—right out, in all its bearings. First I considered the question of finance. I don't want to bore you with my private affairs, but the figures are, I think, instructive and valuable, as they show what a lot can be done with very little. My capital amounted to a little over £4,000, and my yearly income just touched £200. The problem I set out to solve was: can I buy the boat out of my capital and still have sufficient income to live aboard her all the year around, and to maintain the boat and myself adequately? The price of the boat I knew already; she was for sale for £200. If I bought her my income would be reduced to £190, or less than £16 a month. Was this

enough? It did not look like it, by any means. It meant only £3 17s. a week to cover food, clothing, light and heat, and upkeep and repairs to the boat, to say nothing of depreciation and insurance. The figure seemed so ridiculous that I nearly gave up my idea in despair.

'However, I am, thank goodness, a methodical sort of man, and I'd kept a list of my expenses during the time I'd been living aboard the boat. I analysed that list, and found that my food and oil for the lamps and stove had cost me only £7 15s. for the month. I had also spent 30s. on gear for the boat, such as paint, ropes, shackles and such things, while my bill for petrol and lubricating oil came to 15s. only, as I had sailed as much as possible and used the motor as little as I could. Not counting the cost of hiring the boat, my total expenditure had, therefore, been only £10 for the month, or £120 a year. This left £70 over for repairs, accidents, depreciation and insurance. As far as the finance was concerned, the thing began to look possible after all.

'I was very cheered by this discovery, and I then asked myself: "Can I continue to live aboard this little boat from year's end to year's end in health and comfort of body and mind?" As far as the summers were concerned I knew I could answer that with a whole-hearted "Yes." But what about the winters? Could I endure being shut up in a small confined space while the gales blew and it was cold and wet, and the nights were long and dark? I wondered. And I had to admit to myself, very much against the grain, that I probably would not be able to endure these things. I remember I went to bed after that, feeling very miserable. But when I woke up next morning the first thing I said to myself was "but why stay in England in the winter: Why be cold and wet when all you have to do is to follow the sun and sail your boat—your Home—south?"

'To cut all this short, I sailed back to Harwich and sent to London for a map of the French canals. And when it came I found my idea of following the sun south was entirely feasible. All I had to do was to choose a fine day in early autumn and sail across the Channel from Dover to Calais. From Calais the map showed me a network of canals and navigable rivers spreading over the whole face of France, and I discovered that a boat of this size and draught could proceed through those inland waterways right through the heart of France to the Mediterranean. I bought this boat that same day. I had a few small alterations made to her, and the following week I sailed from Harwich, bound south—for Ramsgate, Dover, Calais, Paris, Lyons, and the Riviera.'

'Well done!' I cried. And my wife said, 'Hush! And then? Then?'

Our new friend smiled at us again. 'Yes,' he said. 'You're right. It *was* a bit of a rash proceeding—at my age. But I've never regretted it. That first cruise was perfectly delightful and, on the whole, a very simple affair. I had my troubles, of course. I got to Dover easily enough by coasting all round the Thames Estuary and putting in somewhere snug every night. But I stayed in Dover for ten days before I judged the weather was fine enough for me to sail to Calais. The truth is, I was rather scared. The passage is only twenty-one miles, but I felt a regular Christopher Columbus when I ventured across the Channel at last. It was a fine day, with a light north-east wind, and under sail and motor I got across in four hours. But I assure you Columbus was nothing to me when I sailed into Calais harbour! I felt I had triumphantly accomplished a most tremendous adventure, and I was immensely pleased and proud. And I can assure you it's rather remarkable for anything to make a cynical and disillusioned old man of my age feel like that.

'From Calais onward it was all canal and river work. It took me two months to get to Marseilles, because I went a round-about way and took my time over it. I had no need to hurry, of course, but I don't think anything could have made me hurry through the lovely country in which I found myself. I wandered down the Oise to Paris, where I stayed a week, moored in the Seine almost in the Shadow of the Champs-Elysées' tree. It was amusing and comfortable, too, living in the middle of Paris like that. I could dine ashore if I wanted to and go to a theatre, and then walk back and go to bed in my own floating hotel without any fuss or bother. And when I got tired of the city I just moved on, hotel and all. I went up the Marne to Chalons, along the canals to Bar-le-Duc and Epinal, and down through the Haute-Saône and Côte d'Or country to Macon and Lyons. I mention these towns to show you the route I took, but it was all the little out-of-the-world places between them that I used to stop at and which I found so interesting. I met all sorts of people and everyone was very helpful and kind, and by the time I got to Lyons I could speak about four different brands of French quite well.

'The passage down the Rhone to Arles was rather strenuous. The current is very strong and I had to take a pilot, which spoilt my fun; but it was soon over, and I got to Marseilles without any more bother. I had got as far south then as I could get, so I spent the rest of the winter in most of those delightful little harbours which sprinkle the coast between Marseilles and Fréjus. I found practically no winter along that stretch of coast, which is much better, I think, than the Riviera proper. I can recommend Porquerolles if ever you find yourselves down that way, while Port Cros must be one of the loveliest places there are on this earth. I enjoyed every minute of that first winter, and by the time the spring came round I knew I had discovered the perfect life. I was happier than I ever hoped to be, and healthier than I had ever been. I found myself looking forward to each day, and every day had some new interest. Life was, without exaggeration, nearly perfect. If I found myself anywhere or amongst people I did not care for, all I had to do was to heave up my anchor and go somewhere else. That's one of the many advantages of living aboard a boat. When you want to go away there's no packing, no taxis, no tips, no trains and no bother. And you haven't got to find a place to lay your head when you get to your journey's end. In a boat you just move on, and

your sitting-room, your kitchen, your bedroom and all your little personal comforts and conveniences move on with you. And when you get to your destination there you are—at Home.

'It added to my peace of mind, too, to find I was living well within my income, in spite of the fact that I was living very well and doing myself a great deal better than I had , for instance, in my Harwich lodgings. Of course I had to be careful and not go in for too many luxuries, but I lived as I wanted to live, and it surprised me to find how little it cost me to do it. I'll show you my account book, if it will interest you, but first I'll show you where I've been during these last ten years.

'Look at this! It's the official French canal map, showing all the canals and navigable rivers in the country. You'll notice there's very little of France you can't get at by water. It's almost unbelievable where you can go; everywhere, practically, except to the tops of the mountains. It's the same in Belgium and Holland, and in Germany, too, and until I got these canal maps I had no idea of the extraordinary manner the inland waterways of Europe have been developed. The ordinary maps don't give the details, so perhaps it's not surprising that people in England don't realise they can travel in a yacht from Calais through every country in Europe, except Spain and Italy, entirely by river and canal. It sounds incredible, doesn't it? But I've done it myself, in this boat. Including Switzerland!'

'Switzerland!' cried my wife. 'How *did* you?'

'There are two ways of getting there,' said our extraordinary friend. 'Up the Rhine Lateral canal, or the way I went—up the Rhine-Rhone canal from Strassburg to Mulhause and along the Huningue canal to Basle. That was as far as I could conveniently get then, but I believe the new canal is open now, running right through to Lake Constance and Bregenz. But I'm ahead of my yarn. When the spring came round that first year I went from Marseilles by canal all the way to Bordeaux. I spent that summer cruising up the coast to L'Orient and from there along the canals, right through Central Brittany from Brest to Nantes. Then I came south again, away from the cold, and spent the winter exploring South-West France, along the Dordogne and the Garrone and its tributaries. I saw most of that lovely country between Perigueux and Bordeaux in the north, Floirac and Albi in the east, and from Carcassonne in the south to Lacave, which is pretty well on the Spanish border. The whole country down there flows with milk and honey, to say nothing of the wine and the scenery. I had a good time.

'Then I went up north *via* the Midi canal and the Rhone, got into the Rhine at Strassburg, sailed all down that river to Rotterdam, and spent the summer in Holland. I liked this country and the people so much that I stayed here all that winter. Then I branched out. I was beginning to see the possibilities of this game by then, and I had gained confidence in myself and the boat. I won't bore you with all the details of my travels, but I went through North

Germany to the Mecklenburg lakes. You ought to go there. More lakes than you could explore in two years, set in a park-like country. Perfect. But take a mosquito-net. Then I sailed south to Dresden and Prague, then north to the Danish archipelago and the Swedish islands. I wintered in the Moselle valley, explored Central France and tried to go through the Loire country, but found a difficulty there owing to the shallowness of those particular rivers. After that I pottered about in Belgium and up the Rhine to Mainz, and from there up the Main and through the Ludwigs canal into the headwaters of the Danube. I can recommend Bavaria and all the lost country around there. It's the Middle Ages. And, of course, once I got on the Danube I had to go down it. And I am glad I did, because it's a wonderful river and the scenery is magnificent. I drifted down it, taking my time and meaning to go as far as Vienna, or maybe Budapesth. But you know how it is. There was the river, going on and on all across Europe, so I went on too—to Belgrade, the Iron Gates, Rustchuck and Galatz, until I came to Sulina and the Black Sea.

'I turned back that time, because I did not like the idea of venturing into Russian waters, the political situation being what it was. So I went up the Danube again. It took me two years to get to Passau on the German border. The Danube runs very swiftly, so progress was slow, and at times I had to take a tow, but the real reason I took so long was the number of side trips I felt I simply had to take up the various tributaries. I could write a book about it all, and some day I think I must, but so far I've been so busy moving about and enjoying life that I never have time for writing. And I wonder if my book would be readable if I wrote it? You see, I've had few "interesting adventures" or things like that. I got thoroughly lost once on the willow swamps on the lower Tisza, and went down with a bad go of fever in the middle of it. But I got out all right. And some Bulgarians above Sistove fired at me one day, but it turned out they were Customs guards and thought I was a smuggler, and we finished up the best of friends. Beyond that, and a little unpleasantness with a Ruthenian gentleman who tried to steal my dinghy, nothing much out of the ordinary happened. But I met a lot of very strange and interesting people. I had a wonderfully good time. In fact the country and the people along the Danube fascinated me; so much so that, after sailing about over Eastern Germany and a little of Poland, I went down the Danube again. This time I went as far as Odessa. I wanted to go on , either up the Dnieper, or through the Sea of Azoff, up the Don, through the Katchalinskay canal, and then either up the Volga to Nijni Novgorod, or down river to Astrakhan and the Caspian. Unfortunately I could not get permission from the Russians to make either of those trips. Perhaps it is just as well, as the country was rather disturbed and I might have got into trouble. But one of these days, when things have settled down, I intend to make that trip yet, because, bar politics, there's absolutely nothing to prevent it.'

I remember it was at this point in our friend's discourse that I interrupted him by crying out in a loud voice, 'By God!' and hitting the cabin table hard with my fist. My wife said nothing, but there was a look in her eyes and a light in them that showed me she understood and approved the wild and fascinating thought that had flashed into my mind. And our friend, it appeared, understood me also, for said he, 'Yes. Why not? All you need is a boat drawing less than four feet, with a motor in her for choice and her mast in a tabernacle. That and the—well, let's call it courage; the courage to step out of your rut. It looks hard; but a mere step does it—as I found out. Of course, it costs money. Following the seasons all over Europe in your own home is a millionaire's life; but I've managed to live it at an average cost, over the last ten years, of less than £150 per annum. Look at this!'

He put an open book before us on the table. It was his account book, and it contained. in full detail, his daily expenditures during all the years he had been living aboard his boat. It was, I can assure you, a most engrossing work, and was full of items such as these, which I found on a single page and copied there and then. And I shall regret it till I die that I had no time to copy any more:—

'*Sept*. 5. Capdenac. 8 duck eggs and 1 duck (cooked), 3*s*. 1*d*. 7*th*. 10 lb. grapes in fine willow basket, gratis. 6 boxes matches, 2*s*.! Sulphur at that! Note: Smuggle in big stock of matches when next I come to France. 8*th*. Very hard cheese, 1 ft. in dia., 1 basket peaches, 1 jeroboam peach brandy, 1 kiss on both cheeks, gratis, or perhaps fee for removing flint from farmer's eye. 9*th*. Mule hire, 10*d*. Alms to leper, 1*s*., interesting case. Castets, 15*th*. 6 feet of bread, 1*s*., 1 pint turps, ½*d*. 16*th*. 2 gallons turps, 8*d*. Castelsarrasin. *Oct. 2nd.* Bribe to gendarme, 5*d*.' I should dearly love to publish that account book, just as it stands, without any comment or explanation. It would, I think, make fascinating and suggestive reading.

'Look here,' said our friend, turning over the unique pages and exposing the following figures to our devouring eyes. 'This is a summary of my first twelve months' income and outgoings: —

	£	*s.*	*d.*
Income	190	0	0

Expenditure:

	£	*s.*	*d.*
Upkeep of boat (at 9*s*. per week)	23	8	0
Petrol and oil	10	4	0
(distance covered under motor 1220 miles)			
Charts, canal dues	13	8	0
Food, drink, clothes, light and heat	100	0	0
(at just under £ 2 a week)			
	147	0	0
Balance	43	0	0
	£190	0	0

'I managed to save £43, you see, that first year—enough to buy a new boat like this one, every five years, if I continued to save at the same rate. I was extra careful that year. I didn't spend much on myself, but I bought the boat all she needed and kept her up in first-class shape. I painted her inside once and three times outside, doing it all myself, and I had her sails tanned to preserve them. The tanning was done by a fisherman I made friends with in Toulon. He did a good job. In the end he wouldn't let me pay for anything except the cost of the materials, because he said we were *amis* and he liked English sailors. And one day I came across a broken-down motor-boat, drifting off Cape Camaret, and towed her into port. Her owner was scared to death, and very grateful accordingly. He was no sailor, but he was a mighty good mechanic, and he insisted on giving my little engine a first-class overhaul, just to show his gratitude.

'My fuel bill was very small, because I never use the motor if I can sail. The £13 odd for dues, etc., was mostly spent on maps and charts, not that many charts are necessary, but I simply can't resist buying the things. I spend hours poring over them, and planning more voyages than I shall ever have time to make. As for the canal and harbour dues—they're ridiculous; generally some fraction of a penny per ton. And this boat's registered tonnage is only two ton. The only expensive piece of water to travel over in Europe is the Rhone. It's got a terrific current, pilotage is compulsory, and to get up it you have to be towed. But everywhere else the only trouble about the charges is to find change small enough to pay them with. £2 a week for food and so on sounds very little, but all I can say is I live well on that sum. You see, if I want, say vegetables I don't go to a shop in a city for them. No. Perhaps I see a good-looking garden on the river bank. I stop and have a yarn with the owner, and when I depart I'm richer by a basket full of fresh vegetables, and maybe a chicken and some eggs and fruit as well, while the gardener is left with a fair price for his produce and something to talk about for weeks. He's pleased and I'm pleased. I've paid less than I would if I bought from a shop, and he's received more than he would if he sold to a dealer. And when I say I've got fresh vegetables I mean *fresh*—which is something you can't get from a shop.

'Clothes don't bother me much. It's not essential to dress in the latest style, living this life. I keep my go-ashore clothes in that tin uniform case, and when I get to a city and want to see the sights I put on a civilised suit. Otherwise I use soft shirts, jerseys and flannel trousers. I do my washing myself; half an hour a fortnight does it, which is nothing to grumble about. I use paraffin oil for light and cooking in the summer, and in the winter I keep that little stove going on coal and wood. I find I burn wood mostly, because I've got a passion, apparently, for collecting any odd pieces I find drifting about. There must be a strain of longshoreman blood in me somewhere, I think, for I can't resist picking up bits of driftwood, even though I have to throw most of them overboard again, and I generally have a bigger collection of the stuff on deck than I can ever hope to burn.

'So you see, one way and another, my expenses are very small. The £30 or £40 I save every year I put by for accidents, major repairs, depreciation and a sort of insurance fund. I've bought a new suit of sails and had the whole boat surveyed and recaulked and the engine practically renewed, all out of the fund, and I've still got enough left to buy a new boat if I want one. I'm getting so rich, in fact, that I don't know what to do with all my money. I tried to get rid of some of it by buying extra fine gear for the boat, but I found that scheme merely saved me more money in the long-run. For instance, I scrapped my Manilla running rigging and replaced it with best hemp at twice the cost, but I'll be bothered if the hemp hasn't lasted four times as long as the Manilla already! And to make it worse, people will persist in *giving* me things, bless 'em. I've made a lot of friends in pretty well every corner of Europe. Can't help it, living this sort of life, it seems. And most of them have an idea that, living as I do, I am to be regarded with compassion. A poor old man, living all alone aboard a little boat—that's how they seem to feel about me, I fear. So, whenever I turn up, my compassionate friends appear, bearing gifts! It's quite embarrassing sometimes. And sometimes it's a real nuisance. The Middelburg canal is barred to me, for instance, because the keeper of one of the swing bridges refuses to let me through until he's been aboard to greet me and give me a box of cigars or a jar of schnapps; which things he really can't afford, as he's a poor man with a very large family. He does it, it seems, because I'm leading just the kind of life *he*'d like to lead if he hadn't been blessed with a wife, his mother-in-law and nine children. The result is I have to go round now by Terneuzen, instead of through Middelburg, whenever I want to pass from Holland into Belgium. And I always have to go through Strassburg by night to dodge a dear old gentleman, who invariably presses on me about a stone of the smelliest cheese on earth whenever he catches sight of me. He calls me his brave ancient *ami* so lonely. Lonely! Why, I should think I must have a larger and more varied assortment of friends than any man in Europe. And I keep on making more all the time. For instance, I hope I've made two to-day.'

He had; and we are glad to say he dined with them that evening, entrancing them with his talk until far into the night. He talked of gentle rivers wandering through valleys of everlasting peace; of a quiet canal, lost amongst scented reeds and covered with a pink-and white carpet of water-lilies; of a string of tiny lakes, their blue waters ringed with the green of forest pines; of a narrow canal, built by old Romans, but navigable still, that climbs up through clouds into the high mountains; of aqueducts spanning bottomless ravines and a view from the yacht's deck of half Southern Germany; of a Red Ensign flying at the peak and a Black Forest eagle's screamings at that sight; of the Croatian mayor who had never heard of a certain country called England; of a thousand square miles of bloodred swamp, studded with giant willows; of

Wallachian water-gipsies and their cats who catch fish; of the mile-long log raft commanded by a Russian ex-admiral; of a spiked helmet dredged from out the Meuse by the yacht's anchor; of the warm-hearted kindliness of Bulgarian brigands and the barbarous fines of Frs. 25,000 extorted (unsuccessfully) by 'the most civilised country in Europe'; of pack-ice and ice-breakers in the heart of old Amsterdam; of the 1000 ton motor-barge that trades each year between Groningen and Sulina; of the 300-ton barge proceeding from Bruges to Dunkerque in tow of a jolly old lady of seventy; of a spilliken-like traffic jam in the old moat at Furnes and the Fordson tractor that extricated twenty-eight barges; of the Flemish barge named *No. 27 Park Lane*, because the wounds of her skipper had been succoured at that address in 1914; of pig-manure, chemical fumes and rotting flax on the Lys, and the barge with a deck-load of potted hyacinths that outdid all those scents; of the ten-knot currents on the Rhone and the silent waters of the Oude Ryn that ebb and flow no more; of the charm of this old earth and the fun of living on it, if only you understand the proper way to live. Said our friend, 'I've found one good way to live and be happy. There must be other ways, too, but I don't know 'em, so I mean to stick to my way—till I come to the end of it. The secret seems to be, to do everything you can *yourself*. It's difficult to explain, but take an example. Take travel. Allow yourself to be carried about the world in Wagon-Lits and cabins-de-luxe, and what do you get out of it? You get bored to death. Everything is done for you and you don't even have to think. All you have to do is to pay. You're carried about with the greatest care and wrapped up and fed and insulated from—from everything. You see about as much of life as a suckling in the arms of its nurse. No wonder you get bored! But get yourself about the world, on your own feet, or in your own boat, and you're bound, you're *bound* to fill your life with interest and charm and fun—and beauty. You'll have your disagreeable and uncomfortable times, of course, but they merely serve to make the good times taste better. "Sleep after toyle, port after stormie seas——." Old Spenser knew. He'd been through it. Sail all day in the wet and cold, then bring up in some quiet harbour and go below and toast your feet before the galley fire and you'll realise what bliss means. Travel in a steam-heated Pullman and then put up at the Ritz and see if you find any bliss there! You see what I mean? Stewart Edward White put it all much better than I can. He wrote, "I've often noted two things about trees: the stunted little twisted fellows have had a hard time, what with wind and snow and poor soil; and they grow farthest up on the big peaks." '

Next morning our friend must have risen with the sun, and we were still beneath our blankets when the incense of his coffee and bacon drifted down our cabin hatch. Presently the sound of ropes falling on deck warned us he was getting under weigh, and we arose to say good-bye to him. 'Good morning,' said he. 'I'm sorry to disturb you so early, but I want to catch the first of the flood. With luck it'll carry me into the Rhine and I'll be in Germany by evening. Now I'll cast off and go—and see what this good day's got in store for me. A fair tide and a fair wind is a fine beginning, anyway. Good-bye, you two. We'll meet again somewhere, for certain, if only you follow that impulse you had last night. I don't want to influence you unduly; but, remember—one step does it and you're out of the rut for good. Good-bye. God bless you both.'

He set his jib and the little green yacht fell off before the wind and headed for the harbour entrance. She sailed away with the sun shining bright upon her, and upon the white head of the man at her helm. Presently she entered the broad river, and we saw our friend look back and wave his hand in farewell. Then the boat was hidden by a bank of golden sand, and the last we saw of her was her little Red Ensign, a tiny flame outlined against the sky.

This seems to be the end of the story—but I do not know. I am not sure. I am not sure, because the words of that elderly adventurer seem to have set us thinking. I notice we do not say very much, but I know we think a lot. For, at intervals during the cold and fogs of this last winter, there have passed between my wife and me some detached but significant utterances—such as: 'I don't see why I couldn't get on with my writing aboard a boat just as well as I can inside this flat.'

'Only £200 a year! Hang it! We *ought* to be able to earn that much between us, you'd think?'

'I think, my dear, one of those steam-cookers would be a splendid thing to have if we—for anyone living aboard a small boat.'

'What a foul fog! It hurts to think of the sun shining, *now*, in the south of France.'

'May the Devil run away with that damned loud-speaker next door. You know, if this flat was a boat, we could move it out of hearing.'

'If I get bronchitis again next winter—My dear, I don't think I *could* stand another winter here.'

Also we have purchased a monumental work entitled, *Guide Officiel de la Navigation Intérieure*, published by the Ministère des Travaux Publiques. This is a fascinating work, heartily to be recommended. It has a lovely map.

Also we have just heard of a little boat. In fact, we have been to look at her. She is sound and very strong. She has two good berths and a galley and lots of stowage space. Also she has a little auxiliary motor. And her mast is in a tabernacle. And she is for sale. And we have fallen in love with her. So perhaps this is not the end of this story. In fact, we hope and we pray this story has only just begun.

Index